DAT

Museums, Zoos & Botanical Gardens of Wisconsin: a Comprehensive Guidebook

An Illustrated Guidebook to Collections of History, Culture, Art, Zoology, Natural History, Botany, and the Environment, in the Badger State.

Anto

Fine Arts Publishing
in cooperation with
University of Wisconsin Press
Madison, Wisconsin

Dedication

This book is dedicated to my grandparents: Anton Rajer (1879-1959) and Mary Pust Rajer (1891-1976). They immigrated separately from the Austro- Hungary province of Slovenia early in the 20th century and met in Sheboygan. He was a cabinetmaker and she an apprentice blacksmith and woodworker. They were married in Sheboygan at Saints Cyril and Methodius Church on July 1, 1912 and had three boys. Anton's favorite book was a pre-World War I atlas of the world.

His favorite hobby was making wine and Mary's was gardening and raising rabbits and birds.

Includes bibliographical reference and indices
© 2006 Anton Rajer, Fine Arts Publishing, Madison, Wisconsin
Protected under the 1988 International Berne Convention Copyright Treaty ©
® World Intellectual Property Copyright (WIPO) 2002
® United States Copyright Office

Photos used by permission of the institutions as listed and by the Sheboygan County Historical Research Center, Sheboygan Falls (SCHRC).

Graphic Design: Angela Wix and Christine Style
Cover design by Lynne Bergschultz and Cheryl Gordon

ISBN # 0-9664180-0-X
Banta Book Publishing Corporation, Menasha, Wisconsin
Printed in the United States
Distributed by the University of Wisconsin Press, Madison, Wis. USA
www.wisc.edu/wisconsinpress

SCHRC

Table of Contents

Southeast

Southwest

Northeast

Acknowledgements

The author wishes to thank all those people and places that provided assistance in research and preparation of this book. In particular, I wish to thank my wife Christine Style, Mary Risseeuw, the Wisconsin genealogist, special thanks to U.S. Senator Russ Feingold, Maureen Tillotson, a great friend and family member, Thomas Lidtke for his inspiration in producing this book, Jerry and Gail Tigges, Beth Dippel, Lynn Bergschultz and Cheryl Gordon for their assistance; Ruth Muehlmeier for her encouragement, and of course all my friends and colleagues at the University of Wisconsin Press. Tom McKay and the Office of Affiliated Historical Societies of Wisconsin. Additional thanks to Chad Peters, Erica Becker, Angela Wix, David Eagan, Sue Abing, Chris Foy, Tammy DeCoursin, the Wisconsin Veterans Museum and its director, Dr. Zeitlin, and to the anonymous donors who supported this project. Thanks to all the institutions that responded to the inquiries over the years and provided us with information and photographs to use in the book. Sorry if I forgot anyone, wait for the next edition.

Photo of Sheboygan County Historical Research Center, Sheboygan Falls (SCHRC) Mill House

Special thanks to Sheboygan County Historical Research Center-Archives. The center loaned many photographs to illustrate this book. We appreciate the kindness that was extended to us from one of the primer archival centers in Wisconsin. They house, collect, and preserve thousands of irreplaceable documents and historic materials for the benefit of present and future generations. They also have a friendly and helpful staff that makes research come alive.

Forward! our state motto

This book is a useful guide for anyone who wants to discover more about the wonders of Wisconsin. We have many.

Wisconsin is home to a range of institutions, from our acclaimed public museums to our local historical societies, and "Museums, Zoos and Botanical Gardens of Wisconsin" makes all these destinations easier to find and enjoy.

Representing Wisconsin in the U.S. Senate has been a privilege for many reasons, including the time I have spent getting to know the diverse communities around our state. Time and again, I have had a chance to see how much cultural institutions contribute to the rich character of Wisconsin; what a point of pride a local botanical garden or natural history collection can be for a community; and how dedicated staff make these attractions so rewarding for visitors, year after year.

In every corner of our state, there are unique destinations to celebrate and enjoy. This useful guide helps visitors discover Wisconsin, from some of our most famous attractions to our greatest hidden treasures. I hope this book will encourage more people to explore all that Wisconsin has to offer and, in turn, strengthen the cultural resources that make Wisconsin such a wonderful place to visit, and an even better place to live.

Senator Russ Feingold
United States Congress

Tony's Footnote:

Senator Feingold has visited all over the state on various occasions for his Listening Sessions with the public. We applaud that. In addition, he has held some of these sessions in museums and historical societies. For that reason and many more I asked Senator Feingold to write this Forward to my book. Thanks Russ.

Some of the Listening Session sites have included:
1. The historic Hotel Chequamegon in Ashland
2. The State Capitol in Madison
3. The Wisconsin Black Historical Society/Museum in Milwaukee
4. The Frank Lloyd Wright Visitors Center at Taliesin in Spring Green
5. The Aviation Center at the Experimental Aircraft Association (EAA) in Oshkosh
6. S.C. Johnson Corporation's Golden Rondelle Theater in Racine
7. The Apostle Island Visitors Center in Bayfield
and many more.

Preface

From Madeline Island in the north to Kenosha and Beloit in the south, hundreds of museums and collecting institutions that reside in the cities, towns, and villages throughout Wisconsin help preserve history, teach us about our natural world, and celebrate our achievements. Some contain the common from previous generations and others contain the rare and unique. Collectively, they help us discover and explore the immense diversity that represents the regions of our state, our country, and the world, both past and present.

Until now there has been no single source of printed information that references most, if not all, of Wisconsin's vast museum resources.

In fact, a publication such as this is long overdue because the majority of the public is not aware of the quality and quantity of treasures that rest within Wisconsin's collecting institutions. When people do discover these treasures, they seem pleased they made the effort to seek them out, and now they have a guide to almost all of the cultural resources that collectively make up a vast state-wide treasure-trove.

Most people would be hard pressed to name more than a few museums in Wisconsin outside the half dozen larger museums in the state, and even fewer would be able to name some of the those institutions' most beloved displays or collection items. For this reason, both the public and the museums of Wisconsin should be pleased with this, the first published effort to Reference these wonderful resources.

This indispensable guide will prove to be a valuable reference to teachers, students, museum goers, researchers, scholars, governmental and political leaders and libraries, as well as the general public who will simply enjoy discovering treasures in the Badger state.

This guide is the beginning of a discovery journey that should stimulate the mind as well as entertain. I am sure you will enjoy your discovery journey and the treasures waiting for you within.

Thomas Lidtke
Executive Director
West Bend Art Museum

The Flagellants painting by Carl Von Marr, 1891 at the West Bend Art Museum.

My Introduction to Museums, Zoos and Botanical Gardens of Wisconsin

It has taken me a lifetime to write this book, because I have lived it. The experiences have shaped my life. From my earliest years as a kid growing up in Sheboygan, I have been visiting the museums, zoos, and botanical gardens of Wisconsin. What a wonderful journey it has been!

My parents, Bill and Charlotte Rajer, loved driving around the state on summer weekends touring these sites. It was such an innocent time. My mother loved history and travel and especially enjoyed visiting the Catholic shrines like Dickeyville and Holy Hill. She was always writing away for brochures about historic or cultural destinations. At the supper table she would say to my dad, "We should visit that place, it will help little Tony in school. He can get extra credit for it." My dad traveled for a living — he was involved in trucking — so sometimes it took a lot of coaxing to get him to see a place purely for pleasure, but he often did. Frequently, a visit to a museum would be accompanied by a picnic in a local park with my mom, dad, Judy (my sister), and me.

I still fondly remember our family visits to such places as the original Milwaukee Public Museum and old Milwaukee County Zoo. I loved the Egyptian mummy exhibits which I replicated at home in PlayDoh. Similarly, seeing elephants in the zoo inspired me to try my hand at papier-mache with the Sunday newspaper. With such inspiration, anything was possible!

Wisconsin's state historic sites are part of my family history. Though I was just a baby when the following event occurred, my mom told the story again and again, often with tears in her eyes.

Wisconsin's second state historic site is the Old Wade House, in the village of Greenbush in Sheboygan County. It was given to the State Historical Society in 1953 and the dedication ceremony was quite an event. The Kohler family and their foundation had saved the old abandoned stagecoach hotel and restored it. Actually, it was Ruth DeYoung Kohler (senior) who had done much of the work. She raised the funds and persuaded her husband and others to save the building. She spent three years working on it, but died shortly before it opened. Her passing was a tragic loss.

Herbert V. Kohler, Sr. and his daughter Ruth DeYoung Kohler II presided over the dedication ceremony on June 4, 1953, along with the American poet Carl Sandburg. My parents were members of the audience, looking on. Years later my mother would say, "Oh, it was so sad. Mr. Kohler lost his pretty wife, she did so much to save Old Wade house and she died so young." That day in 1953 was both a day of celebration and sorrow, but because of Mrs. Kohler's love of Wisconsin history we now have the Old Wade House as a historic site. She believed, as I do, that there is a future for the past.

Our family never ventured far; rarely did we go out of state. Since my parents were poor, our excursions were kept close to home and because of that I came to know our Wisconsin museums, zoos, and botanical gardens quite well. Little did I know how those visits would serve as an apprenticeship for my future profession as a museum specialist and heritage conservator.

My earliest museum memory is a family trip to Green Bay. It was when Fort Howard was still downtown, before the creation of Heritage Hill State Park. We drove up to Green Bay to see the old Neville Museum and Library and then went to Fort Howard, a real pre-Civil War gem. While going through the museum with my parents, I admired a black beaver top hat. "Wow," I thought. "That hat is the best!" My mom talked to the curator who let me try the hat on and get my picture taken on the museum's front porch. Unfortunately, I've lost that photo, but the memory is kept alive in my heart and I still chuckle about the moment.

Not all the heritage trips went well, especially the Oshkosh trip in 1965. Mom had written away for brochures about the Paine Art Center and Arboretum. She showed them to me and we begged dad to drive us to Oshkosh to see the incredible house, gardens, and art collection. We eventually drove over on a hot and humid summer day. But when we got to the museum, we saw a very disturbing sign: "No children allowed!" It was as if the ice cream cone had been taken right out my hand, like I was at the doorway of a candy store but couldn't enter. My parents did go in for a visit, while I waited whimpering in the car.

On the way home my mom showed me the wonderful postcards she bought, which only made things worse. I vowed that someday I'd be an adult and would walk right into that museum — which I did, ten years later. (The Paine, fortunately, no longer has such a restriction.)

Beginning in my teen years, I became a museum professional, first working at the Kohler Arts Center in Sheboygan for seven years as a technician and art handler. The experience acquainted me with the inner workings of a museum and I loved it. In college, I studied art history at the University of Wisconsin-Milwaukee. I then studied art conservation at Harvard University where I became a conservator and a heritage preservation specialist, which I still am today. My additional heritage conservation studies took me to London, Paris, and Rome, but I always returned to Wisconsin.

Although my profession has taken me all over the world, I still call Wisconsin home. My five years as conservator at the State Capitol in Madison taught me valuable lessons about how others view history and heritage. What I still love about the museums, zoos, and botanical gardens of Wisconsin is their endless variety and diversity, from world-class facilities to tiny historical society museums chock-full of local history. In total, there are well over 540 institutions in the state. My wife now joins my many heritage excursions, whether to Racine in the south or Phillips in the

Judy Rajer at a zoo with bear.

north, to see art or history, animals, or gardens. We love exploring new places around the state and especially meeting the dedicated people who make it all happen. We attended the opening of the new Milwaukee Art Museum, what a stunning building. We enjoy driving into history.

I hope this guidebook helps you to enjoy, as I have, the wonders of Wisconsin heritage in all its varied forms. For me, art, history, and natural history are alive in every corner of the state. Happy travels!

Anton (Tony) Rajer
Madison, Wisconsin

How to Use This Book

First, thank you for choosing and using this book. I hope it will lead to many memorable adventures in Wisconsin. We are fortunate to have so much to see, experience and learn in this state, a state for all seasons and reasons.

This Guidebook to Museums, Zoos and Botanical Gardens of Wisconsin is meant to be a comprehensive, portable, and readable book. It reviews over 540 venues; no other book offers such detailed information on so many places. To be as inclusive as possible, I have included not only traditional museums, but also specialty museums, one-of-a-kind zoos, petting zoos, nature centers, regional gardens, natural history, college art galleries, and a variety of unorthodox cultural attractions. Notes and highlights about their collections and special holdings will help you decide which places will be most interesting for you to visit.

Star System and Icons

Out of necessity, I rated the cultural institutions listed in this book with a star rating system similar to that used by the Green Michelin Guides. This book is about museums, zoos, and botanical gardens and their intrinsic qualities that are representative, unique, irreplaceable, or distinctly characteristic of an area or place. These institutions enrich the quality of life in Wisconsin and form an important part of the fabric of our culture.

No star: See if possible. A local cultural reference point such as a museum, zoo, or botanical garden.

★One star: a place of note and interest. See it on your journey.

★★Two star: worthy of a detour. Head over to this spot.

★★★Three star: a real destination, a stellar site. Don't miss it. Worth the journey.

In addition, we placed icons, small pictorial images, next to each citation and they come in three types:

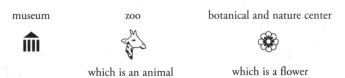

museum	zoo	botanical and nature center
	which is an animal	which is a flower

This should help the user instantly identify the nature of the site that they wish to visit.

The places described in this book are arranged alphabetically — by community and site — in four geographical quadrants of the state. Maps are intended to show approximate locations, but you will likely need a good state map or a Gazetteer to help you find specific sites. Keep in mind that some of the best places are off the beaten track, and many can be visited on a tank of gas or even on your bicycle. We have extensive bike travels throughout the state.

Each entry provides basic information, including name, address, hours, and seasons of operation, accessibility, and admission. Exact admission costs are not given because they often change. It pays to call ahead to confirm hours, admission, and special events because these may have changed, too. To find the museums, zoos, or botanical gardens in particular areas, use the indexes in the back of the book. Indexes are cross-referenced to help you find what you are looking for.

I assume ultimate responsibility for the information contained in this book, and apologize for any errors, omissions, or flights of fancy. Entries are based on data provided by the institution on a written survey form, augmented by my own recollections of the many places I have visited personally. For most sites, descriptions in the book barely begin to convey all there is to see. Whole volumes have been written about some of the museums, gardens, and zoos. Because resources like this book can always be made better, I invite you to contact me or the University of Wisconsin Press with suggestions for additions, corrections and for ways to improve future editions. www.universitywisconsinpress.edu

A work like this is never truly finished and can never be complete. The institutions presented here are like an ever-changing mosaic set against the backdrop of Wisconsin's widely varied cultural and natural landscapes. Each year some are born, some close their doors, others expand their holdings, a few go into hibernation. Budget cuts, staff changes, "angel" donors, historical events, natural disasters, and other factors affect their fate. Having spent six years on the research and writing of this book, I fully realize how time-sensitive the material is.

These places could not exist without you. They depend on people who care deeply about history, art, nature, and wildlife. Each is a unique statement about what is important and worth preserving. Let this book be your guide to these fascinating Wisconsin treasures!

Anton (Tony) Rajer
Madison, Wisconsin

The old Milwaukee Public Museum building, today the Milwaukee Public Library.

Tony's Top Ten Favorite Sites

1.   Milwaukee Public Museum. My all-time favorite since my childhood.

2.   Milwaukee County Zoo. Great animals, fabulous park setting.

3.   West Bend Art Museum. Because it focuses on Wisconsin art.

4.   Circus World Museum in Baraboo. Pure fantasy and fun.

5.   Chazen Art Museum in Madison. One of the best university art museums in America. Keep an eye on them, they're going to be expanding in the near future.

6.   Oneida Nation Museum in the Green Bay area. Great collection, a beautiful setting dedicated to Native American culture and history.

7.   Leigh Yawkey Woodson Art Museum in Wausau. An all around great museum for its collection, building and grounds.

8   Wisconsin Concrete Park. American folk art at its best. now a National Historic site.

9.   Beloit College Museums. A superb anthropology collection and a fine arts museum in a campus setting.

10.   Taliesin: the home of Frank Lloyd Wright in Spring Green. It's an international art and architectural treasure.

Historical photo of the Old Milwaukee Zoo.

Come and see how zoos have changed over 100 years.

Ten Must See Objects

1. The Jesuit 18th Century Monstrance at the Neville Public Museum in Green Bay. French pioneers gifted it to the Catholic mission in De Pere in 1686.

2. The Flagellants painting by Carl Von Marr, 1891 at the West Bend Art Museum. Wow, He was a good painter. The large painting is over 13'x 10' in size.

3. USS Coiba submarine at the Wisconsin Maritime Museum in Manitowoc. You can even arrange to spend a night in the sub. Das boot!

4. B-17 World War II bomber experience at EAA in Oshkosh. It takes flight.

5. The 1895 Apostles Clock at the Oshkosh Public Museum. All handcrafted.

6. The Frida Kahlo Painting at the Madison Museum of Contemporary Art. She was a genius.

7. The tropical plants at "the Domes" Botanical Gardens in Milwaukee. Why go to the tropics, We have it here.

8. The elephants at the Milwaukee County Zoo. Gosh their big.

9. St. Francis of Assisi painting by Francisco Zurbaran from 1630/34 at the Milwaukee Art Museum. It's a haunting picture.

10. Superbowl trophies: I, II, XXXI, in the Packers Hall of Fame in Green Bay.

In 1686 the French commander and interpreter, Nicolas Perrot, presented this stunning religious artifact to the Jesuit Mission in De Pere. It is one of the oldest and most important European cultural artifacts in Wisconsin. This a real must see.

Silver Monstrance, Courtesy of the Neville Public Museum of Brown Countyand the Catholic Diocese of Green Bay.

Welcome to Wisconsin

The State of Wisconsin operates beautiful Welcome Centers at all the main land based entry points to the state. They are staffed by knowledgeable people who can provide accurate information for the traveler. Each center has an ample supply of brochures about sites and places to visit in our state.

Beloit
Interstate 90 Rest Area
P.O. Box 918
Beloit, WI 535512
(608) 364-4823

Genoa City
Hwy 12 Rest Area
P.O. Box 277
Genoa City, WI 53128
(262) 279-6856

Grant County
Visitors Center
P.O. Box 103
Kieler, WI 53812
(262) 748-4484

Hudson
2221 Crestview
Hudson, WI 54016
(715) 386-2571

Hurley
P.O. Box 327
Hurley, WI 54534
(715) 561-5310

Kenosha
Interstate I-94
10519 120 Ave.
Pleasant Prairie, WI 53158
(262) 857-7164

La Crosse
Interstate I-90 Rest Area
2323 Lakeshore Dr.
La Crosse, WI 54603
(608)783-6403

Marinette
1680 Bridge street
P.O. Box 1077
Marinette, WI 54143
(715) 732-4333

Prairie Du Chien
Visitors Center
211 s. Main St.
Prairie du Chien, WI 53821
(608) 326-2241

Superior
Hwy 53 and Hwy 2
P.O. Box 35
Superior, WI 54880
(715) 392-1662

Lake Superior

UpperMichigan

Minnesota

Northwest

Northeast

Lake
Michigan

Southwest

Iowa

Southeast

Illinois

 State of Wisconsin Travel Information Centers

Wisconsin Department of Tourism
(800) 432-8747, www.travelwisconsin.com/winter

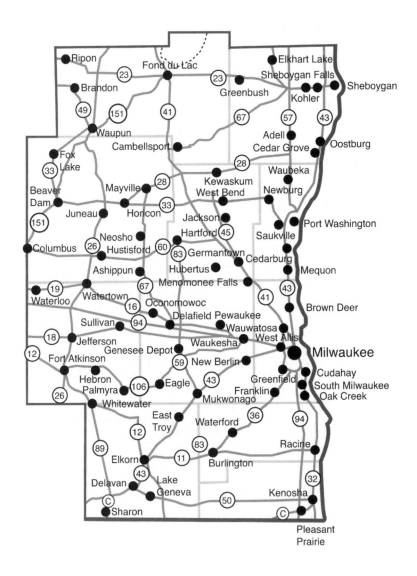

Southeast

courtesy of Ten Chimneys

Adell

Correctly pronounced "yamas," not lamas, these beasts are worth their fleece!

Pleasure Valley Llamas
W7757 S. Hwy A
Adell, WI 53001

Phone: (920) 994-9294 [Fax: 920-994-9602]
Email: llamas@execpc.com
Website: www.execpc.com/PleasureValleyLlamas
Open: April 1 – October 31 by reservation only
Admission: Yes, discount for groups of thirty-five people or more

Ashippun

This is a sweet little place in the middle of the prairie that really knows bees. Hive some honey!

Honey Acres "Honey of a Museum"
N1557 Hwy 67 (2 miles north of Ashippun)
Ashippun, WI 53003

Mailing address: P.O. Box 346, Ashippun, WI 53003
Phone: (920) 474-4411 [Fax: 920-474-4018]
Contact: Ashippun Business Association
(920) 474 - 7143
Email: sales@honeyacres.com
Website: www.honeyacres.com
Open: Daily, Monday – Friday, 9am to 3:30pm.
Mid-May through October: Saturday and Sunday, noon to 4pm.
Admission: Free

Important works: American and European honey-making equipment.

About the museum: Honey Acres was founded in 1852, this unusual farm turned museum highlights bees, beekeepers and the making of honey. Now in its fifth generation, Honey Acres began in 1852 when C.F. Diehnelt arrived in Milwaukee from his native Germany with his beekeeping talents. Today, Honey Acres is a large honey making operation located on a forty-acre property in rural Ashippun, midway between Milwaukee and Madison. The museum has all kinds of facts and trivia concerning the making of honey and the bees that do the work. You can sample different kinds of honey and see honey-making artifacts from Europe.

Fascinating Facts

Kringles are a type of Danish pastry made with nuts, honey, and dough. Kringles also come in fruit fillings and in Racine County there are several bakeries that specialize in kringles. My favorite Racine bakeries: Racine Danish Kringle, the Owen H. Danish Bakery, and Lehmann's Bakery.

Beaver Dam

Dam, this is a good little historic museum only one hour from Madison!

Dodge County Historical Society Museum
105 Park Ave.
Beaver Dam, WI 53916

Phone: (920) 887-1266
Contact: Beaver Dam Area Commerce (920) 887-8879
Email: dchs@powercom.net
Website: http://www2.powercom.net/~dchs/Index.htm
Open: Tuesday through Saturday, 1pm to 4pm.
Special tours by appointment.

Important works: 1902 Rambler automobile, rocks & minerals
collection, one-room schoolhouse, and war memorabilia.

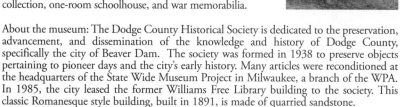

About the museum: The Dodge County Historical Society is dedicated to the preservation, advancement, and dissemination of the knowledge and history of Dodge County, specifically the city of Beaver Dam. The society was formed in 1938 to preserve objects pertaining to pioneer days and the city's early history. Many articles were reconditioned at the headquarters of the State Wide Museum Project in Milwaukee, a branch of the WPA. In 1985, the city leased the former Williams Free Library building to the society. This classic Romanesque style building, built in 1891, is made of quarried sandstone.

Exhibits include a recreation of a One Room School House of the late 1800's and early 1900's. Although scaled down, the room has original desks, maps, chalkboards, and displays chronicling the history of area schools. A new exhibit honors veterans and displays numerous items from the Civil War, Spanish-American War, World War I, World War II, Korean War, and Vietnam War.

A small but lively community art center for ALL to enjoy, Seoppel it!

Seoppel Homestead and Center for the Arts
1605 N. Spring St.
Beaver Dam, WI 53916

Mailing address: P.O. Box 442, Beaver Dam, WI 53916
Email: bdaaa@powercom.net
Website: www.bdaaa.org
Open: Gift shop and exhibit: Thursday, 1pm to 7pm; Saturday, 10am to 4pm; Sunday, 1pm to 4pm.

Shows six exhibitions per year in fiber arts, wildlife, and landscape art.

Brandon

Brandon has a diverse history. See it at its best at the historical museum.

Brandon Historical Society Museum
117 East Main Street
Brandon, WI 53919

Mailing address: 125 N. State Street, Brandon, WI 53919

Phone: (920) 346-2962
Contact: Karey Schmidt or Twilah DeBoer
Email: ctdeboer@centurytel.net
Website:
www.wlhn.org/fond_du_lac/communities/brandon/brandon_historical_society.htm
Open: Saturdays, 2pm to 4pm and by appointment.

Important works: County, township, and village archives.

About the museum: The Brandon Historical Society was organized in 1996 to preserve the history of the village of Brandon. Exhibits include many artifacts, antique furniture, and memorabilia donated by the community. There are also historical papers, obituaries, and plat books that are useful to those doing genealogy research.

Brookfield

Only minutes from Milwaukee, this wonderful site is a step back in time. Come live the past.

▲ Dousman Stagecoach Inn Museum
1075 Pilgrim Pkwy
Brookfield, WI 53005

Mailing address: P.O. Box 292, Brookfield, WI 53008
Phone: (262) 782-6312
Contact: Mrs. Marion Bruhn or Greater Brookfield Chamber of Commerce (262) 786-1886 or Brookfield Convention and Visitors Bureau, Inc. (414) 789-0220
Open: May-October, first and third Sunday, 1pm to 4pm. Advanced reservations requested for group tours.

About the museum: This stately Greek Revival Inn once stood at the corner of Bluemound and Watertown Plank Roads. It was built in the 1840s by Talbot Dousman, whose brother (Hercules) later built the Villa Louis in Prairie du Chien. In 1857, Daniel Brown purchased the property and ran it as a stagecoach inn to accommodate travelers using the plank road that sliced through the wilderness from Milwaukee to Watertown. It later became a farm and in 1980 was donated to the historical society. Start your tour at the 1852 William Donaldson log/frame Visitor Center. Walk through the rooms of the Stagecoach Inn furnished with Wisconsin artifacts. Share the experiences of the Browns and the weary travelers who stopped at the Inn during their long horse drawn journey across the state. Stroll the grounds and see the 1852 Log House, the Smoke House, the Ice House, and the Wagon/Blacksmith Shop. Recall school days past with the original 1862 Woodside School Bell Tower. Step back in time to relive an earlier era in Wisconsin history.

Diversity in the arts is the theme of this community arts center.

▲ Sharon Lynne Wilson Center for the Arts
Ploch Art Gallery
19805 W. Capitol Drive
Brookefield, WI 53405

Phone: (262) 781-5470
Open: Monday through Friday 9am to 5pm, Saturday 10am to 2pm.
Admission: Free, donations appreciated

The Ploch Art Gallery is housed in this community based art center that has a reputation for fine cultural activities. The ever-changing art gallery highlights Wisconsin Art as well as unique exhibits from the region. Call ahead for details.

Brown Deer

A well preserved one-room school evokes bygone days in American rural education. Good grades for this museum!

Brown Deer Historical Society
4800 W. Green Brook Dr.
Brown Deer, WI 53223

Mailing address: 8035 N. Grandview Dr., Brown Deer, WI 53223
Phone: (414) 354-4116
Contact: Dorothy Kittleson, Historical Society Historian
Email: earlkittl@aol.com
Open: Preservation week – May 15, 2pm to 4pm; fourth of July, 3pm to 7pm. Also by appointment.

Important works: 1884 one-room school.

About the museum: The 1884 Brown Deer School, a Greek revival 19th century one-room school, was used from 1884 to 1922. It is the only intact one-room schoolhouse from that period in Milwaukee County. Joseph Gill donated the school to the Village of Brown Deer in 1972. The historical society restored the building and developed an educational program and local history museum.

Dorothy Kittleson founded the 4th grade Living Schoolhouse Program in 1976. Spring and Fall terms have been held at the school for twenty-nine years and over 20,000 4th graders from ten communities have experienced "a school day in 1844 in a rural one-room school." The structure is on the National and State Registers of Historic Places and is also a Milwaukee County Landmark.

Burlington

Stop at the Underground Railroad and get a glimpse of local history through hundreds of artifacts and antique buildings. You don't need a ticket; it's free.

★Burlington Historical Society —
Museum, Pioneer Cabin, Whitman School
232 N. Perkins Blvd.
Burlington, WI 53105

Phone: (262) 767-2884 [Fax: 262-767-2844]
Contact: Doug Lind, President or Burlington Area Chamber of Commerce (262) 763-6044
Email: info@burlingtonhistory.org
Website: www.burlingtonhistory.org
Open: Museum: Sunday, 1pm to 4pm; Schoolhouse: by appointment
Pioneer Cabin: May – October, Saturday, 1pm to 4pm.
Admission: Free

SOUTHEAST

Important works: Al-Vista panoramic cameras (made in Burlington from 1897-1908), artifacts from the Burlington Liars Club, extensive archives including photographs (many available on-line), genealogy, and local connections to the Underground Railroad.

About the museum. The Burlington Historical Society was established in 1928 to collect and preserve historical records and artifacts pertaining to the area. It was the first historical society in Racine County. In 1964, a former church building, erected in 1883, was donated for use as a museum. Burlington area artifacts on display include a Victorian-era parlor, turn of the century kitchen, a collection of Indian artifacts, and several items from the Civil War.

The Pioneer Log Cabin is located one block north of the museum in a downtown park. It was dismantled, moved, reassembled and is now furnished as a post-Civil War farm family home. Adjoining the cabin are vegetable and flower gardens, as well as a tool shed with displays on local agricultural history and period hand tools. Whitman School, the first school building in Burlington (1840), was acquired in 1986. This brick structure was renovated and outfitted as a 19th century schoolhouse and special classes are taught there as they were in the 1840s.

This museum tests your ability to solve the puzzles of life.

Logic Puzzle Museum
533 Milwaukee Ave
Burlington, WI 53105

Phone: (262) 763-3946
Contact: Judith Schulz, Director or Burlington Area Chamber of Commerce (262) 763-6044
Email: logicpuzzles1@hotmail.com
Website: www.logicpuzzlemuseum.org
Open: No regular hours. Visitors must call ahead, reservations are required.
Admission: Yes, free parking

About the museum: The Logic Puzzle Museum is a hands-on museum of more than fifty different logic puzzles that also includes exhibits of vintage parlor puzzles, mind teasers, and brain twisters. Join the fun and make one to keep!

Don't get dizzy at this fun "yoyo" adventure destination. We wouldn't string you along.

★Spinning Top and Yo-Yo Museum
533 Milwaukee Ave.
Burlington, WI 53105

Phone: (262) 763-3946
Contact: Judith Schulz, Director or Burlington Area Chamber of Commerce (262) 763-6044
Website: www.topmuseum.org
Open: No regular hours. Visitors must call ahead, reservations are required.
Admission: Yes, free parking

Important works: More than 2,000 antique and modern tops, yo-yos, and gyroscopes.

About the museum: The Spinning Top and Yo-Yo Museum is a unique and lively two-hour "tour/program". See a 2,000 item exhibit, view videos, try thirty-five hands-on tops and top games, and enjoy a live show and demonstrations by the top collector. The collector is also the Tops Expert expert from the MGM movie My Summer Story (sequel to A Christmas Story with Ralphie). The museum has been featured on the crazy PBS show Wild Chicago, Ripley's Believe It Or Not TV, and the highly regarded Discover Wisconsin Television. Features have also appeared in Reminisce Magazine, Collectibles, Toy Collector, Midwest Living Magazine, Contact Kids, and many others. Books Offbeat Museum, Weird Wisconsin, Spinning Toys, and others include this friendly one-of-a-kind museum filled with science, history, optical illusions, and a personal tour. Special events include the Annual Yo-Yo Convention, the Wisconsin State Yo-Yo Contest, the Gyroscope Contest, Top Investing Labs, Yo-Yo classes, old-fashioned Top Spinning Classes, and presentations about working on a movie set.

Campbellsport

Don't get cold feet on this Ice Age glacial adventure!

Henry S. Reuss Ice Age Visitor Center
Kettle Moraine State Forest – Northern Unit
N2875 5th 67 (located half a mile west of Dundee, off Hwy 67)
Campbellsport, WI 53010

Mailing address: N1765 Highway G, Campbellsport, WI 53010
Phone: (920) 533-8322 [Fax: 262-626-2117]
Contact: Jackie Scharfenberg, Naturalist or Campbellsport Area Chamber of Commerce (920) 979-0080
Email: jackie.scharfenberg@dnr.state.wi.us
Open: Weekdays 8:30am to 4pm, Weekends and Holidays 9:30am – 5pm. Weekday hours vary from December to March.

Important works: Displays and natural objects related to Wisconsin's glacial past.

About the center: The Kettle Moraine State Forest - Northern Unit has some of the best glacial features in the world as well as rich, diverse plant communities. Start your visit at the Henry S. Reuss Ice Age Visitor Center to learn more about how glaciers shaped the landscape and what other opportunities are available within the forest. Located half mile west of Dundee on State Highway 67, the center offers forest information, interpretative displays, and a twenty-minute Ice Age film. Naturalist programs are scheduled throughout the year. Group interpretive programs are available upon request.

Cedar Grove

Go Dutch and get a taste of Wisconsin's heritage by visiting here on a summer day. Wooden shoes allowed...

★Het Museum and Te Ronde House
Te Ronde House: 118 Main St.
(at Union and Main Streets)
Het Museum: 1 block south of Te Ronde on Main St.
Cedar Grove, WI 53013

Cedar Grove Het Museum

Mailing address: W2879 Highway G, Cedar Grove, WI 53013
Phone: (920) 668-6746
Email: rjlenz@execpc.com
Contact: Joan Lenz
Open: Mid-June through August, Fridays, 4pm to 8pm. Last weekend in July, Friday, noon to 8pm (Holland Festival).

Important works: The museum has country school items, artifacts from military and industry, and archives. The house contains furnishings circa 1920s including pump organs, period clothing, and kitchenware.

About the museum: The Het Museum, which opened in 1976, is dedicated to collecting and preserving the information, records, and artifacts relating to the history of the Village of Cedar Grove. At one time the village was largely of Dutch descent, so many of the objects are from the Netherlands. Exhibits of memorabilia plus household and commercial artifacts from Dutch settlements portray daily life during the early years of the community.

The Te Ronde House, a beautifully restored home built in 1875, is furnished to show local household scenes from the period 1920-1930. It houses the organ from the First Presbyterian Church as well as the family organ used to give lessons in the house. An old-fashioned Ice Cream Social is held on the lawn in late June.

Cedarburg

Cedarburg has a reputation for quality. Come see how they preserve their diverse history at many sites.

★Cedarburg Cultural Center — General Store Museum
W62 N546 Washington Ave.
Cedarburg, WI 53012

Mailing address: P.O. Box 84, Cedarburg, WI 53012
Phone: (262) 375-3676 [Fax: 262-375-4120]
Contact: Sarah Hall, Executive Director or Cedarburg Chamber of Commerce (414) 377-5856 or Cedarburg Visitors Information Center (414) 377-9620
Email: cccenter@ameritech.net
Website: http://www.cedarburgculturalcenter.org/History-Museums.htm
Open: Cultural Center: Tuesday - Saturday, 10am to 5pm; Sunday, 1pm to 5pm.
General Store Museum: Monday - Friday, 10am to 4pm; Saturday, 10am to 3pm; Sunday, 11am to 3pm.
Admission: Free, donations appreciated.

Important works: Edward Rappold and Harold Dobberpuhl collections of historic photographs, antique advertising, and packaging art. Properties include the General Store Museum, Kuhefuss House, and restored one-room school.

About the collection: Serving simultaneously as an art gallery, theater, museum, and community gathering place, the Cedarburg Cultural Center is dedicated to preserving the history of Southeastern Wisconsin while enhancing its vital contemporary culture. Performing arts programs, folk heritage celebrations featuring ethnic music and dance, fine arts fairs, and ever-changing exhibits are among the events held at the Center's main facility. It also hosts the Annual Stone and Century House Tour of historic homes and owns and oversees the Kuhefuss House, which is one of Cedarburg's oldest German-American households. It maintains a replica of an early 20th century schoolroom in the Lincoln Building and serves as curator of the Cedarburg General Store Museum.

The General Store Museum, at W61 N480 Washington Ave, is housed in a restored 1860's era frame building on the south end of Cedarburg's main National Historic District. The Roger C. Christensen Collection of antique packaging and advertising art, which is displayed in the museum, dates from the early 1900s through the 1940s and is believed to be one of the most extensive of its kind in the Midwest.

The Kuhefuss House Museum at W63 N627 Washington Ave., is among the oldest and most important residences in Cedarburg. This simple Greek revival structure provided shelter for five generations of one of Cedarburg's oldest families for 150 years. Schoolteacher Marie Kuhefuss, the last surviving member of the family, bequeathed the home to the Cultural Center in 1989. A founding member of the Center, Miss Kuhefuss also left an extensive collection of family photographs and memorabilia that can be seen in the home.

The Lincoln Building, adjacent to the Cedarburg City Hall, was once Cedarburg's only grade school and is the home of the Cultural Center's restored 1920s schoolroom. Filled with ornate desks, slate tablets, and inkwells, this room takes visitors back to a bygone era and a simpler time. School groups participating in the Center's Walking Tours as well as other groups of visitors frequently request to experience this historic little room.

Start your tour of historic Cedarburg at the ever-changing Art Center.

★Ozaukee Art Center
W62 N718-730 River Edge Dr.
Cedarburg, WI 53012

Phone: (262) 377-8230 or (262) 377-7220
Contact: Paul J. Yank, Director or Cedarburg Chamber of Commerce (414) 377-5856 or Cedarburg Visitors Information Center (414) 377-9620
Open: Wednesday – Sunday, 1pm to 4pm. Times will differ during the summer. Call to confirm.
Admission: Free

Important works: Russian art.

About the center: Housed in an 1843 brewery, the center and complex is home to sculptor Paul J. Yank's working studio and the Ozaukee Art Center. Works of art, crafts, and a Russian art collection are on display. The center and complex are open year-round with exhibits changing every six weeks.

Wisconsin Museum of Quilts and Textiles

Mailing address: P.O. Box 562, Cedarburg, WI
Phone: (262) 377-0345
Contact: Kay Walters
Website: www.quiltmuseum.com

No information available.

Cleveland

Discover history in the farming community!

Centreville Settlement, Inc.
Cleveland, WI 53015

Mailing address: P.O. Box 247, Cleveland, WI 53015
Phone: (414) 964-0319
Contact: Janet
Email: janetlutze@worldnet.att.net
Website: centrevillesettlement.homepage.com
Open: Workdays 9am to 5pm. Please call to confirm dates and times.

About the museum: In the 1840s and '50s, immigrants fled Germany to escape war and economic hard times. Many Saxon Germans settled in Centreville. Their fifth and sixth generation original farms using original buildings for their original purpose. Centreville is a unique time capsule of architecture, culture, and traditions of the early settlers.

Centreville Settlement, Inc. is a non-profit organization dedicated to preserving this rural farm heritage through education and preservation. When you come to visit, bring work gloves, wear steady shoes, and be prepared to learn and have fun!

Columbus

Columbus never visited Wisconsin, but his namesake museum tells the whole story, from tragedy to triumph. You can discover antiques in the mall.

Christopher Columbus Museum
239 Whitney St. (in the Columbus Antiques Mall)
Columbus, WI 53925

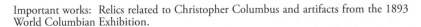

Mailing address: P.O. Box 151, Columbus, WI 53925
Phone: (920) 623-1992 [Fax: 920-623-1992]
Contact: Columbus Area Chamber of Commerce (920) 623-3699
Website: www.columbusantiquemall.com
Open: Daily, 8:15am to 4pm.
Admission: Yes

Important works: Relics related to Christopher Columbus and artifacts from the 1893 World Columbian Exhibition.

About the museum: The museum displays a comprehensive collection of souvenirs from the 1893 World's Fair Columbian Exposition in Chicago, as well as Christopher Columbus memorabilia. Exhibits include statues, silks, lithographs, chinaware, and glassware. Relics related to Christopher Columbus include stones from Columbus' first home and the home of his grandfather (Giovianni Columbo,1420, Italy), a pottery piece from and sketch of the Hospital Le Bon Samaritain (site of LaNavidad, the fort built from the ship-wrecked Santa Maria), and the first coin minted in Spain in 1505 for use in Hispanola. Note: the museum is a small part of an antiques mall. The historic displays need upgrading and proper labels.

Cudahy

Cudahy depot is full of memories, past, present, and future. Stop by and make your own.

Cudahy Historical Society — Cudahy Railroad Depot
4647 S. Kinnickinnic Ave.
Cudahy, WI 53110

Mailing address: P.O. Box 332, Cudahy, WI 53110
Phone: (414) 747-1892
Contact: Cudahy Chamber of Commerce (414) 483-8615
Open: May through October, last Saturday of the month, 10am to noon.

Important works: Historic railroad depot.

About the museum: The Cudahy Depot was once the gate to the City of Milwaukee. At this crossroads, a stream of immigrants arrived from Europe, and Wisconsin farm boys seeking work came down from Northern Wisconsin. In the 1940s, this was the tearful departure point as Wisconsin men and women left to serve in World War II. For decades, this was the shipping and receiving point for Cudahy and area industries, including the Patrick Cudahy Co., the Federal Rubber Co., the Document Error Co., and George J. Meyer Manufacturing Co.

Delafield

A rare pre-Civil War jewel, the Milwaukee stagecoach no longer stops, but you can for a slice of history.

Hawks Inn Historical Society
426 Wells St.
Delafield, WI 53018

Mailing address: P.O. Box 180104, Delafield, WI 53018
Phone: (262) 646-4794
Contact: Jim Babcock or Delafield Chamber of Commerce (414) 646-8100
Website: www.hawksinn.org
Open: May through October, Saturdays, 1pm to 4pm. Call for additional tour information.
Admission: Yes

Important works: Period antiques, blacksmithing equipment.

About the museum: Hawks Inn is an 1846 Greek Revival stage coach inn with eighteen rooms authentically restored and furnished with Federal, American Empire, and early Victorian antiques. Costumed guides provide tours through exhibits, seasonal events, weaving demonstrations on antique looms, a blacksmith and wheelwright shop, and herb and flower gardens.

Military history comes alive at this academy nestled in historic Delafield, a short march away, only forty-five minutes west of Milwaukee.

St. John's Northwestern Military Academy Archives and Museum
1101 N. Genesee St.
Delafield, WI 53018

Phone: (262) 646-7118
Contact: Lynette Ahlgren or Delafield Chamber of Commerce (414) 646-8100
Email: lahlgren@sjnma.org
Website: www.sjnma.org
Open: Open by appointment and during special events

About the museum: In 1995, St. John's Military Academy and Northwestern Military and Naval Academy merged. The Academy's museum presents the past of these academies through historical photographs, documents, memorabilia, and cadet uniforms. The archives are available for research and include such items as yearbooks, publications, photographs, documents, and cadet scrapbooks.

Tony's Tips

If you are near Fond du Lac, stop by Schreiner's Restaurant. With consistently good homemade food, it's one of my favorite restaurants. Find it right off of Johnson Street and the expressway, and don't forget to try the walnut pie!

Delavan

There's something for everyone at this zoo! Pet the animals, ride the carriage, and frolic on the hayrides. The kids, human and animal, love the petting zoo.

Lake Geneva Animal Gardens
5065 Hwy 50
Delavan, WI 53115

Phone: (262) 728-8200
Website: www.animalgardens.com
Open: May, Saturday and Sunday; June, July, and August, Monday-Sunday; September and October, Saturday and Sunday. Presentation shows start at 10am and run until 4pm. Approximately a two-hour event.
Admission: Yes, group discounts available

Come to experience wildlife through this interactive setting with animal shows, animal keeper talks, and a baby-petting barn! Also available are train rides, horse drawn carriage rides, and pony and hayrides.

Eagle

If you are visiting nearby Old World Wisconsin, take the time to see this community-based museum. It's well worth the stop, for heaps of history.

Eagle Historical Society Museum and Research Library
217 West Main Street
Eagle, WI 53119

Mailing address: P.O. Box 454, Eagle, WI 53119
Phone: (262) 594-8961
Contact: Jeff Nowicki or Eagle Business Association (262) 594-3114
E-mail: curator@eaglewi.org
Website: www.eaglehs.org
Open: Friday and Saturday, 9am to noon or call for an appointment.

Beginning in August 2004, an exhibit of Civil War items will be on loan from a private collection. The exhibit includes articles related to the service of William W. Chatterton, a farm boy from rural Oregon. Take advantage of this, and the other collections the Eagle Historical Society has to offer.

This impressive collection of sixty historic buildings is one of Wisconsin's premier historic destinations not to be missed!

★★★Old World Wisconsin
S103 W37890 Highway 67 (1 1/2 miles southwest of Eagle)
Eagle, WI 53119

Phone: (262) 594-6300
Contact: Eagle Business Association (262) 594-3114
Email: oww@whs.wisc.edu
Website: http://www.wisconsinhistory.org/oww/
Open: May 1 – June 10, 10am to 3pm weekdays; 10am to 5pm weekends. June 11 – June 30, 10am to 4pm weekdays; 10am to 5pm weekends. July 1 – August, 10am to 5pm daily. September

SCHRC

1 – October 31, 10am to 4pm weekdays; 10am to 5pm weekends. Open for special postseason holiday events in November and December.
Admission: Yes

Important works: A collection of over sixty historic buildings, plus over 50,000 19th century objects, most of which are on display or in use, including Norwegian decorative arts objects, German-American furniture, pre-Civil War African American church furnishings, and tools and equipment from many occupations.

About the museum: Nestled in the Southern Kettle Moraine Forest, just thirty-five miles southwest of Milwaukee, Old World Wisconsin is one of the nation's largest outdoor museums of living history and is operated by the Wisconsin Historical Society. The museum is home to more than sixty-five historic buildings – farms, houses, churches, and stores of the hardy pioneers who forged a new life in a new land. Features include ten farms and a crossroads village, nine ethnic groups represented, rare historic breeds of animals, hundreds of heirloom plants, miles of nature trails, and diverse wildlife. Staff at OWW dress in period costume and "live" the roles of settlers, craftsmen, cooks, and farmers in and around the buildings.

OWW was developed as Wisconsin's bicentennial project and opened to the public in 1976. Historic houses representing vernacular architectural traditions brought to North America by European immigrants were moved to the site to preserve them from destruction. Many are rare or unique examples of their kind. Structures characteristic of "old stock" Yankee settlers have also been restored at the museum. One of the more recent acquisitions is an African-American chapel, church, and cemetery, extending the institution's interpretive scope beyond white European immigrants and Yankee migrants from the east coast. Together, the buildings and the collections that furnish them exemplify Wisconsin's heritage as the most ethnically diverse state in the union during the 19th century.

Although OWW is best known for its architectural restorations and interpretive programming, it is also the repository of a large and varied collection of historic and ethnic heritage artifacts, approximately 80% of which are housed and exhibited in the historic buildings. Representative examples include a collection of exquisitely carved and painted Norwegian decorative arts objects and Norwegian-American furniture pieces. The museum has an extensive collection of German-American furniture collected in Wisconsin, providing an interesting contrast with the better-known Pennsylvania German furniture found in many east coast museums. OWW has the original furnishings of a church founded by an African American community. This community was made up of freed slaves who migrated from Virginia to southwestern Wisconsin before the Civil War. The pieces from this group are highly important elements of the state's heritage because of their unique provenance. The many objects with ethnic associations are supplemented by a large number of domestic articles, decorative arts objects, agricultural tools and equipment, woodworking and metalworking tools and equipment, factory-produced furniture, and other manufactured items that, taken together, document the material culture of 19th century native and immigrant communities. The collection tells a story of social upheaval, massive migration, the peopling of a continent and far-reaching cultural change, but also documents a unique regional material heritage.

Tony's Tips

If your travels bring you to Kohler Village, see the sites and stop by one of the many fine restaurants. My favorite is Black Wolf Run. It's open to the public for golfing, food, and fun.

East Troy

Experience the romantic ambience of dining by rail aboard America's only all electric dinner train. Dessert is included. All aboard! You might even meet Helen of East Troy.

★East Troy Electric Railroad Museum
2002 Church St.
East Troy, WI 53120

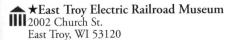

Mailing address: Friends of the East Troy Railroad Museum, Inc., P.O. Box 943, East Troy, WI 53120
Phone: (262) 642-3263 [Fax: 262-642-3197]
Contact: Andy Witkowski, Superintendant of Operations or East Troy Chamber of Commerce (262) 642-3770
Email: ACWTRAINDUDE@aol.com
Website: www.easttroyrr.org
Open: Call for seasonal hours or dining reservations.
Admission: Yes

Important works: Electric trolley and related artifacts.

About the museum: One of the most interesting and short lived chapters of railroading's rich past is that of the electric trolley. In East Troy, this once common mode of transportation is preserved for you to enjoy. Come experience America's only all-electric dinner train in regular service. You'll be taken back to a time when the pace of life was slower and riding the rails was the best way to travel. Your journey begins upon arrival at the museum's historic depot. Once at the museum, your visit includes a self-guided tour of the museum's exhibits inside its historic 1910 depot and power house, an hour-long round-trip trolley ride over Wisconsin's last electric railroad, a tour of the museum's car-barn and restoration facility, shopping at the museum's gift shop, and a visit to The Elegant Farmer bakery and deli.

Call ahead to check out the schedule for the special seasonal exhibits.

East Troy Historical Society
2806 Main St.
East Troy, WI 53120

Mailing address: P.O. Box 861, East Troy, WI 53120
Phone: (262) 642-5701
Contact: Kate Behrens or East Troy Chamber of Commerce (262) 642-3770
Open: Call for current hours

About the museum. This new museum is housed on the upper level of the old Marshall Building. The building was built in 1856 and has a restored, fully working hand pull elevator. There are seasonal exhibitions.

Tony's Tips

There are two seasons in Wisconsin – winter and construction. The Department of Transportation publishes a road construction map annually and they have website links that keep you up to date on road conditions. Check them out, it's worthwhile.

Elkhart Lake

Relax at the lake and see the depot museum, only an hour from Milwaukee.

Elkhart Lake Depot Museum
104 South East Street
Elkhart Lake, WI 53020

Phone: (920) 876-2922
Contact: Elkhart Lake Area Chamber of Commerce (920) 876-2922 or (877) ELKHART
Open: June-Labor Day, Monday - Saturday. Contact the Elkhart Lake Chamber of Commerce for further details.
Admission: Free

Important works: This museum houses photos, newspaper clippings and original depot furnishings as well as other mementos from the Elkhart Lake area.

A contemporary family has preserved the history of countless people from the ancient past, the first inhabitants of the land during the last 10,000 years.

Henschel's Museum of Indian History
N8661 Holstein Rd.
Elkhart Lake, WI 53020

Phone: (920) 876-3193
Contact: Gary or Rosalie Henschel or Elkhart Lake Area Chamber of Commerce (920) 876-2922 or (877) ELKHART

Open: Tuesday - Saturday, 1pm-5pm, Memorial Day to Labor Day and by appointment.

Important works. Extensive collection of Native American artifacts including copper, pottery, and other artifacts dating back to 8000 B.C. A 1996 book entitled Prehistoric Tools, Points, and Arrowheads.

About the museum: The museum, housed in a newly constructed building and built on the archeological site, features a fascinating collection of Native American history and artifacts. Since the first Henschel homesteader settled in Sheboygan County in 1849, the family's land has yielded evidence of 10,000 years of human occupation. Today, the Henschel collection of prehistoric artifacts is one of the most complete in Wisconsin. Items such as chipped stone tools, projectile points, ground stone tools, bone and antler tools, copper implements, and pottery trace the lives and times of the state's prehistoric peoples. The Henschel Indian Museum was started in 1979 by the fifth generation of Henschels, Gary and Rosalie

In the late 1800s, a large burial vault was discovered when Herman Henschel's (second generation) horse broke through the earth. The contents and story of the vault are highlighted during tours. In the summers of 1987-1989, Archaeological Rescue, affiliated with the Milwaukee Public Museum, conducted an archeological field school on the farm. Many of the Early Woodland (dating back to 500 B.C.) materials found during the dig are on display in the museum. The museum hosts two special events each year. An Indian artifact show in late June, features displays of collectors from the Midwest. In October, the "Pumpkin Patch" fall festival is held the second and third weekends of the month, and guests can pick their own pumpkins.

Elkhorn

Music lovers and waterfowl enthusiasts alike enjoy this site! Come see why.

★Walworth County Historical Society — Webster House Museum
9 E. Rockwell St.
Elkhorn, WI 53121

Mailing address: P.O. Box 273, Elkhorn, WI 53121
Phone: (262) 723-4248
Contact: Elkhorn Area Chamber of Commerce (414) 723-5788
E-mail: walcohistory@elknet.net
Website: www.geocities.com/walcohistory/museum.html
Open: Mid-May through mid-October, Wednesday-Saturday, 1pm – 5pm or by appointment.
Admission: Yes

Important works: Furnishings from mid to late 1800s, Civil War era documents, and mounted waterfowl collection.

About the museum: Webster House, the museum of the Walworth County Historical Society, contains Civil War and Victorian period items. Much of the collection belonged to Joseph P. Webster, one of the best-loved composers of the nineteenth century. After moving to this house in 1857, he composed more than 1,000 hymns and ballads. Music lovers will pause in the music room to view its range of instruments and songs. Part of the house was the original Land Grant office, which was created in the public square in 1836 during Wisconsin's territorial period. It has become a repository for rare books, newspapers, documents, and paintings representative of the Civil War period. While on tour, listen carefully; you may hear the lovely melodies that emanated from the square rosewood piano which once belonged to Mr. Webster.

A new acquisition to the museum is one of the most complete collections of mounted waterfowl in the country. The specimens, from the U.S. and abroad, were collected and prepared by a Walworth County resident over a forty-year period. Also new is the Boyd Carriage House, which features historic items depicting the significant achievements and influential pioneer statesmanship of General John W. Boyd.

Saddle up and gallop over! Pick up supplies and hear the old-timers spin a yarn or two.

Watson's Wild West Museum
W4865 Potter Rd.
Elkhorn, WI 53121

Phone: (262) 723-7505
Contact: Doug Watson or Elkhorn Area Chamber of Commerce (414) 723-5788
Website: www.watsonswildwestmuseum.com & www.genevaonline.com/~wildwest
Open: May – October: Tuesday – Saturday, 10am to 5pm; Sunday, 11am to 5pm.
Hours and dates may change.
Admission: Yes

Important works: Historic general store merchandise, 1880s-era cowboy gear and horse tack.

About the museum: Watson's Wild West Museum is a recreation of a unique turn-of-the-century general store. Its sixteen-foot-high shelves are fully stocked with authentic merchandise; medications, confections, crackers, tobacco, coffee, tea, toys, hardware, and horse tack are all on display as in the 1880s. The museum captures your imagination with oral and written tales of yesteryear and the dreams come true of generations gone by. You will see thousands of 1880s-era cowboy artifacts including saddles, harnesses, chaps, guns, gun belts and holsters, branding irons, bear traps, spurs, game heads and life-size mounts of elk, bear, buffalo, wolves, moose, and mountain lions.

Fond du Lac

Discover the origins of Fondy in this huge historic village complex. It's worth the visit, especially during the summer celebration!

★★**Fond du Lac County Historical Society — Galloway House and Village**
336 Old Pioneer Rd.
Fond du Lac, WI 54935

Mailing address: P.O. Box 1284, Fond du Lac, WI 54936
Phone: (920) 922-1166, (920) 922-6390
Email: history@fdl.com
Website: www.fdl.com/history/galloway.iml
Open: Memorial Day weekend through Labor Day, Daily, 10am to 4pm; Also weekends in September.
Admission: Yes

Important works: Extensive collection of Fond du Lac County artifacts exhibited in chronological order, including objects from the Native American era, Civil War, logging industry, World Wars I and II, the Depression, plus special collections featuring General Edward S. Bragg and aviator Steve Wittman. Village contains over thirty historic structures.

About the museum: The Blakely Museum is the focal point of the Fond du Lac County Historical Society's Galloway House and Village. Built in 1981, it provides an overview of Fond du Lac County history and showcases "the best of the best" from the collection. The society also maintains a research library with books, manuscripts, family files, maps, and photos of Fond du Lac County.

The Village has over thirty buildings including a country church, railroad depot and caboose, furnished log cabin, dressmaker's shop, Willow-Lawn School, newspaper and print shop, and toyshop. One of the highlights is the Galloway House, which was built in 1847 and remodeled in 1880. It is a classic Midwest version of an Italianate villa of Victorian elegance. This charming thirty-room home of four generations of Galloways has since remained unchanged. Four fireplaces, hand carved pine, stenciled ceilings, and one of the first bathrooms in the state are some of the features. The Adams House Resource Center is also located on the village grounds and is open year round for Fond du Lac County research and Historical Society business.

You will grow 'fondy' of this many-sided historic house.

Octagon House Museum
276 Linden Street
Fond du Lac, WI 54935

Phone: (920) 922-1608
Website: www.octagonhousefdl.com
Open: April – October, Monday, Wednesday, and Friday from 1pm to 5:30pm. Group tours of six or more by reservation year round.
Admission: Yes

This is a privately owned Victorian house that was built around 1856 by Orson Fowler and Isaac Brown. The unique structure has not only beautiful interiors in the style of the high Victorian, but also a connection with the Underground Railroad as the house has a secret passageway and hiding places. On the grounds are other displays related to pioneer agricultural tools as well as a gift shop.

The Windhover Center promotes performing and visual arts in all its forms, Bravo!

★Windhover Center for the Arts
51 Sheboygan street
Fond du Lac, Wisconsin, 54935

Phone: (920)921-5410 [Fax: 920-926-6742]
Contact: Phillip l. Zimmerman
Email: phil@windhovercenter.com
Website: www.windhovercenter.com
Open: tuesday, wednesday, and friday 10 am to 5pm, thursday 10 am to 8pm, saturday 10am to 2 pm
Admission: Free, donations welcome

About the museum: The Windhover Center for the Arts specializes in promoting live music, theatre performances, exhibiting local and national artistic talent. They have several visual arts galleries. The Fondy Children's Chorale, as well as the Fondy Acoustic Music Alliance (FAMA) also perform here. The most recent addition to the center has been the Arts Education Department, which works closely with the Fond du Lac Children's Museum, also housed in the same historic facility. Sample them all in this former Masonic Lodge in downtown Fond du Lac. A stately building houses this ambitious organization that stimulates, educates and advocates the arts.

Fort Atkinson

Thousands of objects to pique your interests about pioneer life and social customs. Great for the whole family! A dairy delight.

★Hoard Historical Museum and National Dairy Shrine's Visitors' Center
407 Merchants Ave.
Fort Atkinson, WI 53538

Phone: (920) 563-7769 [Fax: 920-568-3203]
Contact: Sue Hartwick
Email: info@hoardmuseum.org
Website: www.hoardmuseum.org
Open: Memorial Day-Labor Day: Tuesday-Saturday, 9:30am to 4:30pm and Sunday, 11am to 3pm. Labor Day-Memorial Day: Tuesday-Saturday, 9:30am to 3:30pm.
Admission: Free, donations welcome

Important works: Jefferson County archeological artifacts, mounted birds, Civil War books, and dairy industry memorabilia.

About the museum: A local history museum, the Hoard Historical Museum was started in 1936 and is now housed in the former home of Luella and Frank Hoard. Built in 1864 by local pharmacist Rueben White, the home includes sixteen period and exhibit rooms. The Indian Artifacts room houses over 4,000 archeological artifacts and outlines of the prehistory of area Indians. A bird collection of over 500 specimens includes mountings by Thure Kulein, noted naturalist of the 1800s who lived near the shore of Lake Koshkonong. Included is a fine example of the extinct passenger pigeon. The textile room exhibits a rotation of quilts, costumes and other textiles from the museum's extensive collection. The Lincoln Era Library holds a collection of over 1,100 books on the Civil War. Exhibits with audiotapes offer brief histories of the Black Hawk War and Jefferson County's involvement in the Civil War. A Tools and Trades exhibit room highlights the trades of the late 19th and early 20th century. Also on the property is the Foster house. The first frame house built in the county features 1840-1870 period rooms.

In addition to the museum, the National Dairy Shrine Visitors Center is located within the complex. The center offers a self-guided multi-media tour of dairy farming past and present along with displays of dairy artifacts. A research room on Jefferson County history and genealogy is open to visitors. Monthly special events are offered.

Fox Lake

In the past, the railroad depot was often the hub of activity for a small town. It still is at this historic site.

Fox Lake Depot Museum
211 W. Cordelia St.
Fox Lake, WI 53933

Mailing address: P.O. Box 493, Fox Lake, WI 53933
Phone: (920) 928-3754
Contact: Scott Frank, President
Open: Memorial Day - September, first and third Sundays, 1pm to 4pm, or call for an appointment.

Important works: American Indian artifacts, railroad memorabilia.

About the museum: Housed in a 1884 Milwaukee Road Railroad depot, the museum features Indian artifacts from local archeological digs and offers a special Veterans display on Memorial Day weekend.

For those who love Wisconsin, this a bona-fide gem.

Fox Lake Library and History Room
117 W State St.
Fox Lake, WI 53933

Mailing address: P.O. Box 47, Fox Lake, WI 53933
Phone: (920) 928-3223
Open: Call ahead for an appointment
Admission: Free

Important works: This small history room is filled with hundreds of fascinating documents related to Wisconsin history.

Located within the Fox Lake Public Library is a room dedicated to local history. It was established nearly 100 years ago by a local group of women who dedicated themselves to collecting, preserving, and documenting Wisconsin and Fox Lake history. Some of the incredible items found within the collection are the original territorial land entry books from 1840, an original copy of the 1829 Winnebago Treaty with Blackhawk's signature, and Civil War letters, battle records, and photographs. There are also birth, death, and marriage certificates. Time your visit to coincide with the Fox Lake History Days and the Civil War Reenactment.

Fascinating Facts

The world's biggest clock face is not Big Ben in London, but the Allen Bradley clock on the south side of Milwaukee.

SOUTHEAST

Franklin

Like a village within a village, Legend Park keeps history in the center of Franklin life.

Franklin Historical Society — Legend Park
9229 W. Loomis (Behind the Franklin City Hall)
Franklin, WI 53132

Phone: (414) 425-0903
Contact: Al Block, President
Open: Summer, first Sunday of the month from 1pm to 4pm. Also, on special holidays.

About the museum: Legend Park, maintained by the Franklin Historical Society, includes St. Peter's Chapel, Franklin Town Hall, Sheehan-Godsell Cabin, and the Whelan School. St. Peter's Chapel was built about 1869 on S. 68th St. The Town Hall was moved to the park in 1975 and has been restored for use as a museum and office for the society. The Sheehan-Godsell Cabin is furnished to reflect the lives of the early settlers of Franklin. The Whelan School served the residents of Franklin from 1878 until consolidation of area school districts in 1953. It now serves as a living museum to remind future generations of one-room rural schools about the past.

Genesee Depot

Wisconsin's version of Gone with the Wind, this is an estate filled with movies, memorials, and memorabilia. A real time capsule of American culture. Chimney cricket.

★★★Ten Chimneys
Genesee Depot, WI 53127

Mailing address: P.O. Box 225, Genesee Depot, WI, 53127
Phone: (262) 968-4161 reservation line: (262) 968-4110
[Fax: 262-968-4267]
Website: www.tenchimneys.org
Open: Mid-April – mid-November, Tuesday – Saturday, 10am to 4pm. Reservations recommended.
Admission: Yes

About the museum: Ten Chimneys, the estate lovingly created by theater legends Alfred Lund and Lynn Fontanne, is a world-class house museum and national resource for theater and theater arts education. Guests will be treated to one of the most inspirational historic house tours in the country. Almost all of the estate's enchantingly personal decor and collections are intact and unchanged since the Lunts first assembled them in the 1930s and 40s. Ten Chimneys is simply overflowing with memorabilia including notes from Laurence Olivier and Charlie Chaplin, mementos from Helen Hayes and Noel Coward, and inscribed first edition books by Edna Ferber and Alexander Woollcott. For decades, this idyllic retreat inspired the country's finest actors, writers, and artists.

Tony's Tips

Bratwurst is a local sausage delicacy, German in origin. A Sheboygan restaurant that serve the best "brats" on hard rolls is the Charcoal Inn on south 8th street.

Germantown

Ding, Dong! 5,000 historic bells are here, one hour from Milwaukee. Ring in the New!

★**Germantown Historical Society — Bast Bell Museum**
N128 W18780 Holy Hill Rd.
Germantown, WI 53022

Germantown Historical Society — Christ Church Museum
W 188 N 12808 Fond du Lac Ave.
Germantown, WI 53022

Mailing address: P.O. Box 31, Germantown, WI 53022
Phone: (262) 628-3170
Open: Bast Bell Museum: April 1 – November 1, Wednesday-Sunday, 1pm to 4pm. Christ Church Museum: June 1 – October 1, Sunday, 1pm to 4pm, and by appointment.
Admission: Yes

SCHRC

Important works: Extensive bell collection, shoe-making equipment, a 1929 Seagrave Pumper Fire Truck.

About the museum: Sila Lydia Bast's collection of 5,000 bells from around the world rings to life in a restored barn nestled in the heart of historic Dheinsville near Germantown. Three historic gems - the Sila Lydia Bast Bell Museum, Christ Church museum, and a shoemaker's shop are all housed in the same settlement and are maintained by the Germantown Historical Society. Sila Bast found her first bell in a field just north of the barn that now houses the collection. Barn exhibits also feature a historic Fire Hall display that includes a pristine 1929 Seagrave Pumper Truck and other memorabilia.

Only minutes from Milwaukee, step back in time to a pioneer experience.

Valentine Wolf Haus Museum
The Dheinsville Settlement
Highway 145
Germantown, WI 53022

Mailing address: P.O. Box 31, Germantown, WI 53022
Phone: (262) 628-3170
Open: Call ahead for current times.

The Valentine Wolf Haus was built in 1845 and is an example of medieval German stucco constructor. Valentine Wolf and his wife Elizabeth Klumb raised twelve children here and operated a cobbler shop. The Dheinsville Settlement reflects German origins of the community. Within the house are the archives of the Germantown Historical Society, which operates the Dheinsville Settlement, and items of local interest. Also to be seen in the area is the 1862 limestone Evangelical Christ Church, the 1892 Victorian parsonage, and the Wolf barn. This is part of the complex of 3,000 Bells from Around the World.

SOUTHEAST

Greenbush

Motels have changed a lot since 1850, and so has transportation. See the past come alive in all its facets at this stellar historic site. Stop and Wade awhile.

★★★**Wade House and Wesley Jung Carriage Museum**
W7824 Center St. (off Highway 32)
Greenbush, WI 53026

Mailing address: P.O. Box 34, Greenbush, WI 53026
Phone: (920) 526-3271 [Fax: 920-526-3626]
Email: wadehouse@whs.wisc.edu
Website: www.wisconsinhistory.org/wadehouse
Open: Mid-May – mid-October, 10am to 5pm.

Important works: Major collection of wagons and horse-drawn vehicles.

About the museum: The rattle and clap of wagon wheels rumbling over a plank road signal the arrival of guests seeking sustenance and shelter. The stately Wade House stagecoach inn provided just that in the 1850s. Relive the dreams New England Yankees Sylvanus and Betsey Wade shared for their roadside inn. Board a horse-drawn wagon for an open-air ride to the Wesley Jung Carriage Museum, home to the state's largest carriage and wagon collection. Costumed interpreters reenact the day-to-day activities of the inn and environs.

Depending on the day and season, visitors may experience fireplace cooking and baking, food preservation, soap making, house cleaning, candle making, gardening, or blacksmithing. The carriage museum contains more than 120 horse drawn vehicles from 1870-1915. They exemplify the careful craftsmanship of wagon-makers from that era. The collection includes elegant carriages of the wealthy to the common buckboard. Of special note is the large collection of working wagons, including butcher's carts, grocery wagons, a coal wagon, a street sprinkler, omnibuses, and firefighting equipment. It is regarded as one of the finest of its kind in the U.S.

Greendale

Visit an Irish cottage filled with lore (no blarney stone) and lots of leprechauns. This is a real pot of gold!

Jeremiah Curtin House
8601 W. Grange Ave.
Greendale, WI 53129

Mailing address: 910 N. Old World 3rd St., Milwaukee, WI 53203
Phone: (414) 273-8288 [Fax: 414-273-3268]
Email: mchs@prodigy.net
Website: www.milwaukeecountyhistsoc.org/homes.htm
Open: Mid-May – Labor Day, 1pm to 4pm.
Admission: Free, donations appreciated

Important works: Irish immigrant furnishings, limestone immigrant cottage.

About the museum: The Jeremiah Curtin House, built in 1846, was the first stone house in the Town of Greenfield. David Curtin, his wife and son Jeremiah, were among a group of Irish immigrants who settled in Greenfield in the 1830s. The limestone structure resembles traditional Irish cottages. The home is furnished with furniture and decorative pieces typical of the period 1846-1866, when the Curtin family resided there. Restoration of the home began as a Bicentennial Project in 1976. It is important historically as a physical reminder of Milwaukee County's early Irish settlement and as the boyhood home of Jeremiah Curtin. Curtin became an accomplished linguist, author, and world traveler. He wrote extensively on the language and folklore of primitive peoples all over the world. His best know work is the translation of the novel Quo Vadis by Polish author Henryk Sienkiewicz.

Take a giant step back into pioneer times with a visit to Trimborn Farm.

Trimborn Farm Park
8881 W. Grange Avenue
Greendale, WI 53129

Phone: (414) 529-7744
Open: Farm open for self-guided tours May 15-
October 1. During these open months, there are
daily-guided tours, except Monday.
Admission: Donations appreciated

Trimborn Farm is the only Milwaukee County Park with an historic theme. The nine buildings that comprise the farm include two large barns. One is the largest stone barn in the state. There is also a restored Greek Revival-style farmhouse that dates to the early 1860s. The most unusual of the structures is a group of lime kilns that produced high quality lime mortar and plaster that were used in the construction of early buildings throughout metropolitan Milwaukee from 1850 to 1900. Other buildings featured are a granary (a structure with a wood exterior and a brick interior) and a barrel-vaulted smokehouse. All of these structures supported the manufacture of lime that contributed to the industrial nature of the property.

Greenfield

Get a sample of Greenfield's diverse past at the historic cabin and cottage.

Greenfield Historical Society
5601 W. Layton Ave.
Greenfield, WI 53220

Mailing address: 3239 S. 58th St. 215, Milwaukee, WI 53219
Phone: (414) 545-1117
Open: June through August, second and fourth Sundays, 2pm to 4pm, and by appointment.

Important works: 19th century log cabin and brick cottage, Native American artifacts.

About the museum: The Greenfield Historical Society, founded in 1968, maintains two historic buildings and conducts educational programs pertaining to the history of the town and city of Greenfield. The society's two historic museum buildings are located at 56th and Layton Avenue: The Finan-Gabel-Bodamer Log Cabin (c. 1832) and the Montag-Boogk Cream Brick Cottage (ca. 1856). The log cabin emphasizes furnishings and artifacts from the period 1835-1870, but also has collections of Native American artifacts. The brick cottage emphasizes furnishings and artifacts from the period 1870-1920. The society also maintains a large collection of local photographs, manuscripts, genealogical data, and public records.

Hales Corners

This is one of the largest botanical gardens in Wisconsin. It blooms all year long!

 ★★**Boerner Botanical Gardens**
9400 Boerner Drive
Hales Corners, WI 53130

Phone: (414) 525-5600
Website: www.countyparks.com/horticulture
Open: Formal Gardens: May-October, daily 8am to sunset; Education and Visitor Center: May-September, daily 8am to 7pm; October – April, Monday – Friday, 8am to 5pm; October – November, Saturday, 9am to 4pm; April, Saturday, 9am to 4pm. Late April and early November, if weather conditions are favorable the gardens may be open earlier in the season or stay open later in the season.
Admission: Yes

About the gardens: Boerner Botanical Gardens, located in Milwaukee's Whitnall Park, is an intimate collection of formal garden spaces which host a variety of plant collections from ornamental grasses to phenomenal peonies. The formal gardens include a perennial, peony, rose, rock, shrub, annual, daylily, and trial garden. This internationally renowned garden also holds one of the largest crabapple tree collections in the country.

The nature writer, Ben Hunt, loved the out of doors. Ben's life and legacy is told here in his humble cabin.

 Hales Corners Historical Society — W. Ben Hunt Cabin and Hale Summer Kitchen
5885 S. 116th St.
Hales Corners, WI 53130

Phone: (414) 529-6150 ext. 24
Contact: Bob Zeit (414) 425-6040
Email: Historical Society: mkochis@execpc.com, Bob Zeit: r-jzeit@one-web.net
Website: www.historichalescorners.org
Open: First Saturday of the month, May - November, 1 - 3
Admission: Free, donations appreciated. Tours of the cabin are available. Call Bob Zeit or print an application from the website.

Important works: Ben Hunt memorabilia, Indian artifacts.

About the museum: W. Ben Hunt (1888-1970) was a leader in the outdoor movement and in the reintroduction of pioneer skills. He introduced subjects such as rustic woodworking, whittling and carving, metalworking, and historic Indian crafts and lore. He was involved with the Boy Scouts locally and nationally. His twenty books and 1,000 magazine articles have been printed in twenty-six languages. His cabin contains interesting artifacts and memorabilia related to Ben Hunt and Native Americans.

Ebenezer Hale and his sons Seneca and William Hale were among the earliest settlers of Hales Corners. The Hale Summer Kitchen was built by Seneca in the 1850s. It provided a place to prepare meals, bake, heat water for bathing and laundry, and keep the heat of a wood-burning stove out of the house during summer months.

Hartford

Yes, Kissel deluxe automobiles were built in Hartford. Come see them and other cars full of history. Drive on over.

▲ ★**Wisconsin Automotive Museum and**
Schauer Art Center
147 N. Rural St.
Hartford, WI 53027

Phone: (262) 673-7999
Contact: Dale W. Anderson
Open: May 1 – September 30: Monday
through Saturday, 10am to 5pm, Sunday noon
to 5pm. October 1 – April 30: Wednesday through Saturday, 10am to 5pm, Sunday
noon to 5pm.
Admission: Yes. Children under eight are free.

Important work: Kissel automobile collection, other historic cars.

About the museum: The Wisconsin Automotive Museum provides a rare opportunity to see the largest assembled group of Kissel luxury automobiles. The Kissel, a high caliber custom-built automobile, was manufactured in Hartford from 1906 to 1931. Of 35,000 produced only 150 are known to exist today. A fine selection of models, including four-passenger, coupes, touring cars, fire engines, and trucks await your inspection. Another featured car is the Nash, which was built in Kenosha, WI. Recently added is the Hudson Essex Terraplane Historical Society New Display Area for those vehicles. The museum's striking art deco interior sets off the more than ninety autos on display: Reos, Pierce Arrows, Pontiacs, Studebakers, Kissels, Chevrolets, and Fords. Many of the autos on display are on loan, thus exhibits change regularly. There is also a growing collection of automotive artifacts such as license plates, spark plugs, oilcans, and signs.

The Schauer Art Center features rotating exhibitions and live performances and is located next to the automobile museum in the same building.

Hebron

If you like fishing, hunting, and pioneer life, see the exhibits at the old Town Hall.

▲ **Bark River Woods Historical Society —**
Old Hebron Town Hall
Green Isle Dr. (off County Hwy D)
Hebron, WI

Mailing address: W4080 State Rd. 106 E, Fort
Atkinson, WI 53538
Phone: (920) 563-4773
Open: First Sunday in May and by appointment.

Important works: Historic town hall with stage
curtains, hunting and fishing artifacts.

About the museum: The Historical Society owns and maintains the Old Hebron Town Hall, built in 1902. The vintage interior of the building has tin ceilings and walls, well-worn wooden floors, and an upstairs stage, which features an original stage curtain, complete with advertising from local businesses. The society's collection includes artifacts from pioneer families, town governments, and schools of Hebron and Cold Springs, as well as hunting, fishing, and Indian artifacts from both township areas.

Horicon

One hour from Milwaukee, three historic buildings chock full of artifacts await your visit.

Horicon Historical Society and Museum — Satterlee Clark House
322 Winter St.
Horicon, WI 53032

Mailing address: P.O. Box 65, Horicon, WI 53032
Phone: (920) 485-2011
Open: May through October, fourth Sunday, 1pm to 4pm or by appointment.
Christmas Open House: first Sunday in December.
Admission: Free

Important works: Period furniture, blacksmith forge, Indian artifacts, pottery, cast iron, clothing and textiles, and a working wooden loom.

About the museum: The Horicon Historical Society was organized in 1972 and the Satterlee Clark House became available for use as the museum in 1974. The house was built in 1863 for the Clark family and is an example of Georgian architecture. It is furnished in the style during which the Clark family resided there. One point of interest is the blacksmith forge, which is used for demonstrations. A newer addition to the museum is a schoolhouse built in 1884. It was once used in the Hustisford School District #6 and was relocated brick by brick to its present site in 1993. The archives holds local documentary material for research, including cemetery records, tax rolls, newspapers, and census records.

Hubertus

Rising into the heavens, the spires of Holy Hill are sure to lift your spirits. Bring the family on a daylong pilgrimage.

★Holy Hill National Shrine of Mary
1525 Carmel Rd.
Hubertus, WI 53033

Phone: (262) 628-1838
Website: www.holyhill.com
Open: Year round, Daily, 6am to 5pm.
Admission: Free

Important works: Stained glass windows and mosaics.

About the museum: Just thirty miles northwest of Milwaukee, the spires of the Holy Hill National Shrine of Mary are a prominent feature of the landscape. The neo-Romanesque church, with priceless stained glass windows and mosaics, boasts a breathtaking view of the southern Kettle Moraine countryside. Pilgrims walk along the half-mile outdoor Way of the Cross with fourteen groups of life-size sculptures representing the Passion of Jesus. Others pray at the Lourdes Grotto or stroll around 400 wooded acres crossed by Wisconsin's Ice Age Trail. During summer and fall, thousands climb 178 steps to the top of the observation tower inside one of the spires for an unparalleled view of the surrounding countryside and skyline of Milwaukee. Special seasonal events include a live nativity, religious concerts and a popular arts and craft fair. Simple but comfortable guest rooms and group retreat facilities are available by reservation. The Holy Hill Cafe is open Friday, Saturday, and Sunday all year, and seven days a week from May 1 until October 31.

Hustisford

This quaint historic house filled with pioneer relics invokes bygone days. Only 1 hour from Milwaukee.

Hustisford Historical Society – John Hustis House/Museum
134 N. Ridge St.
Hustisford, WI

Phone: (920) 349-3501
Website: www.hustisford.com/historic.htm
Open: June - September, second and fourth Sundays, 1pm to 3pm, or by appointment.
Contact: Mary

Important works: Shoe shop artifacts, two-story bandstand, cannon.

About the museum: The Hustisford Historical Society has restored the house that John Hustis built in 1851. Also on the museum grounds you can view the 1889 Roethke Shoe Shop, a unique 1919 two-story bandstand, the fire bell that was used in town from 1908-1936, and an 1894 California cannon.

Jackson

Only sixty minutes from Milwaukee, this church offers historic salvation by appointment.

Mill Road Church Museum
1860 Mill Road
Jackson, WI 53037

Phone: (262) 677-3957
Contact: Mrs. Nancy Ebeling
Open: By appointment (call ahead).

This is a small gem of a collection that's well worth your visit.

Fascinating Facts

According to the 2000 census, the population of Wisconsin was 4,891,769 people. That includes the metropolitan areas of Milwaukee, Madison, Green Bay, the Fox River Valley, La Crosse, and the Racine-Kenosha areas.

Jefferson

Come to school and learn about local history.

Jefferson Historical Society Museum
305 S. Main St. (one block off Main St.)
Jefferson, WI 53549

Phone: (920) 674-7731
Open: Wednesday, 10am to 2pm and Sundays, 1pm to 4pm. Call for special times.

Important works: School and church artifacts

About the museum: The Historical Society is the local history resource serving the City of Jefferson. It maintains two sites: the Jefferson Historical Society Museum and the Bakertown School Museum at 303 E. Ogden St. The society has archives of photographs and a collection of historic artifacts. There is also a significant collection on the churches and schools of the area.

Twenty minutes from Madison, this multi-faceted collection stretches from pre-history to the present.

★★Lake Mills/Aztalan Historical Museum
N6264 County Hwy Q
Jefferson, WI 53549

Mailing address: P.O. Box 122, Lake Mills, WI 53551
Phone: (920) 648-4632
Website: http://www.lakemills.org/museum.htm
Open: May 15 – September 30, Thursday - Sunday, noon to 4pm. Tours and large groups may call for appointments at other times. Also open noon to 4pm Memorial Day and Labor Day.
Admission: Yes

Important works: Archeological artifacts, historic tools and farm equipment, Civil War memorabilia, three pioneer log cabins, one-room schoolhouse.

About the museum: The Aztalan Museum, housed in a pioneer Baptist church located adjacent to Aztalan State Park, contains artifacts from Indian cultures as well as articles, maps, and documents dating from the advent of white settlers. These include clothing, dolls and toys, household utensils and dishes, musical instruments, furniture, Civil War memorabilia (including a uniform), and the original map of the village of Aztalan. Also on the property are three pioneer log homes and the two-story Zickert House equipped with items from the latter half of the 19th century. A fully furnished one-room schoolhouse and the Hansen Granary are also part of the settlement. The Granary and most of its contents (a collection of old tools and farm equipment) are gifts of a Lake Mills family.

Fascinating Facts

The Preamble to the Wisconsin State Constitution reads, " We, the people of Wisconsin, grateful to Almighty God for our freedom, in order to secure its blessings, form a more perfect government, insure domestic tranquility, and promote the general welfare, do establish this constitution."

Juneau

This Juneau museum has something for everyone. Come see why, J'no?

🏛 **Dodge Center Historical Society Museum**
Fair Street and East Oak Grove Street
Juneau, WI 53039

Phone: (920) 386-4915
Contact: Bernice Kuntz
Open: May-October: first and third Sunday, 1pm to 4pm and by appointment.

The Dodge Center Historical Society Museum was established to preserve the history of Juneau and the surrounding area. Items on display include a wedding dress from the early 1900s, a replica of the old Werblow shoe store, a showcase from the former Woodward's jewelry store, and part of tree planted by Native Americans in memory of Paul Juneau.

Kenosha

A stately mansion on Lake Michigan filled with art and culture.

🏛 ★**Anderson Arts Center**
121 66th Street
Kenosha, WI 53143

Phone: (262) 653-0481 [Fax: 262-657-2526]
Email: info@andersonartscenter.com
Website: www.andersonartscenter.com
Open: Tuesday-Sunday, 1pm to 4pm.
Admission: Free, donations are welcome

The structure is a beautiful French Renaissance Revival building made of stone, stucco, and wood. It was built in 1929 by the Chicago architects Ralph Milman and Archibald Morphet for James Anderson, who was an executive with the American Brass Company. The 9,000 square foot structure is located on the shores of Lake Michigan. In 1989 the house and grounds became part of the Kemper Center, which is located immediately across the street and is another cultural and recreational complex. In April of 1992, the mansion opened as the Anderson Art Center and is well known in the region for its varying exhibits of contemporary and traditional arts. Special events include the Gallery of Trees in December when local individuals are invited to decorate Christmas trees placed throughout the house.

The Durkee Mansion is a monument to money, marriage, and historic memories. Come see why.

🏛 ★**Durkee Mansion**
6501 3rd Avenue (Kemper Center)
Kenosha, WI 53143-5111

Phone: (262) 657-6005 [Fax: 262-657-7866]
Website: www.kempercenter.com
Open: Saturday and Sunday, 1pm to 4pm, April through October. Open briefly for "Christmas at Kemper" in the weeks following Thanksgiving. Call to verify date and time.

About the museum: The Durkee Mansion is a cream brick, Italianate Victorian home. It originally had an ornate, wooden, wrap-around porch and a widow's walk. One of the striking features is the suspension stairway located in the foyer. It is the largest stairway of its type in the state. It has been declared an historic landmark and a monument to Charles Durkee, a Kenoshan who has a major influence on national and local politics.

Victorian gingerbread interiors, historic dioramas, and genealogy archives await the visitor only sixty minutes from Chicago.

Kenosha County Historical Society — Kenosha History Center
220 51st Place
Kenosha WI 53140

Phone: (262) 654-5770 [Fax 262: 654-1730]
Email: kchs@acronet.net
Website: www.kenoshahistorycenter.org
Open: Tuesday - Friday, 10am to 4:30pm;
Saturday, 10am to 4pm; Sunday, noon – 4pm.
Admission: Free, donation requested.

Important works: Victorian era furnishings, decorative arts, and extensive archives.

About the museum: Since 1965, the Society has been located in the former home of George and Harriet Yule. George Yule was the superintendent of the Bain Wagon Co., one of the largest wagon makers in the world. Designed to give visitors a taste of turn-of-the-century elegance, the first floor contains late Victorian era period rooms highlighting 19th and early 20th century furnishings and decorative arts. Lower level exhibits tell the story of the earliest pioneer settlers of the Western Frontier. The second floor features dioramas depicting bygone eras, a Native American gallery, decorative arts, and a special exhibit gallery. A modern addition to the building houses an extensive archives of local history, a special exhibit gallery, and an auditorium.

Kenosha History Center: The 1866 Southport Lighthouse and the adjacent 1917 Kenosha Water Utility Pumping Station together now form the campus of the Kenosha History Center on Historic Simmons Island.

10,000 years ago mammoths roamed Kenosha. Now you can see them and many more exhibits at the new public museum.

★★Kenosha Public Museum
5500 First Ave.
Kenosha, WI 53140

Phone: (262) 653-4140 [Fax: 262-653-4143]
E-mail: mpaulat@kenosha.org
Website: www.kenosha.org/departments/museum
Contact: Paula Touhey, Director
Open: Tuesday - Saturday, 9am to 5pm; Sunday and Monday, noon to 5pm.
Admission: Free

Important works: Internationally significant collection of rocks and minerals, natural history specimens and cultural artifacts; full size mammoth replica and mammoth bones.

About the museum: Kenosha's museum of natural history and fine and decorative arts first opened in 1937 in a restored post office, but it moved recently to a spacious new building on First Avenue. The museum's significant and diverse collections in geology, biological science, anthropology, and the arts have grown to over 60,000 items. A replica of the Hebior mammoth (the largest, most complete mammoth ever found in the U.S.) and the bones of the Schaefer mammoth (another mammoth excavated in Kenosha County) are featured in the ice age exhibit. An enormous wall of "glacial ice" cuts through the museum, recalling the last Wisconsin Ice Age 10,000 years ago. The Palumbo Civil War museum will merge with Kenosha Public Museum in 2008. Stay tuned.

Kewaskum

If you are passing through Kewaskum on a summer afternoon, don't miss this fun historic site.

Kewaskum Historical Society Museum and Log Cabin
1202 Parkview Drive
Kewaskum, WI 53040

Phone: (262) 626-4656
Open: May 27 - September 9, Sundays, 2pm to 4pm, group tours by appointment.
Admission: Free, donations appreciated

About the museum: The museum is an old cinder block building which previously functioned as a mild transfer station and then as a village garage. Exhibits include an old-time schoolroom, a general store, doctor's office, carpenter's shop, a cheese factory display, and farm equipment. Visitors will also enjoy the library and photograph collection. The log cabin, which dates back to 1842, was built in the town of Scott and moved to the village in 1980. Set up like the original log cabin with kitchen, parlor, and bedrooms upstairs, the house reflects the period between the 1840s and 1910.

Kohler

Artspace is out of this world, with stunning art displays for the connoisseur.

Artspace
The Shops at Woodlake
725 G Woodlake Road
Kohler, WI 53044

Phone: (920) 452-8602
Website: www.jmkac.org/artspace_artspaceII.htm
Open: Daily, year round.
Admission: Free

Artspace is a gallery of the John Michael Kohler Arts Center and hosts an ever-varying schedule of temporary exhibits that include painting, photography, sculpture, ceramics and jewelry. Exhibitors are Wisconsin artists as well a nationally recognized figures in the arts movement.

This is an exploration of contemporary interior design where they have raised the art of living to new heights.

★★Kohler Design Center
101 Upper Road
Kohler, WI 53044

Phone: (920) 457-3699 or toll free 800-456-4537
Website: www.kohler.com
Open: Monday-Friday: 8am to 5pm; Saturday, Sunday, and Holidays: 10am to 4pm
Admission: Free

About the design center: This innovative facility features more than just bathrooms; it's a showplace for nationally acclaimed interior designers to explore creative solutions to modern design for home and industry. It includes historical displays about the history of Kohler Company, examples of their Arts in Industry products, fine ceramics collections, and if you choose, a wonderful three hour tour of the Kohler foundry, pottery, brass, and enamel shops. Make a day of it and call ahead for details!

Built by Austrian master craftsmen, this huge house is wunderbar!

★Waelderhaus
1100 West Riverside Drive
Kohler, WI 53044

Phone: (920) 452-4079 or (920) 458-1972
Open: Year round, tours at 2pm, 3pm, and 4pm. Call ahead for further details. For groups of more than twenty, call ahead.
Admission: Free

The Waelderhaus is a replica of the childhood home of John Michael Kohler, the founder of the Kohler Company. In 1931, Marie Kohler brought the well-known Austrian sculptor and architect, Kaspar Albrech from Munich, Germany to design and build this memorial to her father. Albrech was from the same area of Austria as Kohler and was known for his carvings, tapestry work, stain glass, custom lighting, and furnishings. The structure is actually two buildings in one. One side is where the family would have resided and the other would have been a barn for animals. In the interior of the residential portion of the building are wonderful pieces of folk art related to the folk traditions of Austria. Waelderhaus is also closely linked to the history of the Girl Scouts of America. In Kohler, Marie Kohler established one of the earliest Girl Scout troups who used Waelderhaus as their meeting place for decades. Today the Grand Hall is used for both Girl Scout get-togethers and for community functions.

Lake Geneva

Your trip to one of Wisconsin's great historic resort towns is not complete until you visit this private mansion turned history museum.

★Geneva Lake Area Museum of History
818 Geneva St.
Lake Geneva, WI 53147

Mailing address: P.O. Box 522, Lake Geneva, WI 53147
Phone: (414) 248-6060
Open: Mid-May to Mid-October, Friday - Sunday and Holidays, 1pm to 5pm. Extended hours mid-June through Labor Day.
Admission: Free, donations appreciated

Important works: Tourism artifacts, Chicago and Northwestern Railroad items, and "Andy Gump" cartoons.

About the museum: This Mediterranean style structure, once a private home, now houses rare and historic memorabilia ranging from our early Indian period to more modern times. The collection includes transportation items from the Chicago and Northwestern Railroad, which played a prominent role in bringing Chicagoans to Lake Geneva's shores. Tourism is well documented with progression from tenting to private clubs and hotels, including Frank Lloyd Wright's "Geneva Hotel." Examples from the collection of Sidney Smith's cartoon caricature "Andy Gump" are on display, along with an 1800 round typewriter manufactured in Lake Geneva. The research room contains rare books, documents, and newspapers.

Mayville

If you are in the vicinity, come see the fascinating collections and soak up the past, especially the ice cream social in June.

▲ Mayville Historical Society Museum — IIII Hollenstein Wagon and Carriage Factory
at Bridge and German Streets
Mayville, WI 53050

Mailing address: P.O. Box 82, Mayville, WI 53050
Phone: (920) 387-2420
Open: May through October, second and fourth Sundays, 1:30pm to 4:30pm.
Admission: Free, donations appreciated

Important works: Wagons, carriages, sleighs, fire trucks, gear, and cigar-making equipment.

About the museum: The museum complex, which opened in 1973, began with the building that once housed the John Hollenstein Wagon, Carriage Factory, and the adjoining Hollenstein house. In 1978, two local buildings, a firehouse and the Brunke Cigar Factory, were moved to the museum grounds. Holdings include artifacts, pictures, and documents that illustrate the history of Mayville and surrounding area. The wagon factory houses carriages, wagons, and sleighs manufactured by the Hollensteins in that building. There are also displays of memorabilia from local businesses and industries, past and present. Exhibits illustrate the history of local newspapers and small displays give viewers an idea of Mayville's musical, dramatic, and literary past.

In the Hollenstein house, the first floor has six rooms of furniture and artifacts from the past. Exhibits of paintings and needlework done by Mayville residents can be found in the living and music rooms. The second floor contains a variety of exhibits, including vintage clothing and hats, children's toys, a wedding gown, and memorabilia. In the Firehouse, a Stutz fire truck and other firefighting materials are on display, along with pictures and records of the local fire department. The upper floor shows artifacts and histories of local churches. The Brunke Cigar Factory features items originally used in the factory and information about several prominent local cigar makers of the past.

The community of Mayville honors its proud educational past at this school museum.

▲ Mayville Limestone School Museum
IIII North Main and Buchanan Streets
Mayville, WI 53050

Mailing Address: P.O. Box 82, Mayville, WI 53050
Phone: (920) 387-2420 or (800) 256-7670
Open: May-October, first and third Sunday of the month or by appointment

Housed in a magnificent 1857-77 Greek revival building, the Mayville Limestone School Museum presents a glimpse of the past displayed in ten rooms and galleries. These include a furnished and restored 19th century classroom, the Edgar G. Mueller photo gallery, Hugo Fenske Wild Game Room, Elsmer Pieper's Boy Scout memorabilia, the Charles Henderson Collection of Indian Relics, the Dick Ruedebusch Jazz exhibit, the Cap Blohm art gallery, Ted Bachhuber's African collection, and the "When Iron was King" history room.

Menomonee Falls

Like a magnet, this historical park has drawn rare old buildings to a central spot for everyone to enjoy.

★Old Falls Village Historical Park and Museum
Corner of Pilgrim and County Line (Hwy Q) Roads
Menomonee Falls, WI 53051

Mailing address: P.O. Box 91, Menomonee Falls, WI 53052
Phone: (262) 255-1114
Contact: Jeff Steliga
Email: jsteliga@wi.rr.com
Website: www.oldfallsvillage.com
Open: May – September, Saturday and Sunday, 1pm to 4pm
or by appointment. Call to verify hours.
Admission: Yes

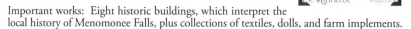

Important works: Eight historic buildings, which interpret the
local history of Menomonee Falls, plus collections of textiles, dolls, and farm implements.

About the museum: Nestled on the grounds of a beautiful seventeen-acre park, Old Falls Village invites visitors to step back in time and glimpse life of the mid-1800s to the early 1900s. Featuring a variety of historic homes and buildings, this living history museum includes a log home, schoolhouse, barn, railroad depot, log cabin, and dairy. Each of the buildings showcases antiques and artifacts from the time. An annual series of special events, such as Woodworkers Day in May and Old Haunted Village in October, encourages involvement by area residents.

The museum complex, established in 1966, began with the Miller-Davidson House. Built in 1858, this Greek revival style house was made of locally quarried limestone with mortar from nearby lime kilns. This early American farm home is special in many ways, beginning with an unusual arched foundation. In 1935 it was selected by the federal government's Historic American Building Survey and in 1973 was listed on the National Register of Historic Places. An 1850s barn, also original to the site, showcases time-honored pioneer craftsmanship in its framework, with timbers hewn and fitted by old-world hand tools. Inside, the barn holds an exhibit of small farm, industrial, and household implements.

Over the years, several other buildings were moved to the site. These include the 1890 Milwaukee Road Depot, marking a time when the railroad brought a new commercial and industrial prosperity to Menomonee Falls. A two-story log cabin, the Umhoefer House, dates from 1856 and features a handprint from a soldier returning from the Civil War. There is a one-room schoolhouse built in 1851 at a cost of $55, in which students spanning eight grades were taught by one teacher. The 1842 Brogan Cabin is a rare example of the primitive but sturdy dwellings erected by the earliest Irish immigrants to the area. Another log structure, the Koch House, built in 1873, is unique because its logs were not hand-hewn. Instead they were produced in a local sawmill. Its additions and clapboard siding reveal how living spaces evolve over time. There is also a historic Carriage House that offers an exhibit of antique vehicles and transportation artifacts.

Tony's Tips

Wisconsin has 15, 000 lakes plus two Great Lakes: Michigan and Superior. All that water makes fishing in this state a world-class event all year-round - spring, summer, fall, and even in winter, for ice fishing. Bring your ice shack and drill!

Mequon

A pleasant setting enhances the rotating exhibition schedule. Call for details.

Concordia University Art Museum
12800 N. Lakeshore Dr.
Mequon, WI 53097

Phone: (262) 243-4552 [Fax: 262-243-4351]
Contact: Jeffrey Shawhan
Email: jeff.shawhan@cuw.edu
Website: www.cuw.edu
Open: Sunday – Friday, noon to 4pm; Thursday evenings, 6pm to 8pm.

This museum fills a void in understanding the importance of traditional crafts in modern life.

Crafts Museum
Mequon
Traveling exhibit

Phone: (262) 242-1571
Contact: Bob Seigel, Jr. Director
Open: Please call for appointment between 7am to 9pm,

Important works: Wooden shoe-making equipment, ice-harvesting tools, and sheet music.

About the museum: Since 1969 the Crafts Museum has roamed the U.S. It is a traveling museum offering seven authentic historical, educational, and entertaining programs for groups and events in Wisconsin and the Midwest. The focus is now on bringing programs to locations in Wisconsin. Programs include: America's Last Wooden Shoe Carver – from log to Dutch shoe in twenty-eight minutes using only three antique traditional tools; Wisconsin Ice Story – harvesting, storage in ice houses, and wagon delivery to home ice boxes; Variety Show with country stories, humor, antiques and Appalachian Buck Dancing; 1940s Movie Musical Memories, featuring major stars born and raised in Wisconsin (Spencer Tracy, Pat O'Brien, Fred MacMurray, Don Ameche, Dennis Morgan, Jack Carson, and Les Paul). The museum owns over 2,500 items including America's premier collection of wooden shoes and ice harvesting equipment, and over 3,500 selections of piano sheet music arranged in 135 subject categories.

Call ahead to see this historic house museum.

Isham Day House
Mequon Historical Society
11312 North Cedarburg Road
Mequon, WI 53092

Phone: (262) 242-3290 or Thursdays from 2pm to 5pm, call (262) 242-3107
Open: Call to schedule a tour

One of the first dwelling in Mequon, this house was built in 1839 by Isham Day on the old American Indian trail that extended from Hudson Bay to Florida.

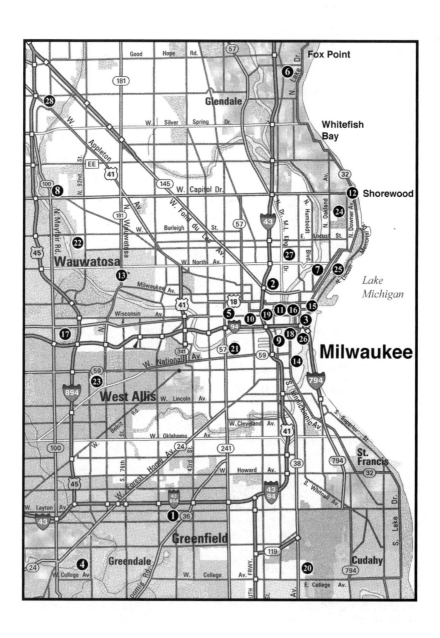

1. Alverno College - Art & Cultures Gallery
2. America's Black Holocaust Museum
3. Betty Brinn Children's Museum
4. Boerner Botanical Gardens
5. Captain Frederick Pabst Mansion
6. Cardinal Stritch University - Art Gallery
7. Charles Allis Art Museum
8. Harley-Davison Engine Plant
9. Harley-Davision Museum *(future)*
10. Marquette University - Haggerty Museum of Art
11. International Clown Hall of Fame
12. Kilbourntown House
13. Kneeland Walker House
14. Latino Arts Gallery
15. Milwaukee Art Museum
16. Milwaukee County Historical Society
17. Milwaukee County Zoo
18. Milwaukee Institute of Art and Design - Eisner Museum of Advertising and Design
19. Milwaukee Public Museum
20. Mitchell Gallery of Flight
21. Mitchell Park Horticultural Conservatory
22. Mount Mary College - Marian Gallery
23. Scout Heritage Museum
24. University of Wisconsin - Milwaukee - INOVA Gallery
25. Villa Terrace Decorative Arts Museum
26. Walker's Point Center for the Arts
27. Wisconsin Black Historical Society & Museum
28. Wisconsin Evangelical Lutheran Synod - WELS Historical Institute Museum

Milwaukee

Powerful exhibits tell the story of our own social and racial history. Everyone should visit this museum. It's good for attitutde adjustment.

★★★America's Black Holocaust Museum
2233 N. 4th St.
Milwaukee, WI 53212

Phone: (414) 264-2500 [Fax: 414-264-0112]
Contact: James Cameron
Email: info@blackholocaustmuseum.org
Website: www.blackholocaustmuseum.org
Open: Tuesday - Saturday, 9am to 5pm; Sunday, open to groups of twenty or more by appointment.
Admission: Yes

Important works: African-American heritage artifacts.

About the museum: America's Black Holocaust Museum was founded in 1988 to educate the general public of the injustices suffered by people of African Heritage in America, and to provide visitors with an opportunity to rethink their assumptions about race and racism. James Cameron is founder of the museum and America's only living survivor of a lynching. Because of this experience, Cameron dedicated his life to promoting civil rights, racial peace, unity and equality. He founded three NAACP chapters in Indiana during the 1940s. The museum's scope continues to grow, but Cameron's most prized possession is a single letter received on February 3, 1993, sixty-two years after his conviction for accessory before the fact to manslaughter. The letter grants a pardon and public apology from the State of Indiana. Exhibits have included The Middle Passage: A Voyage to Slavery, Before Freedom Came: African American Life in the Antebellum South, Cultural Landscape of the Plantation, and Martin Luther King Jr.

College art galleries are often full of surprises and innovation. Come see how they do it the Alverno way.

Art and Cultures Gallery
Alverno College
3400 s. 43 rd street
Milwaukee, WI

Phone: (414) 382-6130, (414) 382-6149
Contact: Linda Sommers

Another small but vibrant college art gallery that is geared to student and faculty development. The Art Gallery promotes a wide and diverse selection of art exhibits throughout the year.

Kids love the hands-on exhibits. There's always something new and exciting!

★★Betty Brinn Children's Museum
929 E. Wisconsin Ave.
Milwaukee, WI 53202

Phone: (414) 390-5437 [Fax: 414-291-0906]
Contact: Kristen Adams or Jacque Long (ext. 243)
Email: questions@bbcmkids.org
Website: www.bbcmkids.org
Open: All year: Tuesday – Saturday, 9am to 5pm; Sunday, noon to 5pm. June – August:

Mondays, 9am to 5pm.
Admission: Yes

Important works: Engaging, hands-on learning exhibits for children

About the museum: The Betty Brinn Children's Museum opened in 1995. Its exhibits provide many fun, hands-on learning opportunities for children ages ten and under. The museum houses a collection of six permanent exhibits, with several traveling exhibitions throughout the year.

World-class art in a fabulous park setting.

★Bradley Sculpture Gardens
2145 W. Brown Deer Road
Milwaukee, WI 53217

Contact: Marjorie Franz
Phone: (414) 276-6840
Open: Tours are given Monday-Friday by appointment. Please call one week in advance.
Admission: Yes

Collector Margaret Bradley molded her home into a beautiful setting for sculpture collection. There are over sixty pieces by more than forty artists including Archipenko, Bill, Etrog, Hepworth, Milkowski, Moore, Noguchi, Pan, Pepper, and Sugarman.

A flourishing art school with a gallery and rotating shows. It includes great artifacts from the hands of famed industrial designer Brooks Stevens who created the Wiener Mobile.

Brooks Stevens and Layton Galleries
Milwaukee Institute of Art and Design
273 E. Erie
Milwaukee, WI 53202

Phone: (414) 847-3350
Contact: Mark Lawson
E-mail: mlawson@miad.edu
Open: Tuesday-Saturday, 10am to 5pm.
Admission: Free

About the galleries: Founded in 1974, MIAD is Wisconsin's only four-year independent art and design college. MIAD offers changing exhibitions of contemporary fine art and presents yearlong exhibitions of product design, from toothbrushes to automobiles, in its Brooks Stevens Gallery of Industrial Design.

Hops on over to the mansion that beer built.

★★Captain Frederick Pabst Mansion
2000 W. Wisconsin Ave.
Milwaukee, WI 53233

Phone: (414) 931-0808 [Fax: 414-931-1005]
Contact: Dawn M. Day Hourigan, Executive Director
Email: pabstman@execpc.com
Website: www.pabstmansion.com
Open: Monday – Saturday, 10am to 4pm; Sunday, noon to 4pm; Closed Mondays, mid-January through February.
Admission: Yes, under age of six free

About the museum: The Pabst Mansion was the home of one of the nation's most famous beer barons. One of its highlights, the Beer Pavilion, was originally built for the 1893 Columbian Exposition in Chicago to display Pabst Brewing Company products. Since 1978, the mansion has been open to the public, hosting changing art exhibits, an annual holiday extravaganza, and festive special events including beer tasting and elegant dinners.

The Pabst art collection includes primarily of late 19th and 20th century decorative and fine arts. Artists featured in the collection include William Bouguereau, Eugene Von Blaas, Robert Schade, Richard Lorenz, and Otto von Ernst. The art of Emil Blatz, who willed many of his possessions to the citizens of Milwaukee County, also has a home in the Pabst Mansion. Nineteenth century furniture and three original rooms of the house are also highlights for visitors.

The Pabst Archives is an important part of the collection with over 5,000 photos, negatives, documents, and ephemera. In 2001, the archives added George Bowman Ferry's personal collection of drawings, renderings and items from the firm of Ferry and Clas. The collection includes original artist renderings from the Pabst Building, Gustave Pabst residence, Milwaukee Public Library, and Forest Home Cemetery Chapel.

Imagine building an art collection with the sole purpose of leaving it behind for others to enjoy. This is a special place!

★Charles Allis Art Museum
1801 N. Prospect Ave.
Milwaukee, WI 53202

Phone: (414) 278-8295 [Fax: 414-278-0335]
Email: jtemmer@cavtmuseums.org
Website:
http://www.cavtmuseums.org/ca/home.html
Contact: James Temmer, Executive Director
Open: All Year: Wednesday – Sunday, 1pm to 5pm.
Admission: Yes

Important works: International art objects, French and American landscape paintings, antique furniture, Renaissance bronzes.

About the museum: The Charles Allis Art Museum is located in a Tudor-style mansion furnished as it was when completed in 1911. Charles Allis (1853-1918), first president of the Allis Chalmers Company, built the mansion working closely with architect Alexander Eschweiler specifically to house his art collection with the intent to bequeath it all to his fellow Milwaukeeans. Spanning 2,000 years, the permanent collection includes Chinese, Japanese, Korean, Persian, Greek, and Roman art objects, fine French, English, and American period furniture, Renaissance bronzes, and landscapes by major 19th and 20th century French and American painters. Programming includes changing art gallery exhibitions, regularly scheduled tours, concerts, films, performances, talks, workshops, and special events.

Bring the family and discover a full day of fun! The IMAX theme is out of this world.

★★★Discovery World Museum: The James Lovell Museum of Science, Economics, and Technology
815 N. James Lovell St.
Milwaukee, WI 53233

Phone: (414) 765-9966 [Fax: 414-765-0311]
Email: hdq@discoveryworld.org
Website: http://www.discoveryworld.org/

Open: Daily, 9am to 5pm.
Admission: Yes

About the museum: Discovery World was founded in 1984 by four business leaders who were convinced that an interactive, hands-on museum was needed to strengthen Milwaukee's school system and increase public awareness and understanding of the impact that science, economics, and technology have on society. Originally housed in the lower level of the Milwaukee Public Library, the museum is located now in a new, state-of-the-art facility known as the Milwaukee Museum Center, opened in 1996. This facility also houses the Milwaukee Public Museum and the state's only large format theater, the Humphrey IMAX Dome Theater. More than 150 interactive exhibits form the core of the museum's collection. There are also hands-on labs, professional science demonstrations, live theater performances, educational workshops, special events, and thematic weekend experiences. The museum will be moving to a new location on the lake front south of the art museum in the summer of 2006.

Wright in the neighborhood is a Greek church. Let's visit.

▲ Greek Orthodox Church of the Annunciation
|||| 9400 West Congress Street,
Wauwatosa (metropolitan Milwaukee area)
Milwaukee, Wisconsin 53225

Reservations
Phone: (414) 461-9400 [Fax: 414-461-9468]

The church Wright designed for the Annunciation Greek Orthodox Congregation was among the architect's last major commissions. In 1956 Wright showed the original drawings for the new suburban church to the Milwaukee congregation, one of the ten oldest in the country. He died in 1959 before the ground breaking and the dedication of the church in 1961. Wright's circular design represented a radical departure from traditional Byzantine church architecture, yet it retained the concept of a domed space and incorporated symbols and colors associated with the Greek Orthodox faith. The basic design of the church is based on the Greek cross inscribed with a circle. This characteristic motif is repeated in several decorative features which include the gold anodized aluminum icon screen, and the gates to the exterior sunken garden.

Tours are generally not available except during Greek Fest, the annual ethnic food and entertainment festival, held on the church grounds the weekend following July 4. Visitors are always welcome to attend the Divine Liturgy held on Sundays at 9:30am.

Reve up the engine and off we go.

▲ Harley-Davidson Engine Plant
|||| 11700 W. Capitol drive
Milwaukee, WI

Phone: (414) 535-3666
Phone reservation system is hard to operate
Contact: Tour operations
Open: Monday through Friday 9:30am to 1pm
Website: harley-davidson.com
harley-davidsonmuseum.com
Admission: free

Free hour long tours of the engine plant are a real thrill for the Hog lover and amateur alike. A true slice of Americana. The legendary Harley-Davidson corporation is also building a museum, finally, that will open in 2008 in downtown Milwaukee at 6th and Canal streets. In the mean time an engine plant tour will suffice for a trip to Hog Heaven.

Even clowns can get serious about preserving their history and craft. It's no joke.

★International Clown Hall of Fame
Grand Avenue Mall
161 N. Wisconsin Ave., Suite LL700
Milwaukee, WI 53203

Phone: (414) 319-0848 [Fax: 414-319-1070]
Email: mirthcon@juno.com
Website: www.theclownmuseum.org
Contact: Kathryn O'Dell, Executive Director
Open: Monday - Friday, 10am to 4pm.
Admission: Yes, children under six free for self-guided tours only.

Important works: Clown artifacts, artwork, and archival records.

About the museum: The Hall of Fame began in 1987 in Delavan where twenty-seven circuses had their winter quarters. It is dedicated to the preservation and advancement of clown art. Represented by professional and amateur associations, it pays tribute to outstanding clown performers, operates a living museum of clowning with resident clown performers, conducts special events, and maintains a national archive of clown artifacts and history. It houses significant artwork by famous clown artist Jim Howle and owns the Seimor Brothers Miniature Circus, which is a traveling exhibit. The Clown center is a complete city, with three performance rings, a sideshow, circus train, cook tent, and every possible circus feature you could imagine. Successful outreach programs include Clowns for Children's Hospital and a clown humor therapy program designed to reach at-risk teens in the Milwaukee area.

Drift back in time and visit this pioneer home chock full of Milwaukee memories.

Kilbourntown House
4400 Estabrook Dr.
Shorewood, WI 53203

Mailing address: 910 N. Old World 3rd St., Milwaukee, WI 53203
Phone: (414) 273-8288 [Fax: 414-273-3268]
Contact: Aenone Rosario
Website: www.milwaukeecountyhistsoc.org/homes.htm
Open: Mid-June through Labor Day: Tuesday, Thursday, and Saturday, 10am to 5pm; Sunday, 1pm to 5pm.
Admission: Free, donations appreciated

Important works: Mid-19th century furniture and decorative arts.

About the museum: Kilbourntown House was built in 1844 by pioneer carpenter and master builder Benjamin Church and is located in the section of Milwaukee know as Kilbourntown, named after its founder, Byron Kilbourn. It offers an outstanding collection of mid-19th century furniture and decorative arts, as well as an outdoor kitchen herb garden. It has been operated as a museum since 1939.

A community based Hispanic showcase for the Latino Arts... muchas gracias.

Latino Arts Center
1028 south 9th street
Milwaukee, Wisconsin 53204

Phone: (414) 384-3100
Admission: Free, donations appreciated
Hours: Monday through Friday 9am to 8pm

About the center: Opened in 1997 this community based arts center focuses on the Latino Arts in all its many forms. Diverse programming in art, dance, music, poetry, and literature make this a real destination. Good ethnic restaurants nearby. Viva la cultura.

An interesting building enhances this university art collection.

Marquette University - Haggerty Museum of Art
530 N. 13th St.
Milwaukee, WI 53233

Mailing address: P.O. Box 1881, Milwaukee, WI 53201
Phone: (414) 288-1669
Email: haggertym@marquette.edu
Website: www.marquette.edu/haggerty
Open: Monday, Tuesday, Wednesday, Friday, Saturday, 10am to 4:30pm; Thursday, 10am to 8pm; Sunday, noon to 5pm.
Admission: Free

Important works: Old Masters paintings, modern paintings, and sculptures.

About the museum: The Haggerty Museum opened in 1984 as a gift to the Milwaukee community from the Marquette University Women's Council. O'Neil Ford and David Kahler designed the award winning building. The Haggerty presents innovative classical and contemporary exhibitions: an Old Masters salon featuring European paintings from the 15th – 19th centuries, a Modern Gallery with paintings and sculptures by artists including Dali, Chagall, and Man Ray, and a permanent collection of over 8,000 paintings, sculptures, and works on paper. The museum offers a stimulating environment to explore art, with free lectures, artists' visits, and panel discussions. It also hosts hands-on art workshops for all ages, and music, theater, and dance performances.

This is Wisconsin's version of the Louvre. Three joined buildings house a diverse, world-class art collection. Don't miss the new Calatrava wings, it flaps.

★★★Milwaukee Art Museum
700 M. Art Museum Drive
Milwaukee, WI 53202

Phone: (414) 224-3200 [Fax: 414-271-7588]
Contact: David Gordon
Website: www.mam.org
Open: Daily, 10am to 5pm; Thursday, 10am to 8pm.
Admission: Yes

Important works in the collection: Winslow Homer, Auguste Rodin, Edgar Degas, Claude Monet, Henri de Toulouse-Lautrec, Pablo Picasso, Joan Miro, Georgia O'Keefe, Mark Rothko, Jasper Johns, and Andy Warhol and more.

The Milwaukee Art Museum, with a new expansion that combines art, dramatic architecture, and landscape design is a must see destination. Located on the city's lakefront, the Museum is a cultural center of regional and national importance. The addition, the first Santiago Calatrava-designed building completed in the U.S., features the glass-walled Windhover Hall enclosed by the Burke Brise Soleil, a sunscreen that can be raised or lowered creating a unique moving sculpture. In other new areas visitors can watch lectures and films in the auditorium, have lunch in the lakefront café, shop in the Museum store, and enjoy the outdoor terraces and the Cudahy Gardens.

With a history dating back to 1888, the far-reaching collections include nearly 20,000 works from antiquity to the present. The permanent holdings include important collections of Old Masters, 19th and 20th century art, collections of American decorative arts, German Expressionism, folk and Haitian art, and American art after 1960. The permanent collections are exhibited in larger, more spacious galleries organized by time frame. There are also new galleries dedicated to Asian and African art.

Also to be seen is the Milwaukee War Memorial, which occupies the upper level of the original art museum building. This is one of Wisconsin's fine museums dedicated to war veterans.

A beautiful former bank houses Milwaukee's powerhouse of rich history. You won't be disappointed.

 ★★**Milwaukee County Historical Society**
910 N. Old World 3rd St.
Milwaukee, WI 53203

Phone: (414) 273-8288 [Fax: 414-273-3268]
Contact: Aenone Rosario
Website: www.milwaukeecountyhistsoc.org
Open: Daily: Monday – Friday, 9:30am to 4:30pm; Saturday, 10am to 5pm; Sunday, 1pm to 5pm. Library: Monday – Friday, 9:30am to noon and 1pm – 4:30pm; Saturday, 10 am to noon and 1pm to 4:30pm.
Admission: Free, donations appreciated

About the museum: The Milwaukee County Historical Society was organized in 1935. In 1965, the Society acquired the Second Ward Office of the First Wisconsin National Bank and opened to the public. The society includes a center for the study of local history, museum for exhibits on Milwaukee history, and headquarters for activities. An extensive research library aids researchers, genealogists, and scholars who explore its vast collection of manuscripts, records, books, and photos. The society displays exhibits on a rotating basis. Past and current topics include: The Civil War, Milwaukee River, Milwaukee fashions, Milwaukee's founding fathers, ethnic groups in Milwaukee, panorama painters, and the Socialist party.

A visit to the zoo will have you roaming with the rhinos and swinging with the monkeys! It's a stellar facility, and the wildest place in town!

★★★**Milwaukee County Zoo**
10001 W. Blue Mound Rd.
Milwaukee, WI 53226

Phone: (414) 771-5500, (414) 771-3040, or (414) 256-5435 [Fax: 414-256-5410]
Website: www.milwaukeezoo.org
Contact: Jennifer Diliberti, Public Relations Coordinator
Open: January 1-April 30, 9am to 4:30pm; May 1-September 30, Monday – Saturday 9am to 5pm, Sundays and Holidays 9am to 6pm; October 1-April 30, 9am to 4:30pm; Sundays and Holidays, 9am to 6pm.
Admission: Yes

Important works: 300 species of animals.

About the museum: The Milwaukee County Zoo is considered among the finest zoos in the country. It is situated on 200 wooded acres and is home to approximately 2,500 animals representing 300 species of mammals, birds, reptiles, fish, and invertebrates. The zoo began in 1882 as a small mammal and bird display in Milwaukee's Washington Park and recently celebrated its 100th anniversary in 1992. It hosts over twenty special events including celebrations at Easter, Halloween, and the December holiday season. The highlight of the year is the finest food festival in Wisconsin, The Milwaukee Journal Sentinel newspaper's "A la Carte," a real feast with the beasts.

From ancient mummies to modern marvels, this museum is world class. It's one of the finest in the U.S. This is Tony Rajer's all time favorite museum in Wisconsin.

★★★Milwaukee Public Museum
800 W. Wells St.
Milwaukee, WI 53233

Phone: (414) 278-2700 [Fax: 414-278-6100]
Website: www.mpm.edu
Open: Daily, 9am to 5pm. Closed July 4th, Thanksgiving Day and Christmas Day.
Admission: Yes

Important works: Major collections of Native American and international cultural artifacts, dinosaur skeletons, extensive collection of natural history specimens.

About the museum: Step into the museum and journey through time, cultural traditions, and amazing worlds. Stand inches away from a life-sized Tyrannosaurus rex and Stegosaurus in Third Planet: Earth. See the largest dinosaur skull in the world and skeletons of creatures that inhabited our planet millions of years ago. Get wrapped up with Djed-hor, a real Egyptian mummy and see how pyramids were built in Temples, Tells, and Tombs. Let the rhythmic beat of drums lure you to Tribute to Survival, a modern-day Wisconsin Woodlands Indian Powwow, complete with thirty-seven full-size figures cast from tribal members. Stroll lamplite memory lanes in Streets of Old Milwaukee. Feel the thrill of safari as you walk the grasslands and bamboo forests of Africa. Walk amidst elephants, tigers, and other wildlife of the African Serengeti and enjoy the art and music of this culturally rich continent. And you can take a tropical adventure in Rain Forest: Exploring Life on Earth. Climb the two-story forest canopy to learning stations detailing the incredible diversity of life. There are various hands-on activity areas as well as music, animation, and documentary footage at video stations throughout the four floors.

Fly through Wisconsin's aviation and space history. No boarding pass required.

Mitchell Gallery of Flight
In Milwaukee's General Mitchell International Airport
5300 S. Howell Ave.
Milwaukee, WI 53207

Phone: (414) 747-4503 [Fax: 414-747-4525]
Email: info@mitchellgallery.org
Website: www.mitchellgallery.org
Open: Daily, 7am to 10pm, but best viewing times are 8am to 6pm.

About the museum: The Badger State is home to some of the greatest aviation legends of the 20th century. Their courage and foresight are showcased at the Mitchell Gallery of Flight, dedicated to preserving Wisconsin's aviation legacy. Here you will see original artifacts, aeronautical memorabilia, and fantastic models. Exhibit highlights include Milwaukee's own General "Billy" Mitchell. His fantastic story, including his historic aero bombardment of a German battleship, is told with rare photographs, personal memorabilia, and accurately detailed models.

Another aviation legend, air travel visionary Alfred W. Lawson, is featured. Around 1920, Lawson undertook the groundbreaking effort to establish a regularly scheduled, national commercial airline in Milwaukee. Original documents, photographs, and a large-scale model of this first U.S. airliner tell the Lawson Story. Wisconsin also had a role in space flight history. Astronaut Jim Lovell, commander of the Apollo 13 mission, successfully guided his dangerously crippled spacecraft back to earth. St. Mary's of Milwaukee was the first hospital to design a series for medical tests for understanding the effects of zero gravity on crews of the Space Shuttle.

Visit a world-class facility with climates and collections from desert to tropical jungle, all under three domes!

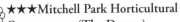★★★**Mitchell Park Horticultural Conservatory (The Domes)**
524 South Layton Blvd.
Milwaukee, WI 53215

Phone: (414) 649-9800
Website: http://www.countyparks.com/
horticulture/domes/
Open: Daily, 9am to 5pm.
Admission: Yes

About the gardens: The Mitchell Park Horticultural Conservatory is comprised of three imposing glass domes located in a sixty-seven-acre park. There are the only conoidal (cone-like) domes in the world. Each of the Domes represents a different habitat. The Tropical Dome showcases rainforest plants and birds as well ads a thirty-five-foot waterfall nestled among the brilliant blooms. It highlights plants that help people survive worldwide. The Arid Dome is delightfully bright and open with unique desert plants from around the world. The desert plantings demonstrate an exotic habitat requiring special adaptations for survival. The Show Dome overwhelms the senses with a themed garden of thousands of flowers blooming at the same time. Changing five times a year, the floral show might be anything from a Japanese Garden to a garden railway or a child's backyard.

College art galleries are often gems. Come see what sparkles in this collection.

▲ **Mount Mary College — Marian Gallery**
2900 N. Menomonee River Parkway
Milwaukee, WI 53222

Phone: (414) 258-4810 or (414) 256-1233
Contact: Lynn Capitan, Chair
Email: lyncha@mtmary.edu
Website: http://www.mtmary.edu/marian.htm
Open: Monday through Friday, 9am to 7pm; Saturday and
Sunday, 1pm to 4pm.

Important works: Georges Rouault – Miserere Series, Richard Hunt – fourteen ft. bronze sculpture "Celestial Conversations," Lambert Rucci – Crucifix and Ceramic Madonna. Collections of carved wood Madonnas and antique silver vessels.

About the gallery: The Marian Gallery, founded in 1929, is an integral part of Mount Mary College's commitment to the fine arts. The original facility, known as the Tower Gallery, was housed in the art department. To be more accessible to the public and expand its display area, the gallery was moved to its present location in 1998. It is used extensively for teaching and for promoting the aesthetic experience through courses and outreach activities.

A series of ten exhibitions each year features the works of Wisconsin artists as well as artists of national and international fame. Works by faculty, students, and alumni are frequently exhibited as part of the series. Prominent artists who have shown their works include Robert von Neuman, Aaron Bohrod, Doris White, Charles Dix, Norman Laliberte, Fred Fenster, Schomer Lichtner, Leo Steppart, Corita Kent, Konstantin Milonadis, John Wilde, Warrington Colescott, John Colt, Tom Uttech, Lee Weiss, Jeanne Crane, and Joanna Poehlmann. The gallery was one of the first in Milwaukee area to exhibit "neon light art" and had major exhibits of stained glass and interior design. To promote better intercultural understanding, the gallery has sponsored shows of Brazilian art, Haitian art, American Indian art, art from Southern France, and works from Russia.

Hey Bud, beer is taken seriously at this museum. No cheap brews allowed, only draft.

★Museum of Beer and Brewing
215 N. Water Street
Milwaukee, WI 53202

Mailing Address: P.O. Box 1376, Milwaukee, WI 53201
Phone: (414) 727-9750
Contact: Jeff Platt, President
Email: milwbrew@execpc.com
Website: http://www.brewingmuseum.org/

A group of dedicated brewers, historians, and enthusiasts noticed that there is no organization in North America devoted to preserving the history of the brewing industry - from grain and hops through the brewing process and packaging, to marketing the finished product. In an effort to preserve and display historical items before they are lost forever, the museum is assembling a treasure trove of breweriana. These include: rare vintage photos, beer related labels and containers, advertising materials, and unique brewery related artifacts on loan or donated by collectors, historians, and breweries throughout North America and the world. Museum plans include a barrel-maker at work, visual presentations reliving the days of large and small breweries, and the stories of the beer barons. Call and check out what exciting plans this new museum has in store for you!

The collection of Outsider Art is one of the finest in the nation and includes wonderful pieces from Europe as well as America. Good job Tony!

★★Petullo Collection of Self-Taught and Outsider Art
219 N. Milwaukee street   3rd floor
Milwaukee, Wis. 53202

Phone: (414) 272-2525 [Fax: 414-272-2528]
Email: kmmurrell@sbcglobal.net
Contact: Katherine Minerath Murrell, curator
Website: www.petulloartcollection.com
Open: Call for appointment

The Anthony Petullo Collection of Self-Taught and Outsider Art is one of the premier collections of its kind in the country. Comprised of more than 450 works, two-thirds of which are European, and continually growing in size, the Petullo Collection includes work ranging from the 1890s to the present. The collection features works by many of the most renowned American artists in the field such as Bill Traylor, Henry Darger, and Minnie Evans. The distinguishing characteristic of the collection, however, is the strong emphasis on the work of European outsider artists including Adolf Wolfli, Alfred Wallis, Scottie Wilson, and artists from the Gugging psychiatric hospital near Vienna. Nearly every artist is represented by multiple works, illustrating the depth of the Petullo Collection. Books about the collection are also available.

The Petullo Collection reflects the driving passion of both the artists and the collector. Self-taught artists, though often isolated, are involved with the world and its influences. They have no professional artistic training and are virtually unaware of the academic traditions of art. Unlike outsiders, however, they are grounded in reality and interactions with others. The term "outsider" is intended to suggest both artists who are institutionalized and those who live outside of mainstream society. Their creations are spontaneous and unstudied.

Located in Milwaukee's Historic Third Ward, the collection is housed in a non-profit study center and gallery devoted to Outsider and Self-Taught art. The gallery is used for student educational groups and non-profit organization meetings.

Scout's promise, this heritage site is worth a jamboree visit.

★Scout Heritage Museum
330 S. 84th St.
Milwaukee, WI 53214

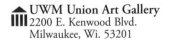

Phone: (414) 774-1776
Open: All year, Monday – Friday, noon to 4pm; Labor Day –
Memorial Day, Saturdays, 9am to 12:30pm.

Important works: Scouting memorabilia, books, photographs,
Ben Hunt Collection.

About the museum: The Scout Heritage Museum features Boy
Scouts of America National and local Council history, historic photographs, rare
Scouting books, unique badges, awards, interesting memorabilia from jamborees and
camporees, uniforms and insignia, camp items, and the famous Ben Hunt Collection of
neckerchief slides and artifacts. The museum contains Scouting memorabilia and
records dating back to Scouting's inception in 1910.

This museum really rocks!

Thomas A. Greene Memorial Museum
University of Wisconsin-Milwaukee
3209 N. Maryland Avenue
Milwaukee, WI 53211

Phone: (414) 229-6171
Contact: Bret Ketter
E-mail: bketter@uwm.edu
Open: Monday through Friday, hours vary. Please call ahead.
Admission: Free

This museum holds a unique place in that it was built and presented to the University
for the purpose of housing a very extensive private collection of minerals and fossils. It
includes nearly all the minerals described in Dana's Mineralogy and the paleontological
collection numbers about 75,000 fossils. At the time of Mr. Greene's death, it was
considered the most valuable collection of its kind west of Philadelphia. If paleontology
is your thing, this is your museum!

UWM-Art History Gallery
Mitchell Hall, room 154
University of Wisconsin-Milwaukee Campus.

Phone: (414) 229-4330 Art History Department
Open: Thursdays noon to 4pm
Admission: Free

The gallery has a diverse range of artifacts in the permanent collection. An active
schedule of temporary shows keeps the students and public well informed about art,
history, and culture. This gallery belongs to the INOVA Art Institute at the University.

The University of Wisconsin-Milwaukee Art Gallery is a small jewel box of artistic treasures.

UWM Union Art Gallery
2200 E. Kenwood Blvd.
Milwaukee, Wi. 53201

SOUTHEAST

Mailing address: P.O. box 413, Milwaukee, WI 53201
Phone: (414) 229-6310
Open: Monday through Wednesday and Friday to Saturday, noon to 5pm; Thursday noon to 7pm.
Admission: Free

The University of Wisconsin-Milwaukee has a fine art gallery in the student union building with an ever-changing series of exhibits on many topics in the visual arts. Stop by and visit. This gallery belongs to the INOVA Art Institute at the University.

Here you will find Milwaukee's Italian villa on the lake with art, gardens, and culture. La doce vita!

★★Villa Terrace Decorative Arts Museum
2220 N. Terrace Ave.
Milwaukee, WI 53202

Phone: (414) 271-3656 [Fax: 414-271-3986]
Contact: James Temmer, Executive Director
Email: jtemmer@cavtmuseums.org
Website: http://www.cavtmuseums.org/vt/home.html
Open: Wednesday – Sunday, 1pm to 5pm.
Admission: Yes

Important works: American and European decorative arts, wrought iron masterpieces, fine art paintings, Renaissance Garden.

About the museum: The Villa Terrace Decorative Arts Museum is located in a magnificent 1923 Italian Renaissance-style villa, once a private residence overlooking Lake Michigan. It was built by Milwaukee architect David Adler for Mr. and Mrs. Lloyd R. Smith. Lloyd Smith was president of the A.O. Smith Corp., the largest manufacturer of automobile frames in the nation. Villa Terrace is the only home Adler designed in Milwaukee. The collection includes 15th through 18th century decorative arts, works by wrought iron master Cyril Colnik, Zuber panoramic wallpaper, and fine art by Spanish, Dutch, Flemish, and Italian painters. The changing gallery often features traveling exhibits or private exhibits of decorative arts.

A restored 16th century Italian Renaissance Garden was recently opened for educational as well as public and private events. One of only a few such gardens in the U.S, it features potted culinary and medicinal herbs, Mediterranean plants, an orchard, meadow, fishpond, secret gardens, statuary, and a tram for public access. Throughout the year, Villa Terrace offers exhibitions, garden/museum tours, youth and family events, concerts, talks, and other special programs.

Vogel Hall is the art museum for the university, buts its much more then that, its a center for art research and artistic innovation with an international reputation. How inova....

Vogel Hall Art Museum
University of Wisconsin -Milwaukee
Art Museum/INOVA
3253 Downer ave
Milwaukee, WI 53211

Phone: (414) 229-5070
Contact: Bruce Knackert
Email: knackert@uwm.edu
WebSite: www3.uwm.edu/arts/about/inova
Admission: free
Open: Call for hours, depending on academic school year.

The mission of the Peck School of the Arts is to provide the highest quality education and professional training in the arts at the baccalaureate and master's degree levels. The school is committed to recruiting faculty, staff, and students who reflect the richness and diversity of art-making in a variety of cultures. As the only school of the arts in Wisconsin in a major urban environment, the Peck School of the Arts encourages collaboration with community arts organizations and artists to provide professional experiences for its students.

INOVA

Since 1996, the Institute of Visual Arts (INOVA) at the University of Wisconsin-Milwaukee has established an international reputation as a contemporary art research center. The mission of the Institute of Visual Arts is to engage the general and university publics with contemporary art from around the world through exhibitions and programs. The Institute is recognized for the high quality of its programs and for the opportunity it offers artists to experiment in the creation of new work, and it is committed to educating audiences by presenting artists who are shaping our visual culture in the present and for the future. According to Artforum magazine, "the Institute of Visual Arts has established itself as one of the most adventuresome venues in the states."

A popular Contemporary Art venue with cutting-edge exhibits.

▲ Walker's Point Center for the Arts
911 W. National Ave.
Milwaukee, WI 53204

Phone: (414) 672-2787 [Fax: 414-672-5399]
Email: staff@wpca-milwaukee.org
Website: www.wpca-milwaukee.org
Open: Tuesday – Saturday, noon to 5pm.
Admission: Free

Important works: Changing exhibits, hands-on art programs for youth.

About the museum: Walker's Point Center for the Arts supports visual and performing arts and learning in a multicultural environment. The center fosters creativity in children through innovative education and encourages audience development and artistic talent with a diverse blend of programming. Special opportunities for children include Hands-On, an after-school program, and Summer Art Camp.

A fascinating display of advertising and design history linked to an art school with changing exhibits.

▲ ★William F. Eisner Museum of Advertising and Design
208 N. Water St.
Milwaukee, WI 53202

Phone: (414) 847-3290
Website: www.eisnermuseum.org
Open: Wednesday and Friday, 11am to 5pm; Thursday, 11am to 8pm; Saturday, noon to 5pm; Sunday, 1pm to 5pm.
Admission: Yes

The William F. Eisner Museum of Advertising and Design is the only national venue focusing on how advertising functions. It is an interactive, archival and educational center focusing on advertising and its impact on popular culture. With its unique emphasis on the social, historical, and aesthetic implications of advertising and design, the Eisner Museum is an important center for research in and discussion of advertising and design. It features changing exhibitions of national and international work and is housed on the campus of the Milwaukee Institute of Art and Design.

At this museum in the heart of Milwaukee, discover the rich history of Wisconsin's African-American community.

▲ ★Wisconsin Black Historical Society and Museum
2620 W. Center St.
Milwaukee, WI 53206

Phone: (414) 372-7677 [Fax: 414-372-4888]
Email: contact@wbhsm.org
Website: www.wbhsm.org
Contact: Clayborn Benson
Open: Tuesday-Friday, noon to 5:30pm; Saturday, 9am to 2pm.

Important works: Mural "Ancient Egypt to Modern Milwaukee" painted by George Gist, African American labor exhibit.

About the museum: The Wisconsin Black Historical Society Museum is dedicated to finding and preserving the history of African Americans in Wisconsin. The museum exhibits, collects, and disseminates materials depicting this heritage. Serving as a resource center for all people interested in Wisconsin's rich African American heritage, the museum's also promotes community and cultural activities.

Take it on faith, the visit is worth it.

▲ Wisconsin Evangelical Lutheran Synod — WELS Historical Institute Museum
6814 N. 107th St.
Milwaukee, WI 53224

Phone: (414) 464-3559
Contact: Char Sampe, Curator
Open: By appointment

Important works: Historical artifacts and archival material from the WELS.

About the museum: This museum preserves the history of the Wisconsin Evangelical Lutheran Synod, founded in 1850 by Germans at this site. The Wisconsin Synod is probably the only major religious group to begin in Wisconsin. Holdings of the synod's archives are located at Wisconsin Lutheran Seminary. The institute is involved in the restoration and preservation of Salem Lutheran Landmark church, built in 1863 and located nearby. The synod museum, on the church's lower level, houses about 1,000 artifacts and pictures from the synod's past.

Mukwonago

If your Sunday drive takes you through Mukwonago, the Red Brick House built in 1842 is a pleasant stop.

▲ Mukwonago Historical Society Museum – "The Red Brick House"
103 Main St.
Mukwonago, WI 53149

Mailing address: Village Hall, 440 River Crest Ct., Mukwonago, WI 53149
Phone: Village Hall, (262) 363-6420 or Carol Hall, (262) 662-3953

Contact: Carol Hall
Open: June through October, Sundays, 1pm to 4pm and the first Saturday of each month, 1pm to 4pm.

Important works: Extensive collection of American Indian artifacts. Historic house furnished to represent 1863-1900.

About the museum: The Mukwonago Historical Society museum is located on the village square in the two-story Sewall Andrews home built in 1842. Locally called "The Red Brick House" museum, it was made using brick from a local brickyard and was the first brick home in Waukesha County. Members offer guided tours of the house, which is furnished in Civil War fashion. Displays include artifacts of the Plains and Hudson Bay Indians, Victorian parlor and furnishings, period kitchen and household items, and paintings by local artists. A log cabin replica of Sewall Andrew's general store is adjacent to the museum.

Muskego

Here you will find a wonderful complex of historic buildings brought to one site for the visitor's pleasure.

Muskego Historical Complex
Old Settler Center: W184 S8092 Racine Avenue
Muskego, WI 53150

Mailing address: P.O. Box 137 Muskego, WI 53150
Phone: (262) 895-7255
Contact: Ronald Peters
Open: Open for special events and holidays. For group tours at other times, call for an appointment.
Admission: Free, donations welcome

Located within the Muskego Historical Complex are the Muskego Town Hall, Heinrich log cabin, tool shed, Mill Valley schoolhouse, Wollman House, farm museum barn, church, machine shed, and log house. All of the buildings except the Town Hall are on the Old Settlement Center.

Neosho

This old village hall serves as the focal point for local history.

Neosho Historical Museum — Old Village Hall Museum
115 South Schuyler Street
Neosho, WI 53059

Mailing address: Neosho Historical Society, P.O. Box 105, Neosho, WI 53059
Phone: (800) 414-0101
Open: April-October: second and fourth Sundays, 1pm to 4pm; November-March: second Sunday, 1pm to 4pm.

The Neosho Museum's collection includes artifacts from an early bank, firehouse, and iron mine.

New Berlin

What would a summer be without an old-fashioned ice-cream social? Get a taste of history at the Annual Open House in July. Two scoops or three?

New Berlin Historical Society - New Berlin Historic Park
19765 W. National Ave.
New Berlin, WI 53146

Mailing address: S46 W22212 Tansdale Rd., Waukesha, WI 53189
Phone: (262) 542-4773 or (262) 679-1783
Contact: Roy Meidenbauer or Jackie Hermann
Website: www.newberlin.org/display/router.asp?docid=632
Open: Call for current hours or to arrange a tour. Special Open Houses in July, September and October (see below).

Important works: Pioneer log cabin, merchant's house and carriage barn, one-room school, other historic buildings, farm equipment, and associated artifacts.

About the museum: The New Berlin Historical Society, organized in 1964, is dedicated to the four Rs – Rescuing, Restoring, Recording, and Recreating New Berlin history. Its collection of buildings is situated in New Berlin Historic Park on Prospect Hill, the site of an early pioneer settlement. The park features an 1870s farmhouse and carriage building, Elger's General Store (1930s), a Coopers Shop, Harness Shop, Prospect Hill Post Office, One-Room School, and an operating windmill that pumps water. Be sure to visit the glass-enclosed lookout tower offering views of four counties.

The society conducts grade school classes in its 1863 one-room school with lessons taught just as they were a century ago, using McGuffey Readers and slates. Three special open houses are held each year. There is an Ice Cream Social (third Sunday in July), Historic Day (second Sunday in September), and Applefest (first Sunday in October). All buildings are open with costumed guides, plus demonstrations of spinning, weaving, and playing of the old organ.

The area around the park has been given Historic Settlement recognition. Wisconsin's first Freewill Baptist Church, built in 1848, is directly across the street. The restored Victorian Peck-Foster-Wiegner home is west of the park and the childhood home of former Wisconsin Governor Julius P. Heil is just down the road. The society's latest project is restoration of the early home of women's suffrage leader Theodora Winton Youman.

Oak Creek

Only minutes from Milwaukee, this complex of historic buildings brings you back in time.

Oak Creek Historical Complex and Pioneer Village
15th Avenue and Forrest Hill
Oak Creek, WI 53154

Mailing address: P.O. Box 243 Oak Creek, WI 53154
Phone: (414) 761-2572
Contact: Elroy Honadel
Email: applenancy@milwpc.com
Website: http://ochistorical.freeservers.com/
Open: Memorial Day-Labor Day, Sundays, 2pm to 4pm. Call for an appointment.

Admission: Free, minimal fee per person for school groups

About the museum: Our museum complex consists of five historical buildings: an 1840 furnished log cabin, 1874 brick town hall, 1886 blacksmith shop, 1890s summer kitchen displaying washing machines, a farm shed containing antique farm tools, and a meeting building which houses a gift shop, archives, print shop, and cobbler shop.

Oconomowoc

This is a perfect destination for a summer drive to local history and heritage.

Oconomowoc and Lake County Museum
103 W. Jefferson Street
Oconomowoc, WI 53066

Mailing Address: P.O. Box 969, Oconomowoc, WI 53066
Phone: (262) 569-0740
Open: Friday, Saturday, and Sunday, 1pm to 5pm.
Admission: Donations

About the museum: Visit the Lake Area Beginnings room, the Sarah Jane Abbott room (a celebration of women's home crafts through the years), the old-time classroom, and an illustrated history of the Oconomowoc mail boat. Other displays include winter sports, toys, antique license plates, arrowheads, sewing machines, and hand tools.

Oostburg

If you can't go to Holland, take a trip to Oostburg to see Dutch heritage come alive.

Oostburg Historical Society and Heritage House
25 N. 10th St.
Oostburg, WI 53070

Mailing address: P.O. Box 33, Oostburg, WI 53070
Phone: June Ver velde (920) 564-2911 or Dale Roerdink (920) 564 – 3148
Contact: June Ver Velde , Secretary; Dale Roerdink, President
Website: www.oostburg.org/organizations/
oostburg_historical_society/oost_hist_soc.htm
Open: Memorial Day – Labor Day: Wednesday and Friday, 6am to 8pm, or by appointment.

Important works: Local schools and businesses artifacts, genealogy resources.

About the museum: The Historical Society and Heritage House, organized in 1990, is housed in a former city firehouse. Changing displays are on topics such as the 100th anniversary of the Oostburg School System, the finale of World War II, and early Oostburg businesses. The society also has a growing collection of genealogical material.

Palmyra

The Biblical Palmyra never had such a fine museum. Come and see what all the fuss is about! Find heritage at one stop.

Palmyra Historical Society — Carlin House and Turner Museum
112 N. Third St.
Palmyra, WI 53156

Mailing address: P.O. Box 265, Palmyra, WI 53156
Phone: (262) 495-2412
Contact: Terry Tutton, (262) 495-4245
Email: cislej@cni-usa.com
Website: http://www.palmyrahistoric.org/
Open: Saturdays, 10am to 2pm, or by appointment.

Important works: Historic house, local artifacts.

About the museum: The Palmyra Historical Society acquired the Carlin House as a gift from Fisk Carlin. Built in 1845, the house is furnished in the style of the late 19th century. In 1998, Paul and Harriet Turner donated money to build the Turner Museum behind the Carlin House. This 3,000 square foot structure contains a display gallery with rotating exhibits, meeting rooms, storage areas, workrooms, and a gift shop. An alcove in the display room houses "Palmyra, Then & Now," a pictorial exhibit.

Pewaukee

Only minutes from Milwaukee, this site is sure to please the visitor.

Clark House Museum
206 E. Wisconsin Avenue
Pewaukee, WI 53072

Mailing address: P.O. Box 105, Pewaukee, WI 53072
Phone: (262) 691-0233
Contact: Sandi Smith
Email: pahs53072@hotmail.com
Website:
http://clarkhousemuseum.lakecountrybusiness.com/ihtml/public/mainframe.ihtml
Open: June-September, Sunday, 1pm to 4pm; Year-round, Wednesday, 7-9 and by appointment.

Built in 1844 by Asa Mosely Clark, son of Pewaukee's first white settler, the Greek revival house served as the community's first hotel. Its location on Watertown Plank Road, the main east/west thoroughfare of the time, made it an ideal stopping place for weary travelers. The Pewaukee Area Historical Society purchased the building from the Clark estate in 1992.

Fascinating Facts

Regarding free speech, the Wisconsin state Constitution reads, "Every person may freely speak, write, and publish his sentiments on all subjects."

SOUTHEAST

Pleasant Prairie

They say, "War is hell." This museum is heaven for military buffs of all ages.

Kenosha Military Museum
11114 120th Ave.
Pleasant Prairie, WI 53158

Phone: (262) 857-3418 [Fax: 262-857-7934]
Contact: Joyce Sonday
Email: msonday@ameritech.net
Website: www.kenoshamilitarymuseum.com
Open: Wednesday - Sunday, 10am to 5pm.
Admission: Yes

Important works: Cobra helicopter used in Vietnam, Desert Storm, and Bosnia, an operating Sherman tank, Sikorsky sky crane used in Vietnam, World War I Schneider cannon.

About the museum: The museum, which opened in 1986, has a small indoor display area with war and military objects including a 1943 Harley Davidson motorcycle mounted with a Thompson machine gun, a gas mask from World War I, and sand from Omaha and Utah beaches from World War II. Also on display is a bulletproof vest from Vietnam and an Iraqi surrender flag from the Gulf War. The museum has about 100 pieces of military hardware including a 110 Howitzer, Sherman tank, 48 Bridge Launcher, 548 tank, and 5-113 armored personnel carriers. Many of its military vehicles have been used in movies and TV commercials. The gift shop sells customized dog tags and other war-related merchandise.

Plymouth

History enthusiasts will love the arrowhead displays and the rocks are worth the Pilgrims landing.

Plymouth Historical Society
520 E. Mill St.
Plymouth, WI 53073

Mailing address: P.O. Box 415, Plymouth, WI 53073
Phone: (920) 892-6228
Email: info@plymouthhistorical.com
Website: http://www.plymouthhistoricalsociety.com/
Open: Call for available times

Important works: Local Indian artifacts.

The society has an extensive collection of Indian arrowheads found locally.

Port Washington

Judge for yourself the richness of this heritage site. It's a closed case!

Judge Eghert House
302 Grand Avenue
Port Washington, WI 53074

Phone: (262) 284-2875 or (262) 284-2897
Open: Memorial Day-Labor Day: Sundays, 1pm to 4pm. Please call to arrange a tour.
Admission: Yes

The Victorian cottage, which is set high on a hill looking towards Lake Michigan, was built by Louis Teed for his brother Byron in 1872. The Teed and Lewis families lived in the house until 1881 when it was purchased by Leopold Eghert, an Austrian immigrant who became a judge in Port Washington. The house was occupied by his descendants until 1969 when the W.J. Niderkorn Foundation acquired it and began restoring the cottage to its late 1880s appearance.

Arrive at Port and see the light at this historic station. It glows.

Port Washington Light Station
Shore of Lake Michigan
Port Washington, WI 53074

Mailing address: Port Washington Historical Society, P.O. Box 491, Port Washington, WI 53074
Phone: (262) 284-7240
Email: portwashhistorical@yahoo.com
Website: www.portwashingtonhistoricalsociety.org
Open: Late spring, summer and early fall: Saturdays and Sundays. Call ahead for details and to make an appointment.
Admission: Yes

The Port Washington Light Station was constructed in 1860 and has been a central focal point for the community for many decades. This was the second lighthouse built on the site. The fourteen-foot wooden tower has a nine-sided lantern and it housed a fourth order of the fresnel lens lamp. It has a focal point of 125 feet above lake level and the structure was decommissioned in 1903.

The Port Washington Historical Society is a group of dedicated volunteers who maintain the light station and promote the activities of the society.

Racine

Find two great art museums in one! The new downtown facility is a showcase for crafts and the country estate is a place for education, nature, and enjoyment. Both are worthwhile destinations that should be seen and Reseen!

★★★Racine Art Museum
441 Main Street
Racine, WI 53401

Phone: (262) 638-8300
Website: www.ramart.org
Open: Tuesday-Saturday, 10am to 5pm; Sunday, noon to 5pm.
Admission: Yes

About the museum: Racine Art Museum is a new museum featuring one of North America's most significant collections of contemporary crafts. With a permanent collection of more than 3,000 objects, half of these pieces represent the museum's focus on contemporary crafts in ceramics, fibers, glass, metals, and wood. The remainder of the collection is a combination of 1930s art from the WPA Federal Art Project, which was the museum's first acquisition, along with works on paper, paintings, and sculpture. This permanent collection was formerly housed in the Charles A. Wustum Museum of

Fine Arts. When the collection outgrew the Wustum campus, the new Racine Art Museum was established. The Wustum campus, at 2519 Northwestern Avenue, now houses the community outreach programs and studio art workshops taught by nationally known artists working in craft media. The facility includes exhibition galleries, a sculpture courtyard, a museum store, and an art library and research center.

Visit this rich collection of local heritage that includes industry, inventions, boating, transportation, and genealogy. Come sample its vast treasures!

★Racine Heritage Museum
701 Main St.
Racine, WI 53403

Phone: (262) 636-3926 [Fax: 262-636-3940]
Contact: Chris Paulson, Executive Director
Email: inquire@clmail.com
Website: www.racine.org/rcmuseum.html
Open: Tuesday, Wednesday, Friday, 9am to 5pm; Thursday, 9am to 8pm; Saturday, 10am to 3pm; Sunday, noon to 4pm. Research Center: Tuesday and Wednesday, 3pm to 4:30pm; Thursday, 5pm to 7:30pm, also by appointment. Hours subject to change.

Important works: Local business and shipbuilding history, Frank Lloyd Wright exhibit, historic vehicles, and extensive archives.

About the museum: The museum offers three floors of entertaining and interesting exhibits celebrating Racine's rich heritage. Stories are told of local people and businesses including Hamilton-Beach, S.C. Johnson, Case, Modine Manufacturing, and Horlick's Malted Milk. A newly opened, award-winning maritime exhibit features Racine's boat-building heritage, with harbor history and the story of the USS Racine naval ship. The popular Sesquicentennial Exhibit Series features the fascinating stories of several Racine inventors and entrepreneurs. Other displays include a 1905 Mitchell automobile, 1870s wagon, Racine County in the Civil War, African-American history, the Racine Belles of the All American Girls Baseball League, and Frank Lloyd Wright's architecture in the Racine area. The Local History Research Center is home to a vast collection of photographs, documents, and reference materials, which is widely used for genealogical and historical research.

It's a jungle out there, but a free zoo in here! They'll make a monkey out of you.

★Racine Zoological Gardens
2131 N. Main St.
Racine, WI 53402

Phone: (262) 636-9189 [Fax: 262-636-9307]
Contact: Jay Christie, President and CEO
Email: info@racinezoo.org
Website: www.racinezoo.org
Open: Labor Day - Memorial Day, 9am to 4pm; Memorial Day - Labor Day, 9am to 8pm.
Admission: Free

About the museum: The Racine Zoological Gardens began in 1923 with a small collection of monkeys and goats. It has expanded to thirty-two acres, providing a home for over 250 animals. This is one of the few remaining zoos providing free admission to over 250,000 visitors each year.

Another great example of Frank Lloyd Wright's genius - real gold. Wright in the neighborhood are other historic Wright buildings like the Hardy House.

★★★S.C. Johnson/Golden Rondelle Theater
1525 Howe Street
Racine, WI 53403

Phone: (262) 260-2154
Website: http://www.racinecounty.com/golden/
Open: Tours on Fridays by reservation.
SC Johnson Wax Tour Office
Telephone: (262) 260-2154
Email: rondelle@scj.com

The Golden Rondelle was originally designed by Lippincott and Margulies as the S.C. Johnson Pavilion at the New York World's Fair in 1964-65. It was as architecturally different then as it is today. After the Fair, the theater was brought to Racine. Taliesen Associate Architects, the architectural group founded by Frank Lloyd Wright, was commissioned to redesign the structure to complement the company's existing Wright designed Administration Building. The tour highlights the main architectural points of interest and gives a broad overview of S.C. Johnson.

Since its opening on April 22, 1939, the SC Johnson Wax Administration Building has been a "mecca" for tourists, architects and Frank Lloyd Wright devotees from around the world. Today the building remains in use as the international headquarters for SC Johnson Wax.

The bricks used in the building are unusual in that more than 200 sizes and shapes of brick were made to form the angles and curves used by Wright. Even their color, Cherokee Red, was specified by Wright. The Great Workroom, which covers nearly one-half acre, is the main office area. Though it has many unique features, two of the most prominent are the slim dendriform columns that support the roof, and glass tubing which replaces conventional windows.

This is one of Frank Lloyd Wright's domestic masterpieces. It's a private home turned conference center for everyone to enjoy.

★★Wings Spread Conference Center
33 Four Mile Road
Racine, WI 53402

Phone: (262) 681-3353
Open: Open to the public when conferences are not in session. Call ahead for an appointment. General hours of operation are Tuesday - Thursday, 9:30am to 3pm.
Admission: Free

Wings Spread was designed by Wisconsin's well-known architect Frank Lloyd Wright in 1939 for Herbert F. Johnson, the grandson of the founder of S.C. Johnson Wax Company. The 14,000 square foot structure has four distinct wings, which Mr. Wright described as zoned housing. There are well-defined public and private areas and all come together under the central wigwam. Only the two wings that contain the bedrooms are currently open to visitors. The wigwam area of the structure contains a library, dining room, sitting rooms, living room, and a small observatory. The famous barrel chairs and octagon shaped ottomans are hallmarks of this important structure. The Johnson Foundation, which was established in 1959, has turned the house into an international conference center. The house is on the National Register of Historic Places and is truly a one-of-a-kind home.

Ripon

This birthplace of the Republican Party is a place of worship for some!

★Little White Schoolhouse
303 Blackburn St.
Ripon, WI 54971

Mailing address: P.O. Box 305, Ripon, WI 54971
Phone: (920) 748-6764 [Fax: 920-748-6784]
Email: chamber@ripon-wi.com
Website: www.littlewhiteschoolhouse.com
Contact: Paula T. Price, Executive Director

Important works: 1850 one-room schoolhouse, History of the Republican Party.

About the museum: In this schoolhouse on March 20, 1854, the nation's first group meeting was held to advocate a new political party under the name "Republican." It brought together a dedicated following of individuals who pledged to organize and fight against the spread of slavery. The Schoolhouse tells the intriguing story of how the Republican Party came into existence. Visitors receive a history lesson in a warm atmosphere surrounded by images and artifacts from days gone by.

Ripon good college history!

Ripon College Historical Museum
300 Seward St.
Ripon, WI 54971

Mailing address: P.O. Box 248, Ripon, WI 54971
Phone: (920) 748-8752
Website: www.ripon.edu/library/archives/museum
Open: Monday - Friday, 8am to noon and 1pm to 5pm, when Ripon College is in session.

Important works: Ripon College memorabilia.

About the museum: The mission of the museum is to preserve the artifacts and history of Ripon College. It features a thematic exhibit that changes each Spring semester. For Alumni Weekend, in addition to the museum exhibit, an informal display for alumni is set up in adjoining classrooms.

A Ripon good history museum!

Ripon Historical Society
508 Watson Street
Ripon, WI 54971

Mailing address: P.O. Box 274, Ripon, WI 54971
Phone: (920) 748-5354
Email: woolley611@yahoo.com
Website: http://my.core.com/~riponhistsoc/
Open: By appointment
Admission: Free

About the museum: The Ripon Historical Museum comprises three buildings. The main building is furnished as a 1910 house museum. A new addition to the building houses a meeting room, library, and historical society archives. A second building is on the National Register of Historic Places. Built in 1858, the grout building is furnished to reflect an 1875 house. The third building, a barn, displays miscellaneous items, including farm and sporting equipment and an antique sleigh, among other historic items. This museum offers a glance into Ripon's past, its effects on the abolitionist and suffragette movements, and its heritage as the birthplace of the Republican Party.

Saukville

Step back in time and feel what life was like nearly two centuries ago.

▲★Ozaukee County Historical Society -
IIII Ozaukee County Pioneer Village
4880 County Hwy I
Saukville, WI 53080

Mailing address: P.O. Box 206, Cedarburg, WI 53012
Phone: (262) 377-4510
Contact: Mary Sayner, President
Website: http://www.co.ozaukee.wi.us/ochs/
pioneervillage.htm
Open: Memorial Day through Labor Day,
Saturdays and Sundays, noon to 5pm; tours when scheduled.
Admission: Yes

Important works: Twenty pioneer and early settlement buildings, trapping and Indian trade goods, and extensive archives.

About the museum: Ozaukee County Pioneer Village is home to a collection of 20 historically significant log, stone, and frame structures dating from the mid to late 19th century. Each represents a particular style or method of construction used by the immigrant groups who settled Southeastern Wisconsin and shaped our present communities. The buildings are furnished with artifacts that enhance understanding of the early pioneer settlers. The Draeger House, built in 1847, is a fine example of early German construction called fachwerbau, or half-timbered work. An authentic 1848 Indian trading post from Fillmore, WI contains calico bolts, oil lamps, trapper supplies, and a display of Indian artifacts including beadwork from the wife of Chief Waubeka. Other buildings include a train depot, summer kitchen, blacksmith shop, carpenter shop, dental office, chapel, and schoolhouse situated in a rural, park-like setting. The village hosts a number of events, including Civil War and Revolutionary War re-enactments and an old-time fiddlers' contest.

The Historical Society also operates the one-room Stony Hill School, birthplace of National Flag Day, a few miles north of Pioneer Village in the Town of Fredonia. An educational school tour program offers elementary students the opportunity to experience life and learning in a one room school. The society is restoring the old Interurban Depot in downtown Cedarburg to serve as the new headquarters for the society and Ozaukee County Archives Research Center.

Sheboygan

The place for kids and families in Sheboygan County and beyond. What fun!

▲ ★Above and Beyond Children's Museum
IIII 902 N. 8th St.
Sheboygan, WI 53081

Phone: (920) 458-4263 [Fax: 920-458-3492]
Website: www.abkids.org
Open: Monday, Wednesday, Friday, and Saturday, 10am to 5pm; Tuesday and Thursday, 10am to 7pm.
Admission: Yes

About the museum: Above and Beyond is a hands-on learning and discovery center for families designed to provide fun, interactive exhibits that complement children's formal education. This non-traditional learning environment encourages exploration, stimulates creativity, and motivates all visitors to appreciate the adventure of lifelong learning.

A local art educational gallery for everyone to share! Call ahead for hours.

Bradley Gallery of Fine Art
W3767 North Drive
Lakeland College Campus
12 miles northwest of Sheboygan

Mailing address: Lakeland College, P.O. Box 359, Sheboygan, WI 53082-0359
Phone: (920) 565-1280
Email: weidnerw@lakeland.edu, presnellweidner@lakeland.edu
Website: http://www.lakeland.edu/Academics/Art/bradley-gallery.html
Open: September - May: Monday – Friday, 1pm to 5pm.
Admission: Free

The Bradley Art Gallery exhibits art by Lakeland College faculty and students in a stimulating educational environment.

It is amazing what a person can do with a lifetime of summer holidays in the woods.

★James Tellen Woodland Sculpture Garden
Evergreen Drive (Black River community)
Sheboygan, WI 53081

Contact: Alice Maffongelli, John Michael Kohler Arts Center
Phone: (920) 458-6144
Email: amaffongelli@jmkac.org

In a sun-dappled wooded lot just south of Sheboygan and a stone's throw from the Lake Michigan shoreline stands a rustic log cabin surrounded by realistic, and often fanciful, concrete statues. It was the summer home of James Tellen, a furniture factory worker with a passionate avocation. The woods are filled with figures depicting prairie settlers, country life, and subjects of religious devotion.

SCHRC

You gotta see the bathrooms! They're works of art, like everything else in this first class place.

★★★John Michael Kohler Arts Center
608 New York Ave.
Sheboygan, WI 53082

Mailing address: P.O. Box 489, Sheboygan, WI 53082
Phone: (920) 458-6144 [Fax: 920-458-4473]
Contact: Ruth DeYoung Kohler, Director, ext. 143
Website: www.jmkac.org
Open: Monday, Wednesday, and Friday, 10am to 5pm; Tuesday and Thursday, 10am to 8pm; Saturday and Sunday, 10am to 4pm.
Admission: Free, donations appreciated

Important works: Changing art exhibits, sculpture garden, theater and music performances.

About the museum: The Kohler Arts Center is housed in a 100,000 square foot complex, completed in 1999, that unites three historic structures with contemporary architecture. The original structure, an 1882 Italianate home built by 19th century entrepreneur John Michael Kohler, is connected to the new building by a glass breezeway surrounded by gardens. A turn-of-the-century carriage house serves as the café, and the exterior walls of an early 20th century Carnegie library form the perimeter of an outdoor sculpture garden and concert stage. The Arts Center is one of relatively few major arts organizations in the U.S. devoted to both the visual and performing arts. Artists, musicians, dancers, theater directors, and actors are regularly in residence creating new works, often in collaboration with area adults and children.

Special events are held year round. Visitors can see up to twenty-seven changing exhibitions throughout the year, with nine or ten occurring at one time. The Arts Center is nationally recognized for innovative exhibitions that explore a range of contemporary art forms, including sculpture, painting, video, photography, crafts, installation works, and new genres. The Kohler has one of the largest public collections of works by renowned self-taught and folk artists such as India's Nek Chand and Wisconsin's Fred Smith and Eugene Von Bruenchhein. For twenty-eight years, the Arts/Industry program, considered the most unusual and successful melding of industry and arts in the U.S., has given artists from around the world the opportunity to create new works in the nearby Kohler Company factory. Visitors can tour artist studios at the factory and see completed works at the Arts Center, such as its six artist-designed public washrooms. Education programs include tours of exhibitions, art classes, and an arts-based preschool and day camp. An interactive gallery allows children to explore the arts through hands-on activities.

What a fabulous environmental park for all to enjoy, and its Free!

★Maywood
3615 Mueller Road
Sheboygan, WI 53083

Phone: (920) 459-3906 [Fax: 920-459-4089]
Website: www.gomaywood.org
Open: Monday through Friday, 9am to 4pm and
Saturday through Sundy, 1pm to 5pm.
Admission: Free

About the Park: Ellwood H. May Environmental Park, commonly known as Maywood, is a 120-acre public park. Maywood is open daily year-round; including the Ecology Center. Maywood offers natural history, environmental programs and activities, community events, recreational outings, summer camps, field trips, self-guided walks, cross country skiing and hiking trails, wildlife viewing, and a meeting place for environmental groups. The park is a popular destination for school groups, families, and individuals who love nature and the outdoors.

Diverse habitats at Maywood provide a haven for wildlife throughout the restored prairie, Pigeon River corridor, spring-fed ponds, wetlands, coniferous and deciduous forests. The Maple forest is tapped every March for its sweet maple syrup, which is bottled and sold at the Ecology Center. Great summer camp for kids.

The park is supported by the City of Sheboygan, public grants and The Environmental Park Trust of Sheboygan County through voluntary donations, bequests, and annual fund drives. The Ecology Center, and extensive trail network, and a beautiful setting make Maywood a natural focal point for our environmental programs within Sheboygan County.

Here you'll find six distinct historic buildings for the family to enjoy in a park setting on a hill. Don't miss the circus exhibit!

▲ ★★Sheboygan County Historical Society Museum
3110 Erie Ave.
Sheboygan, WI 53081

Phone: (920) 458-1103 [Fax: 920-458-5152]
Contact: Robert Harker, Executive Director; Nancy Koeppen, Program Assistant and Volunteer Coordinator
Email: koeppnlk@co.sheboygan.wi.us
Open: April 1 through October 31, Tuesday through Saturday, 10am to 5pm.
Admission: Yes

Important works: Historic buildings, Indian artifacts, ice harvesting, and circus displays.

About the museum: The society maintains four historic buildings and two modern exhibit buildings. The historic buildings are the Taylor House (1850s), Weinhold Log House (1860s), Bodenstab Cheese Factory (1860s), and Schuchardt Barn (1890s). Exhibits include Indian history and artifacts, ice harvesting, circus, maritime, and photo galleries. This museum was a Rajer family favorite and still is. Its amazing what they do with a small staff and dedicated volunteers.

Stay tuned for more museum developments in Sheboygan. There's talk of a Spaceport Museum for aerospace technolgy at the Armory building near the lake and Sheboygan river.

Sheboygan Falls

A virtual treasure trove of illuminating historic documents and exhibits. Hundreds of historic photographs and publications for all to enjoy.

▲ ★Sheboygan County Historical Research Center
518 Water Street
Sheboygan Falls, WI 53085

Phone: (920) 467-4667 [Fax: 920-467-1395]
Contact: Beth Dippel, Director
Email: schrc@execpc.com
Website: www.schrc.org
Open: Tuesday-Saturday, 9am to 4pm.

Even the building is historic and so is the neighborhood! And its historical research collection is one of the finest in the state of Wisconsin. An extensive photo collection, genealogies and family files, and more information on Sheboygan County than you could imagine await your perusal.

Tony's Tips

Walker's Restaurant in Beaver Dam is worth a detour, especially for thier fresh pies, which I love! It's right off Hwy 151.

SOUTHEAST

South Milwaukee

Come trace your ethnic roots in this fun heritage museum.

South Milwaukee Historical Society Museum
717 Milwaukee Ave.
South Milwaukee, WI 53172

Phone: (414) 762-7605 or (414) 768-8790
Contact: "JB" Bulley, President
Website: http://www.southmilwaukee.org/historical_society/historic.htm
Open: Memorial Day - Labor Day, Sundays, 2pm to 4pm, and in winter by appointment.

Important works: Local history artifacts and archives.

About the museum: The society maintains files of community and family information and provides displays and exhibits to enhance the understanding and appreciation of the local heritage.

Sullivan

Discover the roots of the Little House on the Prairie television series here in Sullivan.

Concord Historical Society
Concord Town Hall
W1170 Concord Center Dr.
Sullivan, WI 53178

Mailing address: N5863 Hickory Hill Rd., Sullivan, WI 53178
Phone: (262) 593-8099
Contact: Cindy Arbiture
Open: By appointment

About the museum: Concord Township history dates back to 1841 and its pioneer history includes the family roots of author Laura Ingalls Wilder. The society owns an 1850s log cabin originally from the Town of Concord, which was relocated to Sullivan and restored.

Stop on by and visit this fascinating school museum with Civil War memorabilia.

Town of Sullivan Historical Society Museum
N3866 West Street
Sullivan, WI 53178

Phone: (262) 593-8662 or (262) 567-0129
Open: Memorial Day and by appointment from April to mid-October.
Admission: Free, donations accepted

About the museum: The Rome Elementary School was built in 1870 and used as a schoolhouse for a century. Used as a museum since 1976, it has four rooms, including a tool room and schoolroom. Visitors will also see military uniforms from the world wars, a sports hall of fame, antique clothing, and a photograph of Henry Harndon, who was a Civil War General from Rome, WI

Theresa

Milwaukee's founding family built this trading post. Come see how they lived in the 1830s.

Theresa Historical Society — Juneau Homestead
Theresa, WI 53091

Mailing address: P.O. Box 74, Theresa, WI 53091
Phone: (920) 488-4784
Website: http://www.uwgb.edu/wisfrench/photos/junhouse.htm
Open: Memorial Day through September, open last Sunday of the month 1pm to 4:30pm.

Important works: A mousetrap designed by Solomon Juneau, immigrant artifacts, farm, and domestic tools.

About the museum: Solomon Juneau, a French Canadian trader, established a trading post in what is now Milwaukee in 1818. He platted and named the site Juneau Town. He was the first postmaster and in 1846 was elected the first mayor of Milwaukee. In 1833, he established a trading post and home in Theresa, named for his mother. The Juneau's last home has been restored by the Theresa Historical Society. In 1981, the society acquired the 1848 John Schiefer home, located adjacent to the Juneau residence. Its exhibits include farming memorabilia and the steamer trunk used by the Reklaus family on their immigrant journey from Germany. The collection also has farm and carpenter tools, as well as household and kitchen items.

Waterford

Nuzzle up to nature and bring your family!

Bear Den Petting Zoo and Farm
6831 Big Bend Rd. (Hwy 164)
Waterford, WI 53185

Mailing address: P.O. Box 322, Waterford, WI 53185
Phone: (262) 895-6430
Website: http://www.beardenzoo.com
Open: Saturdays and Sundays: May through October, 11am to 4pm. Call ahead. Weekday hours vary.
Admission: Free

About the museum: Visitors delight in the denizens of this family-owned petting zoo. They can cuddle the newborn animals in spring and explore the pumpkin patch in the fall.

Green Meadows Farm
Waterford, WI

Phone: (262) 534-2891
Open: May 11 – June 25, Tuesday – Friday, 10am to noon; Saturday, 10 am to 1pm; school groups, 9am to 2pm. July 7 – August 14, Tuesday – Sunday, 10am to 1pm. October 1 – October 30, group reservation required.
Admission: Yes

People of all ages can come here to interact with various farm animals in an educational environment. Come see over 300 farm animals and enjoy pony and tractor rides!

Waterloo

Napoleon never attended services at this church museum, but we hope you will. You never know who you will meet.

Waterloo Area Historical Society and Public Museum
Corner of Polk and S. Monroe Streets
Waterloo, WI 53594

Mailing address: P.O. Box 52, Waterloo, WI 53594
Phone: (920) 478-2328 or (920) 478-2969
Open: June through mid-September, 1:30pm to 4pm, or by appointment.

Important works: 1869 Catholic Church, local historical artifacts.

About the museum: The society was established in 1976 and maintains the original St. Joseph's Catholic Church building, built in 1869. This renovated structure includes a mural painted by Fred Wurzbach and a collection of local artifacts including furniture, dishes, clothing, and photographs.

Watertown

Here you will find an eight-sided wonder of history, including the nation's first kindergarten and much more.

★Watertown Historical Society — Octagon House
919 Charles St.
Watertown, WI 53094

Phone: (920) 261-2796
Website: www.watertownhistory.org
Open: Daily. June – August, 10am to 4pm; September, October, and May, 11am to 3pm.
Admission: Yes

Important works: Five-story Octagon House, first Kindergarten building, Plank Road Barn, pioneer and farm tools.

About the museum: The Octagon House, five floors of solid brick construction completed in 1854, was designed and built by John Richards, a pioneer Watertown settler. The house is one of the largest single-family residences of pre-Civil War Wisconsin. Its construction includes central heating, running water, and ventilating systems. The house also features a central spiral staircase, rising from the first floor to the tower room. Occupied only by Richards family members, the house was given to the Watertown Historical Society and has been open to the public since 1938.

Other properties maintained by the society include the first kindergarten in the U.S., which was started in Watertown in 1856 by Margarethe Meyer Schurz, whose husband was the German-American statesman, Carl Schurz. The building was moved from downtown Watertown to its present location in 1956. Its interior represents an early kindergarten class in session. The Plank Road Barn, originally built along the Watertown-Milwaukee Plank Road, was relocated to a nearby site. It now houses a collection of pioneer tools and farm implements.

Waubeka

This place is small but rewarding. Come and discover a local treasure!

Waubeka Museum and Cultural Center
In the former Grandview School, a half mile from Stoney Hill School
on the Milwaukee River
Waubeka, WI 53021

Open: Call for details
Admission: Donations appreciated

About the museum: The National Flag Day Foundation established the Waubeka
Museum and Cultural Center to celebrate the importance of Flag Day in the U.S. Local
patriot, Bernard Cigrand, began celebrating this day in 1885. The organization also
celebrates the importance of Native American history in the area and the cultural heritage
of the people who have lived and worked in this vicinity over the years. They also seek to
promote patriotism, historic interest, cultural awareness, and pride in their community.

Waukesha

Fly into the past and join the aviator's club.

O'Brien/Crites Field Aviation Museum
2525 Aviation Dr.
Waukesha, WI 53188

Phone: (414) 305-0565
Contact: Dennis Mohr, Chairman of the Museum Community
Open: The museum is open when the terminal is open, which is normally 6am to 9pm, daily.

Important works: Photos and memorabilia of early aviation in Waukesha County.

About the museum: The museum is devoted to the history of aviation in Waukesha
County and is sponsored and operated by the Waukesha Aviation Club. The club was
organized in 1931 and is the oldest aviation club in Wisconsin. The museum has
photographs by Warren O'Brien dating back to the 1930s.

West of Milwaukee, WCM brings local history alive with wonderful exhibits.

★Waukesha County Historical Society and Museum
101 W. Main St.
Waukesha, WI 53186

Phone: (262) 521-2859 [Fax: 262-521-2865]
Contact: Susan Baker, Executive Director ext. 225
Email: sbaker@wchsm.org
Website: http://www.waukeshacountymuseum.org/
Open: Tuesday – Saturday, 10am to 4:30pm. Research
Center: Tuesday, Friday, and Saturday, 10am to noon and
12:30om to 4:30pm; Thursday, 12:30pm to 4:30pm.
Admission: Free, donations appreciated

Important works: Exhibits on the Civil War, toys, and the fur trade era. Extensive
archives of documents and photos.

About the museum: Established in 1911, the Waukesha County Museum is located in the county's 1893 courthouse. The museum tells Waukesha County's history through exhibits, programs for schools and the public, and special events. Current exhibits include the American Civil War, toys through the ages, Waukesha's Springs Era, and early settlement including fur trading. Historic documents and photographs are preserved and available to the public in the museum's Research Center.

Keep the engine running is the motto at this historical society. Call ahead for details.

Waukesha Engine Historical Society
1000 W. Saint Paul Ave.
Waukesha, WI 53188

Phone: (262) 549-2606 [Fax: 262-549-2970]
Contact: Ronald Long, President
Open: No regular hours, but society-produced exhibits are available in several locations.

Important works: Historical displays on Waukesha Engine Division accomplishments.

About the museum: Founded in 1906, the Waukesha Engine Division of the Dresser Equipment Group, Inc. (formerly the Waukesha Motor Company), has compiled an impressive record of achievements in both the engineering and industrial fields. Its historical society was formed in 1992. There are presently over fifty members who work on preserving company history. Members have created and placed displays at the Dresser company, the Waukesha County Museum and the Machine Shed Restaurant in Waukesha. During the annual Waukesha Historic Preservation Week held each May, members put together a large display in the downtown Waukesha area.

Waupun

Housed in a former Carnegie Library, this quaint museum focuses on local heritage. Don't miss the city's outdoor sculptures. They're a real eye-opener!

Waupun Historical Society — Heritage Museum
22 S. Madison St.
Waupun, WI 53963

Phone: (920) 324-3878
Contact: Jim Laird, President
Open: First and third Sundays, 1:30pm to 4pm, except for December, January, and February. Call for admission at other times.
Admission: Free, donations appreciated

Important works: Dutch heritage artifacts, prison history, family histories.

About the museum: Artifacts at the Heritage Museum reveal the strong Dutch heritage of the citizens of Waupun. Museum exhibits mark the city's 150-year association with the Department of Corrections, and showcase several prominent citizens such as trick photographer Alfred Stanley Johnson and entrepreneur Clarence Shaler. The Heritage Museum was created in 1971 in the former city library building. This building is one of the few remaining Carnegie buildings in Wisconsin and is on the State List of Historical Buildings. Displays include a post office, kitchen, fire department, pharmacy, military room, and living room.

Wauwatosa

Oliver Damon had a dream in 1844 to build a house for his family. The house is still there filled with family treasures, and it is free and open to the public.

▲ Lowell Damon House
2107 Wauwatosa Ave.
Wauwatosa, WI 53213

Mailing address: 910 N. Old World 3rd St., Milwaukee, WI 53203
Phone: (414) 273-8288 or (414) 257-2145 [Fax: 414-273-3268]
Contact: Art Steadman
Email: mhannan@milwaukeecountyhistsoc.org
Website: http://www.milwaukeecountyhistsoc.org/homes.htm
Open: Wednesday, 3pm to 5pm; Sunday, 1pm to 5pm and by appointment.
Admission: Free, donations appreciated

Important works: Period decorative arts and domestic artifacts.

About the museum: The Lowell Damon House, completed in 1847, is Wauwatosa's oldest home and a classic example of colonial architecture. The rear five rooms were built in 1844 by Oliver Damon, and in 1846 Oliver's son, Lowell, began construction on the front of the house with its typical Early American fieldstone foundation. The front rooms are furnished in period decorative arts and household items and are open as a museum. Rooms on display include a parlor, kitchen, bedroom, and playroom. The rear rooms are used as a caretaker's quarters. The house was given to the Historical Society in 1941 and has operated as a museum home since then.

This elegant, ornate Victorian home and its gardens are treasures to local residents and out-of-town visitors alike. Don't miss the Firefly Arts Festival!

▲ ★★Wauwatosa Historical Society — Kneeland-Walker House
7406 Hillcrest Dr.
Wauwatosa, WI 53213

Phone: (414) 774-8672 [Fax: 414-774-3064]
Email: webinfo@wauwatosahistoricalsociety.org
Website: www.wauwatosahistoricalsociety.org
Open: Office: Monday - Thursday, 9am to 3pm; Research Library: open to the public Wednesday, 10am to 2pm and second Saturdays of each month, 10am to noon. Group tours (minimum of ten people) available by request.

Important works: Oil painting of Wauwatosa and the Menomonee River by immigrant German painter Henry Vianden, called the "Father of Art in Milwaukee." Historic 19th and early 20th century photographs of Wauwatosa and early settlers, extensive archives.

About the museum: The Wauwatosa Historical Society, founded in 1977, is a non-profit, educational organization committed to researching the history of Wauwatosa and to collecting, preserving, and exhibiting objects and documents from its past. The society's offices, research library, and facilities for group use are located in the stately Victorian-era Kneeland-Walker House, built in 1890. Purchased by the society in 1987, staff and volunteers are gradually restoring the house and its magnificent gardens. It is a designated Wauwatosa Landmark, a Milwaukee County Landmark, and is listed on the National Register of Historic Places. The Kneeland-Walker buildings and grounds are popular sites for private functions such as weddings, retirement parties, neighborhood group meetings, garden tours, family reunions, and corporate outings.

The society has a well-organized research library, which focuses on Wauwatosa history and items from Milwaukee County. It contains government documents, WPA records, city directories, newspapers, maps, and photographs, as well as extensive manuscript collections offering information on the community's past and its people. In addition, exhibits and programs in the Kneeland-Walker House feature the society's growing collection of artifacts that help bring Wauwatosa's history into focus. Four major public events are held annually: the Firefly Art Fair in August, Tour of Wauwatosa Homes in October, Christmas House in December, and Blarney Run/Walk in March.

Don't miss the wonderful historical displays at the nearby Wauwatosa East High School, including Art Deco tiles, WPA murals and much more. A real High School Heritage Hall to be proud of. Thanks.

West Allis

This old cream city brick school building, now a Wisconsin Historical Landmark, offers museum visitors wonderful lessons of the past.

West Allis Historical Society and Museum
8405 W. National Ave.
West Allis, WI 53227

Phone: (414) 541-6970 or (414) 821-3452
Contact: Betty Hartwig (414) 258-6346
Email: WAHS@SBCGlobal.net
Website: www.westallishistory.org
Open: Tuesdays, 7am to 9pm; Sundays, 2pm to 4pm.
Admission: Free

Important works: City history, doll collection, pioneer room, blacksmith shop, school classroom, and local manufacturing history. Archival documents include schools, government, maps, obituaries, and buildings, plus an extensive collection of photographs of the Allis-Chalmers Corporation.

About the museum: The current museum is the third building on this property. The first was a log cabin school built in 1838, the second school was built in the 1850s, and the present Richardsonian Romanesque structure, erected in 1887 and made of cream city brick, was used as a school until 1924. Annual events include an ice cream social in June, a banquet in October, and a Christmas Open House in December.

A variety of displays are featured in this expansive museum. There is a doll and toy room, a 1930s-style classroom, and church artifacts and items used in early North Greenfield. Other rooms feature a Civil War gun display, World War I and II artifacts, beaded purses, antique glassware, quilts, domestic life, and an exhibit on electricity. A room on the main floor is dedicated to local industry, including the Allis Chalmers Company, Pressed Steel Tank Company, Kearny & Trecker, and the Rosenthal Cornhusker Company. There are period replicas of a blacksmith shop, pioneer store, 1930s beauty shop, barbershop, funeral parlor, dentist office, and pioneer cabin. Located outside is an herb garden and old cemetery.

The research library has a large collection of city directories, school yearbooks, maps, death notices, church histories, manufacturing company records, state fair documents, historic post cards, and photographs.

Also, don't miss the wonderful WPA era murals at the Post Office in downtown West Allis. They are by Mrs. Francis Foy and portray Wisconsin spring and fall wild flowers.

West Bend

Here you will find a majestic museum setting with hundreds of fascinating artifacts including the historic jail and courtroom. You be the judge!

SOUTHEAST

★★Washington County Historical Society — Old Courthouse Square Museum and Jail
320 S. Fifth Ave.
West Bend, WI 53095

Phone: (262) 335-4678 [Fax: 262-335-4666]
Website: www.historyisfun.com
Contact: Chip Beckford
Open: Wednesday – Friday, 11am to 5pm; Saturday, 9am to 1pm; Sunday, 1am to 4pm.

Important works: Local artifacts, period rooms, archives, and photo collection.

About the museum: With cream city brick spires rising above the city's skyline, the Old Courthouse is a masterpiece of late 19th century Romanesque Revival-style architecture. Designed in 1889 by famous Milwaukee architect H.C. Koch, the building served as the county's courthouse from 1889 until 1962. It offers a variety of exhibits and period rooms, including permanent and temporary galleries and an interpretive center for kids of all ages. The third floor is home to the society's research department. In addition to historical and genealogical documents, the society's collection includes over 5,000 historical images from Washington County.

The city also owns West Bend's Old Jailhouse, built in 1886, which originally served as both the local jail and home for the county sheriff. The collection of jail artifacts was once housed in the courthouse, but is not awaiting renovation of the original jail.

This is one of the finest small art museums in the mid-west and it has a stellar collection devoted to Wisconsin art and history.

★★★West Bend Art Museum
300 S. Sixth Avenue
West Bend, WI 53095

Phone: (262) 334-9638 [Fax: 262-334-8080]
Website: www.wbartmuseum.com
Open: Wednesday-Saturday, 10am to 4:30pm; Sunday, 1pm to 4:30pm.
Admission: Free

The museum collection is dominated by a historical collection of documents and artwork representing the artistic output of Carl von Marr. The collection highlight is the stunning masterpiece by von Marr- The Flagellentes, a must see for art connisseurs. Over 300 works in the collection attest to his remarkable artistic ability. Selections from the Early Wisconsin Art History Collection, is the museum's second continuous collection. Leading Wisconsin artists of the mid-19th to mid-20th century are represented in this collection. Included are artists such as Carl Holty, Edmund Lewandowski, Aaron Bohrod, John Steuart Curry, and Frank Lloyd Wright. The annual schedule of exhibitions reflects the varied genre that makes up the world of visual arts. The Walter S. Zinn Doll House can also be viewed at the museum. This delightful antique dollhouse was built in 1911. It was completed by the family four generations thereafter. Over a thousand miniature items have been handcrafted and collected from around the world to complete the piece. Check the website for classes, workshops, and special events.

Whitewater

Time your visit to coincide with the annual ceramics invitational. You won't be disappointed!

Crossman Gallery
University of Wisconsin-Whitewater
950 W. Main St.
Whitewater, WI 53190

Phone: Office (262) 472-5708 or Gallery (262) 472-1207
Contact: Michael Flanagan
Email: flanagam@uww.edu
Website: http://academics.uww.edu/CAC/art/uww-art%20dept/web2/site/crossman.html
Open: Academic year: September – May, Monday – Friday, 10am to 5pm; Monday – Thursday, 6am to 8pm; Saturday, 1pm to 4pm. Closed Sundays and school holidays.

Important works: Ceramic art, textiles, contemporary fine art works, folk and outsider art pieces.

About the museum: The Crossman Gallery has been at its current location since the early 1970s and was named to honor Katherine Crossman, a former professor at the university whose interest was in textiles and weaving. Her legacy is evident at the annual Weavers & Spinners show held each summer. The gallery hosts four curated shows each year in addition to the service-oriented exhibits typical of a university art department. Major curated shows include an annual ceramics invitational, now in its 32nd year, which features national and international artists and is frequently tied into visiting artist programs in the ceramics area.

Additional shows have included surveys of the books arts, thematic shows, and shows of regionally and nationally known artists. The collection includes contemporary works by Claes Oldenburg, Dennis Nechvatal, Ellen Lanyon, Judy Pfaff, Ed Paschke, Roger Brown, Charles Parness, and Jerry Peart, as well as prints and drawings from the Neue Sachlichkeitera in Weimar, Germany (1920-1930). It also includes many works of American folk and outsider artists including Howard Finster, William Dawson, Jimmie Sudduth, and Jerry Coker. The ceramics area houses a collection of contemporary ceramic artists who have visited the university.

Conduct your own tour into Whitewater family history at this depot museum.

Whitewater Historical Society Museum
Whitewater St.
Whitewater, WI 53190

Phone: (262) 473-6820
Contact: Carol Cartwright
Open: Memorial Day-Labor Day: Sunday, 1:30pm to 4:30pm.
Admission: Free

Important works: Local family artifacts.

About the museum: The 1890 Chicago-Milwaukee-St. Paul Railroad Depot building was obtained in 1973 by the city and Historical Society to be used collaboratively as a local museum. Artifacts on display represent the families who resided in Whitewater and vicinity.

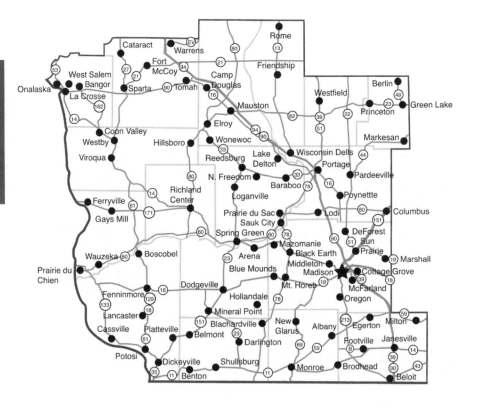

Southwest

Albany

Only an hour from Madison, Albany is chocked full of history.

Albany Historical Society Museum
117-119 N. Water Street
Albany, WI 53502

Mailing address: P.O. Box 464, Albany, WI 53502
Phone: (608) 862-3423
Contact: Ruth L. Beckman, President
Open: Year-round: Saturdays, 9am to noon; Memorial Day – Labor Day: Saturdays, 9am to 3pm.

A wide range of artifacts will pique your imagination at this local museum.

Arena

It's amazing what nature can do with rock! Here you'll find fantastic creations in stone.

Concretions Museum
7571 Highway 14, one mile west of Arena
Arena, WI 53503
Open: Usually from noon to 2pm, daily; sometimes later.

Byron Buckeridge, a retired Northland College philosophy professor, moved to Arena with a collection of over 50,000 concretions. They're rocks like you've never seen before. Some look so much like sculpture it's hard to believe they're a product of nature. During an exhibit in Milwaukee during the 1980s, many of the pieces were removed from the exhibit because they so closely resembled male body parts. But, all of these pieces are the natural results of clay, sand, silt, and iron oxide bonding together in holes in the clay. Buckeridge believes that his rocks are conceptual art. Stop by and decide for yourself!

Bangor

Here is a perfect starting point for local history tours. Call ahead.

Bangor Area Historical Society
1525 Commercial St.
Bangor, WI 54614

Mailing address: P.O. Box 15, Bangor, WI 54614
Phone: (608) 486-2616 or (608) 486-2807
Contact: Bangor Business Club (608) 486-2711
Open: Wednesday, 1pm to 3pm; Saturday, 10am to noon.

About the museum: The museum contains collections of historical items relevant to Bangor and surrounding area. A brochure produced by the society describes over twenty historical sites and structures in the Bangor area that are worth visiting.

SOUTHWEST

Baraboo

Live animals, acrobats, and a real circus atmosphere are daily fare. Let's meet at the Big Top and clown around!

★★★Circus World Museum
550 Water St. (Hwy 113)
Baraboo, WI 53913

Phone: (608) 356-8341, Toll-free (866) 693-1500 [Fax: 608-356-1800]
Contact: Baraboo Area Chamber of Commerce (608) 356-8333 or (800) 277-2266
Email: ringmaster@circusworldmuseum.com
Website: www.circusworldmuseum.com
Open: Museum open all year. Monday-Saturday, hours vary.
Admission: Yes

Important works: Circus history exhibits and memorabilia, real circus shows, live animals, clowns, collection of circus wagons, extensive archives.

About the museum: Located along the Baraboo River, this unique museum features the excitement of the circus every day of the year. Visitors can explore the historic buildings of the original Ringling Brothers Circus, browse through original circus posters, see beautifully restored circus wagons and ongoing restoration projects, and ride a real elephant or antique carousel. During the live show season, an authentic three-ring circus show comes alive twice a day in the big top tent. Meet the clowns, acrobats, ringmaster, animal trainers, and other characters that bring the circus to life.

They called it salvage, but he made it art. He's a true visionary, Tom Every.

★Forevertron Sculpture Park
Hwy 12 south of Baraboo, across the street from the Badger Ammunitions Plant and behind Delaney's Surplus
Baraboo, WI 53913

Mailing address: Evermor Foundation, P.O. Box 22, Prairie du Sac, WI 53578
Contact: Baraboo Area Chamber of Commerce (608) 356-8333 or (800) 277-2266
Email: info@drevermor.com
Website: www.drevermor.com
Open: Monday, Thursday, Friday, Saturday, 9am to 5pm; Sunday, noon to 5pm.
Admission: Free, donation appreciated.

It's possible that Wisconsin has more folk art environments than other states, and one of the most fascinating of these is Dr. Evermor's Foreverton. This structure is the fantasy of Tom Every, who refers to himself as Dr. Evermor. Inventive in vision and astounding in scope, the Forevertron is a gargantuan science fiction landscape. The 320-ton complex is the largest metal scrap sculpture in the world and a monument to the machine age that took the doctor twenty-three years to construct. Six stories high, it was assembled from generators, thrusters, machine components, and factory scrap accumulated by this former industrial salvage dealer. Gathered in the vicinity is the Big Bird Band, a playful crowd of several dozen figures made from musical instruments, old tools, gasoline nozzles, and bedposts. A huge scrap spider is poised nearby waiting to see what will happen next. Dr. Evermore hopes that the Forevertron carries the message that we're scrapping a large part of our energy and that it's important to stay connected to the 'stuff' of our past. Update: The art at this site might be moving to another location. Stay tuned.

SOUTHWEST

Here you'll find more species of living cranes on display than in any other place in the world. Flap your wings and fly on over!

★★★International Crane Foundation, Inc.
E11376 Shady Lane Rd.
Baraboo, WI 53913

Mailing address: P.O. Box 447, Baraboo, WI 53913
Contact: Baraboo Area Chamber of Commerce (608) 356-8333 or (800) 277-2266
Phone: (608) 356-9462, Ext.127 [Fax: 608-356-9465]
Email: korie@savingcranes.org
Website: www.savingcranes.org
Contact: Korie Klink
Open: April 15-October 31: Daily, 9am to 5pm.
Admission: Yes, children four and under free

Important collections and work: Live specimens of graceful and colorful cranes from around the world, captive breeding program to conserve rare species.

About the facility: Take a guided tour and meet the cranes, which are among the largest, most rare, and most beautiful birds on earth. See and photograph the endangered whooping crane, America's tallest bird and foremost symbol of conservation. ICF is the only place in the world where these magnificent birds are exhibited in a natural setting. Watch a crane fly over the prairie and learn more about cranes and their behavior. A crane flight demonstration can be seen daily at 11:45 am.

From timber wolves to bobcats, this zoo features Wisconsin wildlife and is only one hour from Madison.

★Ochsner Park and Zoo
Park St. and Hwy. 33
Baraboo, WI 53913

Mailing address: 903 Park St., Baraboo, WI 53913
Phone: Zoo (608) 355-2767 or Park Dept. (608) 355-2760 [Fax 608-355-2763]
Contact: Tim O'Keefe or Baraboo Area Chamber of Commerce (608) 356-8333 or (800) 277-2266
Email: tokeefe@cityofbaraboo.com
Open: Daily, 7:30 am to dusk. ADA accessible.
Admission: Free

Important collections: Native Wisconsin mammals and birds, plus selected animals from other states and countries.

About the zoo: The Ochsner Park Zoo is operated by the City of Baraboo on land once owned by the Henry Ochsner family. The zoo was created in 1926 by Cliff Campbell, Baraboo Parks Director, for the enjoyment of children and visitors of the Baraboo area. The first animals to make Ochsner Park Zoo their home were two black bear cubs and whitetail deer fawns.

The two-acre zoo and park has developed into a unique recreation and education resource, located next to the Baraboo River. The zoo features native Wisconsin animals, including black bear, timber wolves, bobcat, whitetail deer, great-horned owl, raccoon, and various waterfowl. Other animals include Capuchin monkeys, prairie dogs, llama and domestic livestock, and birds. Improvements over the years have created larger, more naturalistic areas for the animals. In the future, new or renovated facilities will house black bears, grey foxes, porcupines, river otters, and screech owls, along with an education and visitors area.

SOUTHWEST

The Beckman Mill was built in 1868 and early records indicate that a distillery preceded the mill. Evidence of this can be found in the 1840s structure north of the mill. The design and furnishing of the basement are consistent with a cooperage for making barrels. The building also served as the Beckman family's home from 1882 until 1978. The depression and a greater reliance on store bought flour products forced the family to add a general store, dance hall, swimming pool, fishing piers and a vegetable garden. The mill has been restored and the Friends of Beckman Mill have constructed a new dam and fish passage.

Imagine life in simpler times at this 1857 homestead chock full of history.

Beloit Historical Society — Lincoln Center and Hanchett-Bartlett Homestead
845 Hackett St.
Beloit, WI 53511

Phone: (608) 365-7835 [Fax: 608-365-5999]
Contact: Paul Kerr or Greater Beloit Chamber of Commerce (608) 365-8835
Email: beloiths@ticon.net
Website: www.ticon.net/~beloiths
Open: Lincoln Center: Monday - Friday, 9am to 4pm. Hanchett-Bartlett Homestead: June through August, Wednesday – Sunday, 1pm to 4pm and May, September, and October by appointment.
Admission: Lincoln Center - Free. Hanchett-Bartlett Homestead - small fee.

Important works: Information on industries of Beloit, maps, images, city directories, military clothing and artifacts, and a textile collection.

About the museum: The Beloit Historical Society was founded in 1910 and is the oldest historical society in Rock County. It manages two sites: the Lincoln Center on Hackett St. which houses the collections and offices, and the Hanchett-Bartlett Homestead at 2149 St. Lawrence Avenue. The homestead was built in 1857, twenty-one years after the founding of Beloit. The society has roughly 30,000 objects in its collection, not counting files of information on a variety of Beloit subjects and families.

Here you'll find a magnet for worldwide archaeological and anthropological studies. The displays are state of the art and a real must see!

★★★Logan Museum of Anthropology — Beloit College
at College and Bushnell Streets
Beloit, WI 53511

Phone: (608) 363-2677
Contact: William Green, Director (608) 363-2119 or Greater Beloit Chamber of Commerce (608) 365-8835
Website: www.beloit.edu/~museum/logan
Open: Tuesday - Sunday, 11am to 4pm.
Admission: Free

Important works: Extensive collection of American Indian artifacts.

About the museum: The museum was founded in 1893 with a gift from Chicago financier Frank G. Logan of more than 3,000 Indian artifacts that had been displayed at the 1893 World Colombian Exposition. Because of its primary purpose as a research and teaching museum, visitors will not see the usual types of displays. Instead, they will encounter an extraordinary two-story glass cube in which thousands of pieces are on view and through which they can witness the actual workings of a museum. The collections have brought such noted scholars as Margaret Mead and Louis B. Leakey to Beloit for research. Exhibits rotate regularly and visitors are welcome to open storage drawers and examine stone axes, arrowheads, and ceramics from Native American cultures in the Beloit area. Above the display cases, twelve striking mural paintings depict the rise of humanity. Of particular note are 90,000 items of Paleolithic and Neolithic material from Europe and North Africa, and over 100,000 examples of Native American clothing, tools, and implements.

This is a model for college art museums and a cultural treasure that delights new and old visitors alike.

★Wright Museum of Art — Beloit College
at College and Bushnell Sts.
Beloit, WI 53511

Phone: (608) 363-2677
Contact: Judy Newland, Curator (608) 363-2095 or Greater Beloit Chamber of Commerce (608) 365-8835
Email: newlandj@beloit.edu
Website: www.beloit.edu/~museum/wright
Open: Tuesday - Sunday, 11am to 4pm. Irregular hours during school breaks.

About the museum: The Wright Museum of Art traces its origins to 1892 when Helen Brace Emerson donated her extensive art collection to the college. The collection represents Western and Eastern artistic traditions dating to 3,000 B.C. Over the years, the museum has obtained a large collection of Asian decorative arts from Carolyn Pitkin McCready, a large collection of Chinese snuff bottles, Japanese woodblock prints, Japanese sword fittings, Japanese sagemono and netsuke, Korean ceramics, and Buddhist sculpture.

Benton

See what religious faith could build in pioneer times. A real blessing.

Mazzuchelli Rectory Museum
237 E. Main St.
Benton, WI 53803

Phone: (608) 759-2131
Open: Call for hours. St. Patrick's Catholic Church

Important works: Artifacts from Father Samuel Mazzuchelli.

About the museum: This restored building, the last rectory of Father Samuel Mazzuchelli, has been moved to near its original site. Father Mazzuchelli designed and built St. Augustine Church in 1844. The rectory contains many objects associated with the life of the pioneer priest.

Black Earth

Toot your whistle and stop by the Depot Museum.

Black Earth Depot and Museum
934 Mills Street
Black Earth, WI 53515

Phone: (608) 767-2667
Contact: Shirley Danz

Open: Sunday prior to Memorial Day to Sunday prior to Labor Day. Sundays, 1pm to 4pm. Tours by appointment.

About the museum: The Black Earth Depot Museum was constructed sometime between 1857 and 1870. Displays inform and educate the patrons on the history of the community and the surrounding area.

Blanchardville

An historic library full of local flavor.

Blanchardville Historical Society Museum
101 South Main Street
Blanchardville, WI 53516

Mailing Address: P.O. Box 62, Blanchardville, WI 53516
Contact: Blanchardville Chamber of Commerce (608) 523-2274
Open: Special occasions and Saturdays

About the museum: The museum is located in the old library building. Its mission is to preserve and document the history of Blanchardville and the surrounding area.

Blue Mounds

Nature has been working millions of years to create these beautiful caverns for visitors to enjoy. Look but don't touch. Remembers caves are cool.

★Cave of the Mounds
2975 Cave of the Mounds Road,
Blue Mounds, WI 53517

Mailing address: P.O. Box 148, Blue Mounds, WI 53517
Phone: (608) 437-3038
Website: http://www.caveofthemounds.com/
Open: March 15 – Friday before Memorial Day Weekend: Weekdays 10am to 4pm, Weekends 9am to 5pm; Memorial Day Weekend – Labor Day Weekend: 9am to 6pm; after Labor Day Weekend – November 15: Weekdays 10am to 4pm, Weekends 9am to 5pm; November 16 – March 14: Weekends 10am to 4pm, weekdays call for tour times. Call for holiday hours
Admission: Yes

Important works: A varied collection of colorful stalactites, stalagmites, columns, and other formations.

About the cave: It is listed as a National Natural Landmark, is the most significant cave in the upper Midwest, and possesses "exceptional value as an illustration of the nation's natural heritage and contributes to a better understanding of man's environment".

SOUTHWEST

Tony's Tips
Eat in Platteville before you get to Dickeyville! There's great variety, including a Culver's.

Scandinavian heritage is brought to life in this quaint village. Don't miss the Norway pavilion from the 1893 Chicago World's Fair.

★★Little Norway
3576 Hwy JG North
Blue Mounds, WI 53517

Phone: (608) 437-8211 [Fax: 608-437-7827]
Email: swinner@mhtc.net
Website: www.littlenorway.com
Open: May and June, 9am to 5pm; July and August, 9am to 7pm; September and October, 9am to 5pm. Guided tours require forty-five minutes; last guided tour starts forty-five minutes before closing time.
Admission: Yes

Important works: The largest private collection of Norwegian and Norwegian-American artifacts outside of Norway. Displays include full-size traditional Norwegian buildings.

About the museum: An original 1856 Norwegian farmstead houses an outstanding collection of Norwegian-American antiques. Visitors also tour the Norway Building from the Chicago World Fair of 1893 which was built in Norway and patterned after a 12th century "Stavkirke." A traditional Norwegian gift shop and picnic area are on the grounds. Little Norway is on the National Register of Historical Places.

Boscobel

Yes, it says it in the Bible - Boscobel is the birthplace of the salesman's Bible.

Birthplace of the Gideon Bible
Central House/Boscobel Hotel
1005 Wisconsin Avenue
Boscobel, WI 53805

Phone: (608) 375-4714
Contact: Boscobel Chamber of Commerce (608) 375-2672

At almost any hotel in the world you will find a Gideon bible provided by Gideons International. The birthplace of the Gideons was the Center House Hotel on September 14, 1898, in Boscobel. Traveling salesman John H. Nicholson of Janesville, WI and Samuel E. Hill of Beloit, WI discovered they were both Christians while sharing a room and talked about starting a Christian traveling men's association. The name Gideon comes from the Old Testament Book of Judges and refers to a man who was willing to do whatever God asked of him.

Like a multi-plex of rural history, this museum has it all under one roof.

Boscobel Depot Heritage Museum
800 Wisconsin Ave.
Boscobel, WI 53805

Phone: (608) 375-2672 [Fax: 608-375-2672]
Contact: Boscobel Chamber of Commerce (608) 375-2672
Email: boscocc@mwt.net
Website: www.boscobelwisconsin.com/landmarks.html
Open: Monday – Friday, noon to 4pm; Saturday 10am to 2pm.

SOUTHWEST

Admission: Donation

Important works: Recreations of early Boscobel businesses, artifacts from the Milwaukee Road Railway and Boy Scouts.

About the museum: The Boscobel Depot was built in 1857. It was a marshaling point for soldiers leaving the area to fight in the Civil War, World War I, and World War II. In October 1942, a train accident damaged the depot, resulting in the closing of passenger service. In summer 1989 The Depot Restoration Committee was formed and the renovation of the dilapidated historic depot began. After completion in 1994, the depot became home to the Chamber of Commerce, a tourist information center, and the Boscobel Depot Heritage Museum. Today, visitors can experience a stroll back into rural American history at the General Store, Telephone Company, Barbershop. Saloon, Leather and Blacksmith Shops, Creamery, and Bank. Examine other items of interest including artifacts from the Milwaukee Road Railway, a local clown, and Boy Scout troops.

The sound of muskets fills the air during the annual Civil War re-enactment. Veterans of wars enjoy this historic site. Call ahead.

Boscobel Grand Army of the Republic (G.A.R.) Hall
102 Mary St.
Boscobel, WI 53805

Phone: (608) 375-5765
Contact: Gary Young or Boscobel Chamber of Commerce (608) 375-2672
Open: June-August: Saturdays, noon to 3pm, plus special event days in summer and by appointment.
Admission: Yes

Important works: Historic G.A.R. hall and archival material from the post-Civil War era.

About the museum: This is the only remaining Grand Army of the Republic and Women's Relief Corps Hall in use in Wisconsin. The John McDermott G.A.R. Post #101 chartered in 1883 and the Women's Relief Corps #32 chartered in 1886 bought a Baptist church in 1897 and remodeled it. Used ever since as a meeting hall, it contains the original contents with many portraits, flags, a drum, original charters, and information on veterans of Grant County. There is also a monument to Jefferson Coates, a resident of Boscobel who received a Medal of Honor for being wounded at Gettysburg.

The hall hosts a Civil War Reenactment on the first weekend of August. This three-day event has a competition of cannon and rifle marksmanship and a skirmish on Saturday and Sunday. There is a garden party and ball on Saturday.

Brodhead

An hour south of Madison, the Brodhead Museum has many treasures awaiting you.

Brodhead Historical Depot Museum
Downtown Brodhead
1108 First Center Ave.
Brodhead, WI

Mailing address: 1101 E. 6th Avenue, Brodhead, WI 53520
Phone: (608) 897-4150
Contact: Brodhead Chamber of Commerce (608) 897-8411

Open: Memorial Day through September: Wednesday, Saturday, Sunday, 1pm to 4pm or by appointment.

The historical past and memories of days gone by is best seen at the old Wells-Fargo depot in the downtown area. The Brodhead 'Milwaukee Road' depot has a caboose and Fairbanks locomotive on display. While this depot is also an active rail line, the building has been transformed into a museum.

Camp Douglas

Here you'll find a penetrating look at the National Guards contribution to Wisconsin history.

★★Wisconsin National Guard Memorial Library and Museum
Volk Field Air National Guard Base
101 Independence Dr. Volk CRTC
Camp Douglas, WI 54618

Phone: (608) 427-1280
Email: Eric.Lent@dva.state.wi.us
Website: http://www.volkfield.ang.af.mil/museum.htm
Open: Wednesday – Saturday, 9am to 4pm; Sunday, 10am to 2pm.

Important works: National Guard memorabilia, photos, diaries, maps, and documents.

About the museum: The museum is housed in an 1896 log lodge, restored to its original appearance. The modern interior contains 3,000 square feet of exhibits, including full-scale and miniature dioramas, video and slide programs, and a light map of the Buna battlefield. Learn about the first and second Regiments of Civil War Volunteers. Follow Wisconsin soldiers as they fight in Puerto Rico in 1898, and then set the standard for National Guard excellence during the first decade of the 20th century. Two rooms profile fifty years of the Wisconsin Air National Guard. The Memorial Library contains books, diaries, personal histories, scrapbooks, photographs, slides, videos, and maps.

Cassville

Costumed interpreters bring to life this hotspot of early Wisconsin farm and village life.

★★Stonefield Historic Village
12195 Hwy VV (one mile north of Cassville)
Cassville, WI 53806

Mailing address: P.O. Box 125, Cassville, WI 53806
Phone: (608) 725-5210
Contact: Barbara Kienitz or Cassville Civic Club (608) 725-5855
Email: stonefield@whs.wisc.edu
Open: May28 – September 5, 10am to 4pm, daily; September 11 – October 16, Saturday and Sunday, 10am to 4pm.
Admission: Yes

Important works: McCormick collection including large and rare agricultural implements, State Agricultural collection, Governor Nelson Dewey collection, and an 1890s Village Life collection.

About the museum: Stonefield Historic Site, located along the Mississippi River near Cassville, opened in 1952 as part of the Wisconsin Historical Society. Adjacent to Nelson Dewey State Park, it was once part of the 2,000-acre estate of Nelson Dewey, the first Governor of Wisconsin. Four of Dewey's stone outbuildings and miles of stone fences remain at the site, along with a rebuilt 1893 home.

Stonefield is home of the State Agricultural Museum that relates the story of Wisconsin farming in the 19th and early 20th centuries. Exhibits highlight the innovative people and changing technology that were prevalent during this period, including the struggle that Wisconsin farmers faced as they switched from wheat to dairy farming at the end of the 19th century. "The Changing Land" exhibit is located in a reconstruction of Dewey's stone cattle shed.

The site also includes a 1900s progressive farmstead, which explores the role of women on the family farm, and an 1890s agricultural village. The village, a collection of eighteen distinct businesses, illustrates the social, educational, and economic role of towns in rural Wisconsin during this period. The village includes working crafts-people, a gift shop, and old-time confectionery.

Cataract

A German immigrant family embellished their yard with broken glass, plates, and love. We call it Outsider Folk Art; they called it home.

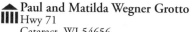**Paul and Matilda Wegner Grotto**
Hwy 71
Cataract, WI 54656

Mailing address: Monroe County Local History Room, 200 W. Main St., Sparta, WI 54645
Phone: (608) 269-8680, Monday-Friday, 9am to 4:30pm
Open: Daylight hours, Memorial Day – Labor Day.

Important works: Sixteen concrete and glass sculptures, including the Peace Memorial, Glass Chapel, and Steamship Bremen.

About the grotto: In the midst of the countryside north of Sparta, an unusual sight suddenly appears: a fantastic garden of concrete sculptures decorated with thousands of glittering glass shards. Transforming ordinary materials into an ambitious series of patriotic and religious monuments, Paul and Matilda Wegner created this remarkable monument in the 1930s. The Wegner Grotto, known locally as the Glass Church, was purchased by the Kohler Foundation in 1986 as part of its commitment to the preservation of significant outsider art environments and folk architecture.

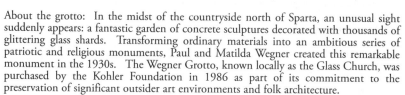

Tony's Tips

I know this is going to sound like an advertisement, but it's not! I love the Butter Burgers at Culver's Restaurants. It's a Wisconsin based restaurant chain that has consistently good food. It started in Sauk City and is now found throughout the state as well as other states. It's good food at a reasonable price.

Coon Valley

This place is a smorgasbord of Scandinavian heritage! Time your visit to see the craft demonstrations or old-fashioned Christmas.

★Norskedalen Nature and Heritage Center
N4550 Ophus Rd.
Coon Valley, WI 54623

Mailing address: P.O. Box 235, Coon Valley, WI 54623
Phone: (608) 452-3424 [Fax: 608-452-3157]
E-mail: info@norskedalen.org
Website: www.norskedalen.org
Open: Norskedalen: May 1 – October 31: Monday
- Friday, 10am to 6pm; Saturday, 10am to 6pm;
Sunday, noon to 6pm. November 1 – April 30: Monday – Friday, 10am to 4pm; Sunday noon to 4pm; closed Saturdays. Skumsrud Heritage Farm: June-August: Monday-Friday, noon to 5pm; Saturday, 10am to 4pm; Sunday, noon to 4pm.
Admission: Yes.

Important works: Features Norwegian and Scandinavian heritage items including the1853 Skumsrud cabin and Bekkum homestead.

About the museum: Exhibits at the Norskedalen Center feature the natural and cultural history of the area. The Skumsrud Heritage Farm offers a self-guided tour through more than eleven historic buildings, including the 1853 Skumsrud Cabin. On weekends you can see artisans displaying, demonstrating, and selling woodcarving, rosemaling, weaving, and more. The Helga Gundersen Arboretum and Nature Trails contain springs, Popular Creek, Gundersen Pond, and more than five miles of trails. "Norskedalen" means Norwegian valley in Norwegian.

Cottage Grove

Bigger than a cottage, Flynn Hall has a diverse collection of local history.

Cottage Grove Area Historical Society
West Reynolds St.
Cottage Grove, WI 53527

Mailing Address: P.O. Box 46, Cottage Grove, WI 53527
Phone: (608) 222-1040
Contact: Fred Volker, Curator
Website: www.cottagegroveonline.com/community/cgahs/
Open: By appointment.

Important works: Artifacts and archives on local history.

About the museum: Located in an old VFW hall, the society's collection primarily includes archival material: photographs, plat books and abstracts, cemetery lists, obituary and wedding clippings, census listings, Civil War battle lists and pension papers, World War II items, histories of schools, churches and families, memorabilia, books, and other small articles.

Cross Plains

Come on over to see Cross Plains history at this community-based museum.

Cross Plains-Berry Historical Society Museum
2204 Brewery Road
Cross Plains, WI 53528

Mailing address: P.O. Box 219, Cross Plains, WI 53528
Contact: John E. Dallman or Cross Plains Business Association (608) 798-3061
Phone: (608) 798-2760
Open: Memorial Day-Labor Day: Sundays, 1pm to 4:30pm or by appointment.
Admission: No admission, donations welcome

The Cross Plains-Berry Historical Society Museum houses artifacts relating to local Cross Plains and Berry history. Visitors can view photographs, family histories from the area, a blacksmith collection, school records, and general items detailing family life since the 1850s.

Darlington

You will have fond memories of your visit to this museum, and it's only ninety minutes from Madison.

Lafayette County Historical Society Museum
525 Main Street
Darlington, WI 53530

Phone: (608) 776-3822
Contact: Janice Ronnerud or Darlington Chamber of Commerce (608) 776-3067 or (888) 506-6553
Email: lchs@mhtc.net
Admission: Free, donations appreciated

Important items in the collection: Historical artifacts that relate to the history of Darlington, including the historic Carnegie Library building and the Railroad Depot.

The Lafayette County Historical Society operates two historic structures, which are under their care. The old Carnegie Library building located on Main Street is a Dutch revival building made of stone and architectural terra cotta. In the collection there are historic art and artifacts related to the history of the community, the American Civil War, veterans associations, Darlington notables, a photography and archives collection, and numerous items donated by the community to enhance and preserve the community's history. The Society also operates the Depot Museum, which is located several blocks from the library. The museum houses collections that revolve around railroad history and the history of Darlington.

Fascinating Facts

The biggest woman in the state is the golden statue of Wisconsin on top of the State Capitol. She weighs three tons and is covered in pure gold. In her hair are corncobs and on her head is a helmet with a badger on top of it. The badger is the tallest architectural feature in the city of Madison.

SOUTHWEST

De Forest

There are four places in town to satisfy your craving for local history. See them all and fill up.

★De Forest Area Historical Society —
Hansen-Newell-Bennett House Museum
119 E. Elm St.
De Forest, WI 53532

Mailing address: P.O. Box 124, De Forest, WI 53532
Phone: (608) 846-5519
Contacts: John Englesby, Archivist or Judy Ewald,
Activities Coordinator or De Forest Area Chamber of
Commerce (608) 846-2922
Website: www.deforest.lib.wi.us/historicalsociety.htm
Open: Museum; second Sundays, 1pm to 3:30pm, June-December. The gallery at the
library site is open during all library hours.

Important works: Boehm Photographs (1912-1915), collection of area obituaries,
and cemetery records.

About the museum: The mission of the De Forest Area Historical Society is to preserve
the historical heritage of the area and to offer related educational materials. The society
maintains and interprets four sites. The primary museum on Elm St., the Hansen-
Newell-Bennett House, has a variety of permanent displays, including information on
the schools, churches, and businesses of the area. A kitchen, parlor, and bedroom are
interpreted from the early 1900s.

A display gallery, office, work, and archival storage area are located on the first floor of
the new De Forest Area Public Library, 203 Library St. This is the primary repository in
the area for vintage photographs, documents, and manuscripts, including information
on genealogy, obituaries, and area cemeteries. The gallery features changing displays and
is open during all library hours. Volunteers are on site each Tuesday and Thursday
morning or by special appointment.

The Adeline Lyster House was recently received as a gift from the family and currently is
being restored. With support from the De Forest Redevelopment Authority, it was
moved from its former site to 201 De Forest St. It will be interpreted as a home from
the pre-World War II era. The society has also recently received the historic De Forest
Depot, constructed in 1872 near the railroad tracks downtown. Future plans call for
restoring the exterior of the building to its original appearance.

Dickeyville

It's amazing what you get when you combine religion and rocks - Viola! A roadside attraction!

★Dickeyville Grotto
US Rt. 151 and West Main Street
one block west of the 151/61 intersection
Dickeyville, WI

Website: http://search.yahoo.com/search?fr=FP-pull-web-t&p=dickeyville+grotto

Father Mathias Wernerus built the "Holy Ghost Grotto" between 1925 and 1931. A
grotto-building frenzy struck the midwest and south in the early 20th century - from

the massive junk glass and stone battlements of the "Grotto of the Redemption", to the landmark miniature of the "Ave Maria Grotto." Although it is smaller and less focused, the Dickeyville Grotto is unique in its combination of religious and patriotic-themed areas. The Grotto wraps around the Holy Ghost Catholic Church, a folk art progression that includes a small artificial cave, statue alcoves, arches, and fountains. The walls and displays feature a wider variety of costume jewelry, shells, and household items than are found in other grottos. The "Patriotism Shrine" radiates around an eagle-topped monument. A marble statue of Christopher Columbus framed in a seashell arch and images of Abraham Lincoln and George Washington complete the trilogy.

Dodgeville

Wander the beautiful nature trails at this site and get stress free.

Bethel Horizons Nature Center
4651 Highway ZZ
Dodgeville, WI

Phone: (608) 935-5885

Come to explore these 473-acres of trails, waterways, rope courses, marshes, ponds, and hillsides.

See how miners lived 100 years ago! It's a rustic experience.

Dodge Mining Camp Cabin
205 E. Fountain Street
Dodgeville, WI 53533

Phone: (608) 935-5557 or (608) 935-7694
Contact: Dodgeville Chamber of Commerce (608) 935-9200
Open: By appointment.

The Dodge Mining Camp Cabin, built circa 1828, is regarded as the oldest building in Iowa County, and certainly ranks among the five oldest surviving structures in Wisconsin. The cabin stands as a rare artifact of the lead mining operations that ensued in a mineral tract, which encompassed most of present-day downtown Dodgeville. This exceptional structure shows the changes wrought in more than 170 years.

Picture yourself in school, turn the clock back 100 years, and then rural education comes alive.

Iowa County Historical Society
1301 Bequette St.
Dodgeville, WI 53533

Mailing address: P.O. Box 44, Dodgeville, WI 53533
Phone: (608) 935-7694
Contact: Dorothy Anderson, Curator or Dodgeville Chamber of Commerce (608) 935-9200
Open: September, 10am to noon and 1pm to 4pm. Other times by appointment.

Important works: Local artifacts and arhives, including photos, genealogies, oral history interviews.

About the museum: The Iowa County Historical Society was organized in 1976 to enhance and preserve the local historical heritage. In 1978 they established their headquarters in the Old Rock School. The collection includes scrapbooks, slides, and over 3,000 pictures from the late 1800s and early 1900s, family genealogies, cemetery records, microfilm of early newspapers, oral history interviews, quilts, clothing, and artifacts from Iowa County. The society conducts yearly bus tours to many points of interest in Iowa County.

Ride the zinc train and dig through mining history. Try to get the lead out.

The Museum of Minerals and Crystals
42285 State Road 23
Dodgeville, WI 53533

Phone: (608) 935-5205
Contact: Dodgeville Chamber of Commerce (608) 935-9200
Open: Daily, April –Memorial Day weekend, 9am to 4pm; Memorial Day Weekend –
November 1, 9am to 5pm; after Labor Day, 9am to 4pm.

Important works: One of the finest collections of rock, mineral, and crystal, including a faceted lead crystal, a 315 lb. Brazilian agate, a 160 lb. fluorite, a 215 lb. amethyst geode, and more.

About the museum: Founded in 1965, this museum offers a variety of exhibits, a tour of an 1845 lead mine and a ride on a 1931 zinc train above ground. Here you will also find a gift shop and Doby Stables, Inc., "a must for the horse and nature lover."

Edgerton

From one-room schools to ivy-covered college campuses, the education system in Wisconsin has always earned high marks. See its history come alive.

Albion Historical Society — Academy Museum and Sheepskin Country School
558 Edgerton Rd.
Edgerton, WI 53534

Phone: (608) 884-3896
Contact: Robert Babcock, President or Edgarton Area Chamber of Commerce (608) 884-4408 or (800) 298-4408
Open: June through August, Sundays, 1pm to 4pm.

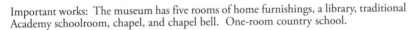

Important works: The museum has five rooms of home furnishings, a library, traditional Academy schoolroom, chapel, and chapel bell. One-room country school.

About the museum: The Albion Academy was the state's first institute of co-educational higher education. It was founded in 1853 by the Northwestern Association of Seventh Day Baptists and administered by them until 1894. By 1959, only one of the original three buildings remained. It was renamed Kumlien Hall in honor of Thure Kumlien, one of the academy's former professors and world-renowned naturalist. Kumlien Hall was deeded to the Albion Historical Society and opened as a museum in 1960. In 1965, Kumlien Hall, where many of the original Sterling North artifacts, along with the birch-bark canoe from the book "Rascal," burned to the ground. A new two-story replica was built and the museum reopened in 1969.

The one-room Sheepskin School, originally located west of Edgerton, was moved to the museum site. It shows a typical Albion/Edgerton country school classroom with the variety and style of education common to the era.

Discover the works of noted naturalist/historian, Sterling North, and how his writing was shaped by life in the Rock River valley. He had a knack for words.

Sterling North Society
409 W. Rollin St.
Edgerton, WI 53534

Mailing address: P.O. Box 173, Edgerton, WI 53534
Phone: (608) 884-3870
Contact: Elizabeth Diedrick or Edgarton Area Chamber of Commerce (608) 884-4408 or (800) 298-4408
Website: www.sterlingnorth.com
Open: April-December: Sundays, 1pm to 4:30pm, or by appointment.
Admission: Yes

Important works: Complete set of author Sterling North's books, biographical materials and family history, restored North boyhood home (site of his most popular book, Rascal).

About the museum: Sterling North was born in 1906 in a farmhouse on the shores of Lake Koshkonong, the second largest lake in Wisconsin, and grew up in nearby Edgerton. He earned his way through the University of Chicago and began his writing career. In 1947, he completed So Dear to My Heart, the best seller that established him as one of America's favorite novelists. Organized in 1989, the Society is committed to preserving and promoting the heritage of Sterling North as it relates to Edgerton and surrounding communities. In 1992, the Society purchased the North childhood home. The home serves as a literary center and museum with programs available to schools and the general public.

Elroy

If you're a political animal, the Governor Thompson exhibit will light your fire, along with farming, bicycling and railroad history from Elroy.

★Elroy Area Historical Museum
259 Main St.
Elroy, WI 53929

Mailing address: P.O. Box 35, Elroy, WI 53929
Phone: (608) 462-8747
Contact: Elroy Area Advancement Corporation (608) 462-2410 or (888) 606-2453
Website: www.elroywi.com/museum.htm
Open: May through September; Saturdays and Sundays, 1pm to 4pm.

Important works: Bronze Eagle by nationally acclaimed sculptor Robert Searles, military artifacts, and Wall of Fame.

About the museum: The museum displays over 400 objects relating to farming, bicycling, family life, and railroading. Highlights are the Wall of Fame featuring former Governor Tommy Thompson, a military exhibit honoring our veterans, Streets of Yesterday, and a farm exhibit. Also included is a miniature reproduction of Elroy when it was a major railroad center in the early 20th century by well-known miniaturist, Dwight W. "Bud" Maher.

SOUTHWEST

Fennimore

Fond childhood memories will come flooding back during a stroll through this unique collection. It's playtime once again!

Fennimore Doll and Toy Museum
1140 Lincoln Ave.
Fennimore, WI 53809

Phone: (888) 867-7935 or (608) 822-4100
Contact: Connie Neal, Director
E-mail: dolltoy@fennimore.com
Website: http://www.fennimore.com/dolltoy/
Open: May through December, Monday – Saturday, 10am to 4pm. Sunday by appointment. Closed holidays. Handicap accessible.
Admission: Yes

Important works: Historic dolls and toys from the early 1800s to present.

About the museum: This charming museum features dolls from as early as 1810, including many of your favorite childhood toys. Featured in the Doll Room are antique china and porcelain/bisque dolls, vinyl, composition, and cloth, plus dolls made from many other materials. The oldest doll is made of paper mache from Germany and is displayed with other German and French fine porcelains. Barbie is present along with Betty Boop, Shirley Temple, Hollywood Stars, Crissy, Ginny, a large display of bride dolls, and dolls from around the world. The toy room is home to a unique collection of Disney film collectibles, plus many Fisher Price toys from the 1930s through the 1950s.

Ferryville

If you like Scandinavian heritage, this is a sterling site!

Hauge Norwegian History Center
2 miles west of Rising Sun on County Road B
Ferryville, WI 54645

Mailing address: P.O. Box 72, Mt. Sterling, WI 54645
Phone: (608) 734-3192
Contact: Jacob Vedvik
Open: By appointment.

The West Prairie Hauge Norwegian Lutheran Church building has been deeded over to the Crawford County Historical Society to be used for a Norwegian History Center. If you're interested in exploring your Norwegian roots, please call ahead for details.

Fascinating Facts

Regarding inherent rights, the Wisconsin state constitution reads, "All people are born equally free and independent, and have certain inherent rights; among these are life, liberty, and the pursuit of happiness."

SOUTHWEST

Footville

Call ahead to see who's in at the telephone museum and archives.

Luther Valley Historical Society
158 Depot St.
Footville, WI 53537

Mailing address: P.O. Box 253, Footville, WI 53537
Phone: (608) 876-6892
Contact: Margorie Boylen
Open: Wednesdays and Saturdays, 9am to noon.

Important works: Early telephone equipment and Rock County archival material.

About the museum: The historical society is dedicated to the collection and preservation of the history of Southwestern Rock County. The Footville State Bank has been restored to its 1910 condition and is used as an archive for the area's local history. The holdings include photos, books, genealogical material, and scrapbooks. The telephone office building located at 115 E. Centre St. is restored to its 1914 condition and used as a "hands on" telephone museum.

Fort McCoy

Military buffs will love this huge museum complex! It's perfect for veterans and families. See the real McCoy.

★★Fort McCoy Historical Center
100 East Headquarters Road
Fort McCoy, WI 54656-5263

Phone: (608) 388-2407
Email: ruth.west@emh2.mccoy.army.mil
Open: Appointments can be made April through October for the WWII buildings and throughout the year for the History Center. They are open to groups of fifteen or more.

About the center: Fort McCoy is named for Major General Robert Bruce McCoy, a prominent local resident who served as a lawyer, district county judge, and mayor of Sparta. Upon returning from the Spanish-American War, McCoy was instrumental in convincing the War Department to establish a military reservation here in 1909.

A variety of exhibits and displays are arranged in chronological order to depict Fort McCoy's history from the time the installation was established in 1909 to the present. Building 839 is a mess hall with a capacity to feed 172 personnel. Building 840 is set up with a chapel display and an extensive exhibit of military training aids. Building 841 is configured as a day room with pictorial exhibits highlighting military history from WWII and the Korean War. Building 842 is furnished as a WWII barracks for enlisted personnel. Display items include office furnishings, potbelly stoves, and period wall art. Equipment Park currently displays forty items, which range from helicopters and howitzers to trucks and trailers.

🏛 Friendship

Brush up on the Gothic Revival style while visiting Wisconsin's friendliest town.

Adams County Historical Society — McGowan House Museum
507 Main St.
Friendship, WI 53934

Mailing address: P.O. Box 264, Friendship, WI 53934
Phone: (608) 339-7732 [Fax: 608-339-3017]
Email: adamsschs@palacenet.net
Website: www.adamschs.org
Open: Saturdays May-September, from 1pm to 4pm. Other times by appointment.

Important works: Adams County artifacts and period furniture, plus extensive archives of school records, photos, newspapers, and documents.

About the museum: This two story, nine room house was built in 1889 and is the best example of vernacular Gothic Revival architecture in the community. Dr. Washington Emmett McGowan purchased the site in 1885. Until 1991 it was home to members of the family, including Katherine McGowan, a long-time supervising teacher for Adams County. The Historical Society was instrumental in restoring the house and adjacent barn to the 1890s period, enabling the history of the McGowan family and Adams County to be exhibited. The society was founded in 1974 as part of a University of Wisconsin-Extension project to organize local historical societies in honor of the U.S. Bicentennial.

Gays Mills

Wooded hills surround this peaceful park, complete with babbling brook and log cabins, it's chock full of history.

🏛 Log Cabin Heritage Park
Hwy 131, County Fairgrounds
Gays Mills, WI 54631

Mailing address: P.O. Box 63, Gays Mills, WI 54631
Phone: (608) 735-4341 (Village of Gays Mills)
Email: gaysmill@mwt.net
Website:
http://www.gaysmills.org/logcabin.html
Open: Call for current times

Important works: Historic log-frame structures.

About the park: The purpose of Log Cabin Heritage Park is to preserve folk architecture of the Kickapoo Valley and celebrate Wisconsin's log cabin era. Adjacent to the county fairgrounds, the park has a playground, picnic areas, and is home to the annual Gays Mills Folk Festival on Mother's Day weekend.

Buildings include: Matti Hen House, McCann House, Barker Cabin, Tucker-O'Brien Log Cabin, Nederlo Granary, Wauzeka Ridge School House, DuCharme House, and the Altenburg-Zweifel Corn Crib.

SOUTHWEST

🏛 Green Lake

Don't miss the pie and ice cream social on July 4th. It's a patriotic celebration! Be a kid again.

Dartford Historical Society
501 Mill St.
Green Lake, WI 54941

Mailing address: P.O. Box 638, Green Lake, WI 54941
Phone: (920) 294-6194
Website: www.wlhn.org/green_lake/dartford_historical_society.htm
Open: Fridays and Saturdays, 10am to 4pm; Sundays, 1pm to 4pm. Additional weekend hours May-October.

Important works: Portrait of Anson Dart by George Catlin, Lizzie Malcolm paintings, c. 1860.

About the museum: The Dartford Historical Society, founded in 1956, operates a museum in the original 1871 railroad depot of Dartford (now Green Lake) at 554 Mill St. and an exhibit gallery and archives at 501 Mill St. The museum has hosted special exhibits of local painters and quilters, and on July 4th each year the society hosts an ice cream and pie social.

Another Wisconsin original: There's artistic glory in these hills.

🏛 ★Gloria Hills Sculpture Garden
W 908 Scott Hill Rd.
Green Lake, WI 54941

Phone: (920) 748-3720
Contact: Schwartz Gallery, P.O. Box 10, Ripon, WI 54971
Admission: Free
Open: Call for current times

Originally from Manitowoc, Lester Schwartz taught art for many years at Ripon College. Before that he spent time studying art in Paris and absorbed European Modernism. He brought that and much more to his teaching. At his home, which he called Gloria Hills he created a most wonderful and unique artistic statement, an art environment in every sense of the word. Using recycled materials such as automobiles and industrial products he made hundreds of outdoor sculptures and arranged them throughout the grounds that overlook Green Lake.. There's also a 1950s inspired house, filled with art. Lester was a man full of energy and his legacy still conveys his love of art and the environment. Lester and Manitowoc artist Rudy Rotter were friends. See Rudy's art environment under Manitowoc, northeast section, page 193.

Hillsboro

Here there are three fascinating historic structures all at one site for the visitor's pleasure.

🏛 Pioneer Log Cabin, Museum, and Schoolhouse
Field Memorial Park
Hillsboro, WI 54634

Contact: Ms. Betty Havlik
Phone: (608) 489-3192 or 489-3225

Open: Memorial Day-Labor Day: Sundays, 1pm to 4pm or by appointment.

Many beautiful and interesting artifacts in this collection will make you glad you stopped.

Hollandale

Nick was a Jack-of-all-trades, but his great legacy is his folk art. A concrete contribution to Wisconsin history. The summer gardens bloom with joy.

★Grandview Sculpture Garden
State Hwy 39 (1 mile west of Hollandale)
Hollandale, WI 53544

Phone: (608) 967-2151
Open: Grounds are open daily. House is open Memorial Day-Labor Day, Tuesday – Sunday, 10am to 4pm and weekends May and October.
Admission: Free

About the museum: Grandview was created by Austro-Hungarian immigrant Nick Englebert, a dairy farmer, musician, storyteller, and self-taught folk artist. He created his first concrete sculpture in the mid-1930s and by the early 1950s his entire yard was transformed into an artistic landscape of over forty concrete sculptures. Many were arranged in tableaux. Subject matter includes human and animal figures, miniature buildings, fantastic urns and planters, birdhouses, fountains, fences, and archways. Elaborate and colorful garden beds created by Englebert's wife further enhanced the impact of the sculptures.

Englebert also decorated the entire exterior of his small farmhouse with a colorful mosaic of concrete embellished with stones, shells, glass shards and fragments of ceramic dinnerware and porcelain figurines. An interpretive exhibit, installed on the first floor of the farmhouse, displays photographic documentation, sculpture remnants, and personal archives. The Kohler Foundation purchased Grandview in 1991 as part of its ongoing commitment to preserve the work of self-taught artists.

Janesville

Another corner stone to Janesville history awaits you. Only 1 hour from Madison.

★Helen Jeffris Wood Museum Center
426 N. Jackson Street
Janesville, WI 53545

Phone: (608) 756-4509
Open: Daily, June 1 – September 30, 9am to 4pm. Closed major holidays.
Admission: Yes

About the museum: If you are looking for a way to complete your historical adventure or add a little culture to your day, pencil in the Helen Jeffris Wood Museum Center on your agenda. Housed in the 1912 Prairie style residence of Stanley Dexter Tallman, it is the Rock County Historical Society's newest facility. This museum provides one-stop shopping for your all history needs!

President Lincoln came for a visit, and so should you. From Greek revival to Italianate treasures, this site is an authentic glimpse into the past.

★★Rock County Historical Society — Lincoln-Tallman and Wilson-King Houses
440 N. Jackson St.
Janesville, WI 53547

Mailing address: P.O. Box 8096, Janesville, WI 53547
Phone: (608) 756-4509 [Fax: 608-741-9596]
Email: rchs@rchs.us
Website: www.rchs.us/
Open: June – September: Daily, 9am to 4pm; off-season, by appointment.

Important works: 1850s Italian Villa and Greek revival houses, period furnishings including the Lincoln bed.

About the museum: The Lincoln-Tallman House, constructed between 1855 and 1857, is a superb example of Italian Villa-style architecture. It offers a view of upper class life during the mid to late 1800s. Most of the home's furnishings are original (including the bed upon which Lincoln slept). Meticulous attention to detail is evident in each of the twenty-six rooms on five levels from basement to cupola. Tours also include the Wilson-King House, which was moved to the site in 1964. This Greek revival style stone house, built in the late 1850s, is furnished to reflect middle class life of the period. There are many special events throughout the year.

Park the car and take a world tour through these gardens. Japan, France, and England are just some of the destinations. Peace and tranquility await you.

★★Rotary Gardens Horticulture Center
825 Sharon Road
Janesville, WI 53545

Rotary Gardens Parker Education Center
1455 Palmer Drive
Janesville, WI 53545

Phone: (608) 754-1779 [Fax: 608-754-1795] or (608) 752-3885 [Fax: 608-752-3853]
Email: Edward.Lyon@rotarygardens.org
Website: www.rotarygardens.org
Open: Gardens open daily, year round, daylight hours. Parker Education Center: April – November, Monday-Friday 8:30am to 4:30pm and weekends 10am to 6pm; December, Monday – Friday 8:30am to 4:30pm and weekends noon to 4pm; January – March, Monday – Friday 8:30am to 4:30pm and closed weekends.
Admission: Donations accepted.

Important works: Internationally-themed gardens.

About the gardens: At Rotary Gardens, twelve internationally-themed garden areas give visitors a sampling of the world's gardening and landscaping styles. Situated on fifteen acres of land, each garden area serves as a valuable educational resource and renowned horticultural showcase for everyone to enjoy.

La Crosse

Kids love to goof off at this place. There's loads of fun for all.

🏛 **The Gertrude Salzer Gordon Children's Museum of La Crosse**
207 Fifth Ave. S
La Crosse, WI 54601

Phone: (608) 784-2652 [Fax: 608-784-6988]
Email: info@childmuseumlax.org
Website: www.childmuseumlax.org
Open: Tuesday through Saturday 10am to 5 pm; Sunday noon to 5pm.
Admission: Yes

About the museum: The museum provides a place where families learn together. It provides interactive, hands-on exhibits, birthday party and meeting rooms, a multipurpose theater, gift shop, and more.

Not everyone lived like this, but you can fantasize about it in this captivating Victorian mansion. Don't miss the oriental room.

🏛 **La Crosse Historical Society -- Hixon House**
429 N. 7th St.
La Crosse, WI 54601

Mailing address: P.O. Box 1272, La Crosse, WI 54602
Phone: (608) 782-1980
Email: LCHS@centurytel.net
Open: Memorial Day through Labor Day: Daily, 1pm to 5pm. Group tours by appointment.
Admission: Yes

Important works: 1860 Italianate-style house, period furnishings, and lumber era artifacts.

About the museum: An architecturally and historically significant house of early La Crosse, this graceful Italianate house reflects an elegant Victorian lifestyle. It was designed by Joseph Twyman, who also designed the Villa Louis in Prairie du Chien, and built in 1860 by successful local lumberman and financier, Gideon Hixon. Donated to the society by Alice Green Hixon in 1965, the house is important to decorative arts history in the upper Midwest. It contains the family's original furnishings spanning the era from the 19th to the early 20th century.

There are fifteen rooms, five beautiful fireplaces, and an adjacent Wash House and Victorian era gardens. Special exhibits include the Hixon family and lumber industry along with many fine pieces from the Hixon's travels to the Orient and Europe. Known for its beautiful woodwork, the house has a "Turkish Nook," designed by Twyman, that is one of the few remaining Victorian era "Oriental Rooms" in the U.S.

Call ahead to see what's on display at the library!

🏛 **La Crosse Public Library**
800 Main St.
La Crosse, WI 54601

Phone: (608) 789-7100
Contact: Kelly Krieg-Sigman, Director
Email: k.krieg-sigman@lacrosse.lib.wi.us
Website: http://www.lacrosselibrary.org/

Open: Monday through Thursday 9am to 9pm; Friday and Saturday 9am to 5pm; Sunday 1pm to 5pm.

Changing exhibits, paintings on loan.

Dig into the past at this Archeology Center!

Mississippi Valley Archeology Center and Laboratories
UW-La Crosse
1725 State St.
La Crosse, WI 54601

Phone: (608) 785-8463 or (608) 785-8454 [Fax: 608-785-6474]
Email: bruce.jody@uwlax.edu
Website: http://www.uwlax.edu/mvac/
Open: Monday through Friday 9am to 5pm. Check in advance to be sure the building will be open.
Admission: Free

See exhibits containing findings from recent excavations, information on the field of archeology, and see paintings depicting previous inhabitants of the area.

Monkeys are but a few of the attractions at this lively zoo.

★Myrick Park Zoo
400 La Crosse St.
La Crosse, WI 54601

Phone: (608) 789-7190
Contact: Barb Peterson, Zookeeper
Open: November – April, daily, 9am to 1pm; May – October, daily, 8am to 8pm.
Admission: Free

Important works: Large variety of animals from the U.S. and world.

About the zoo: The zoo has many outdoor exhibits which house monkeys, bears, foxes, deer, bobcats, sheep, goats, prairie dogs, turkeys, peacocks, and a variety of other birds. The indoor facility has rabbits, chinchillas, and snakes.

A hobby can take many directions, come see how Paul has decorated his yard in his spare time, and made an artistic wonder.

★Paul Hefti's Yard Environment
515 Adams street
La Crosse, WI 54601

Phone: Private phone
Admission: Free
View from the street unless invited in.

Mr Hefti is a gentle soul full of energy. Over the past few decades he has decorated his yard with many wonderful and whimsical creations. Using recycled materials such as dolls and old stuffed animals he's created a true personal art environment. He also gives personal tours with detailed explanations of his work. Outsider Folk Art at its Wisconsin best.

Geared for variety, this Arts Center plays the whole field.

★Pump House Regional Arts Center
119 King St.
La Crosse, WI 54601

Phone: (608) 785-1434
Email: info@thepumphouse.org
Website: www.thepumphouse.org
Open: Tuesday, Wednesday, and Friday, noon to 5pm; Thursday, noon to 7pm; Saturday and Sunday, 10am to 3pm.
Admission: Free

Important works: Changing visual art exhibits and theatrical performances. There is no permanent collection.

About the facility: Founded in 1977, the Pump House presents visual and performing arts with a Midwest emphasis and outreach programming in arts education. It offers two galleries, the Kader Room and the Front Gallery, for artist exhibitions. The 140-seat Dayton Theatre hosts a variety of performance groups. Each month the Pump House's Festival Balcony exhibits artwork of students from area elementary and middle schools. A popular feature of the Balcony is sponsored by a local artist group, the La Crosse Society of Arts and Crafts. Changing monthly, this exhibit features artwork of local significance that is both on display and for sale.

A place of peace and pleasure the world over. It always blooms tranquility.

Riverside International Friendship Gardens, Inc
Riverside Park
La Crosse, WI 54602

Mailing address: P.O. Box 3473, La Crosse, WI 54602
Phone: (608) 791-4769
Website: http://riversidegardens.org/
Open: Call for current hours

Located along the banks of the Mississippi River, the gardens are a reflection of appreciation for the diverse cultures that share the earth. The first gardens to be planted represent the style of a typical garden in each sister city, these being: Epinal, France; Luoyang, China; Friedberg, Germany; and Dubna, Russia.

Meander down and learn about river/town history at the waters edge. Soak up La Crosse heritage.

Riverside Museum
Riverside Park
La Crosse, WI 54601

Mailing address: P.O. Box 1272, La Crosse, WI 54602
Phone: (608) 782-1980 or (608) 782-2366
Contact: Dr. Carl R. Miller
Email: LCHS@centurytel.net
Open: Monday – Friday, 10:30am to 5pm; Saturday, 10:30am to 4:30pm; Sunday, 10:30am to 4pm.
Admission: Yes

Important works: Mississippi River and local artifacts and history, plus natural history of the river valley.

About the museum: Opened in 1990, the museum's purpose is to interpret La Crosse

SOUTHWEST

history with an emphasis on the region's river system and its role in the growth and development of the La Crosse area. Exhibits range from prehistoric artifacts to large collections of area birds and freshwater clams. A video history of La Crosse introduces the museum exhibits and a photography gallery documents the riverboat era. There are also artifacts on display from the steamboat War Eagle, which exploded in 1870. A costume try-on area provides hands-on experience for young visitors.

Touch the past at this small but interesting museum. Bring the kids! Good things come in small packages.

Swarthout Museum
112 S. 9th St. (at Main St.)
La Crosse, WI 54601

Mailing address: P.O. Box 1272, La Crosse, WI 54602
Phone: (608) 782-1980
Contact: Dr. Carl. R. Miller
Email: LCHS@centurytel.net
Open: Tuesday – Friday, 10am to 5pm; Saturday and Sunday, 1pm to 5pm.
Admission: Yes

Important works: Full size room exhibits, Wilma Peter's 1955 Hair Salon, 1945 Doctor's Office.

About the museum: The Swarthout Museum features a variety of permanent and changing exhibits intended to educate and enlighten both children and adults about the history of La Crosse County. The Children's Room is specially designed for young visitors to try on clothing from the past and gain hands-on experience with interesting machines.

Call ahead to see what's up at this university gallery!

UW-La Crosse Art Gallery
16th St. and Vine St.
La Crosse, WI

Phone: (608) 785-8230 or (608) 785 – 8522
Contact: John Ready, Director
Email: ready.john@uwlax.edu
Website: http://www.uwlax.edu/art/gallery/index.htm
Open: Monday through Thursday noon to 8:00pm; Friday through Saturday noon to 5:00pm.

The gallery displays works by student, faculty, regional and nationally known artists in all areas of art. In conjunction with the gallery program, the Art Department presents a visiting artist series of lectures, demonstrations and workshops.

Education comes in many forms at this university art gallery where you'll find a constantly changing array of interesting art shows.

Viterbo University Art Gallery
929 Jackson St.
La Crosse, WI 54601

Phone: (608) 796-3100
Website: http://www.viterbo.edu/academic/ug/sfa/art/features/gallery/
Open: Call for current hours

Throughout the year the gallery features the work of students and faculty, as well as the work of regionally and nationally known artists.

SOUTHWEST

Lake Delton

★Seth Peterson Cottage
E 9982 Fern Dell Rd.
Lake Delton, WI 53940

Mailing address: Sand County Service Company, Box 409, Lake Delton, WI 53940
Phone: (608) 524-6502 or (800) 822-7768 [Fax: 608-254-4400]
Open: by appointment
Website: www.sethpeterson.org

In 1958 young Seth Peterson talked architect Frank Lloyd Wright into building him a cottage on Lake Delton. Poor and depressed Peterson worked on and got the cottage built. Today, setpeterson.org operates the cottage. It can be rented on a nightly basis. Yes you can rent-a-Wright and sleep in the house or have a function there. The setting, year around is special with wonderful vistas and Wright furniture and ambience.

This elegant yet simple and habitable work of art is itself an embodiment of Wright's design principles. It has been described as having "more architecture per square foot than any other building (he) ever designed." Balanced on the edge of a wooded bluff overlooking picturesque Mirror Lake, the Seth Peterson Cottage, a 1958 design, is one of Wright's last commissions. The cottage is perfect for a special getaway, it is available overnight or for longer stays with accommodations for up to four guests. The Cottage will hold 30-40 guests for special events or up to 12 for round-the-table meetings.

Lancaster

If you're interested in social history, race relations, and medicine, you can't miss this captivating heritage site. It's a real eye opener!

Grant County Historical Society — Cunningham Museum
129 E. Maple St.
Lancaster, WI 53813

Phone: (608) 723-4925
E-mail: gcmnhist@runestone.net
Open: Daily, 10am to noon and 1:30pm to 4:30pm, or call for an appointment.

Important works: Story of the Green Colony, as well as medical artifacts, wooden shoes, sewing machines, and stuffed owls.

About the museum: The museum features many local artifacts, including a medical exhibit donated by the late Dr. and Mrs. Wilson Cunningham. Each room of the two-floor museum is organized with its own local history theme. Of special interest is the Green Room, which contains a pictorial history of the Green Colony, near Lancaster. This all-African American colony had a school, which is believed to be the state's first integrated school. One of the colony's most famous residents was Lester Green who became a porter on a commuter train. He was so well liked that he was asked to be porter on a private car owned by stockbrokers. He took the brokers' advice on the stock market and over time his investments made him a millionaire. On display in this room is a set of freedom papers.

Another room is devoted to the medical practice of Dr. Cunningham. A collection of sewing machines dating back to 1846 and a collection from the Sickel Cigar factory located in Platteville are on display. Visitors will delight in the collection of wooden shoes, a display of stuffed owls of Wisconsin, and a beaded Indian blanket used at Custer's Last Stand.

ᥩ Lodi

It started with a log cabin on the prairie...

Jolivette Memorial House
173 South Main Street
Lodi, WI 53555

Phone: (608) 592-4392
Open: Special days and by appointment
Admission: Free

About the museum: In 1846, Isaac Palmer built a log cabin on this site. It was the first house built in what is now the City of Lodi. The museum displays artifacts from the Lodi Valley area, emphasizing the heritage and traditions of the community.

ᥩ Loganville

The three R's were taught at this school - reading, writing, and 'ritmatic. Come for a lesson!

Friendship Rural School Museum
3 miles south of Loganville on Hwy 23, 0.5 miles west on Friendship Road
Loganville, WI 53943

Phone: (608) 727-2941
Open: By appointment only.

This small gem of a museum is worthy of a stop. Please call ahead.

SOUTHWEST

Fascinating Facts

Enjoy a free ferry ride! Yup. Crossing the Wisconsin River on State Highway 113, you will encounter a free ferry. This is one of the few remaining state owned ferries in the United States. Leave Madison on Highway 12 to Highway 78 which runs along the Wisconsin River. Until you get to Hwy 113. You will find it to be an enjoyable and pleasant ride. The ferry operates from mid-April to early December.

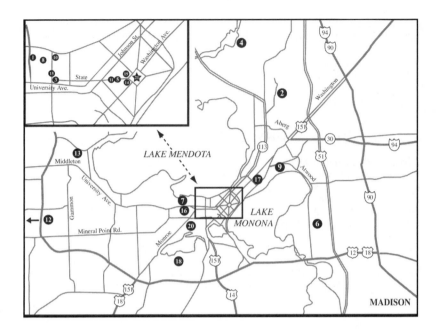

①   Allen Textile Collection
②   Airport Art Court
③   Chazen Museum of Art
④   Cherokee Marsh
⑤   Children's Museum
⑥   Dean House
⑦   Forest Products Labatory
⑧   Geology Museum
⑨   Olbrich Gardens
⑩   Union Galleries
⑪   Overture Center for the Arts
       -Wisconsin Academy Gallery
       -Museum of Contemporary Art
⑫   Owen Park
⑬   Rowley House
⑭   State Historical Museum
⑮   State Historical Society
⑯   Steinbach Gallery
⑰   Tandem Press
⑱   UW Arboretum
⑲   Wisconsin Veterans Museum
⑳   Vilas Zoo
☆   State Capital

SOUTHWEST

Madison

Don't miss the Victorian dollhouse and other fascinating exhibits only minutes from Madison.

Blooming Grove Historical Society — Dean House
4718 Monona Dr.
Monona (suburb of Madison), WI 53716

Mailing address: P.O. Box 6704, Monona, WI 53716-0704
Monona is a suburb of Madison.
Phone: (608) 222-5783
Website: http://www.wlhn.org/daneco/hbg/deanhouse/index.html
Open: Monthly on second Sundays, 2pm to 4pm, and by appointment.

Important works: Doll house, period furnishings, and archives.

About the museum: The Nathaniel Dean House was built in 1856 and has been restored and furnished in the style of the late 19th century. Special features of the house include a large ten-room dollhouse furnished in the Victorian style and an exhibit room with rotating thematic displays using items donated to the society. The society also maintains an archive of records and photographs of area families, businesses, and organizations.

The whole history of art is here under one roof with quality permanent and rotating exhibits and a great art library.

★★★Chazen Museum of Art
800 University Ave.
Madison, WI 53706

Phone: (608) 263-2246 [Fax: 608-263-8188]
Website: http://chazen.wisc.edu/
Open: Tuesday - Friday, 9am to 5pm; Saturday and Sunday, 11am to 5pm.

Important works: Bernardo Strozzi's Christ's Charge to St. Peter, Corot's Hymn to Dawn, 4,000 prints in the Van Vleck Japanese print collection, Vasari altarpiece, extensive art library. Superb collection. One of the finest university art museums in America.

About the museum: The Chazen Art Museum, formerly the Elvehjem Museum, was founded in 1970 to conserve, study, and exhibit the art collections of the University of Wisconsin-Madison. Consolidation of the university's art holdings enabled the museum to catalogue and conserve the 1,600 objects that it originally received. Over time, the museum has cultivated its holdings into a comprehensive collection, global in scope and ranging from old masters to contemporary works, with no specialization in any one culture, period, medium, or genre. The permanent collection includes some 18,100 works of art that represent aspects of the entire spectrum of art history. The museum presents fourteen to eighteen temporary exhibitions each year. Note: Stay tuned for upcoming major expansion. The museum will double in size in the next few years.

Come soak up nature at this restful retreat where the beauty of wet lands can be appreciated.

Cherokee Marsh
6000 N. Sherman Ave
Madison, WI

Phone: (608) 249-4255

At this conservation park you will find prairie restorations, old-field and edge habitats, observation platforms for wildlife viewing, and more.

SOUTHWEST

Recently expanded and upgraded the regional airport now features an art court where contemporary and traditional arts mingle. No boarding pass required.

▲ Dane County Airport Art Court
IIII Art Court
4000 International Lane
Madison, WI 53704

Phone: 608- 263-3437, 608-661-6485
Fax: 608-246-3385
web site: www.msnairport.com

Step into the new Prairie School inspired Madison Airport and fly off to your dream destination. The airport is your portal to the world. It now features a sophisticated art gallery where the best in Contemporary Art can be seen, admired, and purchased. Adjoining the Art Court is a visitors lounge where you can rest your feet, feel the heat, and admire a WPA era mural of the Madison airport in 1938. How's that for Welcome Home.

Though not a museum in the real sense the Wood Anatomy Lab will pique your interest in a product we all use and need: wood. No wood grained formica allowed.

▲ Forest Products Laboratory Wood Anatomy Lab
IIII 1 Gifford Pinchot Place
Madison, Wis 53726

Phone: 608-231-9200
Web site: www.fpl.fs.fed.us
Open: by appintment
Admission: free

The laboratory was founded in 1910 and has been collecting wood samples and specimens since that date. They now have an estimated 50,000 samples from throughout the world. Its fascinating to take a tour of this place and talk with the busy scientists who eagerly cut apart the wood and dissect its structure. The laboratory is a gigantic complex of buildings doing research for the Federal government as a part of the USDA. Ask for an appointment in the Wood Anatomy Lab. If you like wood this is the place to be.

Dig into geology with rock hard history and dinos to boot!

▲ Geology Museum — University of Wisconsin-Madison
IIII 1215 W. Dayton St. (corner of Charter and W. Dayton Streets)
Madison, WI 53706

Phone: (608) 262-2399, Tour Office (608) 262-1412
[Fax: 608-262-0693]
Contacts: Rich Slaughter, Director or Brooke Swanson
Website: www.geology.wisc.edu/~museum
Open: Monday through Friday, 8:30am to 4:30pm;
Saturday, 9am to 1pm. For guided group tours, call the tour number.
Admission: Free

Important works: Meteorites, gems, and minerals of the world, walk-through model of a Wisconsin limestone cave, skeletons of dinosaurs, a Wisconsin mastodon and many other fossils, plus a six-foot diameter rotating model of planet Earth.

About the museum: In 1981, the Geology Museum moved from its original location in Science Hall (where it began in 1848) to its present site in the Lewis G. Weeks Hall for Geological Sciences. While few of the museum's specimens date from the 1800s, most have been acquired since 1970. From 1973 on, the museum staff has conducted annual expeditions to South Dakota, Kansas, Montana, and other states to excavate fossil vertebrates. The results of this fieldwork include the skeleton of an extinct shark, the rare skeleton of the flightless toothed bird Hesperornis, a mosasaur, plus the skulls and skeletons of a variety of other long-extinct mammals. A thirty-three-foot-long skeleton of the duckbill dinosaur Edmontosaurus from South Dakota, unearthed in the 1980s, dominates the museum's fossil section. Visitors can observe the cleaning and restoration of bones and other fossils through a viewing window into the preparation room.

About 20,000 visitors tour the museum every year, including more than 10,000 school children who come for a tour. For the past twelve years, the museum has hosted guest exhibits featuring significant selections of minerals on loan from other institutions, including the Smithsonian and the Carnegie Museum. A long-standing tradition is the museum's annual Open House on a Sunday afternoon in late April or early May. Highlights include demonstrations on fossil preparation and mineral identification, slide lectures, and the ever-popular Free Rock Pile for Kids.

Weave your way through this fabric mecca.

★Helen Louise Allen Textile Collection — University of Wisconsin-Madison
1300 Linden Dr.
Madison, WI 53706

Phone: (608) 262-1162 [Fax: 608-265-5099]
Contact: Mary Ann Fitzgerald
Website: http://sohe.wisc.edu/depts/hlatc/
Open: Open for scheduled exhibitions. The collection office is open Mondays, Tuesdays, and Wednesdays, 9am to 5pm. Call to make an appointment.

Important works: Archeological textile artifacts, 19th century coverlets, quilts and needlework, textiles from many cultures.

About the museum: The collection features 10,000 textiles and costumes representing many eras, places, and techniques, making it one of the largest university textile collections in the U.S. Pre-Columbian and Coptic archaeological textiles are among the collection's earliest pieces. Other major holdings include 19th century American and European coverlets, quilts and needlework, and sub-collections of ethnographic textiles from South and Southeast Asia, Latin America, and Turkey. The collection features both handmade and industrially produced objects created from a wide range of weaving, printing, lace making, and embroidery techniques, including works by Jack Lenor Larson and Dorothy Liebes. Exhibitions drawn from the collection are held biannually in the Gallery of Design, located on the first floor of the School of Human Ecology Building. Past exhibitions have featured textiles from the highland Maya of Guatemala, ikats from Indonesia, and overviews of the collection based on themes such as animal imagery.

Hungry goats are always eager for the healthy snacks human kids can offer them in the Children's Zoo.

★★Henry Vilas Zoo
702 S. Randall Ave.
Madison, WI 53715

Phone: (608) 266-4733 [Fax: 608-266-5923]
Website: www.vilaszoo.org
Contact: Jim Hubing, Director
Open: Zoo Grounds: Daily, 9:30am to pm. Building: 10am to 4pm.
Admission: Free

Important works: More than 700 animals, plus endangered species and a hands-on education center.

About the zoo: The Vilas Zoo is surrounded by a city park and nestled in a quiet neighborhood. Since 1911, the zoo has been providing visitors an experience with a focus on conservation, education, and recreation. One of only ten fully accredited free zoos in the country, the Vilas Zoo is home to over 700 animals including many endangered species such as the Siberian tiger, the orangutan, and the spectacled bear. Favorite places are the polar bear exhibit, primate house, and penguin pen. Beautiful new exhibits enliven the visitors experience.

Find hands on fun and excitement for kids of all ages. This place inspires everyone to learn!

★Madison Children's Museum
100 State St.
Madison, WI 53703

Phone: (608) 256-6445 [Fax: 608-256-3226]
Email: mcm@kidskiosk.org
Website: www.madisonchildrensmuseum.com
Contact: Ruth Shelly, Education Director
Open: Tuesday-Friday, 9am to 4pm; Saturday, 9am to 5pm; Sunday, noon to 5pm.
Admission: Yes. First Sunday of each month free. All times: admission rate of twenty-five cents for families receiving any form of public assistance, live in subsidized or transitional housing, with disabilities, care for foster children, or who participate in Big Brothers/Big Sisters. First Sunday of each month free.

Important works: Hands-on exhibits, including First Feats, Let's Grow, The Milking Parlor.

About the museum: Madison Children's Museum offers innovative, interactive exhibits and programs for children and the child inside us all. Learning and having fun go hand-in-hand at MCM. Its exhibits and programs engage the imagination and all the senses in an exploration of our fascinating world. A day at MCM might find kids milking a cow, jumping at the shadow wall, playing a giant thumb piano, traveling through time, or unearthing a giant dinosaur skeleton. Museum programs offer activities for all ages. Test the laws of physics, make a sculpture or take part in celebrations from around the world. There are weekly toddler programs, day camps and overnight programs for school-age children, changing exhibits and a wide array of performances and special events for all ages. MCM was rated the 10th Best Children's Museum in the country according to Child magazine. By 2006, the museum will move into a new building at Wisconsin Ave. and Dayton St.

This is a world-class facility showcasing cutting edge contemporary art, a sophisticated place for everyone. In the same building is the Community Gallery and Wisconsin Academy Art Gallery. One stop; three art sites.

★★★Madison Museum of Contemporary Art
222 W. Washington Ave. #350
Madison, WI 53703

will reopen in April 2006 at
227 State St.
Madison, WI 53703

Phone: (608) 257-0158
Contact: Katie Kazan
Email: info@mmoca.org
Website: www.madisonartcenter.org
Open: Once reopened, hours will be Tuesday and Wednesday, 11am to 5pm; Thursday and

Friday, 11am to 8pm; Saturday, 10am to 8pm; Sunday, noon to 5pm. Handicapped accessible. Admission: Free.

Important works: American drawings and paintings, annual series of temporary exhibitions.

About the museum: One of the city's oldest cultural organizations, the Madison Museum or Contemporary Art (formerly the Madison Art Center) began in 1901. It is a leading force in the region for presenting the work of new artists and investigating major artistic directions of the 20th century. The permanent collection contains more than 4,500 works of art with a solid core of American drawings and paintings, as well as photographs and sculpture.

Typically, there are ten changing exhibitions annually, displayed on several floors of galleries that are reconfigured to create unique viewing spaces for each show. The Education Department offers innovative programs for all ages. The Art Talks series brings prominent artists, curators, and historians to the museum to share their insights on current exhibitions. Gallery Games and Express It! art workshops introduce children and families to the artworks on exhibit through creative and playful activities. Come see the stunning new building and enlarged galleries. Wow!

The Wright place for your convention or afternoon stroll.

★Monona Terrace
Monona Terrace Community and Convention Center
One John Nolen Drive
Madison, WI 53703

Phone: (608) 261-4000 or TTY (608) 261-4150 [Fax: 608-261-4049]
email: info@mononaterrace.com
Open: Monona Terrace is open daily from 8 a.m. to 5 p.m. Tours Daily at 1 p.m. Gift Shop Sunday–Saturday 10 a.m.–5 p.m. GrandView Café Monday–Saturday 8 a.m.–2 p.m. Rooftop Garden Open Sunday - Thursday 8 a.m. - 10 p.m. Friday and Saturday 8 a.m. - midnight (closed during inclement weather). "The Wright Picture" Photo exhibit on display in East and West Promenades
Daily 8 a.m.–5 p.m.

On July 18, 1997, Monona Terrace Community and Convention Center opened its doors after nearly 60 years of debate. It was first designed by Wisconsin native and internationally renowned architect Frank Lloyd Wright in 1938 as a cultural, governmental and recreational building. Wright reworked the design several times between 1938 and 1958 before signing off on the final plans seven weeks before his death in 1959.

In 1992, Madison voters approved referenda to construct Monona Terrace—on the same site Wright had originally proposed—as a community and convention center. While Wright's design was used for the building's exterior, the interior was redesigned by Wright apprentice and Taliesin architect Tony Puttnam to house state-of-the-art exhibition, meeting and public space.

Monona Terrace Community and Convention Center represents the final cultural contribution of Frank Lloyd Wright's brilliant career. We invite individuals, as well as adult and student groups, to take a guided tour of this magnificent building. The facility is accessible to visitors with disabilities.

SOUTHWEST

Fascinating Facts

The Wisconsin state constitution upholds the right that for elections, "All votes shall be by secret ballot."

Tiptoe through the flowers, and through a tropical paradise, no matter what the weather may be outside!

★★★Olbrich Botanical Gardens
3330 Atwood Ave.
Madison, WI 53704

Phone: (608) 246-4550
Contact: Sharon Cybart
Website: www.olbrich.org
Open: Outdoor gardens: Year-round, April through September, 8am to 8pm; October through March, 9am to 4pm. Bolz Conservatory: Monday through Saturday, 10am to 4pm; Sunday, 10am to 5pm. Admission: Outdoor gardens, free. Conservatory, yes, but free Wednesday and Saturday, 10am to noon.

Important works: Thai Pavilion, award-winning rose garden, all season tropical conservatory, outdoor sculptures.

About the gardens: Olbrich Botanical Gardens is owned and operated by the City of Madison Parks Division in partnership with the nonprofit Olbrich Botanical Society. With sixteen acres of outdoor display gardens, glass-enclosed conservatory, authentic Thailand pavilion, and busy schedule of special events, it is one of Madison's most-visited places.

The outdoor areas include a sunken garden, perennial garden, rock garden, herb garden, prairie garden, and woodland wildflower garden. In 1997, Olbrich's Rose Garden was awarded the All-America Rose Selections (AARS) President's Award honoring the most outstanding AARS-designated public rose garden in the U.S. The two-acre Perennial Garden features a meandering stream surrounded by perennial plants that are hardy to the upper Midwest.

Visitors can experience the exquisite artisanship and exotic culture of Thailand in Olbrich's Thai Pavilion and Garden. It is one of only four such pavilions located outside of Thailand and the only one surrounded by a garden. The wood pavilion features a lacquer finish with intricate decorations and ornate gold leaf accents. A traditional Thai-style garden with serene reflecting pools surrounds the open-air pavilion.

The Bolz Conservatory, a sunny fifty-foot-high glass pyramid, houses a diverse tropical collection of ferns, palms, and flowering plants growing in a naturalized setting. A rushing waterfall, bamboo arbors, and free-flying birds give a realistic feel. In July and August, the place comes alive with the Blooming Butterflies exhibit. Live butterflies emerge from chrysalises daily to fly freely inside the conservatory. Other annual events include a fall flower and quilt show, holiday model train and poinsettia show, spring flower show, weekly concerts during the winter and summer months, and classes for adults and children. The beautiful Thai pavilion, a gift from Thai UW alumni, is covered in gold and set in a beautiful garden.

Find nature at its best with 100 acres of enjoyment!

Owen Conservation Park
6021 Old Sauk Rd
Madison, WI

Phone: (608) 267-4918
Enjoy 100-acres of nature, with 3.4 miles of trails to explore.

A fabulous wildlife museum in a funeral home.

★Sam's Wildlife Museum
Located at the Cress Funeral Home at 6021 University Avenue
Madison, WI 53705

Phone: (608) 238-8406
Open: 8am to 4pm Monday through Friday, but call ahead.
Note: Public visits are discouraged during funeral services.
Admission: Free, but call ahead.

About the museum: Located in the basement of a funeral home is a unique museum of wildlife stuffed animals, taxidermy, and hunting memorabilia. Located in five galleries are an estimated 1,500 specimens, many of which are set in amusing tableaux such as squirrels biking and animals sitting in a bar. The collection has been amassed by Mr. Sam Sanfillippo, an energetic sportsman who opened his first fishing display gallery in 1972 in his newly constructed funeral home. As Sam says, "People love coming here to visit and during funeral showings, many of them wander down and take a look and enjoy the various displays. They light up and come to life." It's notable that Governor Knowles, Governor Dreyfuss, Governor Tommy Thompson, and even Presidents Ford, George Bush Sr, and George Bush Jr. have been friends and acquaintances with Mr. Sanfillippo who was born and raised in Oconomowoc, Wisconsin. It is truly an extraordinary setting. Plan ahead and contact Sam directly for a personal guided tour. His enthusiasm brings it all to life.

Fine Arts Printing at its best in America where artists, faculty, students, and the public can come and learn. A+ for this art workshop.

Tandem Press
201 Dickson street
Madison, Wi 53703

Phone (608)263-3437
Contact: Paula McCarthy Panczenko
www.tandempress.wisc.edu
info@tandempress.wisc.edu

Tandem Press is associated with the University of Wisconsin Art Department as an independent Fine Arts printing facility. Known for its wide ranging and innovative techniques in the field, Tandem Press is a national leader. Founded by American artist William Weege in 1986, the press has continued to grow at a swift pace and invites proposals from artists who wish to collaborate and experiment in the printmaking field. Though not an art museum, the press produces and exhibits art in a wide variety of mediums. When you step in the door you realize this is a special place, full of energy, inventiveness, and artistic creativity.

The real heroes of this church are the congregation members that hauled tons of stone to build this edifice to God. What a blessing.

★★Unitarian Meeting House
900 University Bay Drive,
Madison, Wisconsin 53705

Information: (608) 238-1680 or (608) 233-9774
Open: Season May through October. Days and hours Monday through Friday 10-4 pm Saturday 9am-12pm Sunday after services until 4pm. Reservations Required for ten or more
Admission: yes

Frank Lloyd Wright designed this church. The First Unitarian Society of Madison commissioned this sprawling suburban church in 1946 and participated in its construction. As a means of reducing costs, Society members hauled tons of stone for the thick walls from a nearby quarry and later helped construct furnishings and finish the interior. The original single-level building, constructed of native limestone, copper, and glass, features a multipurpose auditorium and adjoining social area and kitchen. A unique angular hall, one of the many examples of the triangle shape associated with the building and its furnishings, connects this area with offices, classrooms, and another social hall. Two later additions were designed by Taliesin Associated Architects in 1964 and 1990.

Visitors are always welcome at Sunday morning services held during the winter at 9am and 11am, and during the summer at 10am. Access to the building is restricted during weddings and church related events. Building is closed the first two weeks in August.

More than just flowers, this arboretum is a garden paradise for rest, relaxation, and education. Bike, jog, or stroll through nature.

★★University of Wisconsin Arboretum
1207 Seminole Highway
Madison, WI 53711

Phone: (608) 263-7888 [Fax: 608-262-5209]
Website: http://wiscinfo.doit.wisc.edu/arboretum/
Open: McKay Visitor Center: Weekdays, 9:30am to 4pm;
weekends, 12:30pm to 4pm. Grounds: 7am to 10pm, daily.

Important works: World's oldest restored prairies, flowering trees collection, native plants garden, miles of hiking and ski trails.

About the arboretum: Featuring the restored prairies, forests, and wetlands of pre-settlement Wisconsin, this 1,260-acre research and study area borders Lake Wingra. Widely recognized as the site of historic research in ecological restoration, the arboretum includes the oldest and most varied collection of restored ecological communities in the world, including tall grass prairies, savannas, several forest types, and wetlands. The fifty-acre Longenecker Horticultural Garden contains the most extensive woody plant collection in Wisconsin and one of its most colorful, especially when the lilacs, crabapples, and other flowering trees and shrubs are blooming in May. Educational tours and science and nature-based classes for all ages are offered. Running and cross-country skiing are permitted on marked trails.

Located in the stunning new Overture Center for the Arts, the Wisconsin Academy Gallery is sure to please all visitors with its diverse and interesting exhibit schedule. Standing ovation for this art crowd!

★Wisconsin Academy of Sciences, Arts, and Letters Gallery James Watrous Gallery
Overture Center for the Arts
201 State Street
Madison, WI 53703

Phone: (608) 265-2500 [Fax: 608-265-3039]
Contact: Martha Glowacki or Randall Berndt
Website: www.wisconsinacademy.org/gallery
Admission: free
Open: Tuesday, Wednesday, Thursday 11am to 5pm; Friday 11am to 9 pm; Saturday 11am to 9pm; Sunday 1pm to 5pm.

The James Watrous Gallery is operated by the Wisconsin Academy. The Acdemy Gallery is a showcase for a wide ranging and diverse selection of the Fine Arts. A real eye-opener on Wisconsin arts.

SOUTHWEST

Overture Center for the Arts Rotunda Lobby Galleries
201 State Street
Madison, WI 53703

Phone: (608) 258-4177
Email: galleries@overturecenter.com
Open: Overture Center for the Arts Rotunda lobby gallery hours: monday to thursday10:30 am -5:30 pm, friday-saturday 10:30 am to 9 pm, sunday noon-5 pm
Admission: free

In the Overture Center Rotunda lobby are three galleries, each run by different organizations. The lobby is also connected to the Madison Museum of Contemporary Art, as they share the same building. The museum portion of the Overture Center is scheduled to open in April, 2006.

Steenbock Gallery at Wisconsin Academy Headquarters
1922 Old University Drive
Madison, WI 53726

Phone: (608) 263-1692 [Fax: 608-265-3039]
Admission: Free
Open: Monday-Friday 8am to 4pm

Remember that the Academy headquarters and the Steenbock Gallery are located on 1922 old university drive. That's approximately 2 miles west of the Overture Center.

The Smithsonian of Wisconsin has lots for everyone to enjoy! With thousands of objects, each has a story that enlightens our view of the past.

★★★Wisconsin Historical Society and Museum
Historical Society
816 State St. (at Park and Langdon)
Madison, WI 53706

State Museum
30 N. Carroll St. (on the Capitol Square)
Madison, WI 53703

Phone: Museum (608) 264-6555 or Society (608) 264-6400   [Fax: 608-264-6575]
Contact: Ann Koski, Museum Director
Email: museum@whs.wisc.edu
Website: www.wisconsinhistory.org/museum
Open: Tuesday through Saturday, 9am to 4pm.
Admission: Yes

About the museum: Explore Wisconsin's distinctive heritage and a variety of other American history topics through artifacts, photographs, audio-visual presentations, and interactive multimedia programs. The collections of the Museum contain 107,000 historical objects and about 393,000 archeological artifacts. They are used by staff, academic scholars, collectors, local historians, authors, and the general public to document the history of what is now Wisconsin, from pre-historic times to the present. The collections help us understand important trends and events of daily life within diverse social, ethnic, and religious backgrounds. Permanent exhibits include: People of the Woodlands, Wisconsin Indian Ways and On Common Ground, and Two Hundred Years of Wisconsin History. There are also changing exhibits throughout the year. Programs at the Museum include A Taste of Wisconsin Traditions, an adult lecture and dinner series, and History Sandwiched In, an informal brown-bag lunch-and-lecture series.

SOUTHWEST

In Madison, the home of state government is a monumental work of art and a temple for the people!

★★★Wisconsin State Capitol
Capitol Square
Madison, WI 53703

Phone: (608) 266-0382
Website: http://www.wisconsin.gov/state/capfacts/tour_select.html (check out the virtual tour)
Open: Open 365 days a year: weekdays, 8am to 6pm; weekends, 8am to 4pm. Capitol museum open weekdays, 10am to 2pm. Free tours offered hourly, year round.
Admission: Free

Important works: Wisconsin's historic state capitol building. Fabulous art collection.

About the capitol: This majestic granite structure is Wisconsin's third Capitol building. The present Capitol, designed by George B. Post & Sons, was built between 1906 and 1917 at a cost of $7.25 million. The Capitol dome is topped by Daniel Chester French's gilded bronze statue, "Wisconsin." The dome is the only granite dome in the United States and the largest by volume. The interior of the Capitol features forty-three varieties of stone from around the world, decorative murals, glass mosaics, and hand-carved furniture. In the rotunda of the Capitol, one can see Edwin Blashfield's "Resources of Wisconsin" mural two hundred feet overhead. The walls and ceilings of the Governor's Conference Room are decorated with twenty-six historical and allegorical paintings by Hugo Ballin. The State Supreme Court room is decorated with German and Italian marble and four murals by Albert Herter. The Senate Chamber is decorated with French and Italian marble and a Kenyon Cox mural depicting the opening of the Panama Canal.

Constantly rotating exhibits augment the superb collections of Wisconsin art. After your visit here, stop by the Terrace for ice cream!

★Wisconsin Union Galleries
University of Wisconsin-Madison
Wisconsin Union
800 Langdon St.
Madison, WI 53706

Phone: (608) 262-5969, 265-3000
[Fax: 608-262-8862]
Contact: Robin Schmoldt
Email: schmoldt@wisc.edu
Website: www.union.wisc.edu
Open: Memorial Union building, when UW-Madison classes are in session: Monday - Wednesday, 7am to midnight; Thursday - Friday, 7am to 2am; Saturday, 8am to 2 am; Sunday, 8am to midnight. In summer, the union closes one hour earlier. Porter Butts Gallery, open daily 10am to 8pm.

Important works: Wisconsin artist paintings, drawings and sculpture, plus temporary exhibits.

About the galleries: One of the largest collections of original Wisconsin art in the state, the Wisconsin Union Art Collection contains artworks gathered over the past seven decades reflecting the joys and pains of many generations of Wisconsin residents. More than 1,300 works by over 500 artists with Wisconsin roots make up this living and dynamic collection. Work from the permanent collection can be seen through the Memorial Union. The Porter Butts Gallery on the second floor features works of established artists and promising new talent, as well as student work.

See one of Wisconsin's best museums where the drama, heroism, and tragedy of war are all presented in vivid and engaging exhibits.

★★★Wisconsin Veterans Museum
30 W. Mifflin St. (on the Capitol Square)
Madison, WI 53703

Phone: (608) 267-1799 or Research Center (608) 267-1790
[Fax: 608-264-7615]
Contact: Richard Zeitlin, Director
Email: veterans.museum@dva.state.wi.us
Website: museum.dva.state.wi.us
Open: All year: Monday - Saturday, 9am to 4:30pm. Sundays (April through September), noon to 4pm.
Admission: Free

Important works: Wisconsin Civil War battle flag collection, State military uniforms, arms, and equipment from the Civil War through the Persian Gulf War.

About the museum: Established in 1901, the Wisconsin Veterans Museum commemorates the role of Wisconsin citizen-soldiers who served in the military from 1861 to the present. The new museum was built across from the state capitol in the early 1990s and contains 10,000 square feet of exhibit space, a library, archives, and collections storage. Dramatic recreations of battle scenes with life-size figures and equipment transport visitors from the battlefields of the Civil War to the snowy forests of the World War II. A submarine periscope goes up through the roof, and three aircraft are suspended from the ceiling: a World War I Sop with Camel, World War II P-51 Mustang, and a Vietnam War era Huey helicopter. The museum operates the Wisconsin National Guard Museum at Volk Field, just off Interstate 90/94 near Camp Douglas, which preserves the state guard's history from its inception in the 1800s through today. A display area is also housed at the Marden Center at the Wisconsin Veterans Home at King, WI in Waupaca County.

Markesan

Markesan Historical Society — Grand River Valley Museum
214 E. John St.
Markesan, WI 53946

Mailing address: P.O. Box 264, Markesan, WI 53946
Phone: (920) 398-3945 or (920) 398-3554 [Fax: 920-398-3991]
Contact: Don Leider
Email: cmarkesan@vbe.com
Website: http://www.markesanwi.com/HistoricalSociety.htm
Open: May 1 – November 1, Friday – Sunday, 1pm to 4pm, or by appointment.

About the museum: No current information

SOUTHWEST

Tony's Tips

Wisconsin is famous for dairy products, including cheese. Fresh cheese curds are a squeaky treat! Mmm, that's good.

Marshall

Marshall takes its history seriously. They even have a museum in the elementary school for kids of all ages to enjoy.

Local History Room 33
Marshall Elementary School
Williams Street
Marshall, WI 53559

Phone: (608) 655-3610
Contact: Mrs. Nancy Biegel
Open: First and third Tuesday of each month, 1pm to 3pm and by appointment.

A wide range of artifacts will pique your imagination at this local history museum.

Mauston

This is a haven for local genealogy and Juneau County history. "Ja Noo?"

Juneau County Historical Society -- Boorman House
211 N. Union St.
Mauston, WI 53948

Mailing address: P.O. Box 321, Mauston, WI 53948
Phone: (608) 847-4450 or (608) 847-4142
Contact: Rose Clark
Email: rclarkjco@hotmail.com
Website: http://www.rootsweb/com/~wijuneau/JCHSoc.html
Open: Memorial Day through Labor Day, Saturday and Sunday, 1pm to 4pm or by appointment.
Admission: Free, donations appreciated.

Important works: Late 1800s period furnishings, archive material including local church, country school attendance, obituary, marriage, and birth records.

About the museum: The 125-year-old Boorman house is furnished with period antiques. It also houses many scrapbooks and records pertaining to Juneau County and a genealogy collection of area families.

Mazomanie

Eenie, meenie, Mazomanie...Here you will find four rooms and a jail full of diverse local history!

Mazomanie Historical Society Museum
118 Brodhead St.
Mazomanie, WI 53560

Mailing address: P.O. Box 248, Mazomanie, WI 53560
Phone: (608) 795-2992
Contact: Rita Frakes, Curator
Website: www.rootsweb.com/~wimhs
Open: Memorial Day – Labor Day, Wednesday and Sunday, 1pm to 4pm or call to arrange a time.

SOUTHWEST

Important works: Quilts and quilting artifacts, extensive blacksmith tool collection, and an old-fashioned jail building.

About the museum: The museum has four rooms of displays and an attached jail. It was originally constructed in 1900 to house an electrical generation plant for the village. Room One portrays the settlement of the area and development of the village. Room Two contains signature quilts in a setting of sewing, cleaning, laundering, and quilting artifacts. There is also an extensive collection of Mazomanie High School class pictures and memorabilia. Room Three has new exhibits that include an elegant dining room scene. There is also a display of Hull pottery and donated items. Room Four is named the Thiers Room in honor of Werner and Ada Thiers. Werner, a blacksmith and first president of the historical society, collected a vast number of tools during his career. Other exhibits include black smithing, cobbler's tools, bee keeping, a print shop, kitchen, and soda fountain shop. The jail is accessible from outside the museum. Because of its stone construction and outer door with iron bars, it has the flavor of an old-west style "hoosegow."

McFarland

Communities have changed a lot in 100 years. Step back in time with us at the McFarland Museum.

McFarland Historical Society Museum
5814 Main Street
McFarland, WI 53558

Mailing address: P.O. Box 94, McFarland, WI 53558
Phone: (608) 838-3992
Email: bluebee@madtown.net
Website: http://www.madison.com/communities/mhs/index.php
Open: Memorial Day to last Sunday in September, 1pm to 4pm, or by appointment.
Admission: Free

The McFarland Historical Society Museum has an extensive collection of artifacts dating from the mid-1800s up to the 1930s including Native American spear points. The collection focuses on the history of the McFarland area and includes exhibits on Native Americans, William McFarland, a Norwegian settlement, a pioneer kitchen, 1930s kitchen, turn-of-the-century parlor, and blacksmith and cobbler shops. The museum also includes a log cabin from the 1850s, which was moved to the site from a local farm. There is also a display of a timeline of McFarland history dating from the end of the last Ice Age up the present time.

Middleton

For those longing for the horse and buggy days of yesteryear, this museum has a replica carriage house, authentic doctor's residence built in 1868, and many historic artifacts.

Middleton Area Historical Society Museum — Rowley House
7410 Hubbard Ave.
Middleton, WI 53562

Phone: (608) 836-7614
Contact: John Skinner, President (836-1375)

Website: www.madison.com/communities/mahs/
Open: Mid-April to mid-October, Tuesdays and Saturdays, 1pm to 4pm, and by appointment.
Admission: Free

Important works: Largest collection of Depression Glass in the Midwest, 165 patterns identified to maker and manufacture, major collection of egg cups from around the world, farming tools, doctor's carriage house, buggy, and horse.

About the museum: The Middleton Area Historical Society is headquartered in a historic house downtown. The building was constructed in 1868 by Dr. Neuman C. Rowley as a residence in which three generations of Rowleys, all Middleton doctors, once lived. The nine-room house was acquired in 1989 and converted to a museum. An archive of material on Middleton history and families is on site. In 2001, an 1890s-style carriage house was built on the property. Such structures were typical of doctors at the time to provide ready access to transportation for emergency calls. In the carriage house there is an 1890s doctor's buggy and full size model horse with harness stand ready for action.

Milton

The Underground Railroad stopped here. So should you!

★Milton House Museum
18 S. Janesville St.
Milton, WI 53563

Mailing address: P.O. Box 245, Milton, WI 53563
Phone: (608) 868-7772 [Fax: 608-868-1698]
Email: miltonhouse@miltonhouse.org
Website: www.miltonhouse.org
Contact: Dr. David McKay, Director
Open: Weekends in May, 10am to 5pm; Memorial Day – Labor Day, daily, 10am to 5pm; Labor Day – October 15, by appointment.
Admission: Yes

Important works: Hexagonal building, Underground Railroad stopover.

About the museum: The Milton House is an 1844 stagecoach inn built by Milton's founder, Joseph Goodrich, and was deeded by his family to the historical society in 1948. The building is unique for its shape and building materials. The inn portion of the building is a hexagon and the rectangular portion once had five sections, each with a store or business on the lower level and two one-room apartments upstairs. The building is made from a lime mortar material that is as hard as limestone. Joseph Goodrich was an abolitionist and used the cellar of the inn to hide runaway slaves. A tunnel linking the inn's cellar to the cabin in back was used to sneak runaways to the cellar. In 1998, the Milton House Museum was designated a National Historic Landmarks for its role in the Underground Railroad, one of only twelve such places in the nation. The site is also home to the oldest grout building in the U.S., an 1837 log cabin, country store, and blacksmith shop.

Fascinating Facts

Lutefisk is a dried cod that has been preserved in lye and soda. It is particular to the people of Scandinavia and they much relish this unusual local delicacy.

SOUTHWEST

Mineral Point

See Victorian splendor at its best with this house, home, farm, and family in a rural setting.

 ★Mineral Point Historical Society - Orchard Lawn/Gundry House
225 High St.
Mineral Point, WI 53565

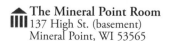

Orchard Lawn
234 Madison St
two blocks east of the Tourist Information Center and Water Tower Park

Mailing address: P.O. Box 188, Mineral Point, WI 53565
Phone: (608) 987-3201 Toll-free (888) 764-6894
Email: info@mineralpoint.com
Website: www.mineralpoint.com/hist.html
Open: May through October, Thursday - Sunday, 1pm to 5pm, and by appointment.

Important works: Mineral Point and Gundry family artifacts, period furnishings, clothing, musical instruments, and elaborate woodwork.

About the museum: The Mineral Point Historical Society maintains Orchard Lawn, previously known as the Gundry House Museum, to preserve Mineral Point's history and display the Gundry House in its Victorian splendor. The house, built in 1868, is an impressive example of an Italianate-style home made of finely crafted local sandstone. Joseph and Sarah Gundry came to Mineral Point in the 1840s from Cornwall, England and their eleven-acre estate was locally known as "Orchard Lawn" due to its apple orchard, pasture, and gardens.

Features include an expansive front porch, tall arched windows, and a bracketed hip roof topped with a belvedere. A library, parlor, music room, and dining room all have high ceilings, elaborate woodwork, furniture, fireplaces, drapes, and musical instruments typical of the Victorian era. An elaborate upstairs bedroom contains furniture and clothing from the 1890s and a collection of notable artifacts from Mineral Point's history.

Jump on board for this destination!

The Mineral Point Railroad Museum

Contact: Dave Kjelland
Email: kjelland@mhtc.net
Website: http://www.mineralpointrailroads.com/museumpage
Open: Thursday through Sunday 10am to 4pm.
Admission: Yes

Important works: telegrapher's office, railroad lantern collection, photographs, maps, and other artifacts from people who worked for the railroad.

About the museum: The museum, located inside the depot, displays artifacts from Southwest Wisconsin railroading history.

Come learn about Point history.

The Mineral Point Room
137 High St. (basement)
Mineral Point, WI 53565

SOUTHWEST

Phone: (608) 987-2447
Contact: Mary Alice Moore, Curator
Email: minptroom@hotmail.com
Website: http://www.swls.org/member.mi_localhistory.html
Open: Saturday 10:00am to 4:00pm and Thursday noon to 4:00pm. Additional hours
May through October 7:00am to 8:30pm.

About the room: It is a secure repository of local history that includes books, maps, local
newspapers, photographs, letters, and other documents relating to the Mineral Point area.

Strange rituals and odd fellows inhabit this locale.

▲ The Odd Fellows and Rebekah Museum
Mineral Point, WI 53565

Phone: (608) 987-3093
Open: 9am to 3pm daily from Memorial Day through Labor Day.

About the museum: The building was constructed in 1835, served as a hall for IOOF
Iowa Lodge No. 1, and now serves as a museum.

Discover Wisconsin's early Welsh history at this historic gem!

▲ ★★Pendarvis Historic Site
114 Shake Rag St.
Mineral Point, WI 53565

Mailing address: P.O. Box 270, Mineral Point, WI 53565
Phone: (608) 987-2122 or Toll-free (866) 944-7483
Contact: Allen Schroeder
Email: pendarvis@whs.wisc.edu
Website: www.wisconsinhistory.org/pendarvis/
Open: Mid-May – October 31, 10am to 5pm. Last tour
begins at 4pm. Open seven days a week during this time.

Important works: Artifacts of Cornish lead mining, lead mine structures, log and stone
buildings, and period furnishings.

About the museum: Discover a rare gem of Wisconsin history nestled into a wooded
hillside where immigrant Cornish lead miners and their families put down roots in a new
homeland in the 1830s and '40s. See the treasures of their Old World culture, preserved
for future generations in the stone and log houses they crafted many years ago.
Connected by winding footpaths that pass by blooming gardens of native flora, the
houses of Pendarvis speak volumes about the pioneer spirit that tamed a wild Wisconsin.
A one-hour interpretive walking trail provides up-close views of one of the shafts of the
Merry Christmas Mine, the mine trailings pile and ore cart railway, the ore mill
foundation and a restored prairie overlooking the town below.

Monroe

There's lots of Civil War memorabilia for history buffs of all ages!

▲ Green County Historical Museum
1617 Ninth Street
Monroe, WI 53566

Phone: (608) 325-4471 or (608) 325-2924
Contact: Dennis Daulton, President of Society
Open: June-September: Weekends, 9am to 5pm.
Admission: Yes

About the museum: The Green County Historical Museum is located in the Universalist Church building, which was erected in 1861. During the Civil War the building was used to store wheat and wool for the Union Army. The museum displays a general collection of local artifacts, a surveyor's wheels, Civil War items, antique kitchen furnishings, items from the local Joseph Huber Brewery, lithographs of birds-eye views of Monroe, and more. Also located on the museum grounds are a schoolhouse and a building housing antique cheese making equipment.

There's no Limburger here, only cheese history. Take a slice! Wear your cheese-heads.

Historic Cheesemaking Center
2108 Seventh Avenue
Monroe, WI 53566

Phone: (608) 325-4636
Email: info@greencountywelcomecenter.org
Open: March-November, daily, 9am to 4pm; December-February, Thursday-Saturday, 11am to 3pm.
Admission: Suggested donation

About the center: Located in a lovingly restored Milwaukee Railroad Depot, it houses both the Green County Welcome Center and the cheese-making museum. The freight room of the 1888 depot features "an era that was, that will never be again." A replica cheese factory, plus artifacts and photos, trace the Swiss Cheese industry that tells the story of dairy farmers, milk haulers and cheese makers. This industry blossomed in the 1920s and 30s to the extent that the area produced 70% of the Swiss cheese marketed in the entire United States. This center is a tribute to the Wisconsin forbearers who made Wisconsin "the dairy state."

Mount Horeb

Mount Horeb is a special shrine to the co-mingling of seven ethnic cultures to make a community. Come see how it was done.

Mount Horeb Area Historical Society and Museum
Museum: 100 S. Second St.
Archives: 138 E. Main St.
Mount Horeb, WI 53517

Phone: (608) 437-6486
Website: http://www.mounthoreb.org/
Open: January - April, Saturday and Sunday, 12:30pm to 4pm; summer hours, Friday and Saturday, 10am to 4pm, Sunday, 12:30pm to 4pm. Archives open second and fourth Wednesday of each month, 12:30pm to 3:30pm.
Admission: Free

Important works: Regional folk art, artwork, writings, books, photographs, artifacts and political materials.

About the museum: The Mt. Horeb Area Historical Society was organized in 1975. Two years later, a small museum opened in the municipal building. This space now houses the archives and collections. In 1996, a former hardware store was converted to 4,000 square feet of public museum space.

The museum currently has exhibits telling the stories of the seven ethnic groups predominant in southwestern Dane County: Winnebago, Scotch, Yankee, German, Irish, Swiss, and Norwegian. The museum uses enlarged photographs, background music, interviews, manuscripts, original art, several hundred artifacts, and the actual interior of a Yankee-owned store to reveal the unique local, state, and national contributions by individuals in these ethnic groups. It examines forces which shaped these groups, including war, settlement, industrialization, religions, and languages, as well as how members of different groups shared and adapted to each other's customs and crafts. The museum's Centennial Gallery features changing exhibits on Dane County and Wisconsin history and the gift shop offers regional and state books, cards, and gifts.

This is not just Dijon! Find 4,000 other types of mustard for all occasions and tastes. M'm, dats good! Bring brats and buns.

★★Mount Horeb Mustard Museum
100 W. Main St.
Mount Horeb, WI 53572

Mailing address: P.O. Box 468, Mount Horeb, WI 53572
Phone: (800) 438-6878
Contact: Barry Levenson, Curator or Michael Carr, President
Email: customerservice@mustardmuseum.com
Website: http://www.mustardmuseum.com/
Open: Daily, 10am to 5pm.
Admission: Free

Important works: The world's only museum devoted entirely to mustard, with thousands of mustard products.

About the museum: The Mount Horeb Mustard Museum is home of the world's largest collection of mustards. There are nearly 4,000 different mustards from all fifty states and over sixty countries. The museum also is home to many items of mustard historical importance, including over 1,500 antique mustard pots, mustard advertisements, and other mustard memorabilia. In addition to the permanent collection, the museum hosts special topical exhibits. These include the History of Mustard, Mustard and Medicine, Mustard in the U.S. Supreme Court, and the Mustard Geography Quiz. There are many types of mustard for sale along with other unique gifts, including items from Poupon U, the school for mustard lovers.

New Glarus

Visit a true wonderland of historic Swiss treasures; you won't get fleeced!

Chalet of the Golden Fleece
618 2nd Street
New Glarus, WI 53574

Phone: (608) 527-2095
Open: For bus and group tours by appointment, May-October.
Admission: Yes

Important works: Jeweled watch owned by King Louis XVI, 2,000-year-old Etruscan earrings, Gregorian chants on parchment from 1485, a 300-year-old Swiss slate and wood inlaid table.

Edwin Barlow, founder of the Wilhelm Tell drama in New Glarus, built the chalet in 1937 as his private residence. His world travels contributed to his ever-expanding and

SOUTHWEST

unique collection. Visitors will be amazed at the size of the collection, which fills three floors. It includes painted furniture, antique silver and pewter, original artwork, paintings and etchings, samplers, Swiss scissors cutting, quilts, antique glass and china, coins, stamps, Swiss woodcarvings and Swiss dolls. The chalet itself is an authentic copy of a Swiss Bernese mountain chalet. The intricately detailed woodwork pays tribute to Swiss woodworking, craftsmanship. Barlow donated the Chalet and his collection to the village of New Glarus.

If you can't go to Switzerland, this is the next best thing! Visit these fourteen clean and tidy historic buildings and you'll find a real Swiss village!

★Swiss Historical Village
612 7th Ave.
New Glarus, WI 53574

Phone: (608) 527-2317
Email: blbeal@tds.net
Website: www.swisshistoricalvillage.com
Contact: John Marty, President
Open: May 1 – November 1, daily, 10am to 4pm. Call to schedule group tours.
Admission: Yes

Important works: Historic buildings, Swiss artifacts, period furnishings, and tools.

About the museum: The Swiss Historical Village provides a unique glimpse into America's heartland. The museum complex has fourteen buildings representing many facets of daily life in the 19th century Midwest. The centerpiece of the museum is the Hall of History, displaying American history, the story of immigration and colonization, and life in New Glarus. Buildings include an authentic settler's log home, traditional bee house, log community building, replica cheese factory, blacksmith shop, original schoolhouse, smoke house, farm implement building, fire house, general store, and log church. The Entrance Building offers changing exhibits about New Glarus and related historical topics.

North Freedom

When the massive steam engines rumble past blowing their whistles, you hear the same train music enjoyed by your ancestors a century ago. Tickets please!

★Mid-Continent Railway Museum
E8948nDiamond Hill Rd.
North Freedom, WI 53951

Mailing address: P.O. Box 358, North Freedom, WI 53951
Phone: (608) 522-4261 or (800) 930-1385 [Fax: 608-522-4490]
Email: inquiries@midcontinent.org
Website: www.mcrwy.com
Open: May-September: Museum open daily 9:30am to 5pm. Trains run May-October on weekends. Call for specific opening dates and times.
Admission: Yes

Important works: Authentic working train engines and cars, extensive collection of railroad artifacts, and photographs.

About the museum: Take a memorable, seven-mile, fifty-minute round-trip ride on a former branch line of the Chicago and North Western Railway through the scenic Baraboo Hills. Passengers ride in restored steel coaches built in 1915. An authentically attired conductor calls, "all aboard!" before the train leaves from the historic wooden depot built in 1894. The depot has a gift shop and fascinating displays. The museum grounds and buildings house steam engines, vintage railroad coaches, freight cars, cabooses, many of which are artfully restored and nationally renowned. This is one of the few places in the U.S. where you can experience the sights and sounds of early 1900s railroading.

Onalaska

Like an ever-flowing stream, history in this Mississippi River town goes way back. Don't miss the Holzhuber art exhibit!

Onalaska Area Historical Society Museum
741 Oak Ave. S., Museum Suite
Onalaska, WI 54650

Phone: (608) 781-9568 or (608) 783-0440
Contact: Neale Horman
Website: http://www.historyofonalaska.com/onalaska_historical.html
Open: Wednesday through Friday, 2pm to 4pm; Saturday, 9am to noon; October-March, Monday, 6pm to 8pm.

Important works: Sketches and paintings by Franz Holzlhuber with regional scenes from the mid-1800s, logging era and Native American artifacts, fire department exhibit.

About the museum: The Onalaska Area Historical Society was founded in 1985 and in 1990 opened a museum in the city library building. Within the museum is a Settler's Cabin whose displays change to reflect the changing seasons. Artifacts from the Indian and lumbering eras are exhibited to interpret the earliest history of the river valley region. Onalaska sits astride two rivers: the Black River and the Mississippi. Accounts of the lumber industry from forest to sawmill are featured in the Black River Boomtown exhibit. A display of logging tools and photographs depicts life in the old logging camps, and a section on sawmills shows gang saw, rotary saw blades, and illustrations of sawmills past and present.

Of particular interest is artwork by Franz Holzlhuber, a young Austrian who spent the years 1856-1860 in America, the "land beyond the sea." With a sketch pad and water colors, Holzlhuber captured "living history" by painting what he saw: Indian Life, Buffalos, the Coulee Region, Logging in the Woods, Paddlewheelers, Rafting on the River, and Railroad beginnings.

Oregon

Come visit anytime. We are open all year long and living history.

Oregon Area Historical Society Museum
159 West Lincoln Street
Oregon, WI 53575

Phone: (608) 835-8961
Open: Year-round: Tuesday, 1pm to 3pm; Memorial Day-Labor Day: Sunday, 1pm to 4pm.
Admission: Free, donations welcome

SOUTHWEST

The museum is located in an old grain mill in the heart of Oregon. There is a comprehensive collection of historical items on display that define the history and genealogy of the community. Oregon is proud to boast the first World War I monument in America. Native son, Nathaniel Ames, is one of only seven Revolutionary War soldiers known to call Wisconsin home.

Pardeeville

An old hotel holds many secrets. Mysteries abound in Pardeeville!

Myrtle Lintner Spear Museum
112 North Main Street
Pardeeville, WI 53954

Phone: (608) 429-1447
Open: June-September, Tuesday-Saturday, 1pm to 4pm; groups by appointment.

About the museum: The Myrtle Lintner Spear Museum has exhibits on three floors of an old hotel. Recall early life in Columbia County by viewing this interesting collection that is maintained by the Columbia County Historical Society.

Platteville

Visit this wonderful pre-Civil War time capsule of Wisconsin life. Don't take it for granted.

Grant County Historical Society — Mitchell-Rountree Stone Cottage
Corner of W. Madison and Hwy 81
Platteville, WI 53818

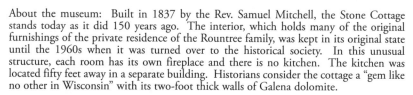

Phone: (608) 723-4925
Website: www.platteville.com/attract.htm
Open: Tours available Memorial Day through Labor Day, or by appointment.

Important works: Historic stone structure, period furnishings.

About the museum: Built in 1837 by the Rev. Samuel Mitchell, the Stone Cottage stands today as it did 150 years ago. The interior, which holds many of the original furnishings of the private residence of the Rountree family, was kept in its original state until the 1960s when it was turned over to the historical society. In this unusual structure, each room has its own fireplace and there is no kitchen. The kitchen was located fifty feet away in a separate building. Historians consider the cottage a "gem like no other in Wisconsin" with its two-foot thick walls of Galena dolomite.

Get the lead out and step into mining history at this 1845 mine or Rollo on over to the Jamison Museum. It's a gold mine of heritage.

★Mining Museum and Rollo Jamison Museum
405 E. Main St.
Platteville, WI 53818

Mailing address: P.O. Box 780, Platteville, WI 53818

Phone: (608) 348-3301 [Fax: 608-348-4640]
Contact: Stephanie Saager-Bourret
Website: www.platteville.com/mining_museum.htm
and www.platteville.com/rollo_jamison_museum.htm
Open: May through October, daily, 9am to 5pm. Changing galleries open Monday -
Friday, 9am to 4pm, November through April. Tours by appointment.
Admission: Yes

Important works: 1845 Bevans Lead Mine, 1931 Whitcomb five-ton locomotive, folk
art portraits by William Bonnell, late 1800s domestic artifacts and musical instruments,
medicine wagon, pioneer oral histories.

About the Mining Museum: The Museum Department of the City of Platteville was
established in 1964 to collect, preserve, and interpret artifacts and documents
relating to the history of mining in the Upper Mississippi Valley Lead-Zinc District.
By 1966, the museum had acquired a historic building and began developing
museum exhibits and public programs. In 1976, the museum excavated and re-
opened an authentic 1845 lead mine, the Bevans Lead Mine, adjacent to the
museum building. The museum also reconstructed a head frame, or hoisting
building, over the mine and acquired a working mine train. The Mining Museum
traces the development of lead and zinc mining through models, dioramas, artifacts,
and photographs. A guided tour includes a walk down into the Bevans Mine, which
produced over two million pounds of lead ore in one year (there are ninety steps into
the mine where it is fifty-two degrees year round). You will also visit the head frame
to see how zinc ore was hoisted from a mine and hand sorted and, weather-
permitting, take a train ride around the museum grounds in ore cars pulled by a
1931 Whitcomb locomotive.

About the Jamison Museum: The Rollo Jamison Museum began as a private, one-
person collection of artifacts of Southwest Wisconsin history that was the result of
over seventy years of active collecting. Rollo Jamison, born in Beetown, WI in
1899, started collecting arrowheads on the family farm as a boy. In 1980, the City
of Platteville authorized the Mining Museum to accept responsibility for this
20,000-item collection as a new museum. The artifacts were moved into quarters
adjacent to the museum, interpretive exhibits were developed, and educational
programs were instituted. Guided tours of the Rollo Jamison Museum will take you
back to the turn of the last century with exhibits of carriages, farm implements,
tools, small businesses, a kitchen and parlor, musical instruments, mechanical
music boxes, and more.

Portage

*The multi-faceted exhibits come alive during summer Canal Days when re-enactment players
live the past. Call ahead to rendevous!*

★Fort Winnebago Surgeon's Quarters
W8687 State Hwy 33
Portage, WI 53901

Phone: (608) 742-2949
Contact: Rachel Wynn
Email: surgeonsquarters@network2010.net
Open: May 15 – October 15, Monday – Saturday,
10am to 4pm; Sunday, noon to 4pm.

Important works: Historic fort building, fort furnishings, medical artifacts, quilts and
dolls, American glass, archives.

About the museum: Surgeons Quarters was built by Francis LeRoy between 1819 and 1824. It is the last remaining building of historic Fort Winnebago and the oldest building in Portage. The house is furnished as a home of army occupation days of Territorial Wisconsin. Original pieces from Fort Winnebago include a wooden eagle from the fort gate, two desks and chairs made by soldiers, the surgeon's operating table, blacksmith bellows, and a sideboard and articles of clothing that belonged to the Captain Gideon Low family. There are copies of farm building reports and other fort records. Among the authentic period furnishings are stitchwork samplers, quilts, dolls, collections of pewter, early American glass, and tools of various trades. Each year during the Portage area Canal Days, the museum hosts guests who reenact U.S. soldiers or fur traders of the period.

Meticulous restoration is the hallmark of this heritage site where Native American and pioneer life are celebrated.

Historic Indian Agency House
Agency House Road
Portage, WI 53901

Mailing address: P.O. Box 84, Portage, WI 53901
Phone: (608) 742-6362
Open: May 15-October 15, Monday-Saturday, 10-4, Sunday, 11-4. Off-season by appointment.
Admission: Yes

About the museum: The Historic Indian Agency House was built by the U.S. Government in 1832 for the Indian Agent to the Ho-Chunk (Winnebago), John Kinzie. His wife, Juliette Magill Kinzie wrote "Wau-Bun," an account of their voyage to Fort Winnebago, their home, pioneer life, and the Indians. Their granddaughter was Juliette Gordon Low, who founded the Girl Scouts of the U.S.A. The Agency House stands near the site of Fort Winnebago and the portage between the Fox and Wisconsin Rivers. It has been carefully restored and furnished with antiques, none later than 1833, the year the Kinzies left the Agency House.

The writer Zona Gale flourished here and so will you on your visit to the Portage Museum!

Museum at the Portage/Zona Gale House
804 Macfarlane Rd.
Portage, WI 53901

Mailing address: P.O. Box 727, Portage, WI 53901
Phone: (608) 742-6682
Open: Saturdays and Sundays, 1pm to 4pm, other times by appointment.
Admission: Free

Important works: Writing room of author Zona Gale (1874-1938), local history artifacts.

About the museum: The William L. and Zona Gale Breese home was donated to the city in 1946 to house the Portage Public Library. In 1996, the Museum at the Portage was established in this house to showcase displays relevant to the history of the city. Within the museum, the Zona Gale Study is preserved as it was when Zona lived in the house and wrote many of her lasting works. The Wisconsin Writers hold writer's workshops here during the year. Included in the permanent collection and display area at various times during the year are photographs and artifacts representing historical events in the city's history. Come on the third Saturday in August for Gale's birthday celebration.

Visit a dynamic cultural center full of artistic life!

★Portage Center for the Arts (Zona Gale Center)
301 East Cook Street
Portage, WI 53901

Mailing address: PO Box 866, Portage, WI 53901 (Portage Center for the Arts)
Phone: (608) 742-5655   [Fax: 608-742-0246]
Email: bschuetz@jvlnet.com
Website: http://www.portagearts.jvlnet.com/
Open: Call ahead for details for special exhibits
Admission: Free

About the museum: The Portage Center for the Arts is dedicated to promoting not only the fine arts, but also the performing arts in the community. There is a small gallery, which has a lively schedule of exhibitions. It is amazing what can be accomplished in a small community that really gets behind promoting the arts, including children's theater, adult education, and high school art exhibits.

Potosi

Time travel to the past, watch the clock.

Passage Thru Time Museum
116 N Main St.
Potosi, WI 53820

Phone: (608) 763-2745
Email: potosihistory@hotmail.com
Website: www.vangrafx.com/PTHS/museum/museum.html

About the museum: Experience the rich heritage of the Potosi Township with an emphasis on mining, farming, the historic Potosi Brewery, and the Mississippi River. Other displays include arrowheads, war memorabilia, former businesses, and John Deere toy tractors. This museum also houses an extensive collection of photos and historic records.

Poynette

From the fire tower platform overlooking MacKenzie, you can watch grazing bison and see the hills roll to the horizon. Poynette it out to me!

★★MacKenzie Environmental Education Center
W7303 County Hwy CS
Poynette, WI 53955

Phone: (608) 635-8110   [Fax: 608-635-8107]
Website: www.naturenet.com/mackenzie
Open: Grounds: Daily, dawn to dusk. Closed during deer gun season. Wildlife Exhibits and Museums: May 1 – mid-October, daily 8am to 4pm; mid-October – April 30, Monday – Friday 8am to 4pm.
Admission: Free

Important works: Wisconsin animals, pheasant farm, logging museum, maple sugaring camp, "aliens and oddities" natural history collection, Wisconsin conservation history.

SOUTHWEST

About the center: Animals in the wildlife exhibit are all native to Wisconsin. There are more than twenty species represented, including bald eagle, owls, hawks, wolves, bison, cougars, deer, and a badger. The logging museum is housed in a log cabin built in the 1880s by Peder and Bergetta Nelson. Exhibits include logging tools, historic photos of logging operations, and two dioramas. Across from the museum are outdoor exhibits of a sawmill and tree planting machinery. In the Aliens and Oddities Museum, visitors learn about exotic plant and animal species, which have been introduced to Wisconsin. There are also exhibits of albino and other unusual animals. A historic barn houses the conservation museum which houses mounted specimens of the animal life of Wisconsin. There are also exhibits about the conservation warden service, recycling, and pollution.

A small community rich in history awaits the visitor.

Poynette Area Historical Museum
116 North Main Street
Poynette, WI 53955

Phone: (608) 635-9849
Open: Year-round: Wednesday, 1pm to 3pm; Saturday, 10am to 2pm or by appointment.
Admission: Donations welcome

The museum features a large room with a major exhibit detailing the history of Poynette from 1830-1980. A school exhibit and Poynette veterans exhibit are also on permanent display. The museum also has two period rooms, a turn-of-the-century parlor and dining room, and a small library with local history books and family histories.

Prairie du Chien

Furs were sold here along with other dry goods. Come and trade stories, fur the fun of it.

Brisbois Store — Fur Trade Museum
St. Feriole Island, Water St.
Prairie du Chien, WI 53821

Open: In conjunction with Villa Louis, from May - October.

Important works: Fur trade artifacts.

About the museum: Built in 1851-52 by fur trader and merchant, B.W. Brisbois, this stone building sits on land having a long association with the North American fur trade. Prior to the War of 1812, the property was owned by a number of prominent traders. After the war, the property became the site of a U.S. Fur Factory. Through much of the 20th century the building was know as the Riverside Boat Repair. It was acquired in the 1970s and renovated as the Fur Trade Museum.

The old time medical exhibits make you grateful for modern science, no medicare then. This national historic landmark tells valuable lessons about the past.

★Prairie du Chien Historical Society — Fort Crawford Museum and Prairie du Chien Museum
717 S. Beaumont Rd.
Prairie du Chien, WI 53821

Mailing address: P.O. Box 298, Prairie du Chien, WI 53821
Phone: (608) 326-6960

Contact: Joan A. Sheriff
Email: ftcrawmu@mhtc.net
Website: www.fortcrawfordmuseum.com
Open: May, September, October, 10am to 4pm; June, July, August, 10am to 5pm.
Guided group tours available by appointment.
Admission: Yes

Important works: Mid-19th century medical, dental, and hospital equipment (including military medicine) and exhibits on local history and natural history.

About the museums: The second Fort Crawford was authorized by the U.S. Government to be built in 1829 of native rock. It was to replace the first wooden fort constructed near the river. It originally occupied many blocks in the area and housed a garrison of several hundred U.S. Army troops. Its purpose was to settle problems among Indians or between Indians and whites on the frontier. It functioned as a military fort until 1856 and as a recruiting station during the Civil War. In 1933 the hospital portion of the Fort was reconstructed. It includes an 1850s doctor's office, refurbished pharmacy, dioramas on the progress of surgery, 1900s dental office, a history of forts, medical instruments, a hospital wardroom display, and the history of military medicine, and is a National Historical Landmark.

The Prairie du Chien Museum includes drawings of important local historic events and exhibits on Chief Blackhawk, the Treaty of 1825, Campion High School, the river clam industry, Native American artifacts, local fossils, and an iron lung.

Stroll the historic grounds and discover the allure of Victorian Wisconsin on the nearby Mississippi River. It's a millionaire's vision in 1870.

★★★Villa Louis Historic Site
521 N. Villa Louis Rd.
Prairie du Chien, WI 53821

Mailing address: P.O. Box 65, Prairie du Chien, WI 53821
Phone: (608) 326-2721 [Fax: 608-326-5507]
Contact: Michael Douglass, Director
Email: villalouis@whs.wisc.edu
Website: villalouis.wisconsinhistory.org
Open: First week in May – October 31, daily. Tours run on the hour with the first one at 10am and the last at 4pm.
Admission: Yes

Important works: Late 1800s furnishings and decor, the only War of 1812 battlefield in Wisconsin.

About the museum: This hilltop mansion, home to generations of one of Wisconsin's most celebrated frontier families, commands a sweeping view of a landscape steeped in history. Descendants of pioneer fur trader Hercules Louis Dousman built the house in 1870. His son, Louis, and his family operated the estate as the Artesian Stock Farm, breeding and raising fine trotting horses for harness racing. They furnished the mansion with elegant antiques, fine art, and exquisite heirlooms. The Wisconsin Historical Society took title to the property in the early 1950s and a major interior restoration, one of the most authentic in the U.S., has returned the mansion to its storied 1890s heyday. See the annual reenactment of the Battle of Prairie du Chien, the third weekend of July.

A must see historic site.

Prairie du Sac

Built with pride, restored with love, this church museum is a public monument to pioneers, prophets, and paradise. These four wonderful historic sites bring history alive.

Sauk Prairie Area Historical Society
565 Water Street
Prairie du Sac, WI 53578

Our Lady of Loretto Church Museum
Between Denzer and Leland on Hwy C

Old Fire Station
One block north of Hwy 12 on John Adams Street
Sauk City, WI 53583

Tripp Memorial Museum
565 Water Street
Prairie du Sac, WI 53578

Salem Rogatz Church Museum
Corner of Church Rd. and Hwy PF
Prairie du Sac, WI 53578

Phone: (608) 644-8444
Contact: Verlyn Mueller (608) 644-8444 or Lola Huber (608) 643-3805
Email: spahs@verizon.net
Website: www.saukprairiehistory.org/
Open: Church Museums: June through August, Sundays, 1pm to 4pm. A Mass of Remembrance is held each September. Open by appointment for tours and weddings. Tripp Museum: Saturdays, 10am to 4pm; Monday and Wednesday, 9am to 11:30am, Tuesdays, 9am to 5pm. For Loretto, contact Lola Huber. For Salem, contact Verlyn Mueller.

Important works: Story and Clark pump organ (1887), original pews 1880, confessional, statues, church memorabilia.

About the museum: The Our Lady of Loretto Church was built in 1880 by German and Irish Catholic farmers, using native limestone of the area. Original stenciling graces the walls and the arched ceiling appears just as it was 120 years ago. Iron chandeliers were recreated by a local blacksmith according to the memories of those who attended the church in the 1930s and 1940s, and the pulpit was rebuilt according to the markings on the wall. The original confessional, pews with kneelers, Jewel potbelly stove, 1887 Story, and Clark pump organ still remain in the church.

In 1960 the church closed, and in 1974 was donated to the Sauk Prairie Area Historical Society after appeals from local historians. In the 1990s, society members raised funds for restoration. From 1993 to 1999, conservator Tony Rajer and art students from the University of Wisconsin restored the wall stencils, painted murals for the pulpit, installed the stations of the cross, restored statues, and carried out many other tasks to bring the little church back to the days of 1880.

SOUTHWEST

Tony's Tips

Madison abounds with good restaurants. My breakfast favorite Diner is Monte's Blue Plate on Atwood on the east side. Boy it's good!

Princeton

The past comes alive on the special cemetery tour along with the thousands of other artifacts at the various historic sites. It's an Ivy League location!

Princeton Chamber of Commerce – Warnke Building
708 Water St.
Princeton, WI 54968

Princeton Historical Society — Stone House Museum and Warnke Building
632 W. Water St.
Princeton, WI 54968

Phone: Historical Society, (920) 295-6949 or Chamber of Commerce, (920) 295-3877
Contact: Gary Wick
Open: Warnke Building, 10:30am to 2:20pm. Visitors Center: April-October, Monday, Wednesday, and Friday, 9am to 1pm; Saturday, 9am to 3pm. Stone House: Memorial Day – Labor Day, Saturday, 1pm to 4pm.

Important works: 1920s style house, period furnishings, lumber yard artifacts.

About the museum: The Princeton Historical Society was organized in 1983 and in 1984 the Stone House Museum was purchased. The Stone House Museum is an excellent example of an early 20th century home with an old style kitchen, dining room, living room, and bedroom. Calendars, pictures of local personalities, and events are located throughout the building. The Warnke Building, at 708 Water St. (which is owned by the Chamber of Commerce) offers displays of local businesses and pictures from Princeton's days as a lumberyard center.

Historic tours of the Princeton community are conducted on the first Wednesday of the month, May through October. Meet at 10 am in the city parking lot. An annual Cemetery Tour occurs on the Saturday before Memorial Day. Meet at 1:30 pm in the city parking lot.

Reedsburg

If log cabins are your cup of tea, this site will fill you to the brim.

Reedsburg Area Historical Society — Pioneer Log Village and Museum
Highway 23 and 33
three miles east of Reedsburg
Reedsburg, WI 53959

Mailing address: P.O. Box 405, Reedsburg, WI 53959
Phone: (608) 524-3419
Contact: Bob Reed
Website: www.reedsburg.com/log.htm
Open: Memorial Day through September, Saturday and Sunday, 1pm to 4pm. Tours upon request.
Admission: Donation appreciated

Important works: Thirteen-star flag once displayed in the office of President John Adams, Claridge family antiques collection, seven log buildings built between 1850 and 1880.

About the museum: The society was formed in 1965 to preserve log buildings in the Reedsburg area. Some buildings were moved intact while others were taken apart and reconstructed on the site. All were built in the middle to late 1800s. The collection includes seven log buildings plus a log building reconstruction in progress. A blacksmith shop displays the private collection of Ray Palmer who apprenticed as a blacksmith. The General Store was originally the Lichte cabin. The Kruse cabin has a puncheon floor and is furnished with antiques. The Library houses the book collection of the society. The Oetzman cabin was built in 1876 and was moved intact with its wood floors. The Redstone cabin was built in the 1850s and is equipped with a cook stove and Hoosier kitchen cabinet. The Willow Creek Church was built in 1876 as a German Lutheran Church. The museum building collection includes a coat worn by a guard at the funeral of Abraham Lincoln and a desk belonging to John Brown.

Richland Center

Learn wright from wrong at this architectural heritage site in Frank Lloyd Wright's hometown.

★A.D. German Warehouse
300 S. Church St.
Richland Center, WI 53581

Mailing address: P.O. Box 6339, Madison, WI 53716
Phone: (608) 647-2808 or (608) 287-0339
E-mail: info@WrightinWisconsin.org
Website: http://www.wrightinwisconsin.org/old/WisconsinSites/ADGerman/
Open: Call for tour reservations.

Important works: Building designed by Frank Lloyd Wright, architectural photomurals.

About the museum: This massive red brick and concrete building would be impressive in any setting; it is especially so in the small Wisconsin town where Frank Lloyd Wright was born. Designed in 1915 and constructed between 1917 and 1921 for a local commodity wholesaler, Albert Dell German, the four-story warehouse was used to store sugar, flour, coffee, tobacco, and other staples. The warehouse is one of only a few major public buildings designed by Wright during the midteens that was actually constructed and is the only surviving example from that decade in which he employed sculptural ornamentation so extensively. In recent years, the building was modified to accommodate a gift shop and small theater on the first floor, and an exhibition of large photomurals, which illustrate Wright's architectural work on the second floor.

Rome

Not to be confused with Rome, Italy, this place is rich in local Roman heritage. Its Romanesque.

Rome/Sullivan Historical Society
N30866 West St.
Rome, WI 53178

Phone: (262) 593-8662, (262) 567-0129
Open: Memorial Day and by appointment from April to mid-October.
Admission: Free

Important works: Local history artifacts, World War II objects, wedding dresses.

About the museum: The society makes its home at the Old Rome Graded Schoolhouse Museum in Rome. In addition to its local history collection, it features exhibits of World War II artifacts, toys, vintage wedding dresses, and handmade quilts.

Shullsburg

Get the lead out and dig into history at a real Badger lead mine. It's an underground adventure!

▲ Badger Mine and Museum
279 W. Estey St.
Shullsburg, WI 53586
Phone: (608) 965-4860
Website: http://www.shullsburg.com/mine/mine.htm
Open: Memorial Day – Labor Day, Daily, 10am to 4pm. Call ahead for particular time and dates.

About the museum: Jesse W. Shull, the founder of Shullsburg, explored this area for the Hudson Bay Fur Company as early as 1818. Along with the Van Matre brothers, he began mining lead and developed Badger Lot Diggings, now known as the Badger Mine. With a trained guide, visitors descend stairs into the mine, which extends beneath the city of Shullsburg, inside the mine, visitors are instructed in the methods of the pioneer miners. In addition to the mining story, the museum has exhibits of early farm tools and medical equipment, plus a general store, drugstore, tobacco shop, turn-of-the-century kitchen, blacksmith shop, and carpenter's shop.

Sparta

Peddle on over and see space history come alive. Junior astronauts are welcome for a lunar rendezvous!

▲ ★Deke Slayton Memorial Space and Bike Museum
200 W. Main St.
Sparta, WI 54656

Phone: (608) 269-0033 or (888) 200-5302 (toll-free) [Fax: 608-269-4423]
Contact: Sparta Area Chamber of Commerce (608) 269-4123
Email: info@dekeslayton.com
Website: www.dekeslayton.com
Open: Summer: Monday-Saturday, 10am to 4:30pm; Sunday, 1pm to 4pm. Winter: Monday-Friday, 10am to 4pm; Saturday by appointment.

Important works: Historic bicycles, the story of astronaut Deke Slayton.

About the museum: The Deke Slayton Memorial Space and Bike Museum was established in March 1999. It is a local history museum emphasizing two special areas: the history of bicycles and the accomplishments of Mercury astronaut and Monroe County native, Donald "Deke" Slayton. It features three permanent exhibits (Deke Slayton, bicycle history, and county aviation history), plus changing exhibits, and hosts around twenty educational programs each year.

Bring your doll and ride on over to this museum where dress-up is taken seriously.

▲ Little Falls Railroad and Doll Museum
9208 County Hwy II
Sparta, WI 54656-6485

Phone: (608) 272-3266
Contact: Sparta Area Chamber of Commerce (608) 269-4123
Email: raildoll@centurytel.net
Website: http://www.raildoll.org/

SOUTHWEST

Open: April 1 - November 1, 1pm to 5pm, closed Tuesdays and Wednesdays.
Handicapped accessible.
Admission: Yes

Important works: Historic and contemporary dolls, railroad memorabilia, literature, and art.

About the museum: A magical experience begins upon entering the Doll Museum, located on a rural, three-acre site. Hundreds of dolls are on display, from German dolls of the 1800s and reproduction French dolls, to the contemporary Barbie, Gene, Tyler Wentworth, and Betsy McCall. Hands-on exhibits allow visitors to stand next to a Victorian lady in her 1800s walking suit as she wheels her baby in a wicker carriage. Enjoy Christmas morning with Grandma and Grandpa or view the Presidents' First Ladies in their beautiful inaugural gowns on the White House stairs.

The Railroad Museum is home to a reference library of over 1,000 books and magazines dating back 100 years. The walls are covered with railroad memorabilia from the days when steam was king. Exhibit cases hold models of steam locomotives, many in brass. There is telegrapher's equipment on display and lanterns from many railroads. A gallery of railroad art is a featured attraction at the museum.

Recent renovation and expansion have added a new dimension to this community heritage center.

Monroe County Local History Room
200 W. Main St.
Sparta, WI 54656

Phone: (608) 269-8680 [Fax: 608-269-8921]
Contact: Jarrod Roll or Sparta Area Chamber of Commerce (608) 269-4123
Email: MCLHR@centurytel.net
Open: Monday – Friday, 9am to 4:30pm; Saturday, 10am to 4:30pm.

Important works: Local artifacts, Monroe County historical archives.

About the library: The library specializes in the history of Monroe County and its settlers. The collection includes Monroe County federal and state census microfilm, newspapers, and family histories.

Spring Green

Eye goggling and mind boggling, the House on the Rock will overwhelm your senses and leave you awe struck. It's an extreme experience!

★★★House on the Rock
5754 Hwy 23
Spring Green, WI 53588

Phone: (608) 935-3639
Email: info@thehouseontherock.com
Website: www.thehouseontherock.com
Open: March – May 27, 9am to 5pm; May 28 – June 30, 9am to 6pm; July 1 – August 20, 9am to 7pm; August 21 – September 4, 9am to 6pm; September 5 – November 7, 9am to 5pm.
Admission: Yes

Important works: Mechanical musical instruments, doll houses, miniature circus models, Streets of Yesterday, cannons, crown jewel replicas, carved ivory, historic weapons.

SOUTHWEST

About the house: Built atop a sixty-foot rock outcropping, this world-famous museum's out-of-the-ordinary collections and bizarre attractions draw over 500,000 visitors each year. Among its exhibits is the world's largest carousel, thirty-five feet tall with 270 carved animals and illuminated with more than 20,000 lights. There is also the Infinity Room, a glass-walled structure that projects 218 feet out over the valley 150 feet below. Another masterpiece is a giant sea creature whose length is greater than the Statue of Liberty. The Music of Yesterday room houses the greatest collection in the world of animated, automated music machines, and gigantic pipe organs.

If you don't see anything else in Wisconsin, come see how a world-class architect created and lived. He was wright and often frank...

▲ ★★★Taliesin (Frank Lloyd Wright's Home and Workplace)
5607 Cty Hwy C
Spring Green, WI 53588

Mailing address: P.O. Box 399, Spring Green, WI 53588
Phone: (608) 588-7900 or toll free 877-588-7900
Email: visitctr@mhtc.net
Website: www.TaliesinPreservation.org
Open: Visitor Center: May 1 - October 31, daily, 9am to 4:30pm; April, November, December, weekends only, 10am to 4pm.
Admission: Yes

Important works: The home, studio, furnishings, and works of famed architect Frank Lloyd Wright.

About the museum: A variety of tours are offered from May 1 to October 31. The one-hour Hillside Studio tour is the best introduction to architect Frank Lloyd Wright and his work. Wright designed Hillside in 1902 for his aunt's boarding school. It was transformed in 1932 into its current use as the center of activity for the Taliesin architectural studio and school. A two-hour Walking Tour lets visitors experience the beautiful rural landscape that inspired Wright's organic architecture. View the exteriors of all the major buildings including Hillside, Taliesin, Romeo and Juliet Windmill, Tan-y-deri house, and Midway Farm.

The two-hour House Tour features Wright's private residence, Taliesin, called his "autobiography in wood and stone." Here visitors gain insight into the genius of Wright by seeing the rooms he imagined, built, and filled with his furnishings and art collections. Reservations are required for this and the four-hour Estate Tour, which is a comprehensive tour that covers all parts of the property. In 1959 Mr Wright was buried at the nearby private Unitarian Chapel but later his bones were removed and sent to Arizona.

Visitors interested in Mr. Wright's work will also find buildings designed by him in Richland Center, Madison, Lake Delton, Milwaukee, and Racine. Google the web site [www.wrightinwisconsin.com]

Other informational sites about Frank Lloyd Wright for the traveler.

Frank Lloyd Wright Building Conservancy
http://www.SaveWright.org
The Conservancy is an organization dedicated to preserving the remaining buildings designed by Mr. Wright.

Frank Lloyd Wright Foundation
http://www.franklloydwright.org/
Formed by Frank Lloyd Wright himself to carry on the ideas and principles of organic architecture, as well as preserving the legacy of Wright's life and work.

Taliesin Preservation Commission
http://www.taliesinpreservation.org/
The mission of TPC is to preserve the Taliesin estate in Spring Green, Wisconsin.

Travel Wisconsin, Wright related material
http://travelwisconsin.com/
A site designed to help you plan a relaxing and enjoyable trip to Wisconsin. A service of
the Wisconsin Department of Tourism.

Wright Sites

The Bernard Schwartz House, Two Rivers
http://theschwartzhouse.com
In 1938 LIFE magazine commissioned Frank Lloyd Wright to design a dream home for
an American family of median income. The result was a Usonian house, an enduring
model of modest-sized residential architecture. It's available as a rental.

Monona Terrace Community and Convention Center
http://www.mononaterrace.com/
The Center opened in July, 1997 and is located on the shores of Lake Monona in
downtown Madison, Wisconsin. It took sixty years to get it built Wright.

Seth Peterson Cottage
http://www.SethPeterson.org
Located on Lake Delton, Wisconsin. The Web site includes floor plans, photographs,
and information about making reservations.

SOUTHWEST

Stoughton

Velkommen, this fine local history museum awaits you.

Stoughton Historical Museum
324 South Page Street
Stoughton, WI 53589

Phone: (608) 873-8005
Contact: David Kalland
Open: Mid-May to September, Sunday, 1pm to 4pm
or by appointment.
Admission: Donations are requested

The Stoughton Historical Museum was originally the
First Universalist Church, which was built in 1858, on
land donated by Luke Stoughton. The museum displays
Norwegian crafts of hardanger (needlework),
woodcarving, and other plain and fancy needlework.
Displays are also dedicated to Native American
collections and community members in uniform, from the Civil War era to the
present. These periods in Stoughton's history are chronicled with many era fashioned
and uniformed mannequins, diaries, newspapers, picture, and artifacts. The
collection is further enhanced by antique dolls and toys, a 1910 printing press, and a
photograph collection. The "hot" feature of the collection is an operational 1925 fire
truck built in Stoughton and presented to the society by the Stoughton Fire
Department in 1969.

Sun Prairie

▲ Georgia O'Keefe's Birthplace
IIII Town Hall rd and County Highway T
south of Sun Prairie

Call for information (608) 837-2915 or (608)837-2511

A historical marker indicates where the O'Keefe farm house stood. A small exhibit honors this great American artist at the nearby Historical Society in town. She was born here in 1887 and died in Santa Fe, New Mexico in 1986. Remember that the farm is a private residence and not open to the public.

What a beautiful museum; it really shines!

▲ Sun Prairie Historical Library and Museum
IIII 115 E. Main Street
Sun Prairie, WI 53590

Mailing address: P.O. Box 313, Sun Prairie, WI 53590
Phone: (608) 837-2915 or 837-7844
Contact: Ed Addison
Open: May 11 - Labor Day: Wednesday, Friday, and Saturday, 2pm to 4pm; Sunday and Monday, 6:30pm to 8:30pm. September-November: Friday and Saturday, 2pm to 4pm and by appointment.

Sun Prairie has an intriguing history of settlement including the intersection of Native Americans, the Yankee culture, and European immigrants. This museum houses a wonderful small collection of historic items, including 19th and 20th century artifacts. Every year they also hold walking tours of area cemeteries and neighborhoods. Call ahead for details.

Tomah

Call waiting... From crank to wireless, a century of telephones under one roof. It speaks for itself.

▲ ★Harris G. Allen Telecommunication Historical Museum
IIII 306 Arthur St.
Tomah, WI 54660

Mailing address: P.O. Box 427, Tomah, WI 54660
Open: Monday - Friday, 8am to 5pm.

Important works: Historic telephones, early telephone exchange office, hands-on telephone exhibits.

About the museum: Harris Allen served as President of the Wisconsin State Telephone Association for several years and was nationally known for his work as Director of the United States Telephone Association. Exhibits include over 100 telephones from around the world dating back to 1894, including tree-shaped wall phones, Eiffel Tower desk phones, and other unique models. The "old business office" is a recreation of a typical telephone exchange in the era of crank telephones and magneto switchboards. One hundred years of communications progress in Wisconsin is seen in a display representing dozens of companies, which began in Wisconsin. Visitors can use old wall phones, "ring up central," talk through the tube phone, use a mechanical switch to connect one phone to another, and learn the basics of how telephones work.

A zillion historic artifacts bring Tomah history alive. Worth the price of admission.

Tomah Area Historical Society Museum
1112 S. Superior Avenue
Tomah, WI 54660

Phone: (608) 372-1880 or (608) 372-5771
Open: Mid-May through the end of August, Tuesday – Saturday, 10am to 4pm;
September through mid-October, Tuesday – Saturday, 1pm to 4pm and by appointment.

This museum catalogs the history of Tomah with displays from Tomah's native son,
Frank King, creator of the nationally syndicated comic strip, "Gasoline Alley," along with
exhibits on the development of Tomah's businesses and industries. Included are the early
railroad and lumber years and the agriculture and cranberry operations.

Viroqua

See Post-Civil War domestic life comes alive at this beautiful mansion. No buts about it.

Sherry-Butt House
795 N. Main Street
Viroqua, WI 54665

Phone: (608) 637-7396
Website: http://www.frontiernet.net/~vcmuseum/Sherry%20Butt%20House.htm
Open: Memorial Day thru September, Saturday and Sunday, 1pm to 5pm or by appointment.

About the museum: An impressive 19th century mansion, this fully restored home of a
Civil War Colonel and his family is furnished as it was in the late 1880s.

Viroqua is rich in local history. Fascinating displays bring the bygone days alive.

★Vernon County Historical Society and Museum
410 S. Center Ave.
Viroqua, WI 54665

Mailing address: P.O. Box 444, Viroqua, WI 54665
Phone: (608) 637-7396
Contact: Judy Mathison, Curator
Email: vcmuseum@frontiernet.net
Website: http://www.frontiernet.net/~vcmuseum/
Open: Mid-May to mid-September, Monday-Saturday, noon to 4pm. Winter hours:
Tuesday, Wednesday, and Thursday, noon to 4pm or by appointment.

Important works: Historic buildings (schoolhouse Catholic church, historic house),
Civil War memorabilia, genealogy records, and medical equipment.

About the museum: The Vernon County Historical Society was originally organized in
1940 in Viroqua. A museum was housed in several locations until purchasing the
Vernon County Normal School building in 1988. Built 1918-1919, it was used as a
Teacher's College and Model School until 1972. Three stories of displays and an
expansive collection of artifacts and historical records are available. Displays include
tobacco history of the area, equipment used by doctors, druggists, and lawyers, a country
store, turn of the century bedroom, and rural school. There is also a local history room
and research room for genealogists. NASA astronaut Mark Lee was born and raised in
Viroqua and a room is dedicated to NASA artifacts and memorabilia. Another well-

SOUTHWEST

known citizen was Jeremiah Rusk who was Brigadier General in the Civil War and elected to congress from 1871 to 1877. In 1882 he was elected governor of Wisconsin and served until 1889. In 1889 he was appointed the first Secretary of Agriculture. A unique chair given to Mr. Rusk by the Texas Cattlemen's Association is on display along with pictures and the history of his life.

Other properties maintained by the society include the Foreaker Country Schoolhouse, the old St. Mary's Catholic Church and the Sherry-Butt House. At the schoolhouse, visitors can research family roots in the genealogy room and explore Vernon County business, church, school, and government records. The Sherry-Butt house was a family home built by Civil War Colonel Cyrus Butt in the early 1870s. Purchased by Orbec and Hilda Sherry in the 1940s, Orbec lived in the home until his death in 1988. It features furnishings from both families including Col. Butt's Civil War memorabilia.

Don't forget to see the WPA era mural in the Post Office. It's one of the largest in the state.

Warrens

Don't be a sour grape! Visit us at this sweet cranberry museum and get juiced.

★Wisconsin Cranberry Discovery Center
204 Main St.
Warrens, WI 54666

Phone: (608) 378-4878 [Fax: 608-378-3328]
Website: http://www.discovercranberries.com/
Open: April – October 31, daily, 9am to 5pm; November 1 – December 31, Tuesday – Saturday, 10am to 4pm.
Admission: Yes

About the museum: The Cranberry Museum is home to an historical collection of machinery designed, built, and used by Wisconsin cranberry growers. From hand rakes to horse clogs to water reels and harvest boats, you'll walk through the development of tools and machinery used in the cranberry industry from the 1870s to the present. You'll learn how cranberries are planted, tended, harvested, and marketed. You'll also get a sense of the dedicated people who make up the cranberry industry.

Waunakee

Bring the kids and see living history at this farm.

Schumacher Farm
5682 Hwy 19
Waunakee, WI 53597

Contact: Allen Holzhueter (608) 238-0546
Phone: (608) 849-4559
Open: May-October, third Sunday of the month, 1:30pm to 3:30pm. Call for schedule or to book tours.

This 117-acre site is an outdoor museum representing local farm life during the 1920s and 30s. It features a ten-acre prairie restoration, the farmstead with spacious and shady grounds, and related activities. Programming and museum development are sponsored by the Friends of Schumacher Farms, and include heirloom gardening, educational field

SOUTHWEST

trips, prairie tours, old farm machinery, buildings restorations, and special public events reminiscent of rural culture of the time period.

Wauzeka

Native-American culture is adored and celebrated at this site; come see why on your family visit.

Kickapoo Indian Caverns and Native American Museum
Hwy 60
Wauzeka, WI 53826

Website: www.kickapooindiancaverns.com
Open: May 15 – October 31, 9am – last tour 4pm.
Admission: Yes, group rates for school and organizations of twenty or more (except Sundays and holidays)

A natural historic site "where adventures of the past live on today."

West Salem

Our garland will weave you into a literary past.

Hamlin Garland Homestead
357 W. Garland St.
West Salem, WI 54669

Mailing address: P.O. Box 884, West Salem, WI 54669
Phone: (608) 786-1399 or (608) 786-1675
Contact: Errol Kindschy
Open: Memorial Day – Labor Day, Monday – Saturday, 10am to 4:30pm; Sunday, 1pm to 4pm.
Admission: Yes

Important works: Furnishings, artifacts, documents, and books of Hamlin Garland, one of Wisconsin's foremost authors.

About the museum: This structure, built in 1859, was one of the homes of author and Pulitzer Prize winner Hamlin Garland. He purchased it in 1893 for his parents and added a second story and dining room, using the house as a summer residence until 1915. His life on the Wisconsin frontier had a deep influence on his writings. A dozen of his short stories are set in the coulee area around La Crosse. It was also an essential element in his autobiography. Many of the furnishings in the house and in the special museum room created from a visitor's bedroom are actual Garland furnishings. The museum contains pictures of the Garlands, Christmas cards from the family, many of Garland's letters, forty-seven of the fifty-two books that he authored, and magazines containing his articles and short stories.

Fascinating Facts

The Wisconsin state constitution upholds the right that "No person may be held to answer for a criminal offense without due process of law."

Come in groups of eight and enjoy all sides of history. It's more than a pentagon!

▲ **Palmer-Gullickson Octagon House**
358 N. Leonard St.
West Salem, WI 54669

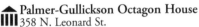

Mailing address: P.O. Box 884, West Salem, WI 54669
Phone: (608) 786-1675
Contact: Errol Kindschy
Open: Memorial Day - Labor Day, Monday - Saturday,
10am to 4:30pm; Sunday, 1pm to 4pm.
Admission: Yes

Important works: Period furnishings, octagonal architecture.

About the museum: The Palmer-Gullickson Octagon house was built in 1856 by Dr. Horace Palmer, the first resident doctor of Neshonoc. When residents of Neshonoc moved to West Salem because of the new railroad, the house was moved to its present location. The process of moving the house took three weeks, during which the Palmer family continued to live in it. One very unusual feature of the house was the attachment of the barn directly to the house. The house was sold in 1876 to Dr. Mary Lottridge, the second woman doctor in the U.S. In 1921 the Gullickson family purchased the house. Many pieces of furniture originally purchased for the house are on display.

Westby

Westby has many historic treasures; come see for yourself.

▲ **Westby Area Historical Society Museum — Thoreson House**
101 Black River Avenue
Westby, WI 54667

Mailing address: P.O. Box 42, Westby, WI 54667
Phone: (608) 654-7986
Contact: Roy Jefson, President
Open: By appointment

Many beautiful and interesting things in this collection will make you glad you stopped. A large sampling of historic photographs, kitchen items and heritage pieces await the visitor.

Westfield

A treasure house of local history. Come in the summer and bring the whole family.

▲ **Marquette County Historical Society Museum**
125 Lawrence St.
Westfield, WI 53964

Mailing address: P.O. Box 172, Westfield, WI 53964
Contacts: Ellen Martin, President
Phone: (608) 296-4700 or (608) 296-4094
Email: mchs@co.marquette.wi.us
Website: www.marquettecohistory.org/museum.htm
Open: Wednesdays, 1pm to 4pm year round. Other times by appointment.

Important works: Historic house, extensive local archives, railroad memorabilia, war artifacts, and one-room school records.

About the museum: The Marquette County Historical Society maintains three properties. The Cochrane-Nelson House was built in 1903 by T. Harry Cochrane, son of Robert Cochrane, a settler from Westfield, NY, who built a mill on the local creek about 1850 and owned the land from which Westfield, WI was platted. The Henry Ellis Section House features exhibits of railroad memorabilia. The museum library contains genealogy and cemetery records, newspapers, diaries, letters, photos, and historical albums. The Kerst Memorial Building houses artifacts from Marquette County's seventy-five one-room schools, as well as mementoes, photos, and journals from the Civil War, Spanish-American War, and both World Wars.

Wisconsin Dells

If the Dells is your destination, don't miss this genuine historic attraction. There's even a letter from Abraham Lincoln.

★Dells County Historical Society — Bowman House
714 Broadway St.
Wisconsin Dells, WI 53965

Phone: (608) 254-2254
Contact: Bud Gussel
Open: June 20-September1: Monday - Thursday and Saturday, 1pm to 4:30pm and by appointment.
Admission: Free

Important works: Prairie style house, Civil War General Joseph Bailey memorabilia.

About the museum: The Bowman residence, built at the turn of the century, is an example of Prairie School style architecture. Now the site of the Dells Country Historical Society, it was a vacation home for working women from the late 1930s to the mid 1970s. It houses General Joseph Bailey's Thanks of Congress and commendation by Abraham Lincoln for his Civil War feats. It also contains authentic antique furnishings and area memorabilia.

If a picture is worth a thousand words, this place is an encyclopedia of photographic history.

★★H.H. Bennett Studio and History Center
215 Broadway
Wisconsin Dells, WI 53965

Mailing address: P.O. Box 147, Wisconsin Dells, WI 53965
Phone: (608) 253-3523 [Fax: 608-253-4635]
Email: hhbennett@whs.wisc.edu
Website: http://www.wisconsinhistory.org/hhbennett/
Open: May 1 – October 31, 10am to 5pm. Later evening hours mid-June – mid-August. February – April and November – December, weekends only, 10am to 4pm. Closed January. Tours by reservation.
Admission: Yes

Important works: Bennett cameras and stereographic images, restored photographer's studio, collection of handmade American Indian dolls.

About the museum: In 1875, Henry Hamilton Bennett built a photography studio in the village of Kilbourn City. He spent his career capturing the magnificence of the place, which later became Wisconsin Dells. His pictures of the Dells and scenes of life among the area's native Ho-Chunk (Winnebago) people, particularly his three-dimensional stereo views, drew tourists by the trainload. In his studio they also discovered rural Wisconsin landscapes, raftsmen hauling lumber downriver, and street scenes of Chicago, Milwaukee, and St. Paul. Bennett's restored studio in Wisconsin Dells' River District is now a museum operated by the Wisconsin Historical Society.

This rack is worth a visit!

Nanchas Elk Ranch
County Hwy H
Wisconsin Dells, WI 53965

Mailing address: E7568A Acorn Lane, Lyndon Station, WI 53944
Phone: (608) 524-4355
Email: info@elkranch.net
Website: www.elkranch.net
Open: May 17-October 21: Tuesday-Sunday, 10-5
Admission: Yes

Important holdings: Herd of American elk.

About the ranch: At this working elk ranch, visitors can enjoy a scenic wagon ride and learn about the lives and secret ways of the elk.

Winnebago Indian Museum
3889 River Rd. (Hwy 13 & River Rd.)
Wisconsin Dells, WI 53965

Closed.

No just white tail, but many species of deer and other animals can be found at this park. Like the Garden of Eden you can pet the beasts.

Wisconsin Deer Park
583 Wisconsin Dells Pkwy.
Wisconsin Dells, WI 53965

Phone: (608) 253-2041
Open: Daily 9am to 7pm. Call to verify hours.

About the park: On this twenty-eight acre park, you can feed, pet, and photograph wildlife ranging from deer and elk to game birds and other animals.

Wonewoc

The whole interior of this heritage site is covered in mysterious murals. Call for an appointment to see this painted treasure!

Painted Forest Folk Art Museum
S2110 Woolever Road
Wonewoc, WI 53968

Phone: (608) 983-2352

Open: June-August: Saturdays, 1pm to 3:30pm or by appointment.
Admission: Free, donations accepted

In a small Wisconsin town that's off the beaten path you'll find the Painted Forest. It is a unique reminder of the Modern Woodmen of America's past and simpler time. Hundreds of camp halls (lodge buildings) were built by members of Modern Woodmen of America, a fraternal life insurance organization, in the late 1800s and early 1900s. The buildings provided members with a place to gather for meetings, fellowship, and fun. Murals painted on the camp walls depict historic rituals and tell stories about rural life.

The building is now owned by Edgewood College.

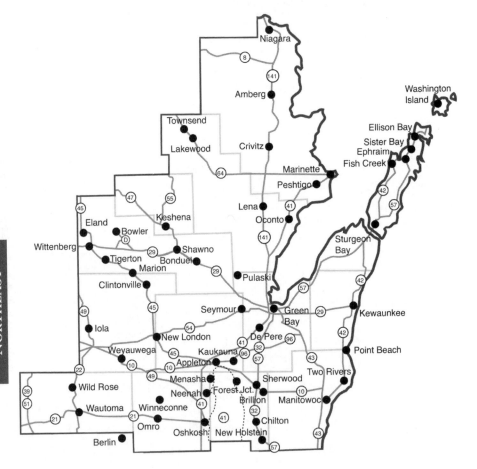

Northeast

Amberg

It's as hard as a rock, and a great display of granite quarrying history and logging lore.

Amberg Museum
Grant St.
Amberg, WI 54102

Mailing address: P.O. Box 1, Amberg, WI 54102
Phone: (715) 759-5281
Contact: Margaret Mattison or Amberg Community
Association (715) 759-5354
Open: Memorial Day - Labor Day, Saturday and
Sunday, 10am to 4pm.
Admission: Free

Important works: Granite quarrying equipment.

About the museum: The Amberg Museum offers exhibits on granite quarrying, logging, turn-of-the-century domestic life, and needlework. Also on display are photographs and documents.

Appleton

This true community based art facility has a large variety of changing exhibits.

★Appleton Art Center
111 W. College Ave.
Appleton, WI 54911

Phone: (920) 733-4089 [Fax: 920-733-4149]
Email: info@appletonartcenter.org
Website: www.appletonartcenter.org
Contact: Tracey Jenks or Fox Cities Chamber of Commerce and Industry, Inc.
(920) 734-7101
Open: Monday - Wednesday, 9am to 5pm; Thursday and Friday, 9am to 9pm; Saturday,
10am to 4pm.

Important works: Changing exhibitions.

About the museum: The Appleton Art Center was founded in 1960 by a group of thirteen local artists dedicated to the visual arts. Their mission is to promote, teach, and nourish the creation and appreciation of the visual arts through exhibitions, educational programs, and information resources. There are eight to ten exhibitions held annually, as well as special educational exhibitions held each fall and spring. Special events include Art in the Park, Art Aid (a silent art auction and benefit dinner), and an antiques showcase and sale.

Exploration and discovery are the themes at this kids museum. Bring Mom and Dad, too!

★Fox Cities Children's Museum
100 W. College Ave.
Appleton, WI 54911

Phone: (920) 734-3226 [Fax: 920-734-0677]
Contact: Fox Cities Chamber of Commerce and Industry, Inc. (920) 734-7101
Email: contact@kidmuseum.org

Website: www.kidmuseum.org
Open: Tuesday - Friday, 9am to 5pm; Saturday, 10am to 5pm; Sunday, noon to 5pm.
Admission: Yes

Important works: Hands-on, interactive arts and sciences exhibits for all ages.

About the museum: The Fox Cities Children's Museum is a special learning center that encourages children to touch, twist, push, and pull their way into new exploration and discovery. Interaction with exhibits will intrigue, involve, and challenge children, and it will expand their awareness, understanding, and enjoyment of the world in which they live. Programs, games, workshops, and demonstrations integrate the arts, sciences, humanities, and technology in ways that are designed to both entertain and educate the young . . . and the young at heart.

Well lit. Come see one of the first electrified homes in America; it's truly illuminating! It sheds light on local history and technology.

★Hearthstone Historic House Museum
625 W. Prospect Ave.
Appleton, WI 54911

Phone: (920) 730-8204 [Fax: 920-730-8266]
Contact: Christine Cross, Executive Director or Fox Cities Chamber of Commerce and Industry, Inc. (920) 734-7101
Email: hearthstonemuseum@athenet.net
Website: www.focol.org/hearthstone
Open: Tuesday - Friday, 10am to 4pm; Saturday, 11am to 4pm. Last tours begin at 3:30pm. Closed last two weeks of January and first two weeks of February.
Admission: Yes

Important works: Original Edison light fixtures, fine woodwork, stained glass windows.

About the museum: Hearthstone's distinction is that it is the first residence in the world to be electrically lighted from an Edison central hydroelectric station. This occurred September 30, 1882. Designed as an architectural showplace, Hearthstone was built between 1881 and 1882 for Henry J. Rogers, a prominent Appleton businessman. The Queen Anne-style building with Eastlake characteristics was designed by William Waters, a leading Wisconsin architect in the late 19th and early 20th centuries. The mansion was purchased in December, 1986 by a group of concerned citizens who feared it was headed for demolition. In 1988, it opened for regular public tours, and since then much of the home has been restored to its original appearance, portraying a home typical of the dawn of the electrical age. Rare, original Thomas Edison light fixtures and period electroliers are still working today. Intricate interior woodwork hand-carved from native Wisconsin woods, nine fireplaces surrounded by imported Minton tiles, exquisite stained glass windows, and restored ceiling decorations add to the elegance of this mansion.

NORTHEAST

Fascinating Facts

Old Abe was the eagle for the Eighth Wisconsin Regiment that took its name from a tame bald eagle which the Unit carried in the Civil War. During the battle the bird would perch on a cannon or fly overhead. The current Old Abe, which is found in the State Assembly room, is actually another bald eagle that has been stuffed and put on display.

A mysterious old Masonic lodge houses the magical Houdini museum where history is on display. See it before it disappears.

★★Houdini Historical Center and Outagamie Museum
330 E. College Ave.
Appleton, WI 54911

Phone: (920) 733-8445
Contact: Fox Cities Chamber of Commerce and Industry, Inc. (920) 734-7101
Website: www.foxvalleyhistory.org/houdini/
Open: Year-round: Tuesday - Saturday, 10am to 4pm; Sunday, noon to 4pm.
Also June, July, and August: Monday, 10am to 4pm.
Admission: Yes

Important works: Magician's equipment, Houdini documents, photos, and memorabilia.

About the museums: The Houdini Historical Center and Outagamie Museum are housed in a Norman Revival-style 1924 Masonic Temple in downtown Appleton. Over sixty years after his death, Harry Houdini continues to fascinate people of all ages. He is the most famous of the world's magicians, past or present, and was perhaps the most successful vaudeville performer of all time. Experience the magical world of Houdini through a unique collection of his personal memorabilia. This includes personal photographs, documents, posters, handbills, handcuffs, leg irons, and lock picks. Among the most prized items are Houdini's earliest known performance contract and the Guiteau handcuffs, which held President Garfield's assassin and from which Houdini escaped. The Center's permanent exhibit features over 120 artifacts and 150 photographic images arranged into the most complete interpretation of Houdini's life ever compiled.

The Outagamie Museum currently houses two long-term exhibits, as well as changing exhibits. The exhibit "Tools of Change" details the changes in people's daily work in the Lower Fox River Valley, and explores how these changes relate to tools, traditions, and values of our ancestors. Exhibit highlights include the country's oldest surviving streetcar motor from 1886, an 1890s mail delivery sled, a 1930s bulletproof bank, the first model dial telephone, and a 1941 doctor's office. Kids (and adventurous adults) can try "History by the Seat of Your Pants," a series of historic seats that includes a milking stool, a Model-T Ford car, and more. The museum's lower level also features a working 19th century reproduction paper shop.

Don't miss the Frank Lloyd Wright inspired visitors center. It's a showcase for Wisconsin plants of all varieties, and a paradise for the plant lover!

★Memorial Park Arboretum and Gardens
1313 Witzke Blvd
Appleton, WI 54911

Phone: (920) 993-1900 [Fax: 920-993-9492]
Contact: Fox Cities Chamber of Commerce and Industry, Inc. (920) 734-7101
Email: info@memorialparkarb.org
Website: www.the-arb.org
Open: Call for days and times

About the gardens: Memorial Park Arboretum and Gardens is designed to foster harmony with nature by developing an understanding of the rich and varied assortment of plants grown in Wisconsin and their role in the environment. A variety of trees and shrubs are displayed in the arboretum, and the gardens offer changing patterns of natural beauty throughout the year. The thirty-three-acre site will eventually recreate or represent all of the plant communities that are native to Wisconsin in order to showcase these ecosystems for generations that may not be familiar with them.

NORTHEAST

Learn all about the history of paper and how the Fox River Cities have played such an important part in its development. History all wrapped up in one site.

★Paper Discovery Center
Come explore the world of paper!
425 W. Water Street
Appleton, WI 54911

Phone: (920) 380-7491
Contact: Daniel Waselchuk, Carrie Feld
Web site: www.paperdiscoverycenter.org
Email: carrie@paperdiscoverycenter.org
Admission: yes
Open:Tuesday – Saturday 10:00 a.m. – 4:00 p.m. Sunday Noon – 4:00 p.m. Closed Mondays. The Paper Discovery Center is closed on these holidays: Christmas Eve, Christmas Day, New Year's Eve, New Year's Day, Easter, Memorial Day, July 4th, Labor Day, Thanksgiving Day.

The Paper Discovery Center invites you to explore the world of paper through a study of science & technology with a look at its past, its future, and the role paper plays in all facets of our lives. Come explore the world of paper! To schedule your visit or to learn more details. Ask for for a Field Trip brochure. The Paper Discovery Center, is located on the banks of the Fox River near downtown Appleton.

In addition to the Paper Discovery Center don't forget to visit the International Paper Hall of Fame. 101 W. Edison, Appleton, Wi. in the old historic Atlas Mill. Proudly displayed on the walls are portraits of the men and women who created the paper industry as we know it today.

What a treasure! Fabulous permanent art collection and interesting temporary exhibits.

★Wriston Art Center — Lawrence University
613 E. College Ave.
Appleton, WI 54911

Mailing address: P.O. Box 599, Appleton, WI 54912
Phone: (920) 832-6621 [Fax: 920-832-7362]
Contact: Fox Cities Chamber of Commerce and Industry, Inc. (920) 734-7101
Website: www.lawrence.edu/news/wriston
Open: Tuesday - Friday, 10am to 4pm; Saturday - Sunday, noon to 4pm.

Important works: Changing exhibits of local, state, and national artists.

About the museum: The Wriston Art Center fulfills the dreams of its namesake. It surrounds students, visitors, and passersby with works of artistic merit. Its galleries sponsor five or six major exhibitions during the academic year. The upper level, devoted to art history and exhibitions, includes a 150-seat auditorium and a serpentine gallery for the display of temporary exhibits and student work. The first floor features the Leech Gallery, Hoffmaster Gallery, and Kohler Gallery. The lower level contains the studio complex and gives access to the outdoor amphitheater.

NORTHEAST

Tony's Tips

After visiting the museums in Sheboygan, take a stroll along the river walk for food, drink, and maritime flavor. It's just south of the downtown and east of 8th Street for fish and ships.

Berlin

Not to be confused with Germany - Berlin, WI has lots of wunderkummer in its two museums.

▲ Berlin Historical Society Museum of Local History
▐▐▐▐ 111 South Adams Avenue
Berlin, WI 54923

Phone: (920) 361-2460 or (920) 361-0807
Contact: Lee Erdmann or Jack Wahlers or Berlin Chamber of Commerce (920) 361-3636
Open: Memorial Day to Labor Day, second and fourth Sundays, 1pm to 3pm. Other times welcome by appointment.

Strolling through the museum's displays you will see Nathan Strong's discovery of the Fox River site where he established Strong's Landing, later renamed Berlin. Walk through a general store and millinery shop and sit down to enjoy slides of Berlin as it was in yesteryear in an old-time theater setting.

Odd Fellows love this place as well as Moose and Elk. So will you, even if you are a mason or knight. Let's shake on it.

▲ Museum of Fraternal Studies
▐▐▐▐ Corner of Huron and S. Adams streets
Berlin, WI 54923

Mailing address: P.O. box 251, Berlin, WI 54923
Phone:(920) 361-1274
Contact: Dan Freimark
Email: Cte47593@centurytel.net
Open: by appintment
Admission: Free, donations appreciated.

About the museum: The many fraternal orders that dot Wisconsin were frequently clouded in a shroud of mystery such as secret ceremonies, handshakes and rituals. The many mysteries are now revealed in the new museum of fraternal studies. It tells the story of how these groups promoted membership well-being, and civic pride. Exhibits include material on the Masonic Order, Knights of Pythias, Odd Fellows, as well as the Elks, Moose Lodge and Knights of Columbus. A real eye opener, considering that it was not long ago when even to speak about these groups was forbidden. It's illuminating.

Bonduel

Surrounding communities have gathered their treasures under one roof for all to enjoy.

▲ Bonduel Community Archives
▐▐▐▐ 108 S First St.
Bonduel, WI 54107

Phone: (715) 758-2687
Open: Wednesday and Saturday 9am to 4pm.

About the archives: The Bonduel Community Archives houses pictures, papers, and information on local and family history for an area which includes Advance, Bonduel, Briarton, Cecil, Landstad, Navarino, Zachow, and surrounding areas.

Drive over to this classic car museum!

Doc's Classic Car and Cycle Museum
W2709 State Hwy 29
Bonduel, WI 54107

Phone: (715) 758-9080 [Fax: 715-758-1340]
Email: docshd@mail.tds.net
Website: http://www.docshd.com/custom/museum.htm
Open: Monday and Thursday 9am to 5pm; Tuesday and Wednesday 9am to 6pm; Friday 9am to 8pm; Saturday 9am to 4pm; Sunday 10am to 3pm.
Admission: Free

About the museum: Located inside Doc's Harley Davidson of Shawno Co, Inc, this museum includes muscle cars, classic cars, and motorcycles as well as old automotive-related signs and antiques. There are also potbelly pigs, buffalo, tortoises, and alligators!

Bowler

Native-American history comes alive at this site.

Arvid E. Miller Memorial Library Museum of the Mohican Nation
N8510 Moh He Con Nuck Rd.
Bowler, WI 54416

Phone: (715) 793-4270
Open: Monday through Friday 8am to 4:30pm. Weekends by appointment.

Come learn about Mohican history at these archives for study and research. Displays will enrich the visit as you learn about Mohican life from pre-European times through the tribe's migration to Wisconsin.

Brillion

Technology and history come together at this company museum.

Ariens Company Museum
109 Calumet St.
Brillion, WI 54110

Phone: (920) 756-2141 [Fax: 920-756-3908]
Contact: Brillion Chamber of Commerce (920) 756-2250
Open: Call to schedule an appointment.

About the museum: The Ariens Company Museum, established in 2003, celebrates decades of Ariens history. Take a look at the evolution of technology and innovation, and learn about the family behind the machines.

NORTHEAST

Tony's Tips

After visiting the sites in Manitowoc, stop by Beernsten's for ice cream on 108 North 8th Street near the Maritime Museum. I love their malts! (920) 684-9616

Interior design buffs will love the historic wallpaper collection and antique furnishings at this museum.

▲ Brillion History House and Museum

110 N. Francis St.
Brillion, WI 54110

Mailing address: P.O. Box 35, Brillion, WI 54110
Phone: (920) 756-2301 or (920) 756-3139
Contact: Brillion Chamber of Commerce (920) 756-2250
Open: By appointment only.

Important works: Brillion wallpaper collection, farm and dairy equipment.

About the museum: The house exhibits turn-of-the-century furnishings, and the museum houses a variety of exhibits including part of the world-famous Brillion wallpaper collection, the largest collection of Victorian wallpaper ever found. Samples of the collection are on display in New York and London. The museum also displays farm equipment and dairy exhibits and has an extensive photo collection.

Chilton

Who better than a country veterinarian to collect and preserve historic rural artifacts and enlist the aid of his community in displaying them?

▲ Calumet County Historical Society and Museum

Corner of Irish Rd. and Hwy 57
2 miles south of Chilton

Mailing address: 1704 Eisenhower, New Holstein, WI 53061
Phone: (920) 898-1333 or (920) 849-2084
Contact: Ronald Zarling, President or Chilton Chamber of Commerce (920) 849-4541
Open: June to September, Sundays 1pm to 4pm, or by appointment.

Important works: A smorgasbord of artifacts pertaining to agriculture, the home, and auto.

About the museum: In the mid-1950s, retired veterinarian Dr. Royal Klafonda began to collect antiques and historical artifacts. He displayed them in a barn behind his house. Eventually he named it the Royal Museum and in 1960 helped establish the county historical society. In 1967 a tornado damaged his barn. The collection of household, farming, and dairy artifacts was moved to a 40 x 100 foot building that was built on land donated to the society. In 1974, a retired auto dealer in Chilton put up another building on the property to display a collection of antique automobiles.

Tony's Tips

Wisconsin Police love to give out speeding tickets, especially to Illinois car plates. Don't speed, enjoy the ride, be safe, and if you get stopped say, "yes, sir," and don't forget to wear your seatbelt.

Clintonville

Put it in gear and drive on over to see this four-wheel shrine to early motorized vehicles. Car enthusiasts will love it!

Four Wheel Drive Museum
105 E. 12th St.
Clintonville, WI 54929

Phone: (715) 823-2141
Contact: Rick Goodell or Clintonville Area Chamber of Commerce (715) 823-4606
Open: Memorial Day through Labor Day, Saturday and Sunday, noon to 4pm.

Important works: First four wheel drive vehicle, first snowmobile.

About the museum: The Four Wheel Drive Museum preserves the work of Otto Zachow and Bill Besendich, inventors of the power wheel drive concept. The museum houses seven vehicles dating back to 1907, with photographs covering the period from 1907 through the 1950s. The vehicles on display were once used for military purposes, civilian construction, pleasure driving, and racing. They include the first four-wheel drive vehicle, the first snowmobile, the truck that mobilized the U.S. Army against Poncho Vila in the Spanish American War, and an Indianapolis racecar. The museum itself is a historic landmark; it is the original blacksmith shop where the four-wheel drive concept was created.

Pioneer Park has three historic buildings. Come see them all!

Pioneer Park
32-11th Street
Clintonville, WI 54929

Phone: (715) 823-4606 (Chamber of Commerce)
Open: Memorial Day-Labor Day: Sundays and holidays, 1pm to 4pm and by appointment.
Contact: Clintonville Area Chamber of Commerce (715) 823-4606
Admission: Donations welcome

The Pioneer Park Village contains three historic houses. The Doty-Besserdich House is a unique structure with walls that are fifteen inches thick. The one-room log cabin was built in 1869 and was the home and factory of Ralph Denn, a local barrel maker. The third structure is called the History House. It was built in 1861 and initially housed the first town hall and fire department. The Kuestner family moved it to its present location and made it their home. The main floor has a formal dining room, parlor, kitchen, and bedroom and is furnished with period items. In the adjoining recreated classroom there are examples of the songwriting of the local Clintonville composer, Eben Rexford, who wrote the song "Silver Threads Among the Gold." In addition, a particular novelty for this collection are stones from many important structures and natural history sites around the world, including the Great Wall of China, Yellowstone National Park, and many others.

Crivitz

Antique objects galore fill every nook and cranny in this historic museum.

Crivitz Area Museum
South St., Off of Hwy 141 (Oak and South Sts.)
Crivitz, WI 54114

Mailing address: P.O. Box 776, Crivitz, WI 54114

Phone: (715) 854-3278
Open: June-August: Wednesday - Saturday, noon to 4pm.
Admission: Free, donations appreciated

Important works: Logging camp building and artifacts, plus re-creations of shops, domestic life, and a schoolroom.

About the museum: The Crivitz Area Museum Complex is a place to take a look back through the history of the Crivitz and Marinette County area. Visitors can travel to eras gone by as they visit an old time kitchen, schoolroom, general store, doctor's office, and communications exhibit. Other exhibits include musical instruments, antique tools, and a collection of farm equipment. A wide variety of manuscripts, photographs, and bits and pieces of local history help bring the story to life. On the property is a historic logging era log building with many artifacts of the lumbering industry.

De Pere

A new art building enhances this small but dynamic college art center with three art galleries.

🔺 Baer Gallery and Godschalx Gallery
Bush Art Center
St. Norbert's College
100 Grant street
De Pere, WI 54115-2099

Phone: (920) 403-3370 [Fax: 920-403-4049]
Email: artgalleries@snc.edu
Admission: free
Open: Call for hours

Three art galleries are found within the Bush Art Center. They rotate the college art collection and sponsor temporary exhibits on a variety of topics throughout the academic year. Call for details.

"Tsi? Kalhakta Luntke To Takwa" means "At the Edge of the Forest They Look. It is one of the finest Native American museums anywhere. A beautiful building houses a fascinating and important collection. It is a real destination!

🔺 ★★★Oneida Nation Museum
W892 County Hwy EE
De Pere, WI 54115

Mailing address: P.O. Box 365, Oneida, WI 54155
Phone: (920) 869-2768 or (800) 236-2214 [Fax: 920-869-2959]
Contact: Rita Lara, Director or Green Bay Area Chamber of Commerce (920) 437-8704
Website: www.oneidanation.org/?page_id=63
Open: September-May, Tuesday-Friday, 9am to 5pm; June – August, Tuesday-Saturday, 9am to 5pm. Closed January.
Handicapped accessible.
Admission: Yes

Important works: Oneida Indian artifacts, photos, interpretive displays, and a full-sized longhouse.

About the museum: The Oneida, People of the Standing Stone, came by water, on foot, and in wagons from New York during implementation of the U.S. Government Indian Removal Policy in the 1820s. They brought to this region their unique culture with deeply rooted matrilineal beliefs in their way of life, their arts, and methods of farming and hunting. The Oneida Nation Museum is one of the largest ongoing exhibitions of Oneida history and artifacts in the world, and it is taking steps toward becoming the recognized world center and repository of Oneida heritage. The story of the Oneida unfolds in a series of displays, which explain the worldview, and history of the Oneida people, and then focuses on expressive culture, social change, and cultural continuity. Exhibits allow visitors to feel the texture of objects like baskets, cornhusk dolls, a stone pipe, and moccasins. Visitors can also make sounds with a wooden rattle and water drum. Departure from the building is through an Oneida longhouse fenced by a stockade where the ancient method of lashing tall poles of poplar can be seen close up. Plan enough time for a pleasant stroll down the nature trail and experience the pine woodlands where Oneida people have lived.

Historic De Pere is one of the oldest European settlements in Wisconsin. The museum preserves this history and much more in a beautiful Greek revival house.

White Pillars Museum
403 N. Broadway
De Pere, WI 54115

Phone: (920) 336-3877
Contact: Laurel Towns or Green Bay Area Chamber of Commerce (920) 437-8704
Open: Monday - Friday, noon to 4pm and other times by appointment. Handicapped accessible.
Admission: No

Important works: Local history artifacts, documents from the fur trade era, extensive archives.

About the museum: This Greek Revival building was built in 1836 and became the home of the De Pere Historical Society and its collections in 1973. Documents, papers, photographs, and objects of local historical value provide the key to unlocking the fascinating history of this century-old city. White Pillars, the oldest building in De Pere, first served as an office for the Fox River Hydraulic Company. It then became the first bank in Wisconsin. It was also a storage room for a cabinet shop and undertaker's business, headquarters for the De Pere Advertiser newspaper, and the first meetinghouse of the First Episcopal Church. Some of the artifacts that link De Pere with its past include: religions articles, personal correspondence of Jacques Porlier and other early fur traders, the Eleazar Williams collection, local family genealogies, funeral card collection, newspaper files about De Pere, and early photographs and postcards.

Ellison Bay

If you're in Door County, stop by and use the nature walk. It's a refreshing change.

★Newport State Park Nature Center
475 County Hwy NP
Ellison Bay, WI 54210

Phone: (920) 854-2500 [Fax: 920-854-1914]
Contact: Michelle Hefty
Website: www.dcty.com/newport

Important works: Variety of native wild animals.

NORTHEAST

Newport offers miles of trails for hiking and off-road bicycles. Winter trails are available for cross-country skiing, snowshoeing, skate skiing, and classical skiing. The park has an interpretive center and naturalist program.

Ephraim

Ephraim is a beautiful community and the museums are no exception. Four sites educate the visitor about this historic town.

★Ephraim Foundation — Anderson Barn and Store Museums, Pioneer Schoolhouse and Goodleston Cabin
3060 Anderson Ln.
Ephraim, WI 54211

Mailing address: P.O. Box 165, Ephraim, WI 54211
Phone: (920) 854-9688 [Fax: 920-854-7232]
Contact: Sally Jacobson
Email: efoundation@itol.com
Website: www.ephraim.org
Open: Mid-June through mid-October, noon to 4pm.

Important works: Re-creation of a general store, local history artifacts, one-room schoolhouse, and pioneer cabin.

About the museum: The Ephraim Foundation was formed in 1949 to preserve historic structures in Door County's Village of Ephraim. It currently maintains four museums: The Anderson Store, Anderson Barn, Pioneer Schoolhouse, and Thomas Goodleston Cabin. The Anderson Barn Museum (3060 Anderson Lane) tells of Ephraim's past through photographs, artwork, artifacts, and stories. Featuring a hands-on children's exhibit, "A Year in the Life of Ephraim," it takes visitors through the work and play activities of a century ago. The Anderson Store Museum (10049 Water St.) retains the original appearance of an early 20th century general store, featuring shelves full of merchandise from days gone by. Chat with storekeepers and take home some candy, books on Ephraim history, or historic postcards. The Pioneer Schoolhouse (9998 Moravia St.) was built in 1880 and was the town's one-room school until 1949. It also features an exhibit on historic clothing. The Goodleston Cabin, constructed originally in 1857, was home to the family of Thomas Goodleston and today is furnished to reflect living conditions in the earliest days of Ephraim.

Fish Creek

The Eagle Bluff Lighthouse illuminates local history with lively tour guides and breathtaking vistas.

★Eagle Bluff Lighthouse
Peninsula State Park
Fish Creek, WI 54212

Mailing address: P.O. Box 218, Fish Creek, WI 54212
Phone: (920) 868-3258
Open: Late May through the third week of October. Call for hours.
Admission: Yes, and state park fee or sticker required

Important works: Authentic lighthouse and original furnishings.

About the museum: In 1960, the Door County Historical Society opened the Eagle Bluff lighthouse after careful historical research and restoration. It is one of the country's first lighthouses to be restored and converted to a museum. Descendants of the original light keepers' families assisted with the renovation and were able to provide original artifacts. Enthusiastic tour guides who interpret the Eagle Bluff Lighthouse enjoy telling about the lives of light keepers William and Julia Duclon and the activities of their seven spirited sons. Due to the isolation of their home, the family had to be very self-sufficient. Present day guests often express a sense of envy for the simplicity of the Duclon family life, yet their home was considered palatial in comparison to the one or two-room cabins used by other pioneer families at the time.

Filled with authentic antiques, this Greek revival house is a pleasure to visit, inside and out.

Noble House Historic Museum
Highway 42 and Main Street
Fish Creek, WI 54212

Phone: (920) 868-2091 (Gilbraltar Historical Society)
Open: Tours Tuesday – Sunday, 11am to 4pm.

The Greek revival house was built in 1875 by Alexander Noble. The Noble House is the oldest dwelling in Fish Creek. Alexander was a Scottish immigrant and a blacksmith in the community. In 1865 he settled in Fish Creek and acted as its first postmaster. The Gibraltar Association bought the house in 1995 and has been undertaking its restoration. Call ahead for tour information as well as details about the structure.

Forest Junction

A small, but diverse, collection of local historic artifacts awaits the visitor.

Haese Memorial Village
East of the Milwaukee Road railroad tracks
Forest Junction, WI 54123

Mailing address: P.O. Box 146, Forest Junction, WI 54123
Phone: (920) 989-1322 or (920) 989-1606
Open: By appointment

The collection spans many eras with items coming from many donors who love local history.

NORTHEAST

Fascinating Facts

Wisconsin is a Native American word with a number of meanings. Interpretations range from the gathering of the waters to wild rice country to homeland. The French spelled it, *Ouiconsin* as it is on many of the early French maps. The French explorer Jean Nicolet arrived in what is today Door County in 1634 dressed in a Chinese robe. He thought that he had arrived in China or Japan…*wow*…was he off the map. Obviously, his *Onstar* was off!

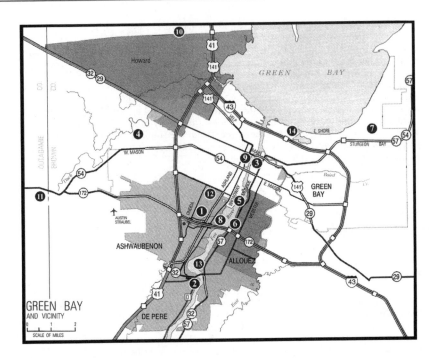

1. Ashwaubenon Historical Society
2. Baer Gallery
3. Children's Museum of Green Bay
4. Green Bay Botanical Gardens
5. Hazelwood Historic House Museum
6. Heritage Hill Historical Park
7. Lawton Gallery
8. National Railroad Museum
9. Neville Public Museum
10. N.E.W. Zoo
11. Onieda Nation of Wisconsin Museum
12. Packer Hall of Fame
13. White Pillars Museum
14. Bay Beach Wildlife Sanctuary

NORTHEAST

Green Bay

This museum has something for everyone, especially during summer heritage day. Call ahead.

Ashwaubenon Historical Cultural Center Museum
737 Cormier Road
Green Bay, WI 54304

Phone: (920) 429-2863
Open: Wednesday and Saturday, 1pm to 4pm and other times by appointment.

About the museum: The Ashwaubenon Historical Society Cultural Center Museum examines activities in Northeast Wisconsin, particularly in the village of Ashwaubenon and the Green Bay metropolitan area. Their exhibit topics include Native American history, WWII artifacts, and scenes from an historic farmhouse (c. 1890) and a schoolhouse (c. 1900). Changing exhibits coincide with planned events, the Summer Heritage Day exhibit, the annual Christmas celebration, and the Summer Heritage Festival. An art gallery, with exhibits of tramp and hobo art, WPA murals, and work by regional artists, is another of the museum's features.

Green Bay pioneer family life is told at this well run house museum.

**★Brown County Historical Society —
Hazelwood Historic House Museum**
1008 S. Monroe Ave.
Green Bay, WI 54301

Mailing address: P.O. Box 1411, Green Bay, WI 54305
Phone: (920) 437-1840 [Fax: 920-455-4518]
Contact: James Emmel
Email: bchs@netnet.net
Website: www.browncohistoricalsoc.org/hazelwood/
Open: May, Saturday and Sunday, 1pm to 4pm. June – August, Monday, Wednesday - Friday, 10am to 2pm; Saturday and Sunday, 1pm to 4pm. December, special days and hours for Christmas.

Important works: Historic house with period furnishings from 1840-1900.

About the museum: Hazelwood, Green Bay's only public historic house still on its 1873 original site overlooking the Fox River, is a fine example of Greek Revival architecture. It was the home of three generations of the Martin family, a political and cultural force in the city and state for a hundred years. This house museum is filled with many original Martin furnishings, works of art, and memorabilia. Its beautiful grounds above the Fox River are an ideal starting place for touring the Astor Historic District. It is also the headquarters of the Brown County Historical Society, historic preservation library, and resource center.

A museum in a mall; what a novel idea! It's where kids can learn while the family shops.

Children's Museum of Green Bay
Washington Commons, 320 N. Adams St.
Green Bay, WI 54305

Phone: (920) 432-4397 [Fax: 920-432-4566]
Email: gbcmuseum@yahoo.com
Website: www.cmuseum.org
Open: Tuesday - Saturday, 10am to 5pm; Sunday, noon to 5pm.

NORTHEAST

Admission: Yes

Important works: Hands-on exhibits for all ages.

About the museum: The Children's Museum of Green Bay, with over 10,000 square feet of exhibits, is designed for two to ten year-olds, but is enjoyed by all ages. Exhibits include: "Dress Me Up and Put on a Show!" where children can dress up in costumes and act out a story; the "S.S. Schierl," a submarine adventure beneath the waters of Lake Michigan; "Safety Street," where kids learn fire safety with a fire truck, fire station, "burning house" and 911 operator; "Kids at Work/Construction Zone," where real building materials can but used to create just about anything; and "Pets are People Too," where participants learn the importance of responsible pet ownership and kindness to animals in an adoption center, veterinary office, and puppet theatre. Set in a historic residential district, Hazelwood is a true Wisconsin historic treasure.

This is the most beautiful and extensive botanical garden in Northeastern Wisconsin. It's perfect for a stroll any day of the year!

★★Green Bay Botanical Garden
2600 Larsen Road
Green Bay, WI 54307

Mailing address: P.O. Box 12644, Green Bay, WI 54307
Phone: (920) 490-9457 [Fax: 920-490-9461]
Email: info@gbbg.org
Website: www.gbbg.org
Open: May 1 - October 31, daily, 9am to 8pm; November 1-April 30, Monday-Friday, 9am to 4pm.
Admission: Yes

About the gardens: Set on forty-seven acres, the garden is designed to provide interest throughout the year with display gardens and natural areas that capture the beauty of Northeastern Wisconsin's four distinct seasons. Outstanding garden architecture sets the stage for an all-star performance by plants specially chosen for their ability to thrive in the upper Midwest.

Plan your visit after the noon Sunday service at Lambeau Field followed by worship at the Hall of Fame shrine. Don't be a couch potato. Be a Packer Backer.

★★★Green Bay Packers Hall of Fame
1265 Lombardi Ave.
Green Bay, WI 54307

Phone: (920) 569-7512
Website: www.packers.com/hall_of_fame
Open: Daily (non-game days), 9am to 6pm.
Admission: Yes

Important works: Green Bay Packers memorabilia and Super Bowl trophies.

About the museum: This is the only sport museum dedicated to a single National Football League team. Its interactive exhibits are designed to entertain and educate all ages on the legendary history of the Green Bay Packers and its famous players and coaches. Among many other sports artifacts and football memorabilia, the Hall of Fame is home to trophies from Packers victories in Super Bowls I, II and XXXI as well as actual championship rings worn by the players. In the hands-on area, visitors can complete a pass, kick a game-winning field goal, or have their picture taken next to life size cutouts of Brett Farve and other Packer favorites. The whole family will love it.

What a breathtaking setting for twenty-five historic structures that display 300 years of Wisconsin history in one stop.

★★★Heritage Hill State Historical Park
2640 S. Webster Ave.
Green Bay, WI 54301

Phone: (920) 448-5150 or (800) 721-5150
Website: www.heritagehillgb.org
Open: Memorial Day - Labor Day, daily. Check for times on guided or self-guided tours.
Admission: Yes

Important works: twenty-five historic buildings with four time periods interpreted.

About the museum: The park boasts twenty-five historic buildings on forty-eight acres of land along the Fox River. Visitors will be transported to the past to explore four time periods of Northeastern Wisconsin's history. Visit La Baye in 1672 and view a Bark Chapel, where French Jesuit missionaries lived and worshiped. Stay to meet the French fur traders at the fur trader's cabin and learn about life and commerce in 1762. Next, travel on to Fort Howard in 1836, the year Wisconsin became a territory, where visitors learn about military life as they talk to officers and soldiers at the Officers' Quarters and Detached Kitchen. The Fort Hospital shows medical knowledge and practices of the time. Visitors can end their tour of the fort by participating in a school lesson at the Schoolhouse.

The third time period is Small Town, 1871. Stroll through town and meet the blacksmith, watch a printing press in action at the DePere News Office or stop by the Baird Law Office. Visitors also see beautiful homes of the period such as Tank Cottage and Beaupre Place. The last stop is the 1905 Belgian Farm. Here visitors learn about life on the farm as well as Green Bay's ethnic heritage. Explore the summer kitchen, which was used in the warm months. Walk through the farmhouse and see how families lived in the early 1900s, and meet the animals at the barn.

Visit this art educational facility geared for university life.

Lawton Gallery (TH331)
University of Wisconsin-Green Bay
2420 Nicolet Drive
Green Bay, WI 54311

Phone: (920) 465-2916
Contact: Stephen Perkins, Curator
Email: perkinss@uwgb.edu
Open: Tuesday-Saturday, 10am to 3pm. Call ahead to confirm times during Fall and Spring semester.
Admission: Free

The Lawton Gallery is the major exhibition facility for the university. It presents a diverse selection of rotating exhibits throughout the academic year and features the work of faculty, students, and art professionals. Time your visit to see their new biennial print show "Refresh."

All aboard! The trains here are fun and the museum overflows with American railroad history.

★★National Railroad Museum
2285 S. Broadway
Green Bay, WI 53404

Phone: (920) 437-7623 [Fax: 920-437-1291]
Email: staff@nationalrrmuseum.org

NORTHEAST

Website: www.nationalrrmuseum.org
Open: Daily, 9am to 5pm. Train Rides: May - September: Departs 10:00am, 11:30am,
1:00pm, 2:30pm, and 4:00pm.
Admission: Yes

Important works: Extensive collection of railroad cars and locomotives, model train,
railroading memorabilia, including the Union Pacific #4017 Big Boy locomotive (the
largest steam locomotive in the world), General Motors Aerotrain (a 1955 futuristic
passenger train) and Gen. Dwight D. Eisenhower's World War II command train.

About the museum: One of the oldest museums of its type in the U.S., the National
Railroad Museum boasts a collection of locomotives and railcars spanning more than a
century of railroading, with over 30,000 artifacts in all. Visitors take a journey through
the technical and historical development of the industry, which built our nation. There
are over seventy locomotive and railcars on display, a railroad video presentation, a 33 x
72-foot HO-scale model railroad exhibit, and an eighty-five-foot observation tower
overlooking the locomotive collection and the Fox River.

*This fabulous facility situated on the Fox River is filled with displays on the history of the
region. Check out the changing exhibits! The famous French colonial period silver Monstrance
is kept on display here. It's one of the most important cultural artifacts in Wisconsin.*

★★Neville Public Museum of Brown County
210 Museum Place
Green Bay, WI 54303

Phone: (920) 448-4460 [Fax: 920-448-4458]
Contact: Marilyn Stasiak, Development/Public Relations Officer
Website: www.co.brown.wi.us/museum/index
Open: Monday, Tuesday, Friday, Saturday, 9am to 5pm; Wednesday and Thursday, 9am
to 8pm; Sunday, noon to 5pm.
Admission: Yes

Important works: Area natural history, Native American artifacts, changing exhibits.

About the museum: As a comprehensive museum, the Neville Public Museum collects
and exhibits in the areas of art, history, and science. Public galleries are located on the
first two floors of the building along with classrooms, a learning center/auditorium, an
educational resource/ orientation room, and gift shop. Educational programs include
interpretive tours for preregistered school groups, gallery talks, workshops, lectures,
classes, demonstrations, and films. The museum's permanent exhibit, On the Edge of the
Inland Sea, is on the second floor. This 7,300 square-foot exhibit leads visitors on a
journey through time from the end of the last Ice Age to the mid-20th century. It utilizes
thousands of artifacts, historic photographs, film, and graphics to describe the natural
history, Native American life, settlement, immigration, industrial development, and daily
life in Northeast Wisconsin. Other galleries are used for semi-permanent and changing
exhibitions that explore the art, history, science, and technology of the people of
Northeast Wisconsin and beyond. Each year, approximately twelve different exhibits can
be seen in the galleries.

*The N.E.W. Zoo is worthy of its name and is a pioneer in the display of animals. In a more
natural setting, similar to their habitants, the expansive setting encourages all sorts of outdoor
activity, from biking to picnics.*

★N.E.W. Zoo

4418 Reforestation Rd.
Green Bay, WI 54313

Mailing address: P.O. Box 23600, Green Bay, WI 54305

Phone: (920) 448-4466
Website: www.co.brown.wi.us/parks/newzoo
Open: April 1 to October 31, daily, 9am to 6pm; November 1 to December 31, daily, 9am to 4pm.
Admission: Yes

Important works: Native and exotic animals in natural settings.

About the museum: The N.E.W. Zoo features a variety of animal species from throughout the world. Exhibits are designed to display animals in natural-style settings characteristic of their native habitats. A special Children's Zoo area is enjoyed by all ages as kids make hands-on discoveries at the animal encounter station, get an up-close look at giant tortoises, or feed the deer, goats, and reindeer. The N.E.W. Zoo is located within the Brown County Reforestation Camp, a 1,560-acre recreation area with hiking, biking, and skiing trails, plus fishing ponds, a playground, picnic areas, and scenic views.

This place is tame compared to some zoos, only wildlife found at this sanctuary.

Wildlife Sanctuary
at Bay Beach
1660 East Shore Drive
Green Bay, WI 54302

Phone: (920) 391-3671
Open: Daily 8am to 4pm all year long
Admission: free
Website: www.green-bay.org
Click on wildlife sanctuary on the Green Bay website

The Wildlife Refuge is set within a well-maintained park at Bay Beach. Several buildings with exhibits explain the ecology of the region, the plant and wildlife, all beautifully arranged and very informative. In addition you can wander amongst the wildlife, see ducks and geese who flock to the area. Bags of corn are available for purchase at the pavilion so you can feed the animals. Best of all its free, and open to the public all year long. In the summers there is a nearby city recreation park that kids and adults can enjoy.

Iola

Track Swiss and Norwegian heritage at this depot museum.

Iola Historical Society Complex
Depot St.
Iola, WI 54945

Mailing address: P.O. Box 111, Iola, WI 54945
Phone: (715) 467-2534 or (715) 445-3445
Contact: Murnell Olson
Email: gomo@gglbbs.com
Website: www.iola.k12.wi.us/iolaHistS/iola_historical_society.htm
Open: Tours by appointment.

Important works: Historic buildings, artifacts from the railroad era and local rural schools.

About the museum: The Iola Historical Society was organized in the early 1950s, nearly 100 years after the first Swiss and Norwegian immigrants moved into the part of

Wisconsin known as the Waupaca Settlement. It began collecting historic buildings in 1979. The Railroad Depot, still in its original location and known as "Station 66," served the village of Iola and surrounding area from 1894 to 1958. It is now a museum for railroad artifacts. Other structures moved to the site include a one-room log house of the type used by immigrants in the 1850s, furnished with 19th century household items. The one-room Country School, built as a reproduction of an area school, contains artifacts from several rural schools in the Iola-Scandinavia area. This new climate-controlled building holds the society's archives of photos, books, and records.

The depot and museum are filled with Iolan treasures; come see for yourself!

▲ Iola Railroad Depot and Museum
Depot Street
Iola, WI 54945

Open: Annual open house in August. Other tours by appointment.

The Iola Railroad Depot and Museum comprises a rural country schoolhouse, which features old books and desks from various Iola country schools, as well as photographs from when the town was young (1860s and 70s). Also featured are items pertaining to the railroad industry, farming and wars, with photos of soldiers. A caboose from the Northern Minnesota Railroad built in 1907 and a log house reconstructed on the site round out the collection.

Kaukauna

Costumed tour guides lead visitors through this "brides" mansion and bring Kaukauna's history alive.

▲ ★Outagamie County Historical Society — Charles A. Grignon Mansion
1313 Augustine St.
Kaukauna, WI 54130

Mailing address: Outagamie Historical Society, 330 E. College Ave., Appleton, WI 54911
Phone: (920) 766-3122 [Fax: 920-766-9834]
Contact: JoEllen Wollangk, Director of Grigon Mansion
Email: ochs@foxvalleyhistory.org
Website: www.foxvalleyhistory.org/mansion.html
Open: Open June –August, Friday, Saturday, and Sunday, noon to 4pm and for group tours year round by appointment.
Admission: Yes

Important works: Fur trade and pioneer era artifacts.

About the museum: In the days before Wisconsin's statehood, the Fox River was an important water highway for travelers and fur traders. The mansion stands at a natural portage point where a trading post was established as early as 1760. Charles A. Grignon, whose family had been active in the fur trade for more than 100 years, took over this post in 1830. In 1837, he built the mansion as a wedding gift for his bride. The Grignon family was familiar to local Native American tribes. The grandson of a Menominee woman, Charles acted as interpreter for the U.S. government at the Treaty of the Cedars, which secured four million acres of land in what is now known as Northeast Wisconsin. Today at the mansion, costumed guides lead tours and tell about the Grignons, their home, and everyday life on the Wisconsin frontier. There are also special events scheduled through the year.

Keshena

Cut your timber and come on over to this logging camp for a cup of history!

Menominee Logging Camp Museum
Hwy 47 and County Trunk VV
Keshena, WI 54135

Phone: (715) 799-5258
Website: http://www.menominee.nsn.us/History/History/HistoryPages/
HistoryLoggingMuseum.htm
Open: Tuesday through Saturday 9am to 3pm; Sunday 11am to 4pm.
Admission: Yes

About the museum: Offers the world's largest collection of artifacts from Wisconsin's logging area. Includes seven log buildings that contain more than 20,000 artifacts. These include saws, musical instruments, axes, gant hooks, and more.

Kewaunee

What was once a county jail now houses rare artifacts and documents including letters from Washington and Lincoln. It's a fascinating local museum. George Washington never slept here.

Kewaunee County Historical Society Museum
613 Dodge St.
Kewaunee, WI 54216

Phone: (920) 388-3858
Contact: Darlene Muellner, Curator or Thomas Schuller
Website: www.rootsweb.com/~wikewaun
Open: Memorial Day through Labor Day, Daily, 12:30pm to 4:30pm. Other times by appointment.

Important works: Jail cell, the Edward Decker collection (including documents signed by Abraham Lincoln), Native American tools, and genealogy records.

About the museum: Built in 1876 as both the sheriff's residence and county jail, this brick building is a rare example of the architecture of William Waters, a prominent Oshkosh architect. It was used as the county jail until 1969. Rooms that once were used as a kitchen and parlor were combined to make a large room to house the Edward Decker Collection. Decker, considered to be the founder of Kewaunee County, came to Wisconsin from Casco, MA in the 1830s. Finding that the area had cheap timberland for sale, he bought enough to begin his own village. During his lifetime, which ended in poverty in 1911, Mr. Decker was involved in establishing three railroads. He was elected to the Wisconsin Senate, served as Kewaunee's first county clerk and during the Civil War served as Adjunct General. Items collected during his worldwide travels include rare masks from Afghanistan, a letter signed by George Washington and land deeds signed by Abraham Lincoln. In addition to the Decker collection, the museum is filled with articles donated by people from the county. One jail cell has been left in its original condition and the rest are used for exhibit space. The upper floor houses an exhibit of Native American tools and woodcarvings.

Tug along and come on board.

Tug Ludington Museum
Kewaunee waterfront
Kewaunee, WI 54216

Phone: 920-388-5000
Contact: City of Kewaunee
Open: Open in the summer
Admission: Yes

Built in 1943 for the U.S. Army the tug served in World War II. In 1947 she was stationed in Kewaunee by the US Corps on Engineers. Since that date the tug has served on construction and maintenance harbors projects throughout the Great lakes. Today it is a museum.

Kiel

A beautiful historic house awaits the visitor in this quaint community.

Kiel Area Historical Society Historic House
227 Fremont Street
Kiel, WI 53042

Phone: (920) 894-2085
Contact: Mrs. Faye Konen, President
Open: Special events and by request. Group tours available.

The house, built about 1907, features two floors decorated in early 20th century style; the basement offers a collection of early tools, early snow blowers, a blacksmith forge, old washing machines and other artifacts.

Lakewood

The bunkhouse, huge saws, and axes are just some of the fascinating items found at this logging museum.

Holt-Balcom Logging Camp Museum
17067 Clubhouse Lane
Lakewood, WI 54138

Phone: (715) 276-7769
Open: July 4-Labor Day, Saturday, 10am to 3pm.

About the museum: Established in 1881, the camp is one of the oldest logging camps in the U.S. A registered National Landmark, the old camp gives a view of how lumberjacks lived and worked until the 1920s.

NORTHEAST

Tony's Tips
Two Rivers has many fine museums, but only one Kurtz's Restaurant. It's well worth the stop for luncheon and dinner! (920) 793-1222

Lena

Though small, this is an authentic log cabin.

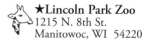**Lena Museum and Log Cabin**
Maple Street
Lena, WI 54139

Phone: (888) 626-6862 (Oconto County Tourism Office) or (920) 829-5242
Open: Summer months: Thursday, 1pm to 4pm.
Admission: Yes

This is a small wooden log cabin that was moved to this site from a nearby farm. It contains historical items related to the history of Lena, including cooking utensils and farming equipment.

Manitowoc

You will see local and exotic animals at this pretty zoo with creatures from around the world. Noah would be envious.

★Lincoln Park Zoo
1215 N. 8th St.
Manitowoc, WI 54220

Mailing address: 930 N. 18th St., Manitowoc, WI 54220
Phone: (920) 683-4685 [Fax: 920-683-4517]
Contact: Joe McLafferty
Open: Memorial Day - Labor Day, Monday – Saturday, 7am to 6pm; Sunday, 9am to 6pm.
Admission: Free

Important works: Native and exotic animals, including bison and snow leopards.

About the museum: The Lincoln Park Zoo is a ten-acre facility within a 100-acre wooded park. From the first animal that was purchased by the Manitowoc Elks Lodge in 1939 (an elk), the zoo has seen a wide variety of species enter its gate. The population fluctuates with the seasons but animals can be seen year-round. The zoo houses bison, white-tailed deer, bald eagle, prairie dogs, cougar, and black bear, plus exotics like snow leopards and African spurred tortoises. The zoo hosts many special events and offers educational programs, including a monthly series to teach visitors about animals from all over the world.

Genealogy is a specialty at this heritage center.

Manitowoc County Historical Society — Heritage Center and Research Library
1701 Michigan Ave.
Manitowoc, WI 54220

Phone: (920) 684-4445 [Fax: 920-684-0573]
Website: www.mchistsoc.org
Open: Tuesday -Friday, 9am to 4pm; Research Library: Tuesday-Friday, 1pm to 4pm, appointment suggested.
Admission: Yes

Important works: Local history artifacts and archives.

About the museum: The Manitowoc County Historical Society, formed in 1906, is one of the oldest societies in Wisconsin. It collects and preserves historical records and artifacts related to Manitowoc County. The Research Library contains the society's archival collection, including books on local and state history as well as manuscripts, maps, and photographs.

After taking the tour you can eat the collection! No 'day olds' here, only fresh history.

★Natural Ovens Farm and Food Museum
4300 County Hwy CR
Manitowoc, WI 54220

Mailing address: P.O. Box 730, Manitowoc, WI 54221
Phone: (920) 758-2500, (800) 558-3535 [Fax: 920-758-2671]
Website: www.naturalovens.com/
Open: Call for days and times. Bakery tours are also available.

Important works: Antique farm tools and tractors, and an heirloom apple orchard.

About the museum: The Farm and Food Museum is located right next to the Natural Ovens Bakery. Stroll the winding path through the beautiful flower garden that connects the bakery with the museum. The museum features antique farm tools and implements and a collection of John Deere tractors. It traces the history of farming and food production in rural Wisconsin. Visitors can take the self-guided tour through nine buildings, including an 1857 log barn, and a small heirloom apple orchard.

You'll love the "Christmas at Pinecrest" event, as well as all the other unique things about this quaint ethnic village!

★Pinecrest Historical Village and Heritage Center Museum
924 Pine Crest Lane
Manitowoc, WI 54220

Mailing address: 1701 Michigan Ave., Manitowoc, WI 54221
Phone: Village: (920) 684-5110 or Heritage Center: (920) 684-4445 [Fax: 920-684-0573]
Contact: Sarah VanLanduyt, Executive Director
Website: www.mchistsoc.org/pinecrest.htm
Open: Pinecrest Historical Village: May-October, 9am to 4pm. Heritage Center: Year round, Tuesday – Friday, 9am to 4pm.
Admission: Yes

Important works: twenty-five historic rural structures, steam locomotive.

About the museum: Step back in time and experience Pinecrest Historical Village, a unique rural village that interprets village and farm life in Manitowoc County from the 1850s to the early 1900s. This sixty-acre outdoor museum of local history features twenty-five historic buildings with period furnishings from Manitowoc County. Authentic Norwegian and Bohemian/German log houses show how immigrant settlers lived more than 125 years ago. There is a one-room school, blacksmith shop, railroad depot (with a locomotive and caboose), country church, and village saloon. A self-guided Nature Trail winds past native trees and shrubs, and interpretive signs provide information on the area's glacial origins, vegetation, and early settlement. Special programs and festivals are held throughout the year. Special monthly events are held May through September, including the German Fest and Fall Harvest Festival. An old-fashioned "Christmas at Pinecrest" is held the first weekend of December.

A wonderful high quality art collection is housed in this Victorian mansion and annex. Don't miss the Georgia O'Keefe!

★★Rahr-West Art Museum
610 N. 8th St.
Manitowoc, WI 54220

Phone: (920) 683-4501
Website: rahrwestartmuseum.org
Open: Monday, Tuesday, Thursday, Friday, 10am to 4pm; Wednesday, 10am to 8pm; Saturday and Sunday, 11am to 4pm.
Admission: Free, donations appreciated.

Important works: 20th century paintings, sculpture, works on paper, and 19th century decorative arts.

About the museum: The Rahr-West Art Museum features changing exhibitions of work by contemporary American artists, as well as a significant permanent collection of 20th century paintings, sculpture, and works on paper. Located in an 1891 Victorian mansion, the museum also holds collections of 19th century paintings and decorative arts.

One of the world's most amazing collections of art, all made by one person! You have to see it to believe it.

★Rudy Rotter Museum of Sculpture
701-705 Buffalo Street
Manitowoc, WI 54220

Contact: Karen Rotter
Phone: (920) 684-8394

This truly amazing collection was produced over forty years and includes over 15,000 sculptures. They range from miniature to life-size and are made of wood, stone, bone, and metal. Call for an appointment to view this unique collection.

You gotta see the submarine and the nautical items in this stunning new facility on the lake. Cruise into the museum and see for yourself.

★★★Wisconsin Maritime Museum
75 Maritime Dr.
Manitowoc, WI 54220

Phone: (920) 684-0218 or (866) 724-2356 [Fax: 920-684-0219]
Website: http://www.wisconsinmaritime.org/
Open: Memorial Day - Labor Day, 9am to 6pm; Labor Day – Memorial Day, 9am to 5pm.
Admission: Yes.

Important works: The U.S.S Cobia, a World War II submarine, shipbuilding and maritime artifacts, model ships collection, children's area.

About the museum: There are over 150 years of Great Lakes maritime history packed into this museum, one of the Midwest's best maritime collections. Visitors can learn about World War II submarines, built in Manitowoc, and other famous Great Lakes sailing ships. They can also see magnificent model ships and look through a real WWII periscope. Two floors of fascinating exhibits are located in the museum's main galleries. Walk the streets of a historic Great Lakes port and relive stories of shipbuilding and commerce. See ship construction methods then and now, and the engines that revolutionized the maritime industry. The gallery of model ships is a special treat for all ages. The precision and detail of these models, of both sail and steam vessels, offer extraordinary examples of old-fashioned shipbuilding on a miniature scale. In a special hands-on children's activity area, kids can relax on a real submarine bunk and talk on sound-powered phones direct from the U.S.S. Hawkbill. Moored adjacent to the museum is the U.S.S. Cobia, a gato-class Navy submarine similar to the twenty-eight submarines built by Manitowoc Shipbuilding during the war. It has been designated a National Historic Landmark and visitors can tour the torpedo room, wardroom, crews quarters, engine room, and more. You can even rent the sub for an overnight stay.

Maribel

Lumber over to this historic mill!

1847 Old Rock Mill Museum
16612 CTH-R
Maribel, WI 54227

Open: Memorial Day through Labor Day with tours on the hour. Sunday 1pm to 4pm, Thursday through Saturday 10am to 4pm. Call for group appointments from May to Memorial Day and Labor Day to October.
Admission: Yes; special group and school rates available

Marinette

If logging history is your love, a visit to this museum is a true affair!

★Marinette County Historical Logging Museum
Stephenson Island
Marinette, WI 54143

Mailing address: P.O. Box 262, Marinette, WI 54143
Phone: (715) 732-0831
Open: Memorial Day through Labor Day, Monday-Friday, 10am to 4:30pm;
Sunday, noon to 4pm.
Admission: Yes

Important works: Replica logging camp, with stable and blacksmith shop.

About the museum: This museum is dedicated to the courageous men who worked the woods from 1856 to 1917, an era when the magnificent pine forests of the north made possible the construction boom that launched some of the largest cities in the Great Lakes states. More than 10,608,230,000 board feet of timber were processed through Marinette and neighboring Menominee, Michigan. A replica of an old logging camp is one of the main attractions at the museum. John B. Mayer of Marinette, a veteran woodsman and riverman, invested approximately 5,000 hours over a six-year period to construct two logging camps, plus a stable and blacksmith shop. All are equipped with the tools of the logging era. Other artifacts and illustrations on logging and its impact on this area are featured. In 1994, the late 1800s Evancheck family log cabin was brought from its original site near Porterfield and reassembled near the museum. Furnishings are typical of the turn-of-the-century.

NORTHEAST

Marion

When given the chance, teenagers can get interested in the past. Bring your teens to see a collection that started as a high school student project. No kidding!

▲ Marion Area Historical Society
620 E. Ramsdell St.
Marion, WI 54950

Mailing address: P.O. Box 321, Marion, WI 54950
Phone: (715) 754-4969 or (715) 754-2118
Contact: Bruce Hofman
Website: http://www.marion.k12.wi.us/
mhs_web_page/site%20Pages/Home/home.htm
Open: May through September, 2 Sundays each
month. Call for days and hours.
Admission: Free

Important works: Reconstructed log cabins, railroad depot, Schoenut Humpty Dumpty Circus toys (mfg. 1910-1915 in Philadelphia), hand tool collection, and railroad memorabilia.

About the museum: It all began with a class on local history at Marion High School in 1987. Ten high school students were given the challenge of creating a videotape on the history of Marion. So much interest was generated in town as students explored Marion's past that area residents experienced a historical renaissance. This led to the creation of the Marion Area Historical Society in November 1988 with almost 100 members, including the ten high school seniors along with their advisor. The students wrote and produced two books on local history, and all sales were donated to the society. Students also designed and maintain a website for the society that offers these and other publications on Marion area history.

The society has been busy creating a history park in Marion. Successful projects include the dismantling, transporting, and reassembly of the two-story Knaack family log cabin, which has been furnished in 1890s style. The local railroad depot was moved from its original location and restored, with exhibit space for railroad artifacts and hand tools. A smaller log cabin was donated and reassembled at the historical site and now is a model of a country school. And high school classes continue to study local history.

Five diverse collections on display for all visitors, including railroads, toys, education, and military history.

▲ Northwestern Railroad Depot Museum and Log Cabins
620 East Ramsdell Street
Marion, WI 54950

Phone: (715) 754-2118 [Fax: 715-754-2651]
Open: May-September, every Saturday, 1pm to 4pm.

About the museum: This historic site includes an original Chicago-Northwestern Depot, a two-story log house built in 1894 and decorated with turn-of-the-century furnishings, and a small log building converted into a one-room school house museum. Exhibits in the depot include railroad furnishings, tools, and wooden toys, including those from the Schoenhut Toy Co. Local memorabilia includes World War I and II items as well as school and business artifacts.

NORTHEAST

Menasha

Offers 3-D shows that stimulate the senses - full color special effects and surround sound have you flying in no time! Gaze into the stars and see your future at this stellar site.

★**Barlow Planetarium**
UW-Fox Valley
1478 Midway Rd.
Menasha, WI 54952

Phone: (920) 832-2848 or (920) 832-2868
Email: barlowplanetarium@uwc.edu
Website: www.fox.uwc.edu/barlow
Open: Shows are forty-five minutes. Call for specific times and to reserve a show.
Admission: Yes
Wheelchair accessible

Offers 3-D shows that stimulate the senses - full color special effects and surround sound have you flying in no time!

Cross on over and see the other side of this bridge museum.

Tayco Street Bridge Museum
Corner of Tayco and Main Sts
Menasha, WI 54952

Phone: (920) 967-5155
Open: May through October from 10am to 7pm.
Important works: historic photos, machinery, and artifacts

About the museum: Explores early use of the Fox River as the main means of navigation for commerce and travel.

Rock on over to this diverse mineralogical site!

Weis Earth Science Museum
University of Wisconsin-Fox Valley
1478 Midway Road
Menasha, WI 54952

Phone: (920) 832-2925 [Fax: 920-832-2664]
Email: jkluesse@uwc.edu
Website: www.uwfoxvalley.uwc.edu
Open: Wednesday and Thursday, noon to 4pm; Friday, noon to 7pm; Saturday, 10am to 5pm; Sunday, 1pm to 5pm. Closed campus holidays.
Admission: Free, donations accepted.

About the museum: The Weis Earth Science Museum is the official State Mineralogical Museum of Wisconsin. This is the only museum dedicated to the geology of Wisconsin and its rich mineral and mining heritage. Interactive and hands-on exhibits, video displays, colorful graphics and specimens of real fossils, minerals, and rocks awaits you. The exciting museum galleries include Geology Basics where you can mobilize continents and create your own quake; A Walk through Geologic Time where you will discover that volcanoes, mountains, oceans, and glaciers were once part of the Wisconsin landscape; Wisconsin's Mining Heritage where you can walk through a 19th century lead mine tunnel and learn how mining gave us our state nickname; the Mineral Gallery where you can marvel at beautiful minerals from around the state and world; and Earth Science and Society where you will learn how important rocks and minerals are to our daily lives. Additional galleries change very few months. There's always something new to see at the Weis.

Neenah

You won't believe it until you see it. Come see the world's largest glass paperweight collection, with over 2,000 stunning examples to hold you down.

★★Bergstrom-Mahler Museum
165 N. Park Ave.
Neenah, WI 54956

Phone: (920) 751-4658 [Fax: 920-751-4755]
Contact: Alex Vance, Director
Email: info@paperweightmuseum.com
Website: www.paperweightmuseum.com
Open: Tuesday-Friday: 10-4:30, Saturday: 9-4:30, Sunday: 1-4:30
Admission: Free

Important works: Extensive collection of glass paperweights, as well as studio art glass.

About the museum: The Bergstrom-Mahler Museum, a historic lakeshore Tudor-style mansion, contains the world's foremost collection of glass paperweights, along with significant Germanic, Victorian, and contemporary studio art glass. By acquiring and preserving nearly 2,000 paperweights, the museum has developed the most comprehensive collection of its kind anywhere. In addition to two permanent collections, there are guest exhibitions that feature contemporary glass, painting, photography, sculpture, and textiles. The museum was the home of John Nelson Bergstrom and his wife Evangeline Hoystradt Bergstrom until it was given to the City of Neenah to be used as a public museum. It also serves as Neenah's community arts center.

Retirement homes have changed a lot in 150 years; come see how Governor Doty spent his sunset years.

Doty Cabin Park — Doty Island
701 Lincoln Street
Neenah, WI 54956

Phone: (920) 751-4614 (Neenah Parks & Recreation Department)
Open: June-August: Daily, noon to 4pm and weekends in May and September.
Admission: Free

The famous Wisconsin pioneer James Duane Doty and his wife Sarah Collin built this log cabin in 1845 as a retirement home. Doty had explored and surveyed the Wisconsin territory and served as Madison's city planner in 1836. President James Tyler appointed him governor of the Wisconsin territory and in 1861 President Abraham Lincoln appointed him superintendent of Indian affairs in the Utah territory. The small log cabin contains memorabilia, photographs, and exhibits about Doty's family, his law office, and other items related to early pioneer life in Wisconsin. The simple structure contains several rooms that are decorated in period furnishings.

This story has eight sides and each one illuminates an aspect of Neenah history.

Neenah Historical Society — Octagon House Museum
336 Main St.
Neenah, WI 54956

NORTHEAST

Mailing address: P.O. Box 343, Neenah, WI 54957
Phone: (920) 729-0244 [Fax: 920-729-7106]
Email: neenahhistoricalsociety@powernetonline.com
Open: By appointment

Important works: Displays include domestic, cultural, and industrial artifacts, plus local history archives.

About the museum: The Octagon House, built around 1852, was the home of Neenah industrialist and banker Hiram Smith. Changing exhibits within the house highlight family, cultural and industrial life in historic Neenah. The society is continually adding to its collection of period furnishings, clothing and artifacts. The site also houses an extensive collection of historic books, maps, photographs, newspaper articles and related publications. The Paper Industry Hall of Fame is also housed at this site.

▲ Velte History Room
City Hall
Neenah, WI 54956

Phone: (920) 751-4614
Open: Call for current hours

Important pieces: tools, dishes, and artifacts of daily life.

About the museum: Learn about the lives of Neenah's early inhabitants, from Native Americans to early European explorers and settlers.

New Holstein

This is a smorgasbord of local history all under one roof.

▲ New Holstein Historical Society — Pioneer Corner Museum
2103 Main Street
New Holstein, WI 53061

Mailing address: P.O. Box 144, New Holstein, WI 53061
Phone: (920) 894-7137
Email: nhref@esls.lib.wi.us
Website: www.geocities.com/nhhistorical
Open: Memorial Day-Labor Day: Sundays, 1pm to 4pm or by appointment.

About the museum: The Pioneer Corner Museum features vintage room displays and a collection of antique artifacts ranging from toys to tools. Highlights include a diorama of old New Holstein, the Lauson (Tecumseh) engine room, the Fenn button collection, Turnverein and Schutzenverein memorabilia, the "Incomparable Hildegarde" display, and much more.

A National Register site for all to enjoy.

▲ The Timm House
1600 Wisconsin Ave.
New Holstein, WI 53061

Phone: (920) 894-7137
Website: http://www.geocities.com/nhhistorical/Timm_House.htm

Open: Closed for renovation until June 2007. Call ahead for details.

About the house: The Timm Family was among the city's early pioneers. Herman C. Timm founded one of the first country grain elevators in the state. The home has earned a place on the National Register for Historic Places and visitors can see rooms and clothing, as they would have appeared in the late 1800s and early 1900s.

New London

The heritage village has many unique historical structures including an octagon house, log cabin, railway depot, triangle school, and village chapel.

★New London Historical Society — Heritage Village
900 Montgomery St. (in Memorial Park)
New London, WI 54961

Mailing address: 101 East Beckert Rd., Apt. 204, New London, WI 54961
Phone: (920) 982-5186 or (920) 982-8557
Contact: Robert Polaske
Website: http://www.newlondonwi.org.hist-society.htm
Open: June - August, first and third Sundays, 1pm to 4pm.
Admission: Donations appreciated.

Important works: Five structures: a log cabin, octagon house, triangle school, train depot, and chapel.

About the museum: Heritage Village is the new home of five historic buildings that have been relocated to this site. The McLaughlin Log Cabin, built around 1850, once housed the McLaughlin family who came from Ireland in 1832. The one story Octagon House, dating from 1867, was considered an architectural feat rather than an oddity. With its eight-sided shape, cupola and fine furnishings, it was quite a showplace in its time. Today the parlor, kitchen, and bedrooms have been furnished in rural, turn-of-the-century style. The Triangle School was built in late 1857 in the Town of Hortonia. It still contains many original furnishings and school pieces including a sand table, clock, and water cooler. The original weather vane and mannequins clothed in vintage attire give the feeling of having just stepped back in time for a day at school. A Chicago & Northwestern Depot is also located in the village. It was built in New London in 1923 and witnessed the last passenger and mail trains that came through town in 1954. Also by the depot is railroad rolling stock. The fifth building is the Village Chapel, which had its first worship services in 1949. The building was originally called the Three Pines School and was located in the Town of Liberty. It has been furnished as a non-denominational chapel set aside for worship and personal meditation. Some entry rooms contain books and other historical collections. Don't forget to visit the nearby diesel locomotive and depot museum with caboose, line care, and box car.

This museum is as good as any you'd find in jolly old London. g'day mate.

New London Public Museum
406 S. Pearl St.
New London, WI 54961

Phone: (920) 982-8520
www.newlondonwi.org/museum
Open: Tuesday, 10am to 8pm; Wednesday through Friday, 10am to 5pm; Saturday, 10am to 1pm.

Important works: Mounted birds and mammals, Indian artifacts, and historic photos.

About the museum: In 1917, amateur naturalist and taxidermist Charles F. Carr gave his collection of mounted birds and animals to the City of New London. At the time, it was considered one of the largest and most complete natural history collections in Wisconsin. Carr's collection, now on display, also contains shells, rocks, guns, war relics, Indian clothing, tools, and many other fascinating items. The museum offers exhibits featuring local natural and cultural history, including an extensive collection of American Indian arrowheads and beadwork. A large photographic display on New London history is popular with museum visitors, as is a series of special exhibits that changes monthly.

Niagara

Near Iron Mountain, Michigan - Niagara, WI (without the falls) has four locations that display local pioneer history. It's on the Wisconsin-Michigan border, not Canada.

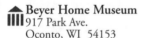
Niagara Historical Museum — Historic Grange Hall
1024 Main Street
Niagara, WI 54151

Historic Grange Hall
Hwy 8
Niagara, WI 54151

Phone: (715) 251-3348

Opening of these facilities is still to be announced, so please call ahead.

Oconto

This museum cures your history hunger. The Victorian house, park, and hall refresh your taste for history.

Beyer Home Museum
917 Park Ave.
Oconto, WI 54153

Mailing address: 4295 County Trunk J, Oconto, WI 54313
Phone: (920) 834-6206
Contact: Peter Stark, President
Open: June 1 - Labor Day: Monday - Saturday, 10am to 4pm; Sunday, noon to 4.
Admission: Yes

Important works: Victorian home furnishings and decor, plus local history exhibits on Native Americans, logging, and early commerce.

About the museum: Preserved in a one-block estate-like setting, the Beyer Home with its carriage house takes visitors back to the 1880s - 1900s. The house was acquired in 1940 for a museum. The George E. Hall Annex was added when space was needed to display items not appropriate to the Beyer Home's Victorian setting. This building contains an "Old Main Street" as well as displays on logging and the prehistoric Native American Copper Culture originally found west of the city.

Omro

What an impressive building; perfect for housing an area heritage collection.

▲ Omro Area Historical Museum
IIII 144 E. Main St.
Omro, WI 54963

Mailing address: P.O. Box 133, Omro, WI 54963
Phone: (920) 685-6123
Open: Memorial Day - Labor Day, Saturdays and Holidays, 10am to 4pm; Sundays, noon to 4pm.

Important works: Local history exhibits, including city jail, and firefighting equipment.

About the museum: The museum is housed in the historic Omro City Hall, built in 1896. The focal point of this Italianate style two-story brick building is a square four-story clock tower with a hipped roof and bracketed eaves. The tower houses a Seth Thomas clock whose bell also once served as the city's fire alarm. The clock still works and is wound by hand every seven days using a metal crank. The first floor of the city hall was used as a fire station and city jail, and city offices were located on the second floor. A fire pumper from 1896 still resides in its original home. Don't miss a visit to the Masonic Lodge Heritage Hall nearby at 160 Main Street.

Oshkosh

Each summer, the EAA Fly-In brings fascinating aircrafts for one of the world's greatest gatherings of aviators. It's a spectacular place. The year-round exhibits are also out of this world! A real must see for any visitors to Wisconsin.

▲ ★★★Experimental Aircraft Association AirVenture Museum, EAA
IIII 3000 Poberezny Rd.
Oshkosh, WI 54901

Mailing address: P.O. Box 3086, Oshkosh, WI 54903
Phone: (920) 426-4848 [Fax: 920-426-6765]
Contact: Adam Smith, Museum Director
Email: museum@eaa.org
Website: www.eaa.org
Open: Monday - Saturday, 8:30am to 5pm; Sunday, 10am to 5pm.
Admission: Yes

Important works: Over ninety airplanes on display, including replicas of the Voyager and Spirit of St. Louis, and an exhibit of working airplane propellers of all sizes.

About the museum: The EAA AirVenture Museum is a gathering place for aviation enthusiasts from around the world. There are more than ninety airplanes on display, from the earliest days of powered flight into the jet age. Additional aircraft are brought in temporarily throughout the year, allowing new restorations or significant aircraft to be displayed. Sections of the museum feature antique and classic airplanes, air racing aircraft, aerobatic airplanes, homebuilt airplanes, and vintage planes from World War II. The majority of these airplanes are still airworthy, though most have been preserved to prevent deterioration. Major exhibits include the Johnson Wax Carnauba Exhibit, commemorating a 1930s journey into the uncharted Amazon in search of carnauba palms to be used for wax, and the Lindbergh Exhibit, honoring Charles Lindbergh and his historic 1927 flight across the Atlantic. A diorama featuring a Spirit of St. Louis replica as it appeared above the 1927 Paris skyline is the exhibit's centerpiece. The Air Racing Gallery features several competitive aircraft banking around a pylon as they would have during a race in the 1930s, and the Women With Wings video gallery offers a twenty-foot wall of video monitors that display the achievements of women in the history of flight. Another favorite is the Voyager exhibit, which features a replica of the aircraft that accomplished aviation's "last great first," a non-stop, non-refueled flight around the world in 1986. Don't forget to visit the EAA AirVenture Convention, the world's largest sport aviation convention.

If you love nature and animals you will love the diverse entertainment at this family farm.

Glen Valley Farm
2561 Vinland Rd.
Oshkosh, WI 54901

Phone: (920) 233-7117 or (920) 231-4053
Contact: Lisa Nolte
Website: www.glenvalleyhorsefarm.com
Open: April through October, call for a reservation (minimum of twenty-five people)
Admission: Yes

Raising, training, and showing fine American Saddlebreds. Tours consist of a hayride, mini horse show, and a cookout. You also have the chance to tour the farm and learn its history, as well as learning about the bedding business.

Fun awaits the whole family at this zoo and playground!

Menominee Park, Zoo, and Little Oshkosh Playground
Hazel St. and Merritt Ave.
Oshkosh, WI 54901

Phone: (920) 236- 5080 or (920) 236-5082
Open: Memorial Day through September 9am to 7pm.
Admission: Zoo: Yes, Playground: Free

Enjoy the miniature train, merry-go-round, amusement rides, and paddleboats at the park, get involved with interactive hands-on exhibits at the zoo, and have a blast at one of the largest playgrounds in the nation! The playground features a gigantic "human" head, lighthouse, castle, airplane, swings, tunnels, and more.

Private individuals have organized a museum dedicated to American military history. We salute this veterans museum!

Military Veteran's Museum
501 City Center
Oshkosh, WI 54901

Phone: (920) 426-8615 [Fax: 920-426-1828]
Email: contact@ mvmwisconsin.com
Website: www.mvmwisconsin.com
Open: Monday - Friday, noon to 5pm, group tours available, call ahead to make sure the building will be open.

Important works: Original ship's log of USS California at Pearl Harbor, 1865 New York Herald headline "Lincoln Shot," plus uniforms from the Civil War to the present.

SCHRC

About the museum: The Military Veterans Museum was founded in 1985 by five local veterans from all branches of military service. The museum opened at its current 6,000 square-foot site in 1991 and features displays of military artifacts and memorabilia. Special events include commemorations of Pearl Harbor, VE Day, VJ Day, Wisconsin's Sesquicentennial in 1998, and the Korean War. The Speakers Bureau reinforces the mission statement "to educate youth and adults concerning the role of the citizen soldier in the wars fought by the United States." Speakers address schools, colleges, universities, and civic and service organizations on our nation's history from the Civil War to Desert Storm. The museum is staffed, in part, by military veteran volunteers who welcome the opportunity to share their stories and reminisce with other veterans.

Oshkosh has many museums; come see the unique displays at Morgan House.

Morgan House – Winnebego County Historical Society
234 Church Ave.
Oshkosh, WI 54901

Phone: (920) 232-0260
Contact: Orv Hando
Website: www.morganhouse.org
Open: Memorial Day – Labor Day: Sunday, 2pm to 4pm or by appointment. Open for group tours by appointment.

Built in 1884 by John Rogers Morgan, the co-founder of Morgan Lumber Products, this Queen Anne-style home features original woodwork, wallpaper, and fireplaces. The museum, home of the Winnebago County Historical and Archeological Society, also features a complete dollhouse, turn-of-the-century activities, and a collection of Oshkosh memorabilia.

Jesus wasn't born here, but the numerous Nativity sets makes you sure think so. Find Christmas all year long! That's heavenly.

The Nativity Collection
Algoma Boulevard United Methodist Church
1174 Algoma Blvd.
Oshkosh, WI 54901

Phone: (920) 231-2800 [Fax: 920-231-9446]
Email: abumc@WisconsinUMC.org
Website: http://www.wisconsinumc.org/oshkosh-algomablvdumc/page10.html
Open: During regular church hours and September through May Wednesday 8am to 8pm. Call to check current times.
Handicapped accessible

Nearly 1,000 nativity sets are displayed here for visitors to see. See nativity sets created from silver, marshmallows, Popsicle sticks, copper, glass, and more! The collection includes antiques, international pieces, home-crafted pieces as well as those made from famed artists, and collections created by young and old alike.

The Apostles clock, as well as the Native American collection, makes this a wonderful destination all year long. History is always in season.

★★Oshkosh Public Museum
1331 Algoma Blvd.
Oshkosh, WI 54901-2799

Phone: (920) 424-4731 or (920) 424-4730
Contact: Bradley Larson, Director
Email: info@publicmuseum.oshkosh.net

NORTHEAST

Website: www.publicmuseum.oshkosh.net
Open: Tuesday - Saturday, 10am to 4:30pm; Sunday, 1pm to 4:30pm.
Admission: Free

Important works: 1895 Apostles Clock, Tiffany stained glass windows, antique vehicles, scale model of Paine Lumber Company, life-size dioramas, decorative arts, and an extensive regional archives.

About the museum: The rich story of the exploration, settlement, and development of the Lake Winnebago region springs to life at the Oshkosh Public Museum. It is the tale of Native Americans, French explorers and fur traders, Yankee settlers, and immigrants from Germany, Poland, Scandinavia, and other countries. The Wetlands & Waterways exhibit, for example, presents the early story of Oshkosh when it was "Sawdust City," the lumber capital of the world. Life-size dioramas of wild marshlands, Native American culture, the adventurous fur trade era, industry and manufacturing, as well as early duck hunting, are included in this exhibit. The Memories & Dreams exhibit features artifacts and the role they played in people's lives. An 1897 Crestmobile and a rare 1913 Harley-Davidson motorcycle are shown on the sliced-log road next to Grandma's Attic where children of all ages can explore the special things of which memories are made through interactive media.

The museum's most popular object is the famous Apostles Clock. Built in 1895 by German immigrant Mathias Kitz, the clock stands over eight feet tall. It comes to life every hour with hand carved figures and the original Regina music box. The museum, founded in 1924, is located in the historic 1908 Edgar Sawyer home, with an attached modern addition. With interiors by New York's famous Tiffany Studios, the magnificent English-style home was once considered one of Wisconsin's finest residences. The museum archive holds approximately 50,000 historic photographs, plus an extensive variety of maps, letters, diaries, and other documentary materials. The museum hosts a major art fair on the grounds the first Sunday after the 4th of July.

Imagine a world-class art collection housed in an English country mansion surrounded by botanical gardens. It's worth the price of admission!

★★★Paine Art Center and Gardens
1410 Algoma Blvd
Oshkosh, WI 54901

Phone: (920) 235-6903 [Fax: 920-235-6303]
Email: info@thepaine.org
Website: www.thepaine.org
Open: Tuesday – Sunday, 11am to 4pm.
Admission: Yes, children under five free

Important works: Excellent artwork by Rousseau, Homer, Whistler, and Remington. Extensive flower gardens and woody plants.

About the museum: This Tudor Revival-style mansion was designed in the 1920s for Oshkosh lumber baron Nathan Paine and his wife, Jessie Kimberly Paine. Without ever having lived within its walls, the Paines donated the building and its contents as an art center. Since it's opening in 1948, visitors from all over the world have toured the beautiful estate regarded as one of "America's Castles." Discover the elegant rooms that boast hand-carved details and sumptuous furnishings. Exceptional craftsmanship is evident in the intricate molded plaster ceilings, oak balustrade staircase, delicately colored stained glass window, and finely woven oriental rugs. Three galleries offer both permanent and changing exhibitions that delight the senses and lift the spirit. The collection includes works by French Barbizon masters such as Corot and Rousseau, American paintings by Inness and Homer, etchings by Whistler and Durer, and sculpture by Frederic Remington and Helen Farnsworth Mears. To complement the art experience, visitors can wander paths through a prairie and formal gardens, enjoying changing scenery and floral displays, including a garden with a dramatic pergola. In summer, there are lawn concerts, garden demonstrations, art lectures, book discussions, and festive plant sales.

Peshtigo

No matches please! The tragic 1871 fire is commemorated at this provocative museum.

★**Peshtigo Fire Museum**
400 Oconto Ave.
Peshtigo, WI 54157

Phone: (715) 582-3244
Contact: Don Hansen, President
Open: Memorial Day to October 8, Daily, 10am to 4:30pm.

Important works: Fire relics, local history artifacts, and fire victim's cemetery.

About the museum: The museum is housed in the first church built in Peshtigo after the deadly forest fire of October 8, 1871. Its purpose is to commemorate the great fire of 1871 and honor those who lost their lives as well as those who survived and rebuilt the city. Exhibits depict the area's past and contain antiques from 1871 to the present, along with artifacts from the fire itself. The Peshtigo Fire Cemetery at this site has a mass grave where over 350 bodies were buried.

Pulaski

Visit a regional repository for local history found in many forms, including genealogy, family, and farming.

Pulaski Area Historical Society and Museum
129 W. Pulaski St.
Pulaski, WI 54162

Contact: Marian Schroeder (920) 822-5856, or Christopher Jaworski (920) 822-3961

Important works: Local history artifacts and archives.

About the museum: The historical society is dedicated to the preservation of the heritage and traditions of the towns of Pulaski, Angelica, Hofa Park, Pittsfield, Krakow, and Sobieski, located in Brown, Oconto, and Shawano counties. The society receives collections and individual items from the public and makes them available for display at the museum. Local history research is made possible through a collection of genealogies, history books, and VHS and cassette tapes.

NORTHEAST

Tony's Tips

Sturgeon Bay is a great starting point for a visit to the Door County penninsula. Stop by at Perry's Cherry Diner for the fresh cherry pie. It's next to the Fairfield Art Center.

Sayner

Come see the world's first snowmobile! Hit the trails.

★Vilas County Historical Museum
Highway 155, 1 block north of Hwy N
Sayner, WI 54560

Mailing address: P.O. Box 217, Sayner, WI 54560
Phone: (715) 542-3388
Website: www.northern-wisconsin.com/museum/
Open: Memorial Day - mid-October, 10am to 4pm.
Admission: Yes

About the museum: Take a walk into the past through exhibits featuring a pioneer kitchen, clothing from the past 100 years, a 1920s post office, formal parlor, and much more. The library offers pictures of the past and stories of towns, people, and a bygone way of life in the area. Exhibits look at military history, music through the years, toys, logging at the turn-of-the-century, Indian heritage, transportation, and more. Sayner is also home of the snowmobile. This exhibit features an extraordinary collection of snowmobiles, including the original machine built by Carl Eliason in 1924. This is undoubtedly the world's most complete collection of Eliason-built snowmobiles.

Seymour

Hold the pickles, it's all in the burgers and the bun. This museum is fried fun.
(Note: the Hamburger Hall of Fame is merging with the community museum, stay tuned for developments. Temporarily closed.

★Hamburger Hall of Fame
126 N. Main St.
Seymour, WI 54165

Open: Sundays, noon to 4pm.
Admission: Free

Important works: Hamburger history and memorabilia, including the grill that cooked the world's largest hamburger.

About the museum: In 1885, fifteen year-old Charles Nagreen set up his food stand at the first community fair in Seymour. Recognizing the need for portable food, he flattened the common meatball into a patty and put it between two slices of bread . . . and the hamburger was born. The Hall of Fame has a large collection of memorabilia, artifacts, and records relating to the history of the hamburger. A notable exhibit is the giant "Charlie Grill" which cooked the world's largest hamburger at the 1989 Hamburger Festival. A model of the future Hamburger Hall of Fame is on display, a hamburger-shaped building that will house even more hamburger lore.

See more of history, including bridal gowns, uniforms, and a casket!

Seymour Community Museum
129 Depot St.
Seymour, WI 54165

Phone: (920) 833-2868

Contact: Rita Gosse
Open: Sundays and Holidays, 1pm to 5pm.
Admission: Free

Important works: Local history displays including a bridal room, military room, and funeral room with an 1870s casket.

About the museum: The museum has a school room, library, millinery shop, picture gallery, funeral room displaying an 1870 casket, old country store, bridal and military rooms, and other items relating to Seymour's history.

Model train enthusiasts love this place! Come take a ride with us!

Seymour Model Railroad Museum
209 Depot St.
Seymour, WI 54165

Phone: (920) 833-7002
Contact: David Fairbanks, Club Secretary/Treasurer
Open: First and third Sundays, 1pm to 3pm.
Admission: Free

Important works: Railroad memorabilia and an HO-scale model train layout.

About the museum: The Model Railroad museum houses a collection of railroad artifacts and an extensive HO-scale model train empire. Freelance layout styling and road representation appeal to all visitors, particularly model train buffs. The layout is located in the former Green Bay and Western depot, which was moved across the street and restored.

Shawano

A quaint heritage park only thirty minutes from Green Bay.

Heritage Park Museum
523 North Franklin Street
Shawano, WI 54166

Phone: (715) 726-3536 or 526-3323
Open: June-August: Wednesday, Saturday, and Sunday, 1:30pm to 4:30pm.
Admission: Yes

The Shawano Heritage Park Museum is located on the Sunset Island Peninsula between the Wolf River and Lake Shawano. It is operated by the Shawano County Historical Society and includes a one-room schoolhouse, a log cabin, and an early stone building. Heritage House, which was built in 1870, is a wood log frame home built by Shawano settler John Kast. In the interior there are authentic Victorian furnishings that represent life in the late 1880s.

NORTHEAST

Tony's Tips

Cheeseheads, what are they? They are extruded yellow foam hats that resemble a large piece of cheese cut in a triangular shape. They're worn by Wisconsin fans the world over!

Sherwood

This general store predates the supermarket. Come in and shop for history!

High Cliff General Store — High Cliff State Park
N7630 State Park Road
Sherwood, WI 54169

Mailing address: P.O. Box 1, Sherwood, WI 54169
Phone: (920) 989-1106
Open: Memorial Day-Labor Day: Saturday, Sunday, and holidays, 1pm to 5pm.

The High Cliff General Store Museum shares history of the park in one of the original buildings from Sherwood's past. The park contains artifacts and items from a time when Sherwood was a mining community, along with other historical items. Additionally, visitors can purchase ice cream, candy, and other items while examining the items in the museum.

Sister Bay

This is rural Victorian life at its best and includes house, home, and garden.

Old Anderson House Museum
Highway 57 at Country Ln.
a mile and a half from downtown Sister Bay
Sister Bay, WI 54234

Phone: (920) 854-7680 or for more information (920) 854-9242
Open: June and September, Sunday, 11am to 3pm. July and August, Friday, 11am to 3pm; Saturday, 9am to 2pm; Sunday, 11am to 3pm.
Admission: Yes

This is an unusual site and structure because the house was actually built in Marinette, WI and towed across frozen Green Bay in the winter of 1895. At that time the house became part of a working farm. Since 1994 the house has been undergoing restoration. There are many restored period rooms on the first floor, including the parlor, kitchen, and bedrooms. The grounds contain gardens and pathways, as well as picnic tables for use during your visit. There are various craft demonstrations that take place throughout the summer, so call ahead for details.

Sturgeon Bay

Knock on the door and come on in! Wildlife dioramas enliven this diverse historical collection.

Door County Historical Museum
18 N. 4th Ave.

Sturgeon Bay, WI 54235

Phone: (920) 743-5809
Contact: Maggie Weir or Ann Jenkins
Open: May 1 – October 31, daily, 10am to 4:30pm.

Cherry Picking Scene, Door County, Wis.

Admission: Free, donation requested for larger groups.

Important works: Fire-fighting equipment, Door County seasonal wildlife dioramas.

About the museum: The people of Door County, from the native Indians to the pioneers who later settled here, are honored in educational and imaginative displays. The original Scandinavian-style building, dedicated in 1939, was expanded in 1984 to incorporate the many artifacts that reflect Door County's past. The Pioneer Fire Company is a replica turn-of-the-century fire station. It houses an 1869 horse-drawn water pumper and three other fully restored trucks. Another wing houses exhibits that feature Door County's unique history, along with displays that depict historical scenes typical of any Wisconsin county. A recent addition is the Door County Wildlife Diorama, created by artist and taxidermist Mike Orthober. All four seasons are portrayed along with birds in appropriate seasonal plumage, native plants and animals.

This museum has three sites filled with local nautical history at its finest. Come visit them all!

★Door County Maritime Museum
120 N. Madison Ave.
Sturgeon Bay, WI 54235

Phone: (920) 743-5958 [Fax: 920-743-9483]
Email: info@dcmm.org
Website: www.dcmm.org
Open: Labor Day – Memorial Day, daily, 10am to 5pm. Memorial Day – Labor Day, 9am to 6pm.
Admission: Yes

Important works: Great Lakes shipbuilding artifacts and history, outboard motor collection, submarine periscope, model boats.

About the museum: Sturgeon Bay has had more ship and boat-building activity than any other city on the Great Lakes. Experience the nautical history of the city and Door County in this modern, 20,000 square-foot museum located on Sturgeon Bay's historic waterfront. The Founders Gallery takes visitors from early Native American canoes to the three masted schooners of the 1800s, the World War II shipbuilding boom (including a working periscope), and the huge ore carriers and mine sweepers built after the war. The Peterson Gallery has an extensive collection of outboard motors and exhibits on wooden boat building. Beautifully crafted model boats are featured in the Baumgartner Gallery along with an exhibit on the many lighthouses of Door County. There are also changing exhibits and special seasonal events. The Door County Maritime Museum also has locations in Baileys Harbor, at the Cana Island Lighthouse, and in Gills Rock. The Gills Rock location features exhibits on commercial fishing and the lifesaving stations of Door County.

Housed in an historic structure, this facility is a showcase for modern art in all its forms.

★Fairfield Center for Contemporary Art
242 Michigan St.
Sturgeon Bay, WI 54235

Phone: (920) 746-0001 [Fax: 920-746-0000]
Email:fairfld@doorpi.net
Website: www.fairfieldcenter.org
Open: Monday – Saturday, 10am to 5pm; Sunday, 10am to 3pm.
Admission: Yes

A diverse selection of cultural and educational programs, plus contemporary art displays.

NORTHEAST

Dynamic programming with an emphasis on regional and national contemporary art are just a few of the many benefits of visiting this art center. Don't forget to visit the gift shop. Call ahead to see what's up.

"The Farm" is a great place to teach kids and adults about nature at work. Go ahead and pet the animals!

★The Farm
4285 Hwy 57
Sturgeon Bay, WI 54235

Mailing address: P.O. Box 44, Sturgeon Bay, WI 54234
Phone: (920) 743-6666 [Fax: 920-743-2266]
Email: thetancks@aol.com
Website: www.thefarmindoorcounty.com
Open: Memorial Day through mid-October, Monday - Sunday, 9am to 5pm.
Admission: Yes

Important works: Farm animals in authentic settings, chicks and other baby animals, petting zoo, restored log buildings.

About the museum: The Farm is a living museum of rural America. It is a composite of cultural, agricultural, ecological, recreational, and educational values and experiences packed into an enjoyable adventure for all ages. Visitors can see farm animals at work and play, and watch goats being milked. Every year, The Farm comes alive with new baby animals including goat kids, piglets, lambs, and calves born throughout the season. Chicks hatch every day in the observation incubator and guests may bottle feed the young animals. There are nature trails through a beautiful forest and prairie, and four restored log cabins. The 1856 Bassford cabin reflects the pioneer days with authentic artifacts and furnishings.

Generous donors gave this museum to Sturgeon Bay for everyone to enjoy. You will not be disappointed!

★Miller Art Museum
107 S. 4th Ave.
Sturgeon Bay, WI 54235

Phone: (920) 746-0707 [Fax: 920-746-0865]
Contact: Bonnie Hartmann
Email: bmam@dcwis.com
Website: www.dcl.lib.wi.us/millerartmuseum.htm
Open: Monday, 10am to 8pm; Tuesday - Saturday, 10am to 5pm.
Admission: Free

Important works: Art by 20th century Wisconsin artists, changing exhibits, and work by famed watercolorist Gerhard Miller. WPA murals.

About the museum: Flourishing for over a quarter century, the Miller Art Museum was originally a 1975 gift from Gerhard and Ruth Miller who nurtured a dream and brought a public, non-profit, year-round art institution to Door County. The museum features seven changing exhibitions each year by local, regional, and national/international artists. A permanent collection of over 500 works by 20th century Wisconsin artists is maintained, exhibited, and expanded by gifts and purchases. A special wing is devoted to the work of Gerhard Miller whose imaginary realism and extraordinary talent has delighted art lovers for decades. He continues to create new egg tempera and watercolor paintings annually. Over the years, the museum has presented more than 190 exhibits covering such areas as landscapes, still life, portraits, maritime art, sculpture, children's' book illustrations, woodworking, wearable art, photography, ceramics, holiday theme exhibits, and Australian, Chinese, Japanese, and Hmong artwork. Lectures, programs, and classes are presented regularly to increase understanding and appreciation of art and art history. Popular events on the museum's annual schedule are a four-county juried exhibit and an exhibit of local high school student art.

This is much more than a nature center. It's an exploration into the sands of time and how plants, animals, and people shaped the land.

★Whitefish Dunes State Park Nature Center
3275 Clark Lake Rd.
Sturgeon Bay, WI 54235

Phone: (920) 823-2400 [Fax: 920-823-2640]
Email: kent.harrison@dnr.state.wi.us
Open: Year-round, daily, 8am to 4pm. Fall, winter, spring, check to verify hours.
Admission: Free with state park admission.

Important works: Recreated Indian village, natural history exhibits.

About the museum: The nature center is the place to learn about the natural and cultural history of the park area. Exhibits and interactive displays cover local plants, animals, and geology. Be sure to see the video, "People of the Dunes," to gain an understanding of who lived there and why. Based on archeological digs in the 1990s, a recreated village site is located nearby showing house structures from the Middle and Late Woodland and Oneota cultures.

Tigerton

Four historic structures bring bygone days to life.

Tigerton Area Historical Society Museum
Corner of Swanke St. and Chestnut St.
Tigerton, WI 54486

Mailing address: 235 Cedar St., P.O. Box 3, Tigerton, WI 54486
Phone: (715) 535-2140 or (800) 235-8528 Shawano Chamber of Commerce
Open: June , July, September, third Sundays, 1pm to 4pm, plus Sundays of Memorial Day and Labor Day weekends. Call ahead for times.
Admission: Free

Important works: Four historic buildings with period furnishings, including a bandstand and a town hall with an exhibit on rural democracy.

About the museum: The Tigerton Museum is a complex of historic structures, all clustered in a downtown location. A wood frame building, formerly a Methodist Church, serves as the main museum, which opened to the public in 1976. The Fairbanks Town Hall, built in 1890, was moved to the park in 1995 along with the eighty year-old Morris Farmer's Club bandstand that still hosts summer concerts. A pioneer log cabin was moved from its original location and reassembled at the museum site in 1996. Exhibits include period settings of a schoolroom, parlor, kitchen, bedroom, and laundry. Displays feature toys, clothing, farm equipment and tools, a workshop, and automotive and power equipment. The Town Hall features an exhibit on rural democracy from territory to town.

Two Rivers

One of Mr. Wright's domestic structures that you can actually rent.

🔺 ★Bernard Schwartz House
⏸ Two Rivers

Website: http://theschwartzhouse.com

In 1938 LIFE magazine commissioned Frank Lloyd Wright to design a dream home for an American family of median income. The result was a Usonian house, an enduring model of modest-sized residential architecture. It's available as a rental.

If printing interests you, this is your type of museum. It's moveable.

🔺 ★Hamilton Wood Type and Printing Museum
⏸ 1619 Jefferson St.
Two Rivers, WI 54241

Phone: (920) 794-6272
Contact: James Van Lanen, Coordinator
Email: hwt@woodtype.org
Website: www.woodtype.org
Open: Monday - Saturday, 9am to 5pm; Sunday, 1pm to 5pm.
Admission: Free

Important works: Complete factory of working historic equipment used to produce wooden type for printing.

About the museum: This is the only wood type museum in the world, preserving the unique story of the Hamilton Manufacturing Company and its role in the printing industry. The Hamilton Company began producing type in 1880 and within twenty years became the largest provider in the United States. The museum is singular in its importance, containing all of James Edward Hamilton's original machinery, operable equipment, type, patterns, and historical memorabilia. The factory setting includes vintage machinery and original patterns for manufacturing multi-lingual wood type. Some of the old equipment still works and is operated to show visitors how wood type was mass-produced. This museum is a unique educational experience that attracts wood type collectors, graphic artists, and lovers of printing nostalgia and wood products.

Visit the Atomic Age in Two Rivers, Power to the People.

🔺 Point Beach Energy Center
⏸ 6400 Nuclear Rd.
Two Rivers, WI

Phone: (920) 755-6400
Open: Tuesday-Saturday 9:30am to 4 pm. Closed Sunday-Monday
Open to the public as well as groups.
Admission: free

Located 7 miles north of Two Rivers off Hwy 42 is the Point Beach Nuclear Power Plant that provides light and electricity for the region. There's a nice visitors center associated with the plant that explains fusion, fission, and nuclear fuel. Splitting the atom is their expertise. Hands-on exhibits and audio-visual presentations enliven the tour. The thorough explanations about nuclear power and how it fits into today's modern world is illuminating. You feel energized after the visit. The Energy Center radiates with light.

Climb aboard the "Buddy O" fishing tug for a nautical adventure into Great Lake fishing history.

⌂ Roger's Street Fishing Village and Great Lakes Coast Guard Museum
2010 Rogers St.
Two Rivers, WI 54241

Phone: (920) 793-5905
Website: www.rogersstreet.com
Open: May through mid-October, 10am to 4pm or by appointment.
Admission: Yes

Important works: forty-foot fishing boat, harbor lighthouse, historic fishing buildings, and artifacts.

About the museum: This museum village and heritage park is located on the banks of the East Twin River, the traditional headquarters of the Two Rivers' commercial fishing fleet. Four historic buildings contain informative exhibits on one of America's most dangerous professions . . . commercial fishing. Visitors can step aboard the 1936 wooden fishing tug "Buddy O," explore the fishing sheds, see the antique Kahlenberg Marine Oil Engine started up, hear the whistles and horns, and climb up the 1886 Two Rivers' North Pier Lighthouse for a bird's eye view of the Fishing Village. The Great Lakes Coast Guard Exhibit, SHIPWRECKS!, features artifacts rescued from the depths of Lake Michigan's most famous shipwrecks such as the "Vernon," which sank in 1887, and the "Rouse Simmons," the legendary Christmas tree ship lost with all hands during a furious storm November 23, 1912.

Three sites, one institution. See the historic ballroom murals, the ever-changing community room, and have an ice cream sundae. Plan to spend the day! There's lots to do.

⌂ ★★Two Rivers History Museum and Historic Washington House
1810 and 1622 Jefferson St.
Two Rivers, WI 54241

Phone: Museum: (920) 793-1103 or Washington House: (920) 793-2490
Contact: Walter Vogl
Open: Museum: Daily, 10am to 4pm. Washington House: Daily; May - October, daily, 9am to 9pm; November - April, 9am to 5pm.
Admission: Free, donation appreciated

Important works: Music and sports memorabilia, ice cream parlor, and local history artifacts.

About the museum: The Two Rivers History Museum (1810 Jefferson St.) is located in St. Luke's Convent, former home of the Sisters of St. Agnes from 1903-1993. The building's community room features changing displays that reflect the art and culture of Two Rivers. The music room has instruments and a collection of antique sheet music. The sports room features an extensive collection of Two Rivers and area sports memorabilia, including the Green Bay Packers. Displays in other rooms include a one-room school, a 1930s art deco room, and Boy and Girl Scout history. Several denominations in the city have displayed religious articles related to the history of their parishes and churches.

The Historic Washington House (1622 Jefferson St.), built in 1850, was once an immigrant hotel and now has six rooms displaying local history and artifacts. Visitors can operate the player piano and sing songs in the old saloon. It was in this house that Ed Berners invented the ice cream sundae in 1881. Today, a replica of his ice cream parlor offers eighteen different sundae flavors. Other exhibits feature an extensive collection of memorabilia from local breweries and rare, early American murals. The ballroom murals were conserved in the 1990s. A second floor ballroom is used for plays, musical performances, silent movies, and other cultural events, as in past years. Original hotel rooms house dental and physician's offices, barbershop, and an 1890 hotel room.

NORTHEAST

Washington Island

A taste of old Washington Island is only a ferry-ride away from the tip of Door County.

Jacobsen's Museum
Washington Island, WI 54246

Phone: (920) 847-2213
Contact: Washington Island Town Office (920) 847-2522
Open: Memorial Day - Columbus Day weekend, daily, 10am to 4pm.

Important works: Local history artifacts, Danish scrollwork, fossils, rocks, and Native American objects from the area.

About the museum: Jacobsen's Museum was founded in 1931 by Danish-born Jens Jacobsen, one of Washington Island's most revered pioneers. Jens came to the U.S. in 1881 from Als Island in Denmark and was sixty-four years old when he built the museum on his lake property. His purpose was to display and share his many collections of native fossils, rocks, and Native American artifacts. One of these artifacts is an unusual map stone. Also on display are many items that Jens himself created depicting history on Washington Island and the surrounding area. This local history can be relived through his artwork, which includes intricate Danish scrollwork, ship models, sketches, and poems. After Jacobsen's death in 1952, his family gave the museum to the people of Washington Island. Additional antiques and artifacts portraying early island life have been donated by gracious islanders, enhancing the original collection.

Waupaca

A lakeside home filled with authentic treasures. What more could you ask for on a summer day?

Hutchinson House Museum — Holly History and Genealogy Center
321 S. Main Street at South Park
Waupaca, WI 54981

Phone: (715) 256-9980
Contact: Waupaca Area Chamber of Commerce (715) 258-7343
Open: Hutchinson House: Memorial Day-Labor Day: Saturday, Sunday, and legal holidays, 1pm to 4pm. Genealogy Center: Wednesday and Friday, noon to 3pm (Sept-May), noon to 4pm (June-Aug); Saturday, 9am to noon. Open for Fall-O-Rama third Saturday in September. Group tours by appointment
Admission: Yes

The Hutchinson House is located overlooking Shadow Lake on the edge of South Park. The structure was built in 1864 and is a fine example of New England Federal architecture. The house was moved from its original location to South Park in 1956. In the summers the grounds are beautifully maintained with gardens or perennials as well as native plants. Costumed guides assist the visitor on their tour through the museum house.

Wisconsin Veterans Museum/Home
located in the Marden Center at the Wisconsin Veterans Home
Hwy QQ (King)
Waupaca, WI 54981

Phone: (715) 258-5586
Open: Daily, 9am to 4pm, 7 days per week.
Collection includes war relics from the first and second World Wars. Photos and uniforms as well as other interesting items for the visitor.

Wautoma

The war room will pique the interest of any visitor. Don't end up in the jail!

Waushara County Historical Society – Jail Museum
221 S. Saint Marie St.
Wautoma, WI 54982

Mailing address: PO Box 616, Wautoma, WI 54982
Phone: (920) 787-3034 or (920) 787-3158
Open: Memorial Day - Labor Day, Wednesdays and Saturdays, 1pm to 4pm. Also open noon to 4pm on Wednesday throughout the winter months.
Admission: Free

Important works: County Jail cell, sheriff's office, guns, and other war memorabilia.

About the museum: Take a step back in time at the Waushara County Historical Society Museum, located in the old Waushara County Jail. The museum is a spacious home for a growing collection of documents, artifacts, and photographs pertaining to Waushara County history. Visitors can see the old jail cell with its original furniture and fixtures, and the sheriff's office with his papers and supplies. The War Room is packed with priceless objects from the Civil, Spanish-American, and World Wars, including a collection of authentic guns and other memorabilia that honor the local men who fought for our country. Other exhibits show antique furniture, clothing, tools, and many local artifacts donated by county residents

Weyauwega

Noah would have liked this place. So will you!

★Animal Haven Zoo and Sanctuary
N1720 Buchholtz Rd.
Weyauwega, WI 54983

Phone: (920) 867-3707
Website: www.visitwaupaca.com/go2animalhavenzoo.html
Open: May 1 - September 30, daily, 10am to 7pm.
Admission: Yes

Important works: Exotic and native animals.

About the museum: This facility includes a wide variety of animals on thirty scenic acres. This is a "Walk Through Zoo" featuring over 100 different species ranging from small chickens to an 800-pound tiger. Some of the animals on display include zebra, camel, bear, lion, cougar, spotted leopard, llama, ponies, wallaby, miniature goats and donkeys, ostrich, emu, and swans. Visitors can feed some of the animals.

Since 1861 people have been learning at this school. Stop by for a lesson in local history!

▲ Little Red Schoolhouse
||| Weyauwega Park
Weyauwega, WI 54983

Mailing address: N2197 River Rd., Weyauwega, WI 54983
Phone: (920) 867-4381
Contact: Suzanne Dyer
Open: By appointment.

Important works: One-room schoolhouse books, desks, and memorabilia.

About the museum: An authentic one-room schoolhouse was moved to Weyauwega's city park and now houses many items related to rural schools, including a large collection of vintage schoolbooks. The floorboards in the entryway and first row of desks are original. The schoolhouse, built in 1861 and originally known as the Baxter School, is the third oldest in Wisconsin. A collection of local memorabilia has grown over the years and is displayed throughout the building.

Wild Rose

Roses are red, violets are blue, this museum's a treasure, and the visitors, too!

▲ Wild Rose Historical Society — Pioneer Museum
||| 479 Main St.
Wild Rose, WI 54984

Mailing address: Wild Rose Historical Society, P.O. Box 63, Wild Rose, WI 54984
Phone: (920) 833-2782
Contact: Pamela Anderson
Website: http://www.1wisconsin.com/wildrose/Museum/museum.htm
Open: June - Labor Day, Wednesday and Saturday, 1pm to 4pm. Last tour starts at 3pm.
Admission: Yes

Important works: Historic buildings with period furnishings and local history artifacts.

About the museum: This cluster of historic structures occupies a prominent place in the town's business district. The charming white frame Elisha Stewart House, built in 1884, is furnished with period artifacts, including a pump organ and original Stewart family photographs. Pioneer Hall, an old bank building, is located next door and features antique dolls, old photographs, and newspaper clippings that tell the story of this once bustling little town. Other buildings include the 1894 Progressive Schoolhouse, carriage house containing a milk wagon and horse-drawn sleigh, smoke house, barn, and blacksmith shop.

Winneconne

Over 500 dolls greet you at the museum and doll cottage.

▲ ★Winneconne Historical Society Museum, Kay Wilde Doll Cottage, and
||| Steamboat House
W. Main St.
Winneconne, WI 54986

NORTHEAST

Phone: Museum (920) 582-4132 or President (920) 582-7643
Contact: Arline Hoenecke
Website: www.winneconne.org/Historical/museum.html
Open: Memorial Day - Labor Day, Sunday, 1:30pm to 4:30pm and by appointment.

Important works: Steam railroading artifacts, county kitchen with wood stove and cistern pump, one-room school memorabilia, and a collection of over 500 antique and contemporary dolls.

About the museum: Explore Winneconne's history by visiting the museum complex composed of the 1871 railroad depot that served the village, a Little House, an 1889 one-room schoolhouse, and the Kay Wilde Doll Cottage. Local history displays in the depot tell the story of the village's beginnings and show artifacts from past Winneconne businesses and organizations. Railroad buffs will find an extensive collection of steam railroading artifacts, railroad lanterns, oilcans, a handcar, and telegraphy equipment. A turn-of-the-century country kitchen in the Little House recalls memories of baking on a wood stove and using a cistern pump for water, in addition to displaying many kitchen utensils from the past. The history of the Winneconne school district is exhibited in the one-room schoolhouse. It features double desks, slate blackboards, wood stoves, an organ, and a collection of children's lunch buckets. The Kay Wilde Doll Cottage houses the doll collection of Kay Wilde of Oshkosh as well as from the historical society's collection. Visitors reminisce about their favorite dolls and learn about the evolution of dolls from antique to contemporary. Over 500 dolls are displayed in theme settings.

Wittenburg

In school we learned about history. Come to Wittenburg and learn about its special historical features.

Wittenberg Area Historical Society
Corner of Vinal and Summit Sts.
Wittenberg, WI 54499

Mailing address: P.O. Box 242, Wittenberg, WI 54499
Phone: (715) 253-3003
Contact: David Jacobson, President or Mario Meverden, Secretary/Treasurer
Open: Memorial Day through Labor Day, Sunday, 1:30pm to 4pm or by appointment.

Important works: Country store exhibit.

About the museum: The Wittenberg Area Historical Society museum is located in the former St. Paul Lutheran Church Parochial School and features displays that provide insight on past ways of life in the area. One of these is a fine collection of photographs from the late nineteenth century through the mid-twentieth century. Others include the original village plat map and exhibits of artifacts from the earliest period of the town's settlement. The popular Country Store exhibit portrays an era a century ago in which country stores truly functioned as community centers.

Northwest

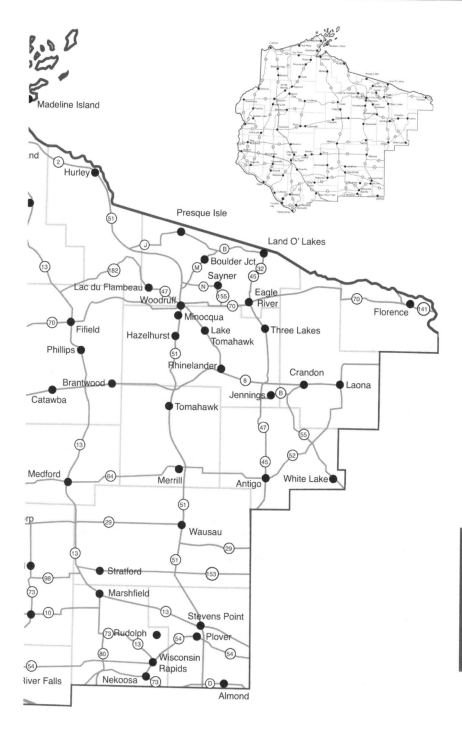

Madeline Island

2 — Hurley

51 — Presque Isle

J — Land O' Lakes

13 — 182 — Lac du Flambeau — 47 — Woodruff

M — Boulder Jct
N — Sayner — 32 — 45
155 — Eagle River
70

70 — Florence — 141

70 — Fifield — Minocqua — Lake Tomahawk — Three Lakes

Hazelhurst

Phillips

51 — Rhinelander — Crandon — Laona

Brantwood — 8 — Jennings — B

Catawba

Tomahawk — 47 — 55

13 — 52 — 45

Medford — 64 — Merrill — Antigo — White Lake

51

rp — 29 — Wausau

29

13 — 51

98 — Stratford — 153

73 — Marshfield

10 — 13 — Stevens Point

73 — Rudolph — 54 — Plover

13

80 — Wisconsin Rapids — 54

54 — Nekoosa — 73
River Falls — D

Almond

NORTHWEST

Alma

Take a memorable step back into local history at this multifaceted museum -. This place has soul and alma!

▲ Alma Historical Society — Alma Area Museum
505 S. Second St.
Alma, WI 54610

Phone: (608) 685-4437
Website: www.almawisconsin.com/local_attractions.htm
Contact: Jane Noll
Open: May – October: Sunday, 1pm to 4pm; Saturday, 1pm to 3pm.

Important works: Doctor's office, logging artifacts, local history memorabilia.

About the museum: The museum houses a wide array of local treasures including Rose Poland's trousseau, Dr. E.A. Meili's office, a detailed logging exhibit, and an original Alma baseball team uniform (complete with cleated shoes) and its 1927 first-place silver cup trophy. The museum also offers a self-guided walking tour brochure for a stroll through Alma's historic district. The Ibach Mansion, Tritsch House, Gallery House and Laue House, are just a few of the stops on the tour.

Almond

Local family history comes alive at this diverse museum. It's history in a nutshell!

▲ Almond Historical Society Museum
Main Street in the Old Bank Building
Almond, WI 54909

Mailing address: Malva Kleist, 319 County A, Almond, WI 54909
Phone: (715) 366-7341
Open: Summer Tuesdays, 1:30pm to 4pm and by request. Open last Saturday in July, 11am to 4pm for Tater Toot.

About the museum: The museum serves as a resource of materials on Almond families with an emphasis on genealogy. The museum's artifacts date back to the Civil War and include an early 20th century dentist's chair, typewriter, adding machine, dishes, clothing, school house artifacts, and farm equipment. There are also displays of early Almond settlers, tracking the early Almond families.

Antigo

This is a true Wisconsin historic treasure. The kids will love it!

▲ Langlade County Historical Society Museum and Deleglise Cabin
404 Superior St.
Antigo, WI 54409

Phone: (715) 627-4464
Contact: Barb MacPhail or Antigo Area Chamber of Commerce (715) 623-4134 or (888) 526-4523

Email: lchs@dwave.net
Website: www.langladehistory.com
Open: Museum: All year, Monday to Friday, 9:30am to 3:30pm; Saturday and Sunday, 10am to 3pm. Deleglise Cabin: May – October, Monday to Friday, 9:30am to 3:30pm, Saturday and Sunday, 10am to 3pm.

Important works: Logging and Indian artifacts, extensive archives, 1878 log cabin.

About the museum: The society was founded in 1905 and was housed in the Antigo Public Library. When the library moved into new quarters in 1997, the museum remained. This outstanding facility houses artifacts from the logging and Indian eras, and early agricultural, woodworking, and lumbering implements. It also contains one of the finest archives in the north woods, with old drawings and photographs of the early days in Langlade County and the city of Antigo. The original 1878 Deleglise Log Cabin is located on the grounds of the museum. It is constructed of hand-hewed native logs and contains pioneer-era furnishings, including some items from the Deleglise household.

Ashland

The Northland's most diverse museum is worthy of a stop! Call ahead for details.

★Ashland Historical Society Museum
509 W. Main St.
Ashland, WI 54806

Phone: (715) 682-4911
Contact: Gloria Lovett or Ashland Area Chamber of Commerce (715) 682-2500 or (800) 284-9484
Email: ashlandhistory@centurytel.net
Website: http://www.ashlandhistory.com/
Open: Monday through Friday, 10am to 4om; other hours by appointment.

About the museum: The Ashland Historical Museum was founded originally by Cora Angvick in 1954. In 2000, the society moved to a new location in downtown Ashland. Features include a wall of fame, early businesses, lifestyles and fashions, dioramas of rail and water transportation, and famous faces of Ashland. Displays change throughout the year and currently include the history of Northland College, history of C.G. Bretting Mfg. Co., and ice harvesting in Chequamegon Bay on Lake Superior.

This is your one-stop kind of place. It will be a memorable adventure to the northland and it's free!

★Northern Great Lakes Visitors Center
29270 County Hwy G (2.5 miles west of Ashland)
Ashland, WI 54806

Phone: Visitors Center: (715) 685-9983 [Fax: 715-685-2680]
History Center and Archives: (715) 685-2649
Contact: Ashland Area Chamber of Commerce (715) 682-2500 or (800) 284-9484
Email: nglbc_mailroom@centurytel.net
Websites: http://www.northerngreatlakescenter.org
Open: Daily, 9am to 5pm.
Admission: Free

Important works: Exhibits on regional history, comprehensive nine-county historical archives and research area.

NORTHWEST

About the museum: Opened in 1998, the center offers state-of-the-art interactive exhibits that show the cultural and natural forces that helped shape the northern region: continental glaciers, the fur trade, Native American culture, mining, lighthouses, Great Lakes shipping, and commercial fishing. Visitors can peek inside an 18th century fur trade post, wander into the head frame of a deep-shaft iron mine where they can push down on a dynamite plunger and hear the rumbling explosion, and listen to Voyageur songs. Temporary, changing exhibits are also featured. Enjoy the view of Lake Superior from the five-story observation tower or take the boardwalk through a cedar wetland.

The History Center and Archives is the northern field office of the Wisconsin Historical Society. An index of its nine-county holdings can be viewed online. The center also is home to several other federal and state offices.

Augusta

Come see an authentic water-powered mill and learn how they ground grain in the 19th century. It wasn't easy!

Dells Mill Museum
E18855 Cty Rd. V
Augusta, WI 54722

Open: May 1 – October 31, 10am to 5pm, daily.
Admission: Yes

Dells Mill is a water-powered museum originating from the 1800s.

Take a carriage ride through time at this museum!

Henning Art Gallery Sleigh and Carriage Museum
E21001 Henning Rd.
Augusta, WI 54722

Phone: (715) 286-2464
Open: By appointment or chance. Call ahead, if possible.

Display includes paintings, antique sleighs, cutters, buggies, and many antiques.

Balsam Lake

Some call it the Smithsonian of the north. It's fifty-seven galleries of history all in one stop!

★★Polk County Museum and Rural School Museum
120 Main St.
Balsam Lake, WI 54810

Mailing address: P.O. Box 41, Balsam Lake, WI 54810
Phone: (715) 483-3979
Contact: Darrell and Rosalie Kittleson or Balsam Lake Community Club (715) 485-3424
Email: radiorey@spacestar.net or darose@centurytel.net
Website: www.co.polk.wi.us/museum
Open: Both museums: Memorial Day weekend through Labor Day, Sunday – Saturday, noon to 4pm.

Admission: Yes

Important works: Native American room with large collection of arrow points, Chief Archie Mosay artifacts, birch bark canoe, and wigwam. Danish heritage artifacts. One-room schoolhouse.

About the museum: The Polk County Museum was opened in 1960 in the Polk County Center Building and in 1976 moved to the Polk County Courthouse. There are fifty-seven galleries on three floors of the 1899 building. Popular exhibits are the ethnic displays that include the Ojibwa Native American room with tools, a wigwam, a birch bark canoe constructed in the 1890s, a chief's feathered headdress, and beadwork. Other ethnic displays include the English, Scottish, Irish, German, Norwegian, Swedish, and the largest Danish display in this part of the country. Other exhibits feature local families, businesses, and organizations, including a 1900s country store and agricultural tools, plus a dining room chair from the home of President Ulysses S. Grant and hanging lamp from the family of President Woodrow Wilson. The Rural Life Museum, located two blocks away in the former Lanesdale School, is used for reenactments of one-room school classrooms. On the fourth Saturdays of June, July, and August, the museum hosts old time musicians, artists, and craftspersons for demonstrations of weaving, soap making, wool spinning, pottery making, and other crafts.

Bayfield

Log on to this heritage center for on-line exhibits where the past meets the present.

★Apostle Islands National Lakeshore Museum
415 Washington Ave.
Bayfield, WI 54814

Phone: (715) 779-3397
Contact: Bayfield Chamber of Commerce (715) 779-3335 or (800) 477-4094 or Bayfield Recreation Business Association (715) 376-2322
Open: Memorial Day – Labor Day: Daily except Mondays, 1pm to 4pm. After Labor Day: Weekends only or by appointment.

Important works: Local history displays, extensive collection of historic photographs.

About the museum: Located in a 19th century cigar factory, the museum displays include an old-fashioned barbershop, telephone switchboard, and exhibits on logging, lumbering, agriculture, and tourism.

Local Great Lakes history comes alive in a beautiful setting. You'll be glad you came.

★Apostle Islands National Lakeshore Visitors Center
415 Washington Ave.
Bayfield, WI 54814

Phone: (715) 779-3397
Contact: Myra Dec or Bayfield Chamber of Commerce (715) 779-3335 or (800) 477-4094 or Bayfield Recreation Business Association (715) 376-2322
Website: www.nps.gov/apis/centers.htm

Important works: Apostle Islands mining, fishing, and cultural history.

About the museum: Located in the old Bayfield County Courthouse, the National Lakeshore Visitor Center is a good place to begin your National Lakeshore visit, whether by car, afoot, or by private boat. Apostle Islands brownstone was used to construct this stately building and to build many other elegant public buildings and residences throughout the Upper Midwest. At the center, visitors can view audiovisual programs and study exhibits about the park's history, natural history, and recreation opportunities.

Thousands of objects bring history alive at this beautiful Bayfield site.

Bayfield Heritage Center
30 N. Broad St.
Bayfield, WI 54814

Mailing address: P.O. Box 137, Bayfield, WI 54814
Phone: (715) 779-5958
Contact: Bayfield Chamber of Commerce (715) 779-3335 or (800) 477-4094 or Bayfield Recreation Business Association (715) 376-2322
Email: info@bayfieldheritage.org
Website: www.bayfieldheritage.org/
Open: Call for hours, open by appointment.

Important works: Sears and Roebuck mahogany pedal organ, barber chair and sink, horse-drawn hearse, plus extensive archives and regional history artifacts.

About the museum: Bayfield Heritage Association was founded in 1974 and is dedicated to promoting awareness, appreciation, and preservation of Bayfield's distinctive history. The association maintains a collection of artifacts and archival materials relating to the history of Bayfield and the Apostle Islands region. The collection focuses on the general themes of settlement, agriculture, logging, lumbering, transportation, and tourism. Archival materials include maps, early city records, photographs, newspapers, brochures, business records, and personal papers. A local history library and research files provide additional resources for research and information. Opened in Summer 2003, the newly built Heritage Center is a community showcase for area history.

If you like fishing, shipwrecks, and boat building, this is a must see.

★Bayfield Maritime Museum
131 First St.
between U.S. Coast Guard Station and City Hall
Bayfield, WI 54814

Mailing address: P.O. Box 1536, Bayfield, WI 54814
Phone: (715) 779-9919 May – early-October, (715) 779-3925 off-season.
Contact: Bayfield Chamber of Commerce (715) 779-3335 or (800) 477-4094 or Bayfield Recreation Business Association (715) 376-2322
Website: www.apostleisland.com/4.htm
Open: Daily, Memorial Day through mid-October. Spring and Fall, 10am to 5pm; July and August, 10am to 7pm.
Admission: Yes

Important works: Lake Superior boats and fishing artifacts.

About the museum: The museum presents 150 years of Bayfield's maritime heritage, featuring hands-on demonstrations, marine equipment, and sailor crafts, plus exhibits on commercial fishing, boatbuilding traditions, lighthouses, and shipwrecks. Special displays honor local fishing families.

NORTHWEST

Get hooked on this turn-of-the-century fishing museum. It's a true great northern.

Hokenson Fishery
Washington Ave.
Bayfield, WI 54814

Phone: (715) 779-3397
Contact: Myra Dec or Bayfield Chamber of Commerce (715) 779-3335 or (800) 477-4094
or Bayfield Recreation Business Association (715) 376-2322
Website: www.nps.gov/apis/hokenson.htm

About the fishery: The rustic buildings and historic artifacts of the Hokenson Fishery at
Little Sand Bay tell the story of a commercial fishery that was operated for more than
thirty years by the Hokenson family. Today, the National Park Service maintains the
fishery complex which includes the Twine Shed, a two story barn-like structure named
for the net building activities it housed, the Pound Net Boat, Ice House, the Dock and
Herring Shed, and the "Twilite," a thirty-eight-foot, diesel-powered fishing tug, typical
of those used throughout the Great Lakes.

Birchwood

From aviation to logging, this museum delights visitors.

Birchwood Area Historical Society — Log Museum and Howard Morey Homestead
Log Museum on Main St., near the Village Hall
Morey Homestead on Park Ave.
Birchwood, WI 54817

Mailing address: P.O. Box 247, Birchwood, WI 54817
Phone: (715) 354-7300
Contact: Arlene Forward or Birchwood Area Lakes Association (715) 354-3771
Open: Log Museum: Memorial Day weekend - Labor Day weekend, Fridays and
Saturdays, 1pm to 4pm, or by appointment. Morey house: by appointment or via the
Log Museum attendant.

Important works: Logging era artifacts, early 20th-century homestead.

About the museum: The Log Museum holds a collection of logging memorabilia as well
as a hand carved replica of a logging camp operation. The Morey house was originally
built in 1901. Howard Morey was an aviation industry pioneer who trained hundreds
of pilots during World War II and played an important role in Wisconsin aviation. One
room of the two-story house gathers Morey memorabilia. The house is restored in the
style of the mid-teens to early-1920s.

Black River Falls

These two exciting historic sites, in two locations, are filled with Black River Falls history.

Jackson County Historical Society Museum and History Room
13 S. First Street and 321 Main Street
Black River Falls, WI 54615

Mailing address: P.O. Box 37, Black River Falls, WI 54615
Phone: (715) 284-5314

Website: www.blackriverfalls.com
Open: Friday & Saturday, 11am to 2pm or by appointment

The museum, at 13 S. First Street, was the gallery belonging to one of the earlier photographers, Charles Van Schaick. The photographs from the widely known book, Wisconsin Death Trip, by Michael Lesy, are from the Van Schaick collection. In addition to the photo collection, there are displays of many artifacts and manuscripts depicting the early history. The museum also has a variety of books that have been compiled about various areas and events in the county.

Bloomer

A patriotic theme celebrates local history.

Bloomer Historical Society Museum
1532 12th Ave.
Bloomer, WI 54724

Phone: (715) 568-3199
Contact: Rodney Jr. Schmidt or Bloomer Chamber of Commerce (715) 568-3339
Open: Memorial Day weekend through Labor Day, Sundays, 2pm to 5pm.

Important works: Historical photographs.

About the museum: Built in celebration of our nations Declaration of Independence, the museum was built through the efforts of the Bloomer Woman's Club. The society's purpose is to collect and store written histories of events, buildings, individuals, and families and to display and provide storage for artifacts of historical interest. The museum houses an unusual collection of amateur photographs and recently added a recorded audio history of Bloomer to its collection.

Boulder Junction

Railroad heritage comes alive in this small, diverse museum. All aboard.

Boulder Junction Area Historical Society — Depot Museum
5370 Park St.
Boulder Junction, WI 54512

Mailing address: 3572 Rockey Reef Ln., Boulder Junction, WI 54512
Phone: (800) 466-8759 [Fax: 715-385-2379]
Contact: Elmer Dahlquist or Boulder Junction Chamber of Commerce (715) 385-2400 or (800) 466-8759
Email: boulderjct@boulderjct.org
Open: Call for hours.
Admission: Free

Important works: Historic railroad depot, railroading artifacts.

About the museum: The Depot Museum occupies the former Milwaukee Road Depot, built in 1903. The historical society relocated and refurbished the structure, and in 2000 it opened as a railroad museum.

Brantwood

Come find a little bit of everything, including an historic sauna!

Knox Creek Heritage Center
N4517 W. Knox Rd.
Brantwood, WI 54513

Mailing address: 4233 W. Knox Rd., Brantwood,
WI 54513
Phone: (715) 564-2525 or (715) 564-2520
Contact: Marcella Braski
Email: mbraski@yahoo.com
Open: Call for appointments and tours.

Important works: Historic buildings, logging era artifacts, school memorabilia.

About the museum: The Center collects, interprets, and preserves the historical, social, cultural, and natural heritage of the area. The original farmhouse, built around 1900, features furniture and accessories that two generations of a family might have accumulated over time. The Keto House also dates from around 1900 and was moved to the farmstead from its original site. The house contains a permanent logging camp display. There is also a collection of desks, books, photographs, and other objects that document the early educational system of the area. The century-old Waahto Sauna, made of hand-hewn logs in typical dovetailed construction, was moved to the site in 1996. In 1998, the Spirit Baptist Church was moved to Knox Creek. Built in 1890, it is used to display artifacts, photographs, and documents that tell the story of early settlers of the area. A hiking/biking/ski trail begins at the center. Don't miss the heritage trail.

Bruce

The written word is a powerful tool for understanding the past. Read all about it in Bruce.

Bruce Area Historical Museum and Genealogical Library
Bruce Newsletter Building - River Avenue
Bruce, WI 54819

Mailing address: P.O. Box 155, Bruce, WI 54819
Phone: (715) 868-5475 or (715) 868-2514
Open: Memorial Day-Labor Day: open Monday – Thursday, 9am to 4pm.

About the museum: The museum's displays change every year and emphasize written histories including area newspapers (dating back to the 19th century), censuses, genealogical files, a photo collection, and plat books. Recent exhibits included a county centennial display.

NORTHWEST

Fascinating Facts

The Wisconsin state constitution states that "Each house of the legislature shall keep a journal of its proceedings and publish the same, except such parts as require secrecy."

Cable

This is a wonderful place for the whole family to explore the diversity of nature.

⌂ Cable Natural History Museum
On County Hwy M, a quarter-mile east of Highway 63

Mailing address: P.O. Box 416, Cable, WI 54821
Phone: (715) 798-3890 [Fax: 715-798-3828]
Contact: Michelle Gostomski or Cable Area Chamber of Commerce (715) 798-3833 or (800) 533-7454
Email: info@cablemuseum.org
Website: www.cablemuseum.org
Open: Year-round, Tuesdays through Saturdays, 10am to 4pm. July and August, Sundays, 11am to 3pm.
Admission: Free.

About the museum: The museum's collections represent the natural history and biological diversity of the upper Midwest. Collections include birds, mammals, fish, insects, reptiles, amphibians, animal skulls and skins, rocks, minerals, casts of animal tracks, bird nests, and more. Museum exhibits include a permanent north woods diorama, a hands-on collections inspection room, and various traveling exhibits. In addition, each year the museum creates a major new exhibit that interprets some notable element of regional natural history. Outdoor resources include the Forest Lodge Nature Trail (an interpretive trail), the Mary Griggs Burke Outdoor Classroom that includes more than 100 species of native plants, and an outdoor Butterfly preserve that attracts a variety of native butterfly species.

Cadott

Come to see a diverse and interesting collection, including a fire truck and antique medical equipment.

⌂ Cadott Area Historical Society and Museum
630 N. Highway 27
Cadott, WI 54727

Mailing address: P.O. Box 1, Cadott, WI 54727
Phone: (715) 289-3867 or (715) 289-3867
Contact: Eugene Harm or Cadott Area Chamber of Commerce (715) 289-3338
Open: Mondays, 9am to 4pm, and by appointment.

Important works: 100 oral histories of local residents, Indian arrowheads, a history and map of the Yellow River, medical equipment.

About the museum: The society was organized in 1986 to preserve and disseminate knowledge of the history of Cadott and surrounding area. The museum's two buildings feature both permanent and temporary exhibits, with themes and materials unique to the Cadott area. Recent exhibits have documented silent movies and barn construction. On permanent display are a wide variety of mementos and artifacts, such as old jewelry, eyeglasses, buttons, gloves, sheet music, instruments, toys, farm tools and machinery, wooden butter churn, band uniforms, and uniforms of World War I and World War II. A fire truck is also on permanent display, along with as is a school exhibit displaying school desks and inkwells. The museum has a collection of photographs of all area residents ninety years or older.

Cameron

Twenty-eight historic buildings are loaded with wondferful artifacts that await the visitor.

★★Barron County Historical Society — Pioneer Village Museum
1870 13-1/2 Ave. (One mile west of Cameron on Hwy W)
Cameron, WI 54822

Phone: (715) 458-2080 or (715) 642-1327
Open: June through Labor Day: Thursday - Sunday, 1pm to 5pm, and by appointment.
Admission: Yes

Important works: Extensive collection of historic buildings, machinery.

About the museum: Go back in time with a stroll through an early pioneer village featuring twenty-eight historic Barron County buildings moved to this museum site. There are five large display buildings and five historic log cabins. Strolling down Pioneer St., visitors will come across an early railroad depot, country school, dentist office, doctor's office, jail, blacksmith shop, newspaper office, library, meetinghouse, general store, post office, the Ebenezer Lutheran Church, and many more authentic structures. Check the website for special weekend events.

Catawba

Jump over to this fun little museum full of local history!

Jump River Valley Museum
W9224 U.S. Hwy 8
Catawba, WI 54515

Phone: (715) 339-2642
Open: Summer: second and fourth Saturdays. For special events and by appointment.

About the museum: The Jump River Valley Museum, a one-story brick building for former Catawba Town Hall, was built in 1920. It displays artifacts covering the period between 1890-1940. Permanent exhibitions explore the history of lumbering in the area, rural schools, and home making. The museum also displays an address machine from Hawkins Telephone Co.

Chippewa Falls

An incredibly diverse collection is housed in a large former convent. Get in the habit of visiting.

★★Chippewa County Historical Society — Area History Center
123 Allen St.
Chippewa Falls, WI 54729

Phone: (715) 723-4399
Contact: James Schumacher, President or Chippewa Falls Area Chamber of Commerce (715) 723-0331
Open: Tuesdays, 9am to 4pm.
Admission: Donation

NORTHWEST

Important works: Extensive archives with photographs, local records, and genealogical data. Relics from the early days of the lumber industry, fur trading, and Native Americans.

About the museum: The History Center is home of the Chippewa County Historical Society and Genealogy Society. The building, which was formerly the Notre Dame Convent, was built in 1883. Adjacent to the center, which has over fifty rooms, is the refurbished Goldsmith Chapel with its beautiful stained glass windows and carved woodwork. Permanent displays at the center include the following rooms: Sea Shell Room, H.S. Allen Room, Victorian Room, Lumberjack Room, and Native American Room. The Historical and Genealogy Library is a center for research featuring local cemetery, probate, and census records. Also found are newspapers, history books, directories, and atlases.

Step back in time to a true Victorian mansion where too much was not enough.

★Chippewa County Historical Society — Cook-Rutledge Mansion

505 W. Grand Ave.
Chippewa Falls, WI 54729

Phone: (715) 723-7181
Contact: Chippewa Falls Area Chamber of Commerce (715) 723-0331
Website: http://www.chippewacounty.com/home/cook_rutledge.html
Open: June - August, Thursday - Sunday, tours at 2 and 3 pm or by appointment.
Admission: Yes. Large group discounts available for twenty-five or more.

About the museum: The mansion is one of the finest examples of high Victorian-Italianate architecture in the Midwest. It was built in 1873 by State Assemblyman James Monroe Bingham who later became Lieutenant Governor. The lavish red brick house is located on a tree-covered lot enclosed by a wrought iron fence. Because of its combination of hand-painted ceilings and walls, ornately carved woodwork, parquet floors, handcrafted silver doorknobs and hinge plates, stained glass windows, crystal chandeliers, and unique fireplaces, it is one of the most unusual historic homes in Wisconsin. The Grand Hall is the focal point of the mansion. It includes a staircase of carved oak and a leaded glass window imported from Europe. The dining room walls are covered with Lincrusta, an embossed version of linoleum, and the linen ceiling is hand painted. The kitchen has been refurbished to include a soapstone sink.

Cray computers were invented here along with many other technological innovations.

★Chippewa Falls Museum of Industry and Technology

21 E. Grand Ave.
Chippewa Falls, WI 54729

Phone: (715) 720-9206
Contact: Yvette Flaten or Chippewa Falls Area Chamber of Commerce (715) 723-0331
Open: Year-round, Tuesday - Friday, 1pm to 5pm; Saturday, 10am to 3pm, and by appointment.
Admission: Yes

Important works: Hands-on exhibits, Cray Supercomputers.

About the museum: The museum interprets the rich, varied history of manufacturing and processing in Chippewa Falls from the 1840s through today, including the beginning of Cray's supercomputers. Featured are local industries and tales of the people

NORTHWEST

who created them. Exhibits include At Work in Chippewa Falls, The Seymour Cray Supercomputer Collection, Nanosecond Knowledge, and Leap into Lakes.

Local Norwegian heritage runs deep at this museum.

Sunny Valley School House Museum and Norwegian Log Home
Bridgewater Ave. & Hwy 124 (in Irvine Park)
Chippewa Falls, WI 54729

Phone: (715) 723-3890
Contact: Chippewa Falls Area Chamber of Commerce (715) 723-0331
Open: Sundays and holidays.

Important works: Historic schoolhouse and log cabin.

About the museum: The Sunny Valley School House was built in 1903. A nearby log cabin is more than 100 years old. These historical buildings are examples of the area's proud heritage.

Clear Lake

Come on a clear day and soak up Clear Lake history.

Clear Lake Historical Museum
Near Hwy 63 in Clear Lake
Clear Lake, WI 54005

Mailing address: 450 5th Avenue, Clear Lake, WI 54005
Phone: (715) 263-3050
Contact: Clear Lake Civic and Commerce Association, mailing address: Box 266, Clear Lake, WI 54005
Contact: Charles T. Clark

The Clear Lake Historical Museum, located in downtown Clear Lake, allows visitors to walk down a recreated Main Street of yesteryear, peek into a pioneer family's log cabin, visit a one-room schoolhouse, admire a century-old church, and view photographs, uniforms, clothing, newspapers, weapons, and other memorabilia of the area's political, athletic, and military activities.

Cochrane

It's amazing what one man with a vision and friends can do!

Prairie Moon Sculpture Garden and Museum
S2663 Prairie Moon Road, off Hwy 35 between Cochrane and Fountain City
Cochrane, WI 54629

Phone: (608) 687-8250
Website: www.kohlerfoundation.org/rusch.html
Open: By appointment.

Important works: Dozens of colorful concrete sculptures

About the museum: Some remember Herman Rusch for his curious view of the natural world, made manifest in his roadside museum. Others recall his lively fiddling at barn dances and weddings. But Rusch is most widely acclaimed for his Prairie Moon Sculpture Garden and Museum, and for the powerful vision, tireless labor, and organic sense of rhythm, form, and color that made such a feat possible.

In 1959, at the age of seventy-four, Rusch, a self-taught artist was inspired to build his first concrete and stone planter. Over time, colorful, hand-sculpted concrete creations began to rise on the landscape in the form of a Hindu temple, watch tower, cactus garden, dinosaurs, bust of Rusch, and 260-foot meandering arch fence, to name a few. By 1974, Rusch had created nearly forty concrete, stone, and rock sculptures, using inventive fabrication techniques and materials including bricks, iron wheels, old grain drills, crockery, glass, and seashells. Miniature replicas of actual buildings in Cochrane, constructed of indigenous stone in the 1930s by the late artist Fred Schlosstein, are the newest addition to the museum.

Colby

Agricultural history is on display in Colby. Sample the cheese.

Rural Arts Museum
Adams Street
Colby, WI 54421

Mailing address: 223 S. 1st Street, Colby, WI 54421
Phone: (715) 223-2264
Contact: Mrs. Pearl Vorland, Curator or Colby Chamber of Commerce (715) 223-4435
Open: Memorial Day- Labor Day: Sunday afternoons and by appointment

The Clark County Historical Society bought the Colby Cheese Box Company land and building, which became the beginning of the Rural Arts Museum. The museum is a collection of buildings that holds the stories, artifacts, and memories of middle Wisconsin. The history of the railroad is complemented by the historical memorabilia of the dairy industry, as well as modes of transportation, machines of the written word, and education. It consists of the original railroad depot from the City of Colby, a one-room country school, and a log home.

Couderay

Gangsters and prohibition come alive in this northern hideout. No guns, please!

The Hideout — Al Capone's Northwoods Retreat
12101 West County Rd. CC
Couderay, WI 54828

Phone: (715) 945-2746
Open: Tours are regularly scheduled May-October. Please call ahead.
Admission: Yes

Al Capone's Hideout is a complex of buildings from the 1920's and was created for him and his gangs from Chicago at the height of his infamous career during the Prohibition Era. The house contains many unique objects left behind when Al Capone was imprisoned for tax evasion. It is located on a private lake with beautiful vistas. Anyone interested in this era or Al Capone and his life will be fascinated and intrigued by a visit to The Hideout in the northwoods of Wisconsin.

Crandon

The Depression era comes alive with people, places, fact, and fiction all under one roof.

Forest County Historical and Genealogical Society — Carter House Museum
105 W. Jackson
Crandon, WI 54520

Mailing address: P.O. Box 432, Crandon, WI 54520
Phone: (715) 478-5900
Contact: Winnie Krueger, 2779 E. Shore Lane, Crandon, WI 54520, (715) 478-3456
Open: Monday through Friday, 10am to 4pm; Saturday, 1pm to 4pm; Memorial Day to mid-September.

Important works: Telephone display, Hiles Post Office counter, clothes irons, logging era artifacts.

About the museum: The society formed in 1990 to preserve historical objects and archival material, and to educate the public on the unique history of Forest County. During its first two years, donated glass bakery cases, whose contents featured local history, were shipped from town to town. In 1994, the society purchased the old Carter House in Crandon to serve as the county museum.

The house was built in 1902 by the Protestant Episcopal Church and through the years this building has seen many facets of life from mission church, to social hall, to private residence, to antique shop. The museum displays reflect everyday life of an average Forest County family in the late 1920s to early 1930s. A comment often heard is, "This is just like my grandma's house." Currently the society is working on the restoration/expansion of the building, which will allow exhibits on the moonshine era in Forest County. It is also compiling histories of county churches and collecting family genealogies for visitors to browse in the genealogy room.

Danbury

Be a voyageur and drift back in time for a French rendezvous.

Forts Folley Avione Historical Park
8500 Highway U
Danbury, WI 54893 (North of Webster)

Phone: (715) 866-8890 or (715) 349-2219
Contact: Danbury Chamber of Commerce (715) 656-3292
Open: Memorial Day-Labor Day: Wednesday - Saturday, 10am to 4pm; Sunday, 11am to 4pm.
Admission: Yes

This is a living history site that recreates an Ojibwa village and fur trading post. Folley Avione means wild rice in French and wild rice has been grown for centuries in this area. The village contains several birch bark wigwams as well as site interpreters that greet the visitors in full Ojibwa costume or in the French speak, 'voyageur costumes.' It is an interesting location that helps bring to life a long lost period in Wisconsin history when the state still belonged to the French empire. There is a beautiful 300-seat amphitheater where lectures and concerts are given. Fur trader rendezvous are held here also in the third weekend in July.

Downsville

About an hour from the twin cities, this site has several historic buildings waiting for the visitor to explore.

▲ The Caddie Woodlawn Home and Park — Dunn County Historical Society
Highway 25
located nine miles south of Menomonie
Downsville, WI 54735

Mailing address: P.O. Box 437, Menomonie, WI 54751
Phone: (715) 232-8685 [Fax: 715-232-8687]
Website: http://discover-net.net/~dchs/sitecw.html
Open: Spring through Fall: Daily during daylight.
Admission: Yes

About the museum: This was the home of Caroline Augusta Woodhouse and was built in 1857. The one and a half story house was moved in 1968 to a five-acre parcel of land owned by the Woodhouse family. The house was restored and painted with the effort of many volunteers. The house inspired the writing of an award winning children's book called Caddie Woodlawn, written by Carol Ryrie Brink in 1935.

The logging industry was dangerous and rough. Come and see its diversity and fascination.

▲ Dunn County Historical Society - Empire in Pine Lumber Museum
County Hwy C (located six miles south of Menomonie on State Highway 25, turn on County C at Downsville)
Downsville, WI 54735

Mailing address: P.O. Box 437, Menomonie, WI 54751
Phone: (715) 232-8685 [Fax: 715-232-8687]
Email: dchs@discover-net.net
Website: http://discover-net.net/~dchs/siteep.html
Open: May - September: Friday-Sunday, noon to 5pm. Guided tours by appointment.
Admission: Yes

About the museum: The Empire in Pine Lumber Museum earned the State Historical Society's "Distinguished Service" award in 1982. Award winning displays show the rich logging history of the Red Cedar Valley. Exhibits include a blacksmith shop, muzzle-loading bunks, a rare up-and-down saw, 1865 Louisville Post Office, and village jail.

Drummond

Discover the history of the area's logging industry, the rough and tumble lumberjack trade, life in a "company town," and northwoods wildlife.

▲ Drummond Historical Museum
14990 Superior St.
Drummond, WI 54832

Mailing address: P.O. Box 8, Drummond, WI 54832
Phone: (715) 739-6500
Email: drummondmuseum@cheqnet.net
Website: http://www.drummandwi.com/museum.asp
Open: Tuesday, Wednesday, Friday, 10am to 5pm; Thursday, 10am to 6pm; Monday

and Saturday (self-guided tours), 9am to 1pm and by appointment.
Admission: Free

Important works: Displays showing conditions in a logging company town, and wildlife.

About the museum: The Drummond Historical Museum, founded in 1962 as a chapter of the Bayfield County Historical Society, contains an outstanding exhibit of Drummond's logging past. The history of this mill town and its surrounding forests is engagingly shown in a wall of dioramas. In 1976 the museum opened its doors and has continued to keep alive the memories of the Drummond area. A new building to house the museum and also the city's public library was designed after the original Rust Owen Company Store. It opened on the site where the store stood from 1884 until it was torn down in the early 1990s. The location and design link the past with the future of the community.

Durand

Stunning 19th century architecture combines with local history at this museum.

Pepin County Historical Society — Old Courthouse Museum
371 W. Madison St.
Durand, WI 54736

Mailing address: P.O. Box 74, Durand, WI 54736
Phone: (715) 672-5423
Open: Memorial Day weekend through mid-October, Saturdays, 1pm to 4pm.
Admission: Donation requested

Important works: Historic wood-framed courthouse, local history artifacts.

About the museum: This Greek Revival style building, built in 1874, and the jail next door, 1895, are both on the National Register of Historic Places. The museum features six rooms of local history and the original second floor courtroom. A museum since 1985, it is operated by the Pepin County Historical Society. This architectural treasure is the last wood-framed courthouse in Wisconsin.

Eagle River

Imagine ... as your car turns on the road to the museum you are greeted by a twenty-five-foot tall carved cowboy...

★★Carl's Wood Art Museum
1230 Sundstein Rd.
Eagle River, WI 54521

Phone: (715) 479-1883 [Fax: 715-479-1883]
Contact: Carolyn and Ken Schels or Eagle River Area Chamber of Commerce and Visitor Center (715) 479-6499 or (800) 359-6315
Website: http://www.carlswoodart.com/
Open: Memorial Day weekend through the second weekend in October, Monday - Saturday, 9am to 5pm; Sunday 10am to 4pm. Handicapped accessible.
Admission: Yes

Important works: Unusual tree formations, "wood oddities," model sawmill, chainsaw collection, and chainsaw carvings.

About the museum: The museum represents a lifelong dream come true. Carl Schels, Sr. came to the U.S. in 1917 from Bavaria. Settling in the north, he became a trapper, logger and sawmill owner. Over the years, Carl collected the wood oddities that nature had designed as he spent long hours in the forests. He saw stories and beauty in pieces of wood that were overlooked by the other loggers. In the mid-1980s, the Schels family decided it was time to create a place where Carl could share his unique collection with the world. They built an assortment of buildings and covered walkways that now house the growing collection. Inspired by Carl's collection, other outdoorsmen have donated additional examples of odd designs found in nature. And chainsaw carvings by Carl's son, Ken, add to the visual appeal.

The museum also features a collection of wood veneers and wood samples, a wall of photos showing trees in their summer greenery and winter outlines, and many skins and mounts of local wildlife. A miniature-operating sawmill made by Carl Schels, Jr., complete with horses and conveyances used to haul logs out of the woods, intrigues even the smallest guest. Displays of antique tools and machinery are a reminder of an era when earning a living was a hands-on experience.

Make a family expedition to Eagle River Museum and have your picture taken in front of Sitting Bull.

▲ Eagle River Historical Society and Museum
IIII 519 Sheridan St.
located at the Trees for Tomorrow Center
Eagle River, WI 54521

Phone: (715) 479-2396
Contact: Eagle River Area Chamber of Commerce and Visitor Center (715) 479-6499 or (800) 359-6315
Open: Mid-May to mid-October, Tuesday - Saturday, 10am to 3pm.

Important works: Five-foot granite sculpture of Sitting Bull.

About the museum: The society was organized in 1988 to collect, preserve, and display memorabilia of local interest from the 1870s to the present. Exhibits and artifacts interpret the timbering era, farming period, and rise of the tourist industry.

Kids learn by having fun in this family friendly museum.

▲ ★Northwoods Children's Museum
IIII 346 W. Division St.
Eagle River, WI 54521

Mailing address: P.O. Box 216, Eagle River, WI 54521
Phone: (715) 479-4623 [Fax: 715-479-3289]
Contact: Mike and Joy Long or Eagle River Area Chamber of Commerce and Visitor Center (715) 479-6499 or (800) 359-6315
Email: ncm@newnorth.net
Website: www.northwoodschildrensmuseum.com
Open: Memorial Day to Labor Day: Monday - Saturday, 10am to 5pm, Sunday, noon to 5pm.
Labor Day to Memorial Day: Tuesday - Friday, 10am to 3pm; Saturday, 10am to 5pm; Sunday, noon to 5pm.
Admission: Yes

Important works: Hands-on exhibits for children of all ages.

About the museum: The Northwoods Children's Museum supports learning, builds confidence, and encourages children to connect with the people, places, and values in their world. A playful, intriguing collection of exhibits, changing themes, and adventures offers hands-on experiences for all learning styles. From the grocery store to the fire tower and ranger station, the museum brings out the child in us all by sparking imaginations and lighting up minds in a friendly, northwoods setting.

Eau Claire

The exhibits at this museum will blow you away. It's a first class act!

★★Chippewa Valley Museum
Carson Park on Menomonee St.
Eau Claire, WI 54702

Mailing address: P.O. Box 1204, Eau Claire, WI 54702
Phone: (715) 834-7871 [Fax: 715-834-6624]
Contact: Susan McLeod, Director or Eau Claire Area Chamber of Commerce (715) 834-1204 or Eau Claire Lakes Business Association (715) 376-2322 or (800) 299-7506
Email: info@cvmuseum.com
Website: www.cvmuseum.com
Open: Memorial Day – Labor Day: Monday - Saturday, 10am to 5pm. Sunday, 1pm to 5pm. School Year: Tuesday - Sunday, 1pm to 5pm. Admission: Yes

Important works: Ojibwe history exhibit, logging artifacts, historic log cabin and schoolhouse, extensive archives.

About the museum: The heritage of the Chippewa River Valley begins with the local Native Americans (called Anishinabe, Ojibwe, or Chippewa), a native people who have lived in the valley for the past 300 years. In an award-winning exhibit, visitors can trace the tribe's history from first settlement through government treaties and boarding schools to the pow wow grounds of the 1990s. Other exhibits portray the flood of immigrants – Yankees, Germans, Norwegians and others – who came to the sawdust cities of the lumber boom to profit from the "inexhaustible pineries" (which lasted only fifty years). There is a "Main Street" with stores and offices from the early 20th century and displays showing turn-on-the-century farm life. The Chippewa Valley Potluck is a sixteen-minute "object theater" production that combines images, sound, and light.

Also on museum grounds are the Sunnyview School, which served grades one through eight from 1882 to 1961, and the two-story Anderson Log House, built in the 1850s, where Lars and Gretha Anderson raised ten children. The museum library serves as a regional archive with 14,000 photographic images and more than 25,000 documents, manuscripts, and other resources available for research.

Stop by this university art gallery for a taste of modern art in all its variety. Call ahead to see what's up!

Foster Gallery — University of Wisconsin-Eau Claire
Haas Fine Arts Center
121 Water St.
Eau Claire, WI 54702

Phone: (715) 836-2328
Contact: Tom Wagener, Director or Eau Claire Area Chamber of Commerce (715) 834-1204 or Eau Claire Lakes Business Association (715) 376-2322 or (800) 299-7506
Email: wagenetk@uwec.edu
Website: www.uwec.edu/Art/featuresc.htm
Open: Monday - Friday 10am to 4:30pm, Saturday and Sunday, 1pm to 4:30pm; Thursday evening, 6pm to 8pm.

NORTHWEST

Admission: Free

Important works: Fine art paintings, drawings, and sculptures, plus changing exhibits.

About the museum: The Foster Gallery is located in the Fine Arts Building. A variety of art exhibitions, including changing works by alumni, bachelor's degree candidates, and internationally known artists, are open to the pubic. The permanent collection, some of which is on display, began in the late 1960s with a major bequest by Emil Arnold of New York. Included in the gift were works by modernist Karl Knaths (a major figure of the Provincetown School), expressionist Jacob Epstein, and figural draftsmen/painters/sculptors Raphael and Moses Soyer. The collection has grown to approximately 700 works.

Birds of a feather see the museum together!

★James Newman Clark Bird Museum
Phillips Science Hall
University of Wisconsin-Eau Claire
Eau Claire, WI 54702

Phone: (715) 836-3523
Contact: Johanna Oosterwyk, Department of Biology or Eau Claire Area Chamber of Commerce (715) 834-1204 or Eau Claire Lakes Business Association (715) 376-2322 or (800) 299-7506
Email: oosterjm@uwec.edu
Open: Weekdays, 8am to 4:30pm.
Admission: Free

About the museum: The Bird Museum, circular in shape, contains four dioramas and surrounds the Planetarium in Phillips Hall. Over 530 species housed in the museum were collected by James Newman Clark from the 1870s through the 1920s. Two popular exhibits are the Bald Eagle and Golden Eagle, which require the University to hold a license to have them. The four dioramas depicting native birds in their natural habitats include a white pine forest with ruffed grouse, a screech owl pouncing on a mouse, the now extinct passenger pigeons, and shorebirds from downtown Eau Claire.

While you are here, don't forget to take a family photo with Paul Bunyan and his Blue Ox, Babe. Family lore is woven here.

★Paul Bunyan Logging Camp
1110 Carson Park Dr.
Eau Claire, WI 54702

Mailing address: P.O. Box 221, Eau Claire, WI 54702
Phone: (715) 835-6200 [Fax: 715-835-6293]
Contact: Norm Kassera or Eau Claire Area Chamber of Commerce (715) 834-1204 or Eau Claire Lakes Business Association (715) 376-2322 or (800) 299-7506
Email: info@paulbunyancamp.org
Website: www.paulbunyancamp.org
Open: Early April to early October, 10am to 4:30pm.
Admission: Yes

Important works: Logging era buildings, tools and artifacts.

About the museum: The echo of the lumberman's call is heard again in this replica 1890s logging camp, complete with authentic tools, equipment, and artifacts. At the camp, which opened in 1931, children find a hands-on introduction to Wisconsin's boisterous logging history in the Henry O. Strand Interpretive Center. A brief video and eye-catching displays and artifacts set the stage for walks through the camp's log buildings. These structures faithfully duplicate the rugged conditions under which early settlers lived while harvesting the white pine forests. Popular stops are the Cook Shanty/Bunkhouse, which was the favored place for loggers at the end of rugged day, and the Blacksmith Shop whose floor is paved with log ends. In the Equipment Shed visitors can examine a go-devil, a rutter, road icer, logging sleigh, and scale-model bateau.

Time your visit for the Teddy Bear Picnic or Christmas Tour. It's worth the wait!

Schlegelmilch House
517 South Farwell Street
Eau Claire, WI 54702

Mailing address: P.O. Box 1204, Eau Claire, WI 54702
Phone: (715) 834-7028 (Chippewa Valley Museum)
Contact: Eau Claire Area Chamber of Commerce (715) 834-1204 or Eau Claire Lakes Business Association (715) 376-2322 or (800) 299-7506
Email: info@cvmuseum.com
Website: http://www.cvmuseum.com/Schlegelmilch.html
Open: Seasonally and by appointment
Admission: Yes

The Schlegelmilch House was built in 1871 by Herman and Augusta Schlegelmilch one year before Eau Claire was incorporated as a city. Herman was trained as a gunsmith in his native Germany and ran a hardware business in Eau Claire. The Chippewa Valley Museum received the donation of the historic property in 1978. The brick Victorian house shows strong Italianate influences and is filled with period furnishings from the Schlegelmilch family as well as other generous donors from the community.

Eland

Come toot your whistle at this depot museum!

Eland Depot Museum – Eland Area Historical Society
Downtown Eland
Eland, WI 54427

Mailing address: P.O. Box 27, Eland, WI 54427
Phone: (715) 253-6040 or (715) 454-6570
Contact: Jerry Van Cauteren, President
Open: Call ahead.

This gem of a depot museum is worth your visit. Please call ahead for details.

Ellsworth

These two sites are only an hour from the Twin Cities. It's double the fun!

Pierce County Historical Association
Archives-Pierce County Courthouse
414 W. Main Street
Ellsworth, WI 54011

Phone: (715) 273-6611
Contact: Ellsworth Chamber of Commerce (715) 273-6442 or (800) 474-3723
Email: retas@spacestar.net
Website: http://www.geocities.com/meire1910/archives.htm
Open: Monday – Thursday, 1pm-4pm.

Pierce County history comes alive at this fun stop! Call ahead.

▲ River Bluffs History Center
Main Street
Bay City, WI 54723

Phone: (715) 273-6611
Email: retas@spacestar.net
Website: http://www.geocities.com/meire1910/historsites.htm
Open: For special events and by appointment.

These collections span many eras with items important to the history of Pierce County.

Fifield

Come in the summer and enjoy the old time ambiance.

▲ Old Town Hall Museum – Price County Historical Society
W7213 Pine St.
Fifield, WI 54524

Mailing address: P.O. Box 156, Fifield, WI 54524
Phone: (715) 339-2254
Contact: Therese Trojak, President
Website: http://pricecountyhistoricalsociety.com/museum.htm
Open: June through Labor Day, Friday and Sunday, 1pm to 5pm.

Important works: Historic artifacts, furnishings, and tools from homes and businesses.

About the museum: The Old Town Hall houses artifacts from the logging days of Price County from 1879 through the 1930s. Beginning on the lower floor, the clerk's office now holds logging tools, camp artifacts, and railroad memorabilia. A Victorian era living room and kitchen occupy the old jail area, and other rooms house changing exhibits, collections of personal and community artifacts, an office, and a gift shop. The upper hall contains farm implements, artifacts of early transportation, ice making, clothing, old Price County Courthouse furniture, and more temporary exhibits.

Florence

Don't get locked up in this jail! Come only for a visit and stay a spell.

▲ Old Florence County Jail
501 Lake Street
Florence, WI 54121

Phone: (715) 696-3700

Open: Year-round: Monday-Friday, 8am to 5pm.
Admission: Donations welcome

The Old Florence County Jail is a small building, built in 1899, which functioned as a jail through the early 1940s. It is a Romanesque influenced structure and has been restored to the way it was in the 1940s.

Fountain City

If old toys fascinate you, you will enjoy this world-class collection of antique toys and automobiles. Come over and play!

Elmer's Auto and Toy Museum
W903 Elmers Rd.
Fountain City, WI 54629

Phone: (608) 687-7221 [Fax: 608-687-7221]
Email: info@ElmersAutoandToyMuseum.com
Website: http://elmersautoandtoymuseum.com/
Open: Scheduled weekends, 9am to 5pm. Call for information.
Admission: Yes

Important works: More than 100 antique and classic cars and 200 antique motorcycles, scooters, and bicycles. 40,000 toys, and the world's largest collection of pedal cars.

About the museum: Housed in four large buildings and a barn is an impressive collection of over 100 muscle, antique, and classic autos and trucks. Old Indian and Harley-Davidson motorcycles, old bicycles, high wheel bikes, racecars, and other antiques are also displayed. In the toyshop, more than 40,000 antique toys are displayed on miles of shelves. There are also special collections of antique tools and antique dolls that will delight young and old.

Zillions of arrowheads await you at this quaint historic museum.

Fountain City Museum
25 N. Main St.
Fountain City, WI 54629

Phone: (608) 687-7541 or (608) 687-4500
Open: Memorial Day to Labor Day, Saturdays and Sundays, 1pm to 4pm, or by appointment.

About the museum: The Fountain City Museum has many items including a collection of arrowheads and Indian artifacts, which is one of the best in the state. The museum also houses dozens of historic items from the community.

Wisconsin has two famous rocks associated with houses: The House ON the Rock in Spring Green and the ROCK in the House in Fountain City. Both worth seeing.

Rock in the House
440 N. Route 35
Fountain City, WI 54629

Contact: John and Fran Burt
Open: Daily 10am to 6pm
Admission: Yes

A day to remember. On April 24, 1995 Maxine Anderson was working in her house when a fifty-five ton boulder from the nearby bluff crashed into her house and stopped midway through the residence. She was not hurt. Viola, instant roadside attraction. Now John and Fran Burt own the house and have opened it up to the public. It's a time capsule. Rock-in-the-House.

Frederic

You can bike to this railroad exhibit and ride the trails.

Frederic Soo Line Depot Museum
210 West Oak St.
Frederic, WI 54837

Mailing address: P.O. Box 1, Frederic, WI 54837
Phone: (715) 327-8324 or (715) 327-4271
Website: http://www.atmebiz.com/fredericwi/historical/sooline.php
Open: Memorial Day through October, Saturday and Sunday, 11am to 4pm.
Admission: Free

Important works: Railroading and local history artifacts.

About the museum: On Main Street in downtown Frederic the newest addition is the renovated Soo Line Depot, the only depot remaining along the abandoned railroad line. This historic corridor is again seeing traffic in its new role as the Gandy Dancer State Recreational Trail. The depot is a designated trail rest stop, and also houses the local museum. It's a 'must see' for railroad and history buffs alike.

Galesville

Local history is multi-faceted at this educational center.

One Room Schoolhouse Museum
County Fairgrounds
Galesville, WI 54630

Phone: (608) 582-2908 Open: For the county fair and by special request
Admission: Donations welcome

A small gem of museum that's worth the visit and worth a diversion from county fair attractions.

Gordon

If you have a few extra hours, stop by the Gordon-Wascott Museum and taste the past. It's sweet like fresh apple pie with milk and honey.

Gordon-Wascott Museum
9672 E. County Road Y
Gordon, WI 54838

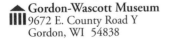

Mailing address: P.O. Box 222, Gordon, WI 54838
Phone: (715) 376-4249
Contact: Rozie Gile, President (715) 376-4767
Open: Memorial Day weekend through Labor Dayweekend, Friday through Monday, 10am to 4pm.

Important works: Railroading, logging, Native American artifacts, memorabilia of Father Phillip Gordon, archival documents, and photos.

About the museum: The museum, run by the Gordon-Wascott Historical Society, was established in the early 1980s. This clapboard building originally was the warehouse for a fur trading post and later was converted to a residence. In 1986, the old Gordon Depot was purchased from the Soo Line Railroad and moved next to the museum. The museum houses a collection of histories and photos of local families, town and school records, stories and photos of area news events, lumbering tools, plus Native American and fur trade items.

Of special significance is memorabilia related to Father Phillip Gordon, the first Native American to become a Catholic priest. Father Gordon is buried in the nearby cemetery along with his father, Antoine, a French-Canadian fur trader who settled in Gordon in the mid-1800s and after whom the town is named. Originally, the Town of Gordon was call Amik, meaning "beaver" in the language of its original Ojibwe (Chippewa) residents. The depot houses a growing collection of railroad memorabilia, and each year the building is used to host an Ice Cream Social during Gordon's Good Neighbor Days in early July.

Grantsburg

Grantsburg has a long history and it's on display at the museum and local heritage room.

Grantsburg Area Historical Society and Museum
133 West Wisconsin Ave.
Grantsburg, WI 54840

Mailing address: P.O. Box 35, Grantsburg, WI 54840
Phone: (715) 689-2374 or (715) 463-2573
Contact: Mrs. Gail Potvin
Open: Memorial Day-Labor Day: Sunday, 1pm to 4pm or by appointment. Handicapped accessible.

The museum is located in a late 1800s Methodist Church. Exhibits change every two years and there are no permanent displays in place. Also located on the property are the original Burnett County Jail, a sawed timber building that contains three cells built in 1870, and the home of one of the villages' blacksmiths, now under renovation. Please call ahead to see what exciting exhibit is in store for you!

Greenwood

Bring along your camera and the kids for a day of fun!

Branstiter Museum — Old Streets of Greenwood
600 S. Main St.
Greenwood, WI 54437

Phone: (715) 267-6368 or (715) 267-6205
Contact: Vic Wagner or Loni Klinke, Greenwood's City Clerk
Website: www.clark-cty-wi.org/BranstiterMuseum.htm
Open: First June – August, Sundays, noon to 3pm; Sunday of Memorial Day weekend, noon to 3pm.

Important works: Dairy and lumber equipment, toy tractors, local photos.

About the museum: Visitors take a step back in time as they walk on wooden sidewalks past seventeen store fronts and a church entrance of early 1900 Greenwood. The museum features a collection of over 400 items, including tools and equipment used in the early lumbering and dairying days. Special exhibits feature collections of toy tractors, antique miniature cars, coins dating back to 1934 and a display of over 170 photographs of early Greenwood people, places, and events.

Hayward

You gotta see it! It's the world's biggest fish at the biggest fishing museum on earth. Get hooked. It's reel action.

★★★National Freshwater Fishing Hall of Fame
10360 Hall of Fame Dr.
Hayward, WI 54843

Mailing address: P.O. Box 690, Hayward, WI 54843
Phone: (715) 634-4440 [Fax: 715-634-4440]
Contact: Ted Dzialo
Email: fishhall@cheqnet.net
Website: www.Freshwater-Fishing.org
Open: April 15 – November 1 plus Labor Day through October, 10am to 5pm.
Handicapped accessible
Admission: Yes, reduced cost for tours of fifteen or more.

Important works: Fishing artifacts and memorabilia, plus Wisconsin's largest outdoor sculpture: an immense muskie fish that visitors can climb inside.

About the museum: This is the world's largest fishing museum. It serves as the official qualifier and recorder of fresh water sport-caught and world record fish, and as a library, education center, and clearinghouse for fishing facts. Exhibits recognize persons and organizations for outstanding achievement in the realm of fishing. The collection includes over 400 fish mounts (representing 200 species), 300 classic and antique outboard motors, 5,000 fishing lures, 200 antique fishing rods, and hundreds of other fishing accessories.

Lumber over this way and get a taste of Northwoods history!

Sawyer County Historical Society and Museum
15715 W. County Rd. B
Hayward, WI 54843

Mailing address: P.O. Box 384, Hayward, WI 54843
Phone: (715) 634-8053
Contact: Andi Wittwer
Email: histbuff@SawyerCountyHist.org
Website: www.sawyercountyhist.org
Open: June to September, Saturday - Wednesday, noon to 4pm or by special arrangement in spring and fall. Handicapped accessible.
Admission: Free, donations accepted

Important works: Over 1,000 photographs with some dating back to 1887, plus resort, farm, and lumber industry artifacts.

About the museum: Exhibits and displays cover nearly every facet of local history at this museum: Ojibwe culture, logging and lumberjacks, homesteading and pioneers, community development, Victorian lifestyles, churches, schools, hunting, fishing, and the resort industry. The building itself, the former DNR Ranger Station built in 1928, is an important part of area history. Children enjoy the diorama of Hayward's Main Street showing how it looked long before they were born. Visitor favorites are the lumberjack displays as well as the detailed homestead and Victorian furniture. New exhibits are added regularly.

Hazelhurst

Take a Northwoods safari and step back in time at this pioneer village and zoo.

Warbonnet Zoo (Closed)
5610 Hwy 51
Hazelhurst, WI 54531

Contact: Gary or Jan Zumach
Website: http://www.north-wis.com/wbzoo/
Open: Daily in summer, 9am to 7pm; Call for winter hours.
Admission: Yes

Important works: Over 300 live animals, and an old-time village.

About the museum: A main attraction of this zoo is the tractor-pulled Northern Safari Wagon that takes visitors on a guided journey through 60 acres of Wisconsin's northwoods. During the ride, wild animals can be viewed at home in their natural habitats. The safari stops at Warbonnet's Pioneer Village, a re-creation of life in the northwoods a century or so ago. The village has a Trading Post, Old-Time Fort, Museum, large Sioux teepee and an Ojibwe cedar bark lodge. Of the many mammals, birds and other animals in the zoo, very few are in cages.

Hudson

There are many sides to this buildings story. Come see them all!

Octagon House Museum
1004 Third St.
Hudson, WI 54016

Phone: (715) 386-6194 or (715) 386-2654
Open: May – October, and in December before Christmas: Tuesday - Saturday, 11am to 4pm; Sunday, 2pm to 4:30pm.
Admission: Yes

Important works: Octagonal structure, period Victorian furnishings, blacksmith shop.

The museum: The Octagon House, originally built for Judge John Shaw Moffat and his family, is a fine example of the novel eight-sided dwelling that was popular in the mid-1800s. The rooms are beautifully furnished with authentic mid-Victorian era pieces. The Children's Room has a fine collection of children's clothing, toys, and a rare doll collection from the turn of the century. The library with its collection of books suggests a leisure haven of days gone by. There is a fully outfitted blacksmith shop along with changing exhibits in the Carriage Museum, adjacent to the house. In addition, country store items and farm equipment are featured in the Garden House.

Hurley

Visit a touch of Finland in this 1921 log cabin.

Harma House Museum -- Little Finland
Highway 2
Hurley, WI 54534

Mailing address: P.O. Box 352, Hurley, WI, 54534
Phone: (715) 561-4360
Website: http://www.littlefinland.com/
Open: June-August: Wednesdays and Saturdays, 10am to 2pm.
Admission: Free

About the museum: The Harman House Log Cabin was built in 1921 by Finnish immigrant Nate Harma and donated by the family as a museum in 1972. The annual Iron County Heritage Festival takes place from late June through the second week of August and features events held at Little Finland.

You won't find this boring, nor get shafted...

Iron County Historical Society Museum
303 Iron St.
Hurley, WI 54534

Phone: (715) 561-2244
Contact: Walter Hoepner
Website: www.hurleywi.com/IronCountyHistory/
Open: Year-round: Monday, Wednesday, Friday, and Saturday, 10am to 2pm.
Admission: Free

Important works: Local history artifacts.

About the museum: The Iron County museum has three floors of engaging and educational exhibits on topics that include logging, mining, farming, weaving, clothing, and home furnishings. Visitors can browse the library to find books, photos, and maps related to area history.

Iron River

You'll get hooked on the historic "Man-O-Robelia."

Western Bayfield County Historical Society Museum
68245 South Main St.
Iron River, WI 54847

Phone: (715) 372-8792
Contact: William Meyer, President
Open: May - September: Wednesday – Saturday, 11am to 3pm, plus holidays, special

weekends, and by request.

Important works: Historic photos, local artifacts.

About the museum: The society is dedicated to preserving the heritage of Iron River and surrounding communities. Through a variety of displays, visitors can experience the rich history of the area's logging, mining, and railroad industries. Photograph exhibits include the Town of Delta's Civilian Conservation Corps camp, Spring Lake hatchery and Delta Brook Trout Resort, as well as military uniforms from the Revolutionary War to the Vietnam War. The area's storied past is found in logging tools and markers, turn of the century clothing, household furnishings, farm tools, veteran's uniforms and memorabilia, and special displays for children.

Jennings

This is a quaint historic building made of short stove wood logs. For the architecture buff, it's worth a visit.

Mecikalski Stovewood Building
County Hwy. B (5 miles east of Pelican Lake)
Jennings, WI

Mailing address: P.O. Box 69, Pelican Lake, WI 54463
Website: www.kohlerfoundation.org/stovewood.html

Important works: Rare stove wood building construction.

About the museum: The Mecikalski Stovewood Building is a unique historical structure with great architectural significance. Built at the turn of the century, it represents a rare example of stove wood construction and is the only known commercial building utilizing this building method. The use of stove wood seems to be a singularly American form of architecture. Found primarily in frontier settlements of German and Polish heritage, Wisconsin has over sixty stove wood structures. As part of the documentation and preservation of outsider art environments and folk architecture, the Kohler Foundation undertook restoration of the building in 1984.

Lac du Flambeau

A Native American cultural center on Peacepipe Road.

★★George W. Brown Jr. Ojibwe Museum and Cultural Center
603 Peacepipe Rd.
Lac du Flambeau, WI 54538

Mailing address: P.O. Box 804, Lac du Flambeau, WI 54538
Phone: (715) 588-3333 [Fax: 715-588-2355]
Email: idspace@newnorth.net
Website: www.ojibwe.com
Open: May through October, Monday - Saturday, 10am to 4pm; November through April, Tuesday - Thursday, 10am to 2pm.
Admission: Yes

Important works: Ojibwe Indian artifacts and archives.

About the museum: In 1995 the Lac du Flambeau Band of Lake Superior Chippewa Indians chose to distinguish an elder who had been a life long proponent of the cultural preservation by naming the center in his honor. The purpose of this center is to preserve and promote the knowledge of local history and culture through the collection of data and artifacts, featured in the development of exhibits and educational programs. The collections at the center find their roots in the cultural history of the Lac du Flambeau Ojibwe. Many of the objects available for exhibit were made by the Lac du Flambeau Ojibwe and other Ojibwe bands. Exhibits are structured around two general themes: Ojibwe history and culture and the fur trade periods. The museum celebrates Ojibwe culture with a four-seasons diorama and other exhibits including a twenty-four-foot dugout canoe, smaller birch-bark canoes, Ojibwe arts and crafts, traditional clothing, a French fur trading post, and a world-record speared sturgeon taken from one of the nearby lakes. Special museum programs include "Beadwork and the Ojibwe," "The Wild Rice Harvest of the Ojibwe," and numerous Ojibwe craft workshops like moccasin and birchbark basket making. Pow-wows are held every Tuesday evening from the end of June through the third week in August.

Ojibwe life comes alive at this re-created village on the shores of Moving Cloud Lake.

★Waswagoning Recreated Ojibwe Village
County H off Hwy 47
Just outside of Lac du Flambeau

Mailing address: P.O. Box 1059, Lac de Flambeau, WI 54538
Phone: (715) 588-3560 or 588-2241 or 588-2615
Email: linda@waswagoning.com or nick@waswagoning.com
Open: mid-June – end of August, Tuesday – Saturday, 10am to 4pm for public tours; school tours, mid-May – end of September.
Admission: Yes

About the museum: Waswanoning is a living history experience of the Ojibwe culture. Nick Hockings is a member of the Lac du Flambeau band of Lake Superior Ojibwe. Realizing that there was a great deal of misinformation about the Ojibwe culture, Hockings and others have been presenting cultural demonstrations at schools and festivals for the last ten years. Hockings has now realized his dream and built an authentic Ojibwe village when eighty acres of the Lac du Flambeau reservation became available. Based on the belief that first-hand experience is the best way to understand and accept different cultures, visitors are able to study and live in the village for several days at a time. During the summers of 1995 and 1996, sixteen members of the Illinois State University community had an opportunity to learn about traditional and contemporary Lac du Flambeau life. They collaborated with the College of Education, the College of Fine Arts, and Hockings to enable students to receive credit in education or art while they learned about historical and cultural life. They also lived on the reservation, participated in construction and maintenance of the village, and learned about the arts, clothing, food, and traditions of the Ojibwe people. This is a fascinating real life experience for those who wish to understand more about the rich cultural heritage of Native Americans in Wisconsin.

Ladysmith

In Rusk County, people's professions connect you to the historic past.

Rusk County Historical Museum
Edgewood Ave. at Fairgrounds
Ladysmith, WI 54848

Phone: (715) 532-6450, (800) 535-7875
Contact: Jenna Platteter, Curator
Open: Memorial Day – Labor Day, Saturday and Sunday, 12:30pm to 4:30pm and by appointment.

Handicapped accessible.
Admission: Free, donations welcome

Important works: One-room schoolhouse, Glen Flora Jail, medical and military artifacts, period businesses and furnishings.

About the museum: The museum's ten buildings, located at the Rusk County Fairgrounds, house thousands of rare, historical, and fascinating artifacts. The Little Red School is the premier exhibit. Exhibits in other buildings include Governor Rusk's desk, Dr. Lea's dental office, an early medical exhibit, turn-of-the-century kitchen, World War I and II weapons and uniforms, 19th century clothing, logging equipment, drafting and survey equipment, a country store, post office, and blacksmith shop. Outside the buildings, visitors can explore horse-drawn logging and farming equipment, the Glen Flora Jail, a Weyerhaeuser railroad car house, the Civilian Conservation Corps Camp Rusk entrance marker, a World War II tank, and mine information center.

Lake Tomahawk

Historic displays bring pioneer life alive at Hofman House.

Hofman House Museum
7247 Kelly Drive
Lake Tomahawk, WI 54539

Mailing address: P.O. Box 325, Lake Tomahawk, WI 54539
Phone: (715) 277-3123
Email: lkhbowen@newnorth.net
Open: Memorial Day-Labor Day: Saturday, 10am to 2pm or by appointment.

Rotating exhibits of collected artifacts are displayed for the pleasure of those who are interested in the historical development of the area.

Land O' Lakes

This is a small, but interesting museum filled with logging history that is captured in photos, tools, and treasures.

Northern Waters Museum
6490 Chippewa Drive
Land O' Lakes, WI 54540

Mailing Address: P.O. Box 541, Land O' Lakes, WI 54540
Phone: (715) 547-6979
Email: info@landolakeshistory.org
Website: www.landolakeshistory.org
Open: July 1 – September 4, Thursday – Saturday, 11am to 3pm. Open for Colorama, 11am to 3pm.

The Northern Waters Museum, housed in the restored 1939 Gateway Ski Chalet, exhibits geological and human history artifacts from the Land O' Lakes area. Additional exhibits are housed in the Gateway Lodge, the Town Hall, and the Library. School tours and other special tours can be arranged.

Laona

Spend a day at our camp and learn to be a lumberjack.

★Camp Five Logging Museum
5480 Connor Farm Rd.
Laona, WI 54541

Phone: (715) 674-3414, (800) 774-3414
Contact: Sara Connor
Email: mverich@camp5museum.org
Website: www.camp5museum.org
Open: June 19 – August 31, Monday - Saturday, 11am to 4pm. Third week in June – last Saturday in August.
Admission: Yes

Important works: Ride-along steam train, logging camp buildings, and artifacts.

About the museum: After a thrilling ride on the steam train, families can experience Camp Five's historic and natural attractions. The Logging Museum's artifacts bring the turn-of-the-century northwoods camps back to life. Visitors can examine tools used by lumberjacks and see how they transported logs to the railroads and rivers. While learning about the hard life of the lumberjack, no one will be surprised that the most important men in the camps were the cooks! The museum site is unique in Wisconsin because no other similar lumber company farm still exits. Today, the farm is still in operation and all the old lumber company farm buildings remain.

Madeline Island

This school is open in summer for continuing education on Wisconsin history.

Lakeview School Museum
273 Colonel Woods Ave.
LaPointe, WI 54850

Phone: (715) 747-5030 or (715) 747-5030
Open: June - September, Wednesday – Sunday, 10am to 3pm.

Important works: One-room school, classroom memorabilia.

About the museum: Lakeview School takes visitors back to the days of the one-room schoolhouse. Built in 1904 at the north end of Madeline Island, the school was moved to its present location and restored. It is filled with authentic furniture, equipment, educational materials, and historic photographs.

Summer time on Madeline Island is magical. History is alive!

★★Madeline Island Historical Museum
226 Colonel Woods Ave.
LaPointe, WI 54850

Mailing address: P.O. Box 9, LaPointe, WI 54850
Phone: (715) 747-2415 [Fax: 715-747-6985]
Contact: Steve Cotherman, Director

Email: madeline@whs.wisc.edu
Open: Memorial Day weekend to early-October, 10am to 5pm. Handicapped accessible.
Admission: Yes

Important works: Exhibits on Native Americans, boat building, and fishing.

About the museum: Experience the rich history of Madeline Island through exhibits and programs that explore three centuries of island life. Exhibits with rare and one-of-a-kind artifacts (many from Madeline Island or the surrounding Apostle Islands that dot Chequamegon Bay in Lake Superior) tell the story of the area's exploration and settlement from pre-history to the present day. Relics from the earliest days of Ojibwa habitation are displayed alongside voyageur trade goods, missionary artifacts, and tools of the lumbering, fishing, and boat building industries.

Marshfield

Beautiful gardens inspired by Oriental, as well as European modelsenhance this pretty location in one of the most scenic parts of Wisconsin.

★Foxfire Gardens
M220 Sugarbush Ln.
Marshfield, WI54449

Phone: (715) 387-3050
Email: foxfire@tznet.com
Website: www.foxfiregardens .com
Open: May through September or by appointment for group tours

East meets West at Foxfire Gardens where the simplicity of Chinese style, symbolic Japanese gardens, and formality of European gardens are mixed.

Step way back in time to this prehistoric dinosaur park. Don't miss the T-Rex...This is a fun filled art park worthy of a destination. You gotta see what Clyde has made out of recycled materials. A Wisconsin original.

★Jurustic Park
222 Sugarbush Lane
Marshfield, WI 54449

E-mail: clyde@jurustic.com or nancy@jurustic.com
Website: www.jurustic.com
Open: Most of spring, summer and fall until 5pm.
Admission: Free

This site documents the efforts of "amateur paleontologist" Clyde Wynia's attempts to recreate the now extinct creatures that inhabited the large McMillan Marsh near Marshfield during a different age. Make note that Wynia works with iron . . . and irony. His park is filled with scrap metal sculptures. Particularly striking are the large "Marsh Dragons," one topped with a continuously rotating propellor. Wynia's workshop is next to his wife Nancy's "Hobbit House," a fanciful cottage where she does glass art and doll making.

Art can be found in surprising places. This community gallery resides in another important community resource . . . a medical clinic.

★New Visions Gallery, Inc.
1000 N. Oak Ave.
located inside Marshfield Clinic
Marshfield, WI 54449

Phone: (715) 387-5562
Email: newvisions.gallery@verizon.net
Website: www.newvisiongallery.org
Open: Monday - Friday, 9am to 5:30pm; Saturday, 11am to 3pm.

Important works: Hiroshige wood block prints, Hasui and Yoshida prints, Yoruba elephant tusk, Australian Aboriginal art, West African sculpture and masks, Marc Chagall signed original posters.

About the gallery: New Visions Gallery is Marshfield's art connection. This non-profit community art museum has been located in the lobby of the Marshfield Clinic since 1975. Changing every six to eight weeks, the gallery offers a dynamic series of exhibitions featuring a variety of art forms along with national traveling shows, significant works on loan from private and public collections, and regional art. In late winter, Marshfield student art is on display and in spring the gallery organizes a national invitational exhibition of art with agricultural themes. New Visions also acquires, displays, and preserves a permanent art collection, notably the Robert & Barbara Bromberg Collection of contemporary art, and offers educational opportunities for the public. Check with the gallery for the current schedule of lectures, demonstrations, workshops, and opportunities to meet artists and discuss their work.

See how Wisconsin Governor Upham lived, in real Victorian splendor from 1880.

★North Wood County Historical Society — Governor Upham Mansion
212 W. Third St.
Marshfield, WI 54449

Phone: (715) 387-3322
E-mail: upham@tznet.com
Website: uphamansion.com
Open: Sunday and Wednesday, 1:30pm to 4pm or special arrangement. Office open Monday, Tuesday, Thursday, Friday, 8am to noon.
Admission: Free

Important works: Period Victorian furnishings.

About the museum: The Upham Mansion, restored home of former Wisconsin Governor William Henry Upham, represents mid-Victorian architecture at its finest. The furnishings of the Mansion are vintage Victorian, many of them left by the Upham family. Constructed in 1880, the mansion now serves as the center for the North Wood County Historical Society's monthly exhibits. You will find unique furniture and design, as well as many antique items such as a 100-year-old dollhouse. There is also a garden open June through September, which showcases thirty-two varieties of roses.

Exotic animals roam this place, so should you.

The Station
10174 Eagle Rd.
Marshfield, WI 54449

Phone: (715) 676-2310
Open: Daily Monday through Friday from 9am to 5pm, Saturday from 10am to 3pm.

Exotic gifts and animals

This is one of the municipal finest zoos in northern Wisconsin and specializes in a wide selection of North-American animals.

Wildwood Park and Zoo
Hwy 13 South (Roddis Ave. – off 17th St.)
Marshfield, WI 54449

Phone: (715) 384-2474
Open: Call for current zoo hours
Park hours: Year-round 6am to 10:30pm.
Admission: Free

About the zoo: Wildwood Zoo is one of the leading municipal zoos in Wisconsin. The park and zoo extend over more than sixty acres that are home to various animals found in North America. The visitor can walk or bike through the grounds and there is also the option to use the drive-by viewing option to see the large animal exhibits. The park also has ponds for fishing, an observation tower, picnic shelters, fountains, playground area, disc golf course, outdoor swimming pool, and woodlands.

Mason

This museum is more than a depot. It is a focal point for railroad, lumber, and immigrant heritage.

Bayfield County Historical Society —
Mason Depot Museum
County Highway E
Mason, WI 54856

Phone: (715) 765-4554 or (262)-534-6596
[Fax: (715) 765-4570]
Contact: Verne Gilles or Marian Schraufnagel
Email: marian_schraufnagel@wetn.pbs.org
Open: Memorial Day - Labor Day, Sundays, 1 - 4, and by appointment.

Important works: Lumber mill artifacts, pioneer tools, and children's playhouse.

About the museum: Housed in a renovated depot built by the Chicago, St. Paul, Minnesota, and Omaha Railway, the Mason Museum chronicles the town's development and history. Mason was established in 1883 as a mill town for the White River Lumber Company, and by 1894 was home to the largest lumber sawmill in northwest Wisconsin. Museum exhibits feature the lumber company, pioneer homesteading, immigrant heritage, historic photos, and an old fashioned children's playhouse.

NORTHWEST

Fascinating Facts

Regarding trial by jury, the Wisconsin state constitution reads, " The right of trail by jury shall remain inviolate."

Medford

The Taylor County Museum has something for everyone, including pioneer life, education history, and wildlife mounts.

Taylor County Historical Society Museum
845A E. Broadway
Medford, WI 54451

Phone: (715) 748-3808
Contact: Elaine Mravik, (715) 748-5812
Open: Thursday and Fridays, 11am to 4pm, also open for group and school tours by appointment.
Admission: Free

Important works: Taxidermy collection, log cabin, one-room school, extensive wildlife exhibit and military display.

About the museum: The Taylor County Historical Society was organized in 1965 and the museum opened in 1989. The museum building, owned by the county, now holds artifacts on railroads, logging, and farming collected during the early years of the society. An important collection of wildlife mounts, donated in 1992 by local taxidermist Edwin Czarneski, are on display. The society also has conserved a log cabin built in 1860 near Medford, adding furnishings that would have typically been around during the turn of the century. A one-room country schoolhouse, built in 1904 and called "The Washington School" was donated in 1991 by the County Homemakers. This is the first school known to have served hot lunches to its students, beginning in 1920.

Mellen

A Victorian City Hall is full of historic jewels!

Mellen Historical Museum
Main and Bennett Streets
Mellen, WI 54546

Phone: (715) 274-3708

About the museum: The Mellen Historical Museum is located in the still functioning 1896 Victorian-style Mellen City Hall. The museum holds a collection of photographs of the logging industry and displays of logging equipment and artifacts. Patrons can visit a fully furnished Victorian room and browse the collection of clothing. Collections also include antique tools for shoemaking and extensive holdings on WWI, WWII, and the Korean and Vietnam Wars.

Menomonie

Diversity is the theme of this museum's vast holdings. They highlight local people, places, and heritage.

★Dunn County Historical Society — Russell J. Rassback Heritage Museum
1820 Wakanda St.
Menomonie, WI 54751

Mailing address: P.O. Box 437, Menominee, WI 54751
Phone: (715) 232-8685
Email: dchs@discover-net.net
Website: discover-net.net/~dchs/sitehm.html
Open: Summer: May 1 – September 30, Wednesday – Sunday, 10am to 5pm. Winter: October 1 – April 30, Friday – Sunday, noon to 4pm. Guided tours any day by appointment.
Admission: Yes

Important works: Children's discovery room, Victorian era furnished rooms.

About the museum: As headquarters of the Dunn County Historical Society, the museum interprets local history through an extensive collection of artifacts and displays. Exhibits cover many topics and feature colorful local characters including prehistoric to modern day settlement, the Kraft State Bank Robbery (interactive), Automotive Genius Harry Miller, Kinetic Folk Artist Tinker Frank, the lumbering era, inventions and industries, and Dunn County in the Civil War. Don't miss the Hilkrest one-room rural school in Dunn County Recreational Park.

Come visit a fabulous historic treasure restored to its ornate Victorian splendor!

★Mabel Tainter Memorial Theater
205 Main St.
Menomonie, WI 54751

Phone: (715) 235-9726 [Fax: 715-235-9736]
Contact: Laura Reisinger or Gary Schuster
Email: mtainter@mabeltainter.com
Website: www.mabeltainter.com
or www.washburn.edu/cas/art/cyoho/archive/MidwestTravel/tainter
Open: Monday - Friday, 10am to 5pm; Saturday and Sunday, 1pm to 5pm. Memorial Day – Labor Day: Saturday and Sunday, 1pm to 5pm.

Important works: Restored theatre with ornate decorations, artifacts from past shows, old projection equipment, Turner tracker pipe organ.

About the museum: The Mabel Tainter Memorial Theater was built in 1889 by Captain and Mrs. Andrew Tainter in memory of their daughter, Mabel, who died in 1886 at the age of nineteen. The glory of this theater is in its detailing: the hand-carved woodwork, the stained glass and leaded glass windows, rich fabrics, intricate stenciling, and gleaming brass. Of special note is a rare fully restored Steere and Turner tracker pipe organ with 1,597 pipes. Originally water-powered, the organ has been modified to run on electricity. From the beginning, the theater was a roadhouse for professional touring companies and lecturers (like Capt. Roald Amundsen and Helen Keller/Anne Sullivan). Later it was used as facility for high school and other local productions. The basement of the theater includes historical displays including old projection equipment, magic lantern slides, and famous acts which have performed at the theater.

This is an extravagant Victorian mansion filled with historic treasures, especially at Christmas time.

Wilson Place Mansion Museum
101 Wilson Court
Menomonie, WI 54751

Phone: (715) 235-2283 or (800) 368-7384
Open: Memorial Day - Labor Day: Friday - Sunday, 1pm to 5pm. Open during holiday season first week before Thanksgiving and last week in December. Groups by appointment. Call for information.
Admission: Yes

NORTHWEST

Important works: Thematic Christmas tree ornament collection, extensive original Victorian-era furnishings.

About the museum: At the mansion, tour guides tell the story of 130 years of changing tastes and lifestyles of the Wilsons, a Midwestern lumber baron family. The Wilson Place experience features the High Victorian era of the family's greatest wealth, though three generations of family members left their mark on the home. Original family furnishings, which include crystal, china, furniture, silver, fabrics and clothing, span the period from 1832 to 1974.

A popular annual event is the "Victorian Christmas," a celebration of decorated holiday trees whose themes teach about history. A unique way of celebrating family history is found on the Family Heritage Tree. Tours are offered for children studying Wisconsin history, and special tours for university students focus on textiles, decorative arts and clothing. A self-guided walking tour of historic Menomonie featuring three significant sites is available.

Merrill

Two wonderful historic structures, a huge mansion and a one-room school, illuminate Merrill history.

★Merrill Historical Museum and Brickyard School Museum
804 E. Third St.
Merrill, WI 54452

Phone: (715) 536-5652
Contact: William Heideman, President
Email: merrillhs@msn.com
Website: www.ci.merrill.wi.us/attractions/museum.html
Open: Wednesday, Saturday, Sunday, 1pm to 4pm. Office open daily, 1pm to 4pm.
Admission: Donations appreciated

Important works: Victorian furnishings, schoolhouse memorabilia.

About the museum: A classic Victorian house, the Merrill Historical Museum was once the home of the Thomas Blythe Scott family. Built in 1881, the "Painted Lady of Third Street" serves as a cultural heritage center for the community. Interpretive programs and exhibits provide an opportunity for all to increase their knowledge and appreciation of Merrill's local history. The museum's galleries feature changing exhibits and its Victorian parlor and bedroom offer glimpses into the lifestyles of families like the Scotts.

The Brickyard School Museum, which was opened in 1983, preserves the history of the one-room school system in Lincoln County from the mid-1800s to 1961. Moved from its original location to the Lincoln County Fairgrounds, the museum hosts an annual open house during the county fair in July. Documents, records, and original photographs are available in the archives of the Scott Resource Center.

Minocqua

This museum highlights Minocqua's unique history and vacation heritage.

Minocqua Museum
503 Flambeau Street
Minocqua, WI 54548

NORTHWEST

Mailing address: P.O. Box 1007, Minoqua, WI 54548
Phone: (715) 356-7666 or (715) 356-5754 or (715) 356-9591
Contact: Rob Hagge, President
Open: Early June - Labor Day, Monday - Friday, 10am to 4pm. Also open by appointment.
Admission: Free

Important works: Displays on fishing, the resort industry, and local history.

About the museum: Established in 1986 as part of the city's centennial celebration, the Minocqua Museum offers a variety of exhibits focused on the "Island City's" unique heritage. It has been dedicated as a memorial to honor Patrick E. Bolger and his family.

Dozens of animals bring this zoo and park alive!

 Wildwood Wildlife Park
two miles west of US 51/I-39 on US 70
Minocqua, WI 54548

Phone: (715) 356-5588
Admission: Yes

Open: May – mid-Ocotber, daily. Call for more information

This is the place to go if you really want to experience nature! You'll find adventure and education wrapped in one with mammals, reptiles, and primates galore!

Mondovi

The friendly people in Mondovi have created several museums that celebrate rural education and local history.

Mondovi Area Historical Society — Country School Museum and Rural Life Museum
Tourist Park
Mondovi, WI 54755

Contact: Geraldine Hageness
Open: Memorial Day – Labor Day, Sundays and holidays, 1:30pm to 4:30pm.

Important works: One-room school artifacts, toys and childhood memorabilia.

About the museum: The two museums contain a wide range of objects related to local and area history. The old schoolhouse offers a glimpse of the days when children of all ages attended school together. Also check out the local history room that housed in the City Hall basement.

NORTHWEST

Tony's Tips

Many fine cultural institutions, in fact some of the best, are within an easy day's drive from Chicago to Milwaukee or Madison. Come visit. Flatlanders Welcome!

Neilsville

Get locked into the past! This museum is more than just a jail, it's local history in one cell.

▲ Jail Museum
215 E. State St.
Neilsville, WI 54456

Mailing address: P.O. Box 41, Neilsville, WI 54456
Phone: (715) 743-6444 or (888) CLARK-WI
Contact: Pat Lacey (715) 743-4799
Website: www.clark-oty-wi.org/JailMuseum.htm
Open: Memorial Day through Labor Day, Sundays, 1pm to 4pm.
Admission: Yes

Important works: Historic re-creations of local shops and businesses, jailhouse artifacts, and military memorabilia.

About the museum: The museum is located in an old jail building, and its three floors of jail cells now feature thematic exhibits with artifacts donated from the area. Displays include authentically furnished Victorian-style rooms, plus a doctor's office, barbershop, library, schoolhouse, judge's chambers, laundry, millinery shop, hardware store, and a jail cell with a prisoner. The third floor has a military exhibit with artifacts and uniforms from the Civil War through Desert Storm.

This is a unique historic house because the current owner still lives there. Great tips on does and don'ts for preserving old houses.

▲ Tufts' Mansion
26 Hewett St.
Neilsville, WI 54456

Phone: (715) 743-3346
Contact: James Voss
Email: info@tuftsMansion.com
Website: www.TaftsMansion.com or www.clark-city-wi.org/TuftsMuseum.htm
Open: June – September, Sunday, 1pm to 4pm or by appointment.
Admission: Yes

Important works: Victorian architectural details, period furnishings.

About the museum: Extensive remodeling has been ongoing at the Tufts' Mansion throughout its history. Built in 1885 for the Bruley family, the structure still contains the original plate glass windows with their etched, brilliant cut-glass borders, initialed "B" for Bruley. Subsequent owners added bay windows, Greek Ionic columns and a colonial portico that replaced the original porch. Colonel and Mrs. William Tufts purchased the house in 1961 and the Joseph Boe family bought it in 1996 and currently lives there. They restored a number of rooms, including the maid's quarters, refinished the original hardwood floors, and have opened parts of the home for visitors interested in historic homes.

NORTHWEST

Fascinating Facts

The Wisconsin state constitution upholds the right that "The military shall be in strict subordination to the civil power."

Nekoosa

Set along the Wisconsin River, this site fills your hunger for Wisconsin history.

Point Basse
W3425 Wakely Road
Nekoosa, WI 54457

Phone: (715) 423-3120
Open: June-October: second Saturday of the month, 1pm to 4:30pm.
Admission: Yes

This is a living history site at Point Basse, which is located near Nekoosa along the Wisconsin River. It is an early settlement from the 1850s. The area was originally settled by Robert Wakely who brought his family from New York in 1837. In 1840 the Wakelys constructed the current house 100 yards from the river. In the 1850s, a shed, log cabin, and schoolhouse were added to this interpretive site for the arts. Costumed guides assist the visitor in exploring the site. There are annual harvest festivals in October that are oriented for family fun.

New Richmond

Nine historic buildings filled with history illuminate New Richmond heritage.

New Richmond Heritage Center
1100 Heritage Drive
New Richmond, WI 54017

Phone: (715) 246-3276 or (888) 320-3276 [Fax: 715-246-7215]
Contact: Amy Lansing
Email: nrpsinc@pressenter.com
Website: www.pressenter.com/~nrpsinc/
Open: All year, Monday - Friday, 10am to 4pm; plus May through October, Saturdays, 7:30am to 2pm and Sundays, noon to 4pm. Also by appointment.
Admission: Yes

Important works: Nine historic buildings, including a turn-of-the-century farmstead.

About the museum: This complex of nine historic buildings gives visitors a feel for how early area residents would have lived. Several of the buildings were once the heart of a working family farm and include a Victorian Italianate farmhouse, a classic barn, and a little grain storage building called a "granary." The creek that runs through the farm even retains its picturesque name, the Paperjack, honoring a man called "Paperjack" who sold rags and once lived on its banks. To augment the collection of farmstead buildings, the museum has added a store, log cabin, country schoolhouse, working man's home, and log barn. Descriptive histories of all buildings are posted outside, and guided tours are available. Kids can burn off energy while hiking the Paperjack Greenway trails on the eleven-acre heritage center property.

NORTHWEST

Osceola

A family home from 1862 now recreates the past with furnishings and memorabilia from the community.

▲ **Osceola Historical Society — Emily Olson House and Osceola Depot**
IIII 114 Depot Road
Osceola, WI 54020

Mailing address: P.O. Box 342, Osceola, WI 54020
Osceola and St. Croix Valley Railway, P.O. Box 176, 114 Depot Rd., Osceola, WI 54020
Phone: For train ticket information: (800) 711-2591 or (715) 755-3570) or (612) 228-0263
Emily House: (715) 294-2480
Contact: Linda Jensen Gordon
Email: ljensengordon@hotmail.com, Depot: oscvrlwy@centurytel.net
Website: www.riversrailsandtrails.org/rrtoscdown2.htm
Depot: hwww.mtmuseum.org/index.html?body=depots/
Open: Emily Olson House: Memorial Day through October, Sundays, 2pm to 4pm and by appointment.
Osceloa Depot: Memorial Day through October, weekdays and weekends.

Important works: Community fair buttons, ticket box from the first bridge, memorabilia from now-closed stores and businesses, postcards, calling cards, and period furniture.

About the museum: Built in 1862, the Emily Olson House is one of the first homes in Osceola. It was built by Andrew Jackson Clark for his bride, Emily Salisbury, and was occupied by the Clark family for more than 100 years. In 1976, Emily Olson, a Clark descendant, historian and archivist, donated the house to the Village of Osceola for use as a library. In the 1980s, thanks to a major bequest in Olson's will, the society acquired the house for its headquarters and purchased the Osceola Depot.

The dining room and parlor in the house have been restored to depict the 1860s. In other rooms, rotating exhibits of artifacts showcase the community's rich history. Major exhibits have featured Bethania Mineral Springs (a mineral water bottling works), and the 674th Air Base. The Osceola Depot, built in 1916, has railroad artifacts and memorabilia on display in the old waiting room. It is the eastern end of the Osceola and St. Croix Valley Railway, which offers daily rides between Osceola and Marine on St. Croix in Minnesota

Pepin

This little house inspired a literary series by Laura Ingalls Wilder. Come read about it.

▲ **The Little House Wayside**
IIII Highway CC (7 miles north of Pepin)
Pepin, WI 54759

Phone: (715) 442-3011 (Pepin Tourism Bureau)
Open: May-October: Daily, daylight hours.
Admission: Free

This small wayside log cabin is a replica of the one Laura Ingalls Wilder described in her book Little House in the Big Woods. She was born near Pepin in 1855 and the other historic house museum in Pepin has additional information about Laura, her life, and the community of Pepin, including the nearby Pepin Railroad Depot Museum and the Pepin Historical Museum on Highway 35.

Little House on the Prairie was written here. Come see why.

Pepin Historical Museum — Laura Ingalls Wilder Museum
306 3rd St.
Pepin, WI 54759
Mailing address: P.O. Box 269, Pepin, WI 54759
Phone: (715) 442-3011
Open: May 15 through October 15: Monday-Sunday, 10am to 5pm. November through April: Thursday-Saturday, 10am to 3pm.

Important works: Books, documents. and memorabilia of Laura Ingalls Wilder.

About the museum: Exhibits highlight the life and work of Laura Ingalls Wilder, famous author of "Little House on the Prairie" and many other children's books. Wilder was born near Pepin in 1867 and her first book, "Little House in the Big Woods" was set in the Pepin area. The museum also features artifacts and displays on the local history of this Mississippi River town.

Phillips

Made with love, embellished with glass, these concrete statues are testimony to one mans ambition to decorate his yard for mankind.

★★★Wisconsin Concrete Park
Hwy 13 (south of Phillips)
Phillips, WI 54555

Mailing address: Friends of Fred Smith, 104 S. Eyder St., Phillips, WI 54555
Phone: (715) 339-6371
Website: www.kohlerfoundation.org/smith.html
Open: All day everyday
Admission: Donations welcome

Important works: Over 250 decorated concrete sculptures.

About the museum: From 1948 until 1964 retired lumberjack Fred Smith spent most of his time creating sculpture throughout his property south of Phillips, in the heart of Wisconsin's north woods. He created over 250 sculptures of concrete, embellished with colorful glass and other materials, and called his folk art environment the Wisconsin Concrete Park. The sculptures include many full-size animal and human figures with historical themes, such as Kit Carson on a horse and an angel with wings. Smith's work is now internationally regarded as a masterwork of American sculpture, created within the context of the artist's home and landscape. Recently it was listed on the National Register of Historic site.

Plover

Drift back into time to this heritage village filled with Portage County history.

★Portage County Historical Society — Heritage Park
Washington St. at Willow Dr.
Plover, WI 54467

NORTHWEST

Phone: (715) 344-4423
Contact: Tim Siebert
Email: pchs_54481@yahoo.com
Website: www.pchswi.org/hpark/Heritagepark.html
Open: June to late September, Saturdays and Sundays, 1pm to 5pm.
Admission: Donation

Important works: Wisconsin's original printing press, plus nine historic buildings including a one-room school, train depot and caboose, church, farmhouse, and blacksmith shop.

About the museum: Heritage Park is the result of the foresight of two historical society members who bought the Old Plover Methodist Church and two plots of land in the late 1970s. This was the beginning of what is now an eight-building village. In 1983, the society purchased the other six lots in the park and moved the Franklin/Calkins House onto the site. The remaining structures have been gathered from all over the county and brought to Heritage Park to show what life in Portage County was like between 1870 and 1910. This "preserve" of historic buildings has rescued structures that would otherwise have been torn down and lost.

The society also runs the Rising Star Gristmill in Nelsonville, which holds arts presentations in the summer, and the Beth Israel Synagogue in Stevens Point. It maintains a collection of over 20,000 photos and an extensive document collection.

Port Edwards

This house museum is rich in local history, from art to archives. There's even a Colt revolver!

▲ The Alexander House Center for Art and History
1131 Wisconsin River Drive
Port Edwards, WI 54469

Phone: (715) 887-3442
Contact: Ed and Mary Hauer, Joe Clark, Joan Clark, Joan Palen, Directors
Open: Year round: Sunday, Tuesday and Thursday, 1pm to 4pm and by appointment.
Admission: Yes

About the museum: The Alexander House Center for Art and History is located along the Wisconsin River in a beautiful house built by Joseph Aucher in 1934. He was an employee at the Nekoosa Edwards Paper Company. The Alexander Charitable Foundation was established in the early 1960s to better for not only care the house, but to promote philanthropic activities in the community. Housed within the building is an extensive archive from the Nekoosa Edwards Paper Company, as well as space for rotating exhibitions. The main floor of the house is used for gallery space and the second floor is for the archives and artifacts related to local history and genealogy.

Port Wing

Port Wing Hall has lots of history - come in and see, it's Superior.

▲ Port Wing Heritage Hall
Port Wing, WI 54865

Mailing address: P.O. Box 113, Port Wing, WI 54865

Phone: (715) 774-3536 or (715) 774-3624
Contact: Sondra Rockenbach, Chair
Open: May-September: Saturday and Sunday, 1pm to 4pm. Thursdays 1-4 pm year round. Call ahead for details.

About the museum: A wide range of artifacts will pique your interest and imagination at this local history museum, with logging, fishing, and geneaology items.

Presque Isle

Be among the first to visit this new museum documenting early life in the northland.

★Presque Isle Vintage Cottage and Museum
8314 Main St.
Presque Isle, WI 54557

Mailing address: P. O. Box 172, Presque Isle, WI 54557
Phone: (715) 686-2481
Email: wiusword@centurytel.net
Contact: Peggy Johnson Wiessner or Sievert, President
Open: Memorial Day – Labor Day, days and times change annually. Call for information.

Important works: Restoration of an early 1900s sawmill worker's home.

About the museum: This new museum of the Presque Isle Heritage Society opened in August 2002 and was designed to show a typical early 1900s cottage in a sawmill town. In addition to rooms restored to reflect the period, it has exhibits on local logging history and the early resort and northwoods vacation era.

Rhinelander

Nestled in a pine grove, this museum specializes in logging history.

Rhinelander Historical Society Museum
9 S. Pelham Street
Rhinelander, WI 54501

Phone: (715) 369-3833 or (715) 282-6180
Contact: June Phiel, President
Open: Summer: Tuesday, Thursday, Friday, 10am to 4pm, or by appointment. Winter: Tuesday, 10am to 4pm. Changes annually.

About the museum: The museum acts as a monument to families of Rhinelander. It reflects the elements of family life found in Rhinelander from around the turn-of-the-century up to the present time. Revolving exhibit: there is now a new exhibit about military, Vietnam War, as tribute to deceased veterans.

Visit a fascinating logging museum in a beautiful park setting!

★Rhinelander Logging Museum
Pioneer Park on Business US 8 (Oneida Ave)
Rhinelander, WI 54501

NORTHWEST

Mailing address: c/o Walter Krause, 810 Keenan St., Rhinelander, WI 54501
Phone: (715) 369-5004 or (715) 369-5121
Contact: Mike Skuhal, President
Website: www.rhinelanderchamber.com/museum/museum.htm
Open: Memorial Day – Labor Day, daily, 10am to 5pm.
Admission: Free, donations appreciated

Important works: An extensive collection of logging equipment, a narrow gauge locomotive, and historic lumbering photos.

About the museum: The Rhinelander Logging Museum has one of the most complete collections of lumber era artifacts in the Midwest. It features tools and artifacts pertaining to the early logger, including peavies, pike poles, cant hooks, and cross-cut saws. The museum grounds hold a wide variety of early logging equipment such as Thunder Lake's No. 5 narrow gauge locomotive, the mill president's private rail car, one of the few steam-powered "snow snakes" used to haul sleds of logs over iced highways, Big Wheels to haul logs to stream or rails, bateaus, a road icer, and an electrically-operated miniature sawmill. Of special interest to visitors is a cage containing a black Hodag, the only genuine replica of this mythical beast to be found in Rhinelander. The archives offer an extensive file of photographs covering the life and work of the old-time logger.

Rudolph

Led by Father Wagner, he and his congregation built the Wonder Cave and many more inspiring tableaux. It's salvation at one stop; rocks, religion, and roses.

★Rudolph Grotto Gardens and Wonder Cave
6957 Grotto Ave.
Rudolph, WI 54475

Phone: (715) 435-3120 or (715) 459-5547 or (715) 435-3247
Contact: Kris Villfahrt
Website: www.wrcs.org/grotto/home.htm
Open: Memorial Day - Labor Day, daily, 10am to 5pm or by appointment. Grounds are always open.
Admission: Yes for Wonder Cave; Grotto Gardens free

Important works: Sculptures and hand-built religious shrines.

About the museum: The Grotto Gardens are a lasting memorial to the faith and devotion of one man, Father Phillip J. Wagner. While at the Grotto in Lourdes, France in 1912, Father Wagner promised to build a shrine to Mother Mary. He began construction in 1928 along with co-builder Edmund Rybicki, and with little mechanical help they painstakingly created the Grotto Gardens over many years. Made of concrete and stone, they built The Wonder Cave, fourteen Stations of the Cross, The Virgin at Fatima, Patriotism, and other scenes of Christ and the saints. Colorful gardens, a chapel, and small but interesting museum are also part of the site.

NORTHWEST

Tony's Tips

Northern Wisconsin has many beautiful cabins to rent in the summer. Call the local chambers of commerce in the area you wish to visit for a reference.

Shell Lake

Joseph Barta was a master carver. Come see his amazing work, including his life-size version of The Last Supper, all in wood. It's worth the price of admission!

★★Museum of Woodcarving
Hwy 63 1/2 mile north of Shell Lake
Shell Lake, WI 54871

Mailing address: P.O. Box 371, Shell Lake, WI 54871
Phone: (715) 468-7100
Contact: Maria McKay, Curator
Website: www.roadsideamerica.com/attract/WISHEwood.html
Open: May 1 - October 30, daily, 9am to 6pm.
Admission: Yes, special group rates.

About the museum: Established in 1948, this is one of the country's largest collections of woodcarvings, all created by Joseph Barta. Woodcarvers from around the world come to see the 100 life-size carvings depicting the life of Christ, as well as over 400 miniature carvings created over a thirty-year period. Barta worked for years on some of the pieces, spending more than four years to complete "The Last Supper." Ponderosa and sugar pine wood is used in all the life-size carvings, while the miniatures are made of hardwoods like oak, poplar, walnut, and basswood.

This heritage site is actually many museums in one, containing a general store, church, school, and home.

Washburn County Historical Museum
102 W. Second Ave.
Shell Lake, WI 54871

Mailing address: P.O. Box 266, Shell Lake, WI 54871
Phone: (715) 468-2982
Contact: Joyce Ripley, President
Website: www.shelllakeonline.com/attractions.htm
Open: Memorial Day - Labor Day, Thursday through Saturday, 11am to 4pm.
Admission: Free, donations appreciated

Important works: Historic church, one-room school, and World War II Sky Watch Hut, plus many local artifacts.

About the museum: The Washburn County Historical Complex depicts the last 150 years of Washburn County. It includes the St. John's Lutheran Church (built in 1888) the former parsonage (now called the Annex, built in 1896) the Beaver Brook School Museum, and the Sky Watch Hut used during World War II. The main room of the museum displays early photos of the towns, homes, farms, and industries that made up Washburn County. Other featured items include antique toys, phones, hotel ledger, clothes, linens, and war memorabilia. The complex also houses period rooms, including a late 1800's farmer's bedroom and kitchen, a 19th century General Store exhibit, and rooms with farming and logging tools.

NORTHWEST

Solon Springs

Stop on by at John Beck's log cabin and sit a spell!

John Beck Log House
Railroad Street and Jackpine Avenue
Solon Springs, WI 54873

Mailing address: P.O. Box 84, Solon Springs, WI 54873
Phone: (715) 378-429
Open: Memorial Day-Labor Day, weekends from 1pm to 4pm and by appointment.

About the museum: The John Beck Log House has been restored with turn-of-the-century furnishings. The display building houses old ledgers and maps, photos of the town (c.1900), logging and family photos, and other artifacts.

Spooner

This old depot, where the era of iron locomotives is kept alive, is a stop on the way to exploring railroad history in the northland.

Railroad Memories Museum
N8425 Island Lake Rd.
Spooner, WI 54801
(Two blocks from Hwys. 70 and 63, in the depot at
Walnut and Front Streets.)

Phone: (715) 635-3325
Contact: Betty Jo Brown, (715) 635-2752
Website: www.washburncounty.com/railroadmuseum/
Hours: Memorial Day - Labor Day, daily, 10am to
5pm, and by appointment.
Admission: Yes

Important works: Railroad tools, equipment, fixtures, uniforms, reference books, art, maps, track inspection vehicles, and collectibles covering all aspects of railroading.

About the museum: The Railroad Memories Museum began operation in 1990, occupying just one room of the old 1902 Chicago and Northwestern Railroad depot. Today, all twelve rooms are packed with artifacts and memorabilia of railroad history. The collection includes rare uniforms, bells, whistles, tools, train interiors, lanterns, signals and lots of photos, books, and videos. Guided tours led by retired railroaders and volunteers are conducted for schools, tour groups and rail enthusiasts. The archives hold many maps, timetables, official documents, and books. "G" and "N" gauge train models are on display. A popular stop is the 8x12-foot diorama of the Spooner Yard from the years when Spooner was a busy rail terminal. The depot now hosts historic train rides on beautifully rebuilt train cars. Train excursions from Spooner to Trego run from April through December and feature a variety of activities and themes.

Fascinating Facts

Regarding slavery, the Wisconsin state constitution reads, "There shall be neither slavery nor involuntary servitude in this state…"

Springbrook

A former Catholic Church is home to this multi-faceted local history museum. A true confession.

Springbrook Church Museum
N8582 Andrews Rd.
Springbrook, WI 54875

Mailing address: P.O. Box 91, Springbrook, WI 54875
Phone: (715) 766-3876
Contact: Joyce Menzel, Museum Manager
Open: June through August, Friday and Saturday, 11am to 4pm.
Admission: Donations welcome

Important works: Restored historic Catholic Church, local history archives.

About the museum: The Springbrook Church Museum is the former St. Mary Magdalene Catholic Church, built in 1906. It was restored as a church and museum and became part of the Washburn County Historical Museum complex in 1993. Exhibits feature a wide range of artifacts from early Springbrook businesses and homes. A large collection of archival material preserves area history through original photos and books, World War II ration books, the American Legion Charter, railroad time schedules, and old maps and documents. There is a different display every month in the summer.

Stanley

Hundreds of objects bring local history alive at this museum.

Stanley Area Historical Museum
228 Helgerson Street
Stanley, WI 54768

Phone: (715) 644-0464 or (715) 644-5109
Contact: Connie Pozdell, President
Open: Memorial Day-Labor Day: Saturday & Sunday, 1-4 and by appointment

This museum collection spans many centuries with items coming from many donors who love local history.

Stevens Point

If you like natural history, don't miss this beautiful museum filled with stuffed animals, creative displays, and rare fossils.

Museum of Natural History
University of Wisconsin-Stevens Point
900 Reserve St.
Stevens Point, WI 54481

Phone: (715) 346-2858 [Fax: 715-346-4213]
Contact: Edward Marks
Email: museum@uwsp.edu
Website: www.uwsp.edu/museum

Open: Monday, 9am to 7pm; Tuesday -Friday, 9am to 4pm; Saturday, 10am to 3pm; Sunday, 1pm to 4pm. Summer and semester break hours may vary.
Admission: Free

Important works: Preserved collections of animals and plants, including an extinct passenger pigeon and collection of bird eggs.

About the museum: At Central Wisconsin's only natural history museum, visitors can explore the origins of the Earth, discover dinosaurs, witness natural habitats and see rare collections of species. A popular stop is the African Savannah exhibit, which reveals how animal and plant life survives the dry season. A variety of exhibits on North America feature golden eagles, grizzly bears, owls, porcupines, foxes, and Canadian geese, all set in their natural habitats. There are also displays of fossils, rocks, and minerals.

In the late 1800s, as many as 136 million passenger pigeons could be found in Central Wisconsin. By 1914, there were none. A mounted passenger pigeon, along with the story of how the species became extinct, is on display. Another highlight is an unusual collection of bird eggs from dozens of species, collected from the 1870s into the early 1900s.

Local Jewish heritage is celebrated here at this historical synagogue.

▲ ★Portage County Historical Society — Beth Israel Synagogue

1475 Water St.
Stevens Point WI 54481

Phone: (715) 344-4423
Contact: Tim Siebert
Email: pchs_54481@yahoo.com
Website: www.pchswi.org/synagogue/synagogue.htm
Open: June thru early September, Saturday and Sunday, 1pm to 5pm.

Important works: Religious artifacts, Jewish history displays.

About the museum: The Congregation Beth Israel Synagogue was built in 1905 and remains on its original site. At one time the congregation had over eighty families as members, many of whom had immigrated from Eastern Europe. Many of the families named in the synagogue's membership lists played key roles in the community's cultural and business affairs. Over the years, most of the early families either moved away or married into other families. By the 1980s, the congregation had shrunk to the point that the remaining members could not maintain the site. To prevent the building from being torn down, the members of the Synagogue donated the building and its land to the historical society. The congregation left the artifacts intact and the society has been able to use them to teach about Jewish traditions and their role in local history.

The society also maintains Heritage Park in Plover, a re-created "village" of nine historic structures, as well as the Rising Star Gristmill in Nelsonville, which hosts arts presentations in the summer.

Come here and see how Wisconsin environmental heritage is commemorated, along with the people who promoted it. If only they could now save the earth.

▲ Wisconsin Conservation Hall of Fame

Schmeeckle Reserve Visitor Center
UW-Stevens Point
North Point Drive
Stevens Point, WI 54481

Phone: (715) 341-4021 or (715) 346-4992
Contact: Ron Zimmerman, Director
Website: www.wchf.org/welcom.html
Open: Daily, 8am to 5pm.
Admission: Free

About the museum: Crackling fires reveal charred stumps and blackened earth...the sharp aroma of sawdust rises from a freshly sawed log ... glaring headlights expose a poacher's camp...and you are in the driver's seat! Stepping through the door of the Conservation Hall of Fame, visitors become part of Wisconsin's environmental history as they discover how resource management has shaped their environment and their lives. Exciting exhibits bring the past to life for all ages. While exploring the Hall of Fame, voices from the past are heard ... voices of those who made Wisconsin a leader in the conservation and environmental movements. Through their actions, philosophies and legislative involvement, people like Aldo Leopold, John Muir, Ernie Swift, and Gaylord Nelson helped redefine our relationship with the land. Exhibits celebrate the contributions of these and other conservation visionaries in Wisconsin history.

Stone Lake

The former town hall now serves as the center of local heritage life.

Stone Lake Area Historical Museum
Main St.
Stone Lake, WI 54876

Contact: Barbara Ruprecht, (715) 865-2750 or Rosemarie Bradley (715) 865-3331
Open: Call for information.

Important works: Local history memorabilia.

About the museum: The museum opened in 1998 in the former Stone Lake Town Hall. Artifacts and pictures depicting history in the greater Stone Lake area are displayed.

Stratford

Time your visit to the June Heritage Days. You won't be disappointed!

Stratford Area Historical Society
Klemme Park – 3rd St.
Stratford, WI 54484

Mailing address: P.O. Box 312, Stratford, WI 54484
Phone: (715) 687-4237
Open: Heritage Days in June, Wednesday evenings in July, 6:30pm to 8:30pm. Memorial Day – October 1 by appointment.

Important works: Local history artifacts and archives.

About the museum: The Society strives to preserve Stratford area history by collecting artifacts, documents, photographs, oral histories, and other relevant information. Exhibits are open and special programs at the museum are held during Heritage Days in June. Displays change yearly and feature various topics and events in Stratford history.

NORTHWEST

Superior

A stunning new facility highlights Douglas County history, past, and present.

▲ Douglas County Historical Society Museum
1101 John Ave.
Superior, WI 54880

Phone: (715) 392-8449 [Fax: (715) 395-5639]
Email: dchs@douglashistory.org
Website: www.douglashistory.org
Open: Contact the museum for current office and exhibit hours or check website.

Important works: Local history artifacts and extensive archives.

About the museum: Occupying new quarters starting in 2002, the Douglas County Historical Museum is in the process of developing exhibits. Past exhibit topics included wedding dresses and a Victorian-era Christmas and toy display. The museum plans to post online exhibits on their website.

Find a great Victorian mansion with views of Lake Superior. What more could you ask for?

▲ ★Fairlawn Mansion and Museum
906 E. Second St.
Superior, WI 54880

Phone: (715) 394-5712 [Fax: 715-394-2043]
Contact: Susan Anderson, Executive Director or Sara Jackson, Administrator Coordinator
Website: www.superiorpublicmuseum.org
Open: Mid-May – December: Monday – Saturday, 9am to 5pm and Sunday, 11am to 5pm. January – Mid-May: Thursday – Sunday, 10am to 4pm.
Admission: Yes

Important works: Victorian era furnishings.

About the museum: Initial construction on the mansion began in 1889 and was finished two years later. The house was built as the private residence for Martin Pattison, an esteemed businessman and community leader. Pattison's wife, Grace, donated the mansion to the Superior Children's Home and Refuge Center after her husband's death in 1918. It remained a children's home until 1962. At present, most of the first floor is restored to its historic 1890s appearance. The second and third floors display period rooms.

Visit an old firehouse turned Hall of Fame for police and firefighters history and heritage.

▲ ★Old Firehouse and Police Museum (Wisconsin Police and Fire Hall of Fame)
402 23rd Ave. E.
Superior, WI 54880
Phone: (715) 394-5712 or (715) 398-7558
Contact: Susan Anderson
Open: Mid-May – October: Thursday – Saturday, 10am to 5pm and Sunday, noon to 5pm. Closed for winter.
Admission: Yes

Important works: Fire and law enforcement artifacts and equipment from Wisconsin and around the world.

About the museum: The Old Firehouse and Police Museum is housed in an authentic City of Superior fire hall. Fire Hall #4, as it was known, provided fire protection to

Superior's eastside until it was decommissioned in 1981. The structure is built of brick and replaced the wooden fire hall that burned down in 1896. A prominent museum site since 1985, the international collection consists of fire and law enforcement artifacts including antique fire engines, police cars, police and fire memorabilia, a hose tower, a jail cell and even a brass pole used by firefighters of long ago. In 1988, the site was officially designed as home of The Wisconsin Police and Fire Hall of Fame.

A most unusual ship serves as focal point to Great Lakes maritime history.

★★S.S. Meteor Maritime Museum
300 Harborview Parkway (Barkers Island)
Superior, WI 54880

Phone: (715) 394-5712 or (715) 392-5742 [Fax: 715-394-2043]
Contact: Susan Anderson
Website: www.superiorpublicmuseums.org
Open: Mid-May – October: Monday – Saturday, 9am to 5pm and Sunday, 11am to 5pm. Closed for winter.
Admission: Yes

Important works: Only whaleback freighter in existence, plus Great Lakes shipbuilding and maritime artifacts.

About the museum: The S.S. Meteor is the last remaining "whaleback" vessel in existence today. It was originally named the Frank Rockefeller. The initial launching of the ship took place in April of 1896 from the American Steel Barbe Company shipyards, located in west Superior. Captain Alexander McDougall engineered the whaleback design, to be able to ship a large amount of cargo at a reduced cost. These steel ships became the forerunners in the design of today's modern boats. The Frank Rockerfeller was the thirty-sixth of forty-three vessels of this type. It sailed the Great Lakes until 1970 and was permanently docked on the shore of Lake Superior in 1972. It became a maritime museum after it was harbored and has artifacts of shipbuilding and sailing history encompassing the entire Great Lakes region.

Thorp

Step into the past and soak up local history in all its forms!

Thorp Area Historical Society Museum
N14945 Gorman Avenue
Thorp, WI 54771

Phone: (715) 669-3307 or (715) 669-3698 or (715) 669-7449
Contact: Lorraine Sitter
Email: lorgss@discover-net.net
Open: Memorial Day-Labor Day, Saturdays, 3pm to 7pm, or by appointment.
Admission: Donations welcome

About the museum: The Thorp area of today developed through the determination of lumbermen, farmers, merchants, and industrialists who contributed to its heritage. When you visit the museum you walk with us in their footprints of the past. The museum, located in the former Old St. Hedwig's Church Rectory, features displays of different themes and historical periods. These include antique dishes, clothing, home furnishings, children's toys, quilts, and needlework. Available research information includes old publications, family histories, and yearbooks. Private collections of historical interest are periodically on loan to the museum. Special theme rooms show how people and industry helped the Thorp area develop.

Three Lakes

The Johnson House, log schoolhouse, and Civilian Conservation Corps buildings are just some of the treasures to visit at this site.

Three Lakes Museum
1798 Huron Street
Three Lakes, WI 54562

Mailing address: p.O. box 250, Three Lakes, Wi. 54562
Phone: (715) 546-2295 or (715) 369-3113
Contact: Marlo Timat, Curator
Website: www.nnet.net/!robwack/museum.htm
Open: Memorial Day-Labor Day: Tuesday – Saturday, 11am to 3pm, also by appointment.
Admission: Donations encouraged

About the museum: The Three Lakes Museum is a grouping of several buildings that represent history in northern Wisconsin. Johnson House, built around 1890, contains period furnishings and exhibits about the history of the early resorts and camping in the north woods. There is also a log cabin schoolhouse that recreates an authentic feel for bygone days. The most interesting group of structures are the Civilian Conservation Corps (CCC) buildings that exhibit maps, artifacts, as well as numerous other documents related to the CCC and their extensive building program that they undertook in the 1930s to put young men and women to work. Call for further details. Call for information on special events.

Tomahawk

Lots of Native American artifacts are here in Tomahawk. Come see them all, with education, pioneer history, and heritage.

Log Cabin Museum
In Washington Park
Tomahawk, WI 54487

Tomahawk's First School Museum
18 E. Washington
Tomahawk, WI 54487

Mailing Address: P.O. Box 655, Tomahawk, WI 54487
Phone: (715) 453-2056
Contact: Mrs. Dixie Zastrow, President of Tomahawk Historical Society
Open: Mid-June – end of August, Wednesday and Thursday, 10am to 4pm; Tuesday, Friday, and Saturday, 10am to 2pm.

These museums contain collections of items, including 19th and 20th century artifacts.

Trempealeau

Hop on over to this historic hotel (pronounced "Trem-Peel-Low") for heritage and lunch.

Historic Trempealeau Hotel
150 Main Street
Trempealeau, WI 54661

Phone: (608) 534-6898
Website: http://www.trempealeauhotel.com/

About the hotel: On the banks of the Mississippi River, it is one of the few buildings to have survived a devastating 1888 fire. Here you can stay for the night in comfort, eat heartily at the four-star restaurant, and enjoy musical entertainment. But don't forget to soak in the history while you are there!

Washburn

For the history buff and art enthusiast, Washburn's best is in one beautiful location!

Washburn Historical Museum and Cultural Center
1 E. Bayfield St.
Washburn, WI 54891

Mailing address: P. O. Box 725, Washburn, WI 54891
Phone: (715) 373-5591
Email: arts@cheqnet.net
Contact: Rachel Coughtry, Cultural Center Director
Open: Summer hours: Monday - Saturday, 10am to 4pm; Sunday, 10am to 2pm. Contact for seasonal changes.

Important works: Monthly exhibits by local artists. Permanent collection features artwork by Wisconsin artists along with artifacts and photographs depicting local and regional history including a diorama of Washburn's historic waterfront.

About the museum: The Museum/Cultural Center is housed in an 1890 historic brownstone structure known as the "Old Bank Building." It features a gallery, banquet, meeting space, gift shop, and historical museum. The Cultural Center sponsors arts and crafts workshops, children's art classes, and art shows year-round. The museum features old-fashioned artifacts including pioneer tools, household items, and travel modes such as bobsleds and horse drawn carriages. The histories of several prominent local families are also on display. The vitality of Washburn's shoreline industry is captured in a diorama created by Harry Peacy. This miniature replica recreates in detail the familiar sights that once dominated the booming waterfront. Special events are scheduled during Washburn's Brownstone Days, an annual celebration of Washburn's history held the last weekend of July.

Wausau

Check out this venue for modern and contemporary art! It's worth a visit.

Center for the Visual Arts
427 N. 4th St.
Wausau, WI 54403

Phone: (715) 842-4545 [Fax: 715-848-8314]
Email: cva@cvawausau.org
Website: www.cvawausau.org
Open: Tuesday – Friday, 10am to 5pm; Saturday and Sunday, noon to 4pm.

Gallery space, gift shop, and classes for children and adults.

▲ ★★★Leigh Yawkey Woodson Art Museum
700 N. 12th St.
Wausau, WI 54403

Phone: (715) 845-7010 [Fax: 715-845-7103]
Contact: Marcia Theel
Email: museum@lywam.org
Website: www.lywam.org
Open: Tuesday - Friday, 9am to 4pm; Saturday and Sunday, noon to 5pm.
Handicapped accessible.
Admission: Free, donations welcome

Important works: Paintings by Robert Bateman, Frank Benson, Albert Bierstadt, Owen Gromme, Bruno Liljefors, and Ogden Pleissner. Sculptures by Antoine-Louis Barye, Deborah Butterfield, Paul Manship, and Kent Ullberg.

About the museum: At the Leigh Yawkey Woodson Art Museum, visitors can sample artworks from every corner of the world through the museum's changing exhibits. Best known is the internationally acclaimed Birds in Art, an annual juried exhibition on birds that showcases a variety of artistic styles - from impressionism to satirical caricature - created by artists the world over. The museum is housed in a 1931 English Tudor period Cotswold-style mansion. The four-acre grounds feature the Margaret Woodson Fisher Sculpture Garden and a formal English garden. An active program of eight to ten changing exhibitions each year encourage frequent visits as does an array of programs for children and adults that complement each exhibition. The permanent collection focuses on birds and nature in paintings, works on paper, and sculpture. Decorative arts make up the balance of the collection. Highlights include more than 125 Victorian glass baskets, hundreds of early 20th century utilitarian and decorative glass and porcelain works, and nearly 100 Royal Worcester porcelain bird figurines by Dorothy Doughty.

Victorian splendor awaits the visitor at this stately home.

▲ Marathon County Historical Museum
410 McIndoe St.
Wausau, WI 54401

Phone: (715) 842-5750 [Fax: (715) 848-0576]
Website: www.marathoncountyhistory.com
Open: Tuesday - Thursday, 9am to 4:30pm, Saturday and Sunday, 1pm to 4:30pm.

About the museum: The museum is located in a Neoclassical, Revival-style mansion built for lumber baron Cyrus Yawkey in 1900 and donated to the historical society in 1954. Victorian charm abound throughout this stately home, with a parlor, reception hall, music room, sun porch, and formal dining room furnished with period antiques. Rotating displays and meeting rooms, plus the historical society library are on the upper floors. A model railroad display in the basement is open on the first and third Sundays of each month.

White Lake

Farming, family, and frontier life are presented in this depot museum. Stop on by.

▲ White Lake Depot Museum
Lake St.
White Lake, WI 54491

Mailing address: P.O. Box 92, White Lake, WI 54491
Phone: (715) 882-8581

Contact: Helen Sanvidge
Open: Memorial Day-Labor Day: Saturday, 9am to 3pm and by appointment.
Admission: Free, donations appreciated

Important works: Railroad and logging artifacts, plus an innovative Pioneer Family History touch-screen exhibit with taped oral history stories of the area.

About the museum: The museum contains artifacts pertaining to transportation, railroading, and logging, plus many other historical items and a collection of old photographs. The newest addition is the Pioneer Family History touch screen exhibit featuring oral history accounts from sixteen individuals who tell stories of the time period from first settlement up to World War II. The oldest participant, who was ninety-seven, came from Kentucky on a wagon train when she was three years old and was an eye witness of the early years of the community. Also included are stories about farming, the Great Depression, prejudice against the Germans in World War I, and the problems of inter-faith marriages.

Wisconsin Rapids

Some thing for everyone at this community based cultural center. Come check it out.

Central Wisconsin Cultural Center
240 Johnson street
Wisconsin Rapids, Wi. 54495

Phone: (715) 421-4552
Contact: director
Open: tuesday-wednesday, friday 10-3 pm, thursday 5-7 pm, saturday 10-12.
Open all year
Admission: free, donations accepted

A small community based cultural center with rotating exhibits on many subjects. They also offer workshops and other educational programs for children and adults throughout the year.

This neoclassical mansion serves as home to a diverse collection of local history including the cranberry industry, railroad heritage, and toys.

South Wood County Historical Museum
540 Third St. S.
Wisconsin Rapids, WI 54494

Phone: (715) 423-1580 [Fax: 715-423-6369]
Contact: Karen Pecher, Director
Email: museum@wctc.net
Website: www.swch-museum.com
Open: Memorial Day – Labor Day: Sunday, Tuesday, and Thursday, 1pm to 4pm.
Admission: Free, donations appreciated

About the museum: The museum is located in a Neoclassical Revival-style mansion built in 1907 by Wisconsin Rapids banker and papermaker, Isaac P. Witter. The family occupied the home until 1943 and it was opened as a museum in 1973. Exhibits illuminate life at the turn of the century and begin with government surveyors who first mapped the area in the 1840s. The people and families who brought commercial cranberry growing to mid-Wisconsin are featured in a display that shows how cranberry cultivation progressed from hand to machine on it way to becoming Wisconsin's number one fruit crop. Other exhibits include the Toy Room with early childhood amusements, a Chicago, Milwaukee, St. Paul, and Pacific Railroad Station where visitors can tap out messages on the telegraph key, and a country kitchen where everything was made from scratch.

From wild animals to the petting zoo, this park has something for everyone! It's alive.

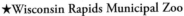

★Wisconsin Rapids Municipal Zoo
1911 Gaynor Ave.
Wisconsin Rapids, WI 54495

Mailing address: 211 12th Ave. S., Wisconsin Rapids, WI 54495
Phone: (715) 421-8240
Contact Person: David Hofs
Open: Mid-May - Labor Day: Tuesday - Sunday, 10am to 7pm.
Admission: Free

About the museum: Petting area plus other displays. Pigs, cows, goats, and other animals will delight the visitors.

Woodruff

This medical museum tells the memorable story of Dr. Kate and a community's desire to build a hospital.

★Dr. Kate Newcomb Museum
923 Second Ave.
Woodruff, WI 54568

Phone: (715) 356-6896 or (715) 356-5562
Contact: Marsha Doud, Curator
Email: drkatmus@Frontiernet.net
Open: Mid-June – Labor Day, 11am to 4pm.
Admission: Free, donations welcome

About the museum: Dr. Kate Pelham Newcomb was a country doctor who played a vital role in the history of Wisconsin's northwoods. "Dr. Kate," as she was called, spearheaded a movement to build a hospital in tiny Woodruff. The lowly penny became a symbol of the project when local children sought to collect a million of them for Dr. Kate's hospital in the early 1950s. The project captured the imagination of the American people and the world and donations of pennies came in from every state and many foreign countries. To preserve this moment when the dedication of one woman and a sense of community made the country cheer, the Dr. Kate Museum was created in 1988.

Some Famous Wisconsinites, movers and shapers

Roy Chapman Andrews (1884-1960) Beloit College explorer who found dinosaur eggs in the Gobi desert in Mongolia. He explored the region between 1922-1930.

John Bardeen (1908-1991) Madison born physicist who developed transistors, twice Nobel prize winner. Graduate of the University of Wisconsin.

Lester Bentley (1908-1972) noted WPA era painter, known for his portraits and Landscapes. He was from Two Rivers.

Eugene von Bruenchenhein (1910-1983), innovative artist, self-taught visionary. He lived in West Allis.

Seymour Cray (1925-1996), scientist, father of the supercomputer. He was born in Chippewa Falls.

John Steuart Curry (1897-1946) regionalist painter and artist in residence at University of Wisconsin-Madison. Known for his images of rural America.

James Duane Doty (1799-1865) territorial governor of Wisconsin, congressman, judge, and land speculator. He laid out Madison and promoted its growth. Retired to Neenah on Doty Island.

Hercules Louis Dousman (1800-1868) was Wisconsin's first millionaire. He was a fur trading expert and built a grand mansion on the Mississippi River that is today a state historic site called Villa Louis. Recently restored.

Dr. Evermor (1938-) self-taught visionary artist and recycling pioneer, who built his great art environment near Prairie du Sac.

Ole Evinrude (1877-1934) Born in Cambridge and resided in Milwaukee. He was the inventor and developed the first practical outboard motor engine.

Edna Ferber (1885-19680) Raised in Appleton and worked in Milwaukee, author and 1925 Pulitzer prize winner for, So Big.

Sister Thomasita Fessler (1912-2005) Milwaukee educator and artist, known for her paintings.

Zona Gale (1874-1938) author and 1921 Pulitzer prize winner for the play Miss Lulu Bett, from Portage.

William T. Green (1863-1911) activist, first black attorney in Wisconsin. Graduated from the University of Wisconsin in 1892 and worked in Milwaukee.

Owen Gromme (1896-1991), born in Fond du Lac, wildlife artist. Resided in Milwaukee.

Ruth Grotenrath, (1912-1988) artist and watercolorist and educator. Lived in Milwaukee.

Cordelia Harvey (1824-1895) humanitarian who helped establish military hospitals in the north during the Civil War who worked in Madison.

Harry Houdini (1874-1926), magician and escape artist. He lived in Appleton briefly.

Vinnie Ream Hoxie (1847-1914) of Madison was the first woman sculptor commissioned by the Congress of the

United States to produce a work of art for Statuary Hall in the Federal Capitol. She carved the statue of the seated Abraham Lincoln which was completed in 1870 and can still be seen in the Federal Capitol in Washington, D.C.

Samuel Johnson (1833-1919) industrialist who founded the Johnson and Johnson Co. in Racine.

John Michael Kohler (1844-1900), Austrian immigrant who prospered by making indoor plumbing fixtures and other industrial products. His family still runs the Kohler Company in the village of Kohler.

Robert M. LaFollette (1855-1925) political leader of the progressive party and USA Senator. Known as "Fighting Bob". He lived in Madison.

Earl L. "Curly" Lambeau (1898-1965) professional football coach, founder of the Green Bay Packers.

Increase Allen Lapham, (1811-1875), pioneer naturalist, inventor, author, established the U.S. Weather Bureau. Moved to Milwaukee in 1836.

Aldo Leopold (1887-1948) teacher, author, pioneer naturalist. He lived near Portage.

Edmund Lewandowski (1914-1998), educator, painter known for his precisionist style. He lived in Milwaukee.

Wladziu Valentino Liberace (1919-1986) musician and pianist from Wauwatosa.

Schomer Lichtner, Milwaukee artist, husband of Ruth Grotenrath. He worked for the WPA and is still active in the world of Wisconsin art.

Vince Lombardi (1913-1970) from 1959-1968 coached the Green Bay Packers.

Carl Von Marr (1858-1936), famous painter, artist. The West Bend Art Museum has the world's largest collection of his art. He lived in Milwaukee.

Helen Farnsworth Mears (1872-1916) artist, sculptor, known for her "Genius of Wisconsin" statue in the State Capitol, Madison.

Golda Meir (1898-1978) political leader from Milwaukee, and prime minister of Isreal (1969-1974).

William "Billy" Mitchell (1879-1936) brigadier general in the U. S. Army and aviator. He lived in Milwaukee.

John Muir (1838-1914) naturalist who promoted the national park system.

Gaylord A. Nelson (1916-2005) father of Earth Day, from Clear Lake.

John Nicolet (1598-1642) French explorer who visited Wisconsin in 1634 and landed near Red Banks, Door County.

George Mann Niedecken (1874-1945), Prairie School artist and interior designer. He lived and worked in Milwaukee. Worked with F.L. Wright.

Mary Nohl (1914-2001) , eccentric Milwaukee artist known for paintings and sculpture.

Georgia O'Keefe (1887-1986), innovative American artist, born in Sun Prairie.

Albert Ringling (1852-1916) circus promoter. Created the "Greatest Show in Earth." To learn more visit Circus World Museum in Baraboo.

Margaretha Meyer Schurz (1833-1876) educator who opened the first kindergarten in the United States in Watertown.

C. Latham Sholes (1819-1890) Milwaukee inventor who built the first practical typewriter.

Donald Kent "Deke" Slayton (1924-1993) U.S. astronaut from Sparta who flew in the first joint U.S.-Soviet space flights.

Brooks Stevens (1911-1995) Milwaukee industrial designer, including the 1956 Oscar Mayer "Wienermobile".tm

Spencer Tracy (1900-1967) Milwaukee born actor and academy award winner.

Orson Wells (1915-1986) Born in Kenosha, actor and director. Famous for his role in the movie Citizen Cane.

Frances Willard (1839-1898), social reformer who organized the Woman's Christian Temperance Union. She promoted equal rights and universal suffrage. She attended Milwaukee Female College.

Frank Lloyd Wright (1867-1959) American architect known for innovative designs, including the Johnson Wax headquarters in Racine. He lived and worked in Spring Green.

APPENDIX

APPENDIX

Wisconsin State Symbols

Thanks to the Wisconsin Legislative Bureau for these images and data.

State Animal
Badger
The badger has been associated with the state since territorial days, but only became the state animal in 1957. Early lead miners were frequently likened to badgers as they lived in burrowed caves as homes and mining sites looking for lead and tin.

State Flower
Wood violet
On Arbor Day in 1909 the wood violet became the state flower after competing with 3 others local flowers.

State Bird
Robin
Between 1926-27 Wisconsin school children voted for a state bird. The robin won out and became the official state bird years later in 1949.

State Tree
Sugar maple
1893 school children voted for the sugar maple, again voting was held in 1948. It became the state tree in 1949.

Shape of Wisconsin
Like an open hand or mitten

State Insect
Honey Bee
Designated as the official state insect in 1977 after being introduced by a third grader from Marinette and the Wisconsin Honey Producers Association. Other contenders included the mosquito, ladybug, and dragonfly. Some still think it's the mosquito.

State Dog
American Water Spaniel
School children again played a role in selecting the official state dog in 1985.

State Mineral: Galena
State Rock: Red Granite
The Kenosha Gem and Mineral Society proposed a state mineral and rock, which was enacted into law in 1971.

State Fossil
Trilobite
The Wisconsin Geological Society proposed a state fossil, which was enacted into law in 1985. It symbolizes Wisconsin's ancient past.

APPENDIX

State Grain
Corn
In 1989 corn was designated the official state grain.

State Beverage
Milk
Milk became the official state beverage in 1987.

State Dance
Polka
In 1993, after intense lobbying by second grade school children from Madison and the Wisconsin Polka Boosters, and others the dance became the official state dance.

State Soil
Antigo Silt Loam
In 1983, after successful lobbying by Prof. Francis Hole and others the Antigo Silt Loam became the official state soil.

State Symbol of Peace
Mourning Dove
In 1971, various organizations dedicated to peace and conservation succeeded in getting the mourning dove designated as the state symbol of peace.

State Wildlife Animal
White-tailed Deer

Wisconsin's nickname
The "Badger State"

State Domesticated Animal
The Holstein and Ayrshire dairy cows
The dairy cow was designated in 1971 as state "domestic animal". Now both cows hold the official designation as state domesticated animal. The Holstein was selected in 2001 followed by the Ayrshire in 2002.

State Fish
Muskellunge
Trout and the Muskellunge competed for years as possible official state fish. The Muskie won out and became the state fish by law in 1955.

State Motto
"Forward"
The motto "Forward" was introduced in 1851 as part of the great seal.

State Song
"On Wisconsin"
Composed in 1909 by William T. Purdy.

APPENDIX

The State Coat of Arms

The coat of arms is historically connected with the great seal. It bears the following images: A sailor of the left, a miner on the right. They flank the state seal in the center. The whole is surmounted by the state animal badger and the state motto "Forward". At the bottom left is a cornucopia and on the right 13 lead ingots that symbolize the 13 original states and mineral wealth. The center is divided into 4 parts with a plow, pick and shovel, arm and hammer, and anchor. In the circular center on a shield is the U.S. coat of arms, symbolizing allegiance to the nation and union. This is surrounded by the Latin motto "E pluribus Unum" (one out of many).

The Wisconsin State Seal

An official seal was created in 1836, then again in 1848 when Wisconsin became a state, then again in 1851, and lastly in 1881. The seal is essentially identical to the state coat of arms, but circular in form with 13 stars at the base that symbolize the 13 original colonies of the American Republic. There is also a sailor and miner supporting a shield that symbolizes manufacturing, navigation, agriculture and mining.

State Flag

The Wisconsin state flag became the official state flag in 1913. The flag, originally designed in 1863 for Wisconsin Civil War regiments, was modified in 1913 and again in 1979.

Wisconsin Museums Affiliated with the American Association of Museums

Langlade County Historical Museum, Antigo
Appleton Art Center, Appleton
Hearthstone Historic House Museum, Appleton
Outagamie Museum, Appleton
Wriston art Center, Appleton
Ashland Historical Museum, Ashland
Ridges Sanctuary, Baileys Harbor
Polk County Museum, Balsam Lake
Circus World Museum, Baraboo
International Crane Foundation, Baraboo
Sauk County Historical Museum, Baraboo
S.S. Meteor Maritime Museum, Barkers Island, Superior
Apostles Islands National Lakeshore, Bayfield
Dodge County Historical Museum, Beaver Dam
Beloit Historical Society, Beloit
Logan Museum of Anthropology, Beloit
Wright Museum of Art, Beloit
Berlin Historical Museum, Berlin
Jackson County Historical Museum, Black River Falls
Little Norway, Blue Mounds
Cable Natural History Museum, Cable

Barron County Historical Pioneer Village, Cameron
Wisconsin National Guard Museum, Camp Douglas
Reuss Ice Age Visitors Center, Campbellsport
Stonefield Historic Site, Cassville
Ozaukee Art Center, Cedarburg
Clear Lake Historical Museum, Clear Lake
Four Wheel Drive Foundation, Clintonville
Forts Folle Avoine Historic Park, Danbury
Oneida Nation Museum, De Pere
White Plains Museum, De Pere
Hawks Inn, Delafield
St. John's Northwestern Military Archives/Museum, Delafield
Old World Wisconsin, Eagle
East Troy Electric Railroad Museum, East Troy
Chippewa Valley Museum, Eau Claire
Foster Art Gallery UW-Eau Claire, Eau Claire
Paul Bunyan Logging Camp, Eau Claire
Albion Academy Museum, Edgerton
Cupola House, Egg Harbor
Webster house Museum, Ekhorn
Newport State Park, Ellison Bay

The Ephraim Foundation, Ephraim
Old Town Hall Museum, Fifield
Eagle Bluff Lighthouse, Fish Creek
Galloway House and Village, Fond du Lac
Hoard Museum and Diary Shrine, Fort Atkinson
Fox Lake Historical Museum, Fox Lake,
Children's Museum of Green Bay, Green Bay
Green Bay Packers Hall of Fame, Green Bay
Heritage Hill State Park, Green Bay
National Railroad Museum, Green Bay
Neville Public Museum, Green Bay
Wade House and Jung Carriage Museum, Greenbush
Greenfield Historical Society, Muskego
Wisconsin Automobile Museum, Hartford
Fishing Hall of Fame, Hayward
Hillsboro Historical Society, Hillsboro
Satterlee Clark House, Horicon
Octagon House, Hudson
Iron County Courthouse Museum, Hurley
Lincoln-Tallman Restorations, Janesville
Rock County Historical Society, Janesville
Aztalan Museum, Jefferson
Grignon Mansion, Kaukauna
Kenosha Historical Museum, Kenosha
Kenosha Public Museum, Kenosha
Kewaunee Historical Museum, Kewaunee
Wisconsin Veterans Museum, King
Hixon House, La Crosse
Pump House Regional Arts Center, La Crosse
Riverside Museum, La Crosse
Swarthout Memorial Museum, La Crosse
Madeline Island Historical Museum, La Pointe
Rusk County Historical Museum, Ladysmith
Northland Historical Society, Lake Tomahawk
Camp five Museum Foundation, Laona
Chazen Art Museum, Madison
Allen Textile Collection, Madison
Vilas Zoo, Madison
Madison Children's Museum, Madison
Madison Museum of Contemporary Art, Madison
Olbrich Botanical Gardens, Madison,
University of Wisconsin Arboretum, Madison
University of Wisconsin, Zoological Museum, Madison
Wisconsin Historical Museum, Madison
Wisconsin Union Galleries-University of Wisconsin, Madison
Wisconsin Veterans Museum, Madison
Lincoln Parl Zoo, Manitowoc
Pinecrest Historical Village, Manitowoc
Rahr-West Art Museum, Manitowoc
Wisconsin Maritime Museum, Manitowoc
Marinette County Historical Museum, Marinette
New Visions Gallery, Marshfield
Upham Mansion, Marshfield
Boorman House, Mauston
Mayville Historical Society, Mayville
Mazomanie Historical Society, Mazomanie
McFarland Historical Society, McFarland
Old Falls Village, Menomonee Falls
John Furlong Gallery, Menomonie
Concordia University Art Gallery, Mequon
Crafts Museum, Mequon
Merrill Historical Museum, Merrill
Milton House Museum, Milton
America's Black Holocaust Museum, Milwaukee
Betty Brinn Children's Museum, Milwaukee
Charles Allis Art Museum, Milwaukee
Discovery World-Lovell Museum of Science,
Economics, and Technology-Milwaukee
Greene Museum, University of Wisconsin-Milwaukee
International Clown Hall of Fame, Milwaukee
Milwaukee Art Museum, Milwaukee
Milwaukee County Historical Society, Milwaukee
Milwaukee County Zoo, Milwaukee
Milwaukee Public Museum, Milwaukee
Michell Gallery of Flight, Milwaukee
Mitchell Park Conservatory (the Domes) Milwaukee
Mount Mary College Costume Collection, Milwaukee
Haggerty art Museum, Milwaukee
UWMUnion Art Galleries, Milwaukee

Villa Terrace Decorative Arts Museum, Milwaukee
Pendarvis, Mineral Point
Bergstrom-Mahler Museum, Neenah
Neenah Historical Museum, Octagon House, Neenah
New Berlin Historical Museum, New Berlin
Chalet of the Golden Fleece, New Glarus
Swiss Historical Village, New Glarus
Calumet County Historical Society, New Holstein
Pioneer Corner Museum, New Holstein
New London Public Museum, New London
New Richmond Preservation Society, New Richmond
Mid-Continent Railway Museum, North Freedom
Oak Creek Pioneer Village, Oak Creek
Beyer Home, Oconto County Historical, Oconto
EAA-Airventure Museum, Oshkosh
Military Veterans Museum, Oshkosh
Oshkosh Public Museum, Oshkosh
Paine art center and Gardens, Oshkosh
Peshtigo Fire Museum, Peshtigo
Platteville Mining Museum, Platteville
Rollo Jamison Museum, Platteville
Bradley Gallery of Art, Plymouth
Fort Winnebago Surgeons Quarters, Portage
Historic Indian Agency House, Portage
MacKenzie Environmental Education Center, Poynette
Fort Crawford Museum, Prairie du Chien
Villa Louis historic Site, Prairie du Chien
Sauk Prairie Historical Society, Prairie du Chien
Racine Art Museum, Racine
Racine Heritage Museum, Racine
Racine Zoo, Racine
Rhinelander Logging Museum, Rhinelander
German Warehouse, Richland Center
Little White School House, Ripon
Gallery 101 University of Wisconsin-River Falls
St. Croix National Scenic Riverway, St. Croix Falls
Ozaukee County Pioneer Village, Cedarburg
Seymour Museum, Seymour
Shawano County Historical Society, Shawano
Kohler Arts Center, Sheboygan,
Sheboygan County Historical Museum, Sheboygan
Museum of woodcarving, Shell Lake
Washburn County Historical Museum, Shell Lake
High Cliff Historical Society, Hilbert
Badger Mine Museum, Shullsburg
South Milwaukee Historical Museum, South Milwaukee
Monroe County History Room, Sparta
House on the Rock, Spring Green
Museum of Natural history, Stevens Point
Stoughton Historical Society, Stoughton
Door County Maritime Museum, Sturgeon Bay
Door County Museum, Sturgeon Bay
The Farm, Sturgeon Bay
Miller Art Museum, Sturgeon Bay
Potawatomi State Park, Sturgeon Bay
Whitefish Dunes Park, Clear Lake
Sun Prairie Historical Museum, Sun Prairie
Douglas County Historical Society, Superior
Vernon County Historical Museum, Viroqua
Washburn Museum and Cultural Center, Washburn
Rock Island State Park, Washington Island
Octagon House First Kindergarten, Watertown
Waukesha County Historical Museum, Waukesha
Holly History Center and Hutchison Museum, Waupaca
Leigh Yawkey Woodson Art Museum, Wausau
Marathon County Historical Museum, Wausau
Lowell Damon House, Wauwatosa
West Allis Historical Museum, West Allis
Washington County Historical Museum, West Bend
West Bend Art Museum, West Bend
Hamlin Garland Homestead, West Salem
Palmer/Gullickson Octagon House, West Salem
Marquette County Historical Society, Westfield
Little Red School House Museum, Weyauwega
Crossman Gallery, UW-Whitewater, Whitewater
Whitewater Historical Museum, Whitewater
Pioneer Museum, Wild Rose
South Wood County Historical Corp, Wisconsin Rapids

Helpful Contacts in Wisconsin

Wisconsin Department of Tourism
800-432-8747, www.travelwisconsin.com/winter

Portal Wisconsin
www.portalwisconsin.org

Wisconsin Department of Natural Resources
www.dnr.state.wi.us

Wisconsin Public Radio
www.wpr.org

Trees For Tomorrow
800-838-9472, www.treesfortomorrow.com

Current information about the lakes area
www.greatlakesonline.com

Chambers of Commerce in Wisconsin

Google or call the following cities for updated information from the local Chamber of Commerce. It has been my experience that the chambers have more current information about the local attractions.

A
Abbotsford Chamber of Commerce: 715/223-0657
Adams County Chamber of Commerce: 608/339-6997 or 888/339-6997
Algoma Area Chamber of Commerce: 920/487-2041 or 800/498-4888
Almena Commercial Club: 715/357-3228
Amberg Community Association: 715/759-5354
Amery Community Club: 715/268-6624
Antigo Area Chamber of Commerce: 715/623-4134 or 888/526-4523
Appleton (Fox Cities Chamber of Commerce & Industry Inc.): 920/734-7101
Arbor Vitae (Minocqua-Arbor Vitae-Woodruff Area Chamber of Commerce): 715/356-5266 or 800/44-NORTH
Arcadia Chamber of Commerce: 608/323-2319
Argyle Chamber of Commerce: 608/543-3233
Ashippun Business Association: 920/474-7143
Ashland Area Chamber of Commerce: 715/682-2500 or 800/284-9484
Athens Area Chamber of Commerce: 715/257-7531

B
Baileys Harbor: 920/839-9487
Baldwin Area Chamber of Commerce: 715/684-2221
Balsam Lake Community Club: 715/485-3424
Bangor Business Club: 608/486-2711
Baraboo Area Chamber of Commerce: 608/356-8333 or 800/227-2266
Barron Community Club: (Mailing address, 307 E LaSalle Ave, Barron, WI 54812)
Bayfield Chamber of Commerce: 715/779-3335 or 800/447-4094
Bayfield Recreation Business Association (Eau Claire Lakes Business Association): 715/376-2322
Beaver Dam Area Chamber of Commerce: 920/887-8879
Belleville Chamber of Commerce: 608/424-3336
Greater Beloit Chamber of Commerce: 608/365-8835
Berlin Chamber of Commerce: 920/361-3636
Birchwood Area Lakes Association: 715/354-3771
Black Creek Advancement Association: 920/984-3575
Black River Area Chamber of Commerce: 715/284-4658
Blair Chamber of Commerce: 608/989-2517
Blanchardville Chamber of Commerce: 608/523-2274
Bloomer Chamber of Commerce: 715/568-3339
Bloomington Business Club: (Mailing address, Bloomington, WI 53804)
Boscobel Chamber of Commerce: 608/375-2672
Boulder Junction Chamber of Commerce: 715/385-2400 or 800/466-8759
Brillion Chamber of Commerce: 920/756-2250
Brodhead Chamber of Commerce: 608/897-8411
Greater Brookfield Chamber of Commerce: 262/786-1886
Brookfield Convention & Visitors Bureau, Inc.: 414/789-0220
Burlington Area Chamber of Commerce: 262/763-6044
Butler Area Chamber of Commerce: 414/781-5195

C
Cable Area Chamber of Commerce: 715/798-3833 or 800/533-7454
Cadott Area Chamber of Commerce: 715/289-3338
Cambria-Friesland Area Chamber of Commerce (Mailing address, Box 143, Cambria, WI 53923-0143)
Cambridge Area Chamber of Commerce: 608/423-3780

Cameron Business Association: (Mailing address, Cameron, WI 54822)
Campbellsport Area Chamber of Commerce: 920/979-0080
Cassville Civic Club: 608/725-5855
Cecil Area Chamber of Commerce: (Mailing address, Cecil, WI 54111)
Cedarburg Chamber of Commerce: 414/377-5856
Cedarburg Visitors Information Center: 414/377-9620
Centuria Commercial Club: (Mailing address, Box 280, Centuria, WI 54824)
Chetek Chamber of Commerce: 715/924-3200 or 800/317-1720
Chilton Chamber of Commerce: 920/849-4541
Chippewa Falls Area Chamber of Commerce: 715/723-0331
Chippewa Valley (Eau Claire Area) Convention & Visitors Bureau: 715/831-2345or 800/344-FUNN
Clear Lake Civic & Commerce Association: (Mailing address, Box 266, Clear Lake, WI 54005-0266)
Cleveland Area Chamber of Commerce: 920/693-8256.
Clintonville Area Chamber of Commerce: 715/823-4606
Colby Chamber of Commerce: 715/223-4435
Coleman-Pound Area Chamber of Commerce: (Mailing address, Box 105, Coleman, WI 54112)
Columbus Area Chamber of Commerce: 920/623-3699
Combined Locks (Heart of the Valley Chamber of Commerce): 920/766-1616
Conover Chamber of Commerce: 715/479-4928 or 800/236-4928
Greater Cornell Area Community Development Association, Inc.: 715/239-3713
Cornucopia Business Association: 715/742-3282
Cottage Grove Economic Development Corporation (CGEDC)
Crandon Area Chamber of Commerce: 715/478-3450 or 800/334-3387
Cross Plains Business Association: 608/798-3961
Cuba City Chamber of Commerce: 608/744-3456
Cudahy Chamber of Commerce: 414/483-8615
Cumberland Area Chamber of Commerce: 715/822-3378

D
Dale Community Club: (Mailing address, Dale, WI 54931)
Dallas Civic Club: 715/837-1186
Kingston-Dalton-Marquette Business Association: 920/394-3544
Danbury Chamber of Commerce: 715/656-3292
Darboy (Heart of the Valley Chamber of Commerce): 920/766-1616
Darlington Chamber of Commerce: 608/776-3067 or 888/506-6553
Deerfield Chamber of Commerce: 608/764-8069
De Forest Area Chamber of Commerce: 608/846-2922
Delafield Chamber of Commerce: 414/646-8100
Delavan-Delavan Lake Area Chamber of Commerce: 414/728-5095 or 800/624-0052
Denmark Community Business Association (mailing address, PO Box 97, Denmark WI 54208-0097)
De Pere (Green Bay Area Chamber of Commerce): 920/437-8704
Dodgeville Chamber of Commerce: 608/935-9200
Door County Chamber of Commerce: 920/743-4456
Douglas County (Superior-Douglas County Chamber of Commerce): 715/394-7716 or 800/942-5313
Dousman Chamber of Commerce: 414/965-3792
Durand Commercial Club: (Mailing address, Durand, WI 54736)

E
Eagle Business Association: 262/594-3114
Eagle River Area Chamber of Commerce & Visitor Center: 715/479-6400 or 800/359-6315
East Troy Area Chamber of Commerce: 262/642-3770
Eau Claire Area Chamber of Commerce: 715/834-1204
Eau Claire Lakes Business Association: 715/376-2322 or 800/299-7506
Edgar Area Business Association: 715/352-2178
Edgerton Area Chamber of Commerce: 608/884-4408 or 800/298-4408
Elkhart Lake Area Chamber of Commerce: 920/876-2922 or 877/ELKHART
Elkhorn Area Chamber of Commerce: 414/723-5788
Ellsworth Chamber of Commerce: 715/273-6442 or 800/474-3723
Elroy Area Advancement Corporation: 608/462-2410 or 888/606-2453
Evansville Chamber of Commerce: 608/882-5131

F
Fennimore Chamber of Commerce: 608/822-3599 or 800/822-1131
Fish Creek Civic Association: 920/868-2316 or 800/577-1880
Fitchburg Chamber of Commerce: 608/288-8284
Florence County Chamber of Commerce: 715/528-3595
Fond du Lac Area Association of Commerce: 920/921-9500
Fond du Lac Area Convention & Visitors Bureau: 920/923-3010 or 800/937-9123
Footville (Orfordville/Footville Chamber of Commerce): (Mailing address, Orfordville, WI 53576)
Forest Junction (Heart of the Valley Chamber of Commerce): 920/766-1616
Fort Atkinson Area Chamber of Commerce: 920/563-3210 or 888/SEE-FORT
Forward Janesville, Inc.: 608/757-3160 or 888/354-8886
Fox Cities Chamber of Commerce & Industry Inc. (Appleton, Menasha, Neenah): 920/734-7101
Fox Cities Convention & Visitors Bureau: 920/734-3358 or 800/236-6673
Fox Lake Chamber of Commerce: 920/928-3777 or 800/858-4904
Franklin Chamber of Commerce: 414/761-8774
Frederic Area Chamber of Commerce: 715/327-4836
Fredonia Chamber of Commerce Committee: 414/692-2466

Freedom (Heart of the Valley Chamber of Commerce): 920/766-1616
Fremont Area Chamber of Commerce: 920/446-3838
Friendship (Adams County Chamber of Commerce): 608/339-6997 or 888/339-6997
Friesland Chamber of Commerce: 920/348-5267

G
Galesville Area Chamber of Commerce: 608/582-2868
Geneva Lake Area Chamber of Commerce: 414/248-4416 or 800/345-1020
Germantown Area Chamber of Commerce: 414/255-1812
Gillett Business Association: 920/855-2255
Gilman Community Betterment Association: 715/447-5723
Gleason Community Club, Inc.: 715/539-9359
Glendale Association of Commerce: 414/228-1716
Glidden Area Chamber of Commerce: 715/264-4304
Grafton Area Chamber of Commerce: 414/377-1650
Grantsburg Chamber of Commerce: 715/463-2405
Green Bay Area Chamber of Commerce: 920/437-8704
Green Lake Area Chamber of Commerce: 920/294-3231 or 800/253-7354
Green Lake County Chamber of Commerce: (Mailing address, Route 1, Box 294, Princeton, WI 54968)
Greendale Chamber of Commerce: 414/423-3900
Greenfield Chamber of Commerce: 414/327-8500
Greenleaf (Heart of the Valley Chamber of Commerce): 920/766-1616
Greenwood Chamber of Commerce: 715/267-7221

H
Hartford Area Chamber of Commerce: 414/673-7002
Hartland Area Chamber of Commerce: 414/367-7059
Hatley Chamber of Commerce: 715/446-3435
Hayward Area Chamber of Commerce: 715/634-8662 or 800/724-2992
Hazelhurst Information Center: 715/356-7350
Heart of the Valley Chamber of Commerce: 920/766-1616 (Kimberly, Kaukauna, Little Chute, Combined Locks, Wrightstown, Freedom, Darboy, Sherwood, Holland, Forest Junction, Greenleaf and Dundas)
Hispanic Chamber of Commerce of Wisconsin: 414/643-6963
Hixton Area Development: (Mailing address, Hixton, WI 54635)
Hollandtown (Heart of the Valley Chamber of Commerce): 920/766-1616
Horicon Chamber of Commerce: 920/485-3200
Hortonville Chamber of Commerce: (Mailing address, Box 430, Hortonville, WI 54944)
Hudson Area Chamber of Commerce & Tourism Bureau: 715/386-8411 or 800/657-6775
Hurley Area Chamber of Commerce: 715/561-4334 or 866/340-4334

I
Iola-Scandinavia Area Chamber of Commerce: 715/445-4000
Iron County Development Zone Council: 715/561-2922

J
Jackson Area Business Association: 262/677-2269
Janesville (Forward Janesville, Inc.): 608/757-3160 or 888/FJI-8886
Janesville Area Convention & Visitors Bureau: 608/757-3171 or 800/487-2757
Jefferson Chamber of Commerce: 920/674-4511
Johnson Creek Area Chamber of Commerce: 920/699-2296
Juda Community Club: (Mailing address, Juda, WI 53550)
Juneau Chamber of Commerce: 920/386-9095

K
Kaukauna (Heart of the Valley Chamber of Commerce): 920/766-1616
Kenosha Area Chamber of Commerce: 262/654-1234
Kenosha Area Convention & Visitors Bureau: 262/654-7307 or 800/654-7309
Kewaskum Area Chamber of Commerce: 262/626-3336
Kewaunee Chamber of Commerce: 920/388-4822 or 800/666-8214
Kickapoo Valley Association, Inc.: 608/872-2504
Kiel Area Association of Commerce: 920/894-4638
Kimberly (Heart of the Valley Chamber of Commerce): 920/766-1616
Kingston - Dalton - Marquette Business Association: 920/394-3544

L
Greater La Crosse Area Chamber of Commerce: 608/784-4880
Lac du Flambeau Chamber of Commerce: 715/588-3346 or 877/588-3346
Greater Ladysmith Area Chamber of Commerce: 715/532-7328 or 800/535-RUSK
Lake Geneva (Geneva Lake Area Chamber of Commerce): 414/248-4416 or 800/345-1020
Lake Mills Area Chamber of Commerce: 920/648-3585
Lake Nebagamon (Nebagamon Community Association): 715/374-2283
Lake Wisconsin Area Chamber of Commerce: 608/635-8070
Lakewood Area Chamber of Commerce: 715/276-6500
Lancaster Chamber of Commerce: 608/723-2820
Land O' Lakes Chamber of Commerce: 715/547-3432 or 800/236-3432
Lena Community Development Corporation: 920/829-5525
Little Chute (Heart of the Valley Chamber of Commerce): 920/766-1616

Lodi Chamber of Commerce: 608/592-4412
Lomira Area Chamber of Commerce: 920/269-7229
Loyal Chamber of Commerce: 715/255-8531
Luck Commercial Club: 715/472-2222 (Village Hall)
Luxemburg Chamber of Commerce: 920/845-2722

M
Madeline Island Chamber of Commerce: 715/747-2801 or 888/475-3386
Greater Madison Chamber of Commerce: 608/256-8348
Manawa Area Chamber of Commerce: 920/596-2495
Manitowish Waters Chamber of Commerce: 715/543-8488 or 888/626-9877
Manitowoc-Two Rivers Area Chamber of Commerce: 920/684-5575
Manitowoc Visitor & Convention Bureau: 920/683-4388 or 800/627-4896
Wausau Area/Marathon County Chamber of Commerce: 715/845-6231
Marinette Area Chamber of Commerce: 715/735-6681 or 800/236-6681
Markesan Area Chamber of Commerce: 920/398-8023
Kingston-Dalton-Marquette Business Association: 920/394-3544
Marshfield Area Chamber of Commerce & Industry: 715/384-3454 or 800/422-4541
Marshfield Visitors & Promotion Bureau: 715/384-3454 or 800/422-4541
Greater Mauston Area Chamber of Commerce: 608/847-4142
Mayville Area Chamber of Commerce: 920/387-5776 or 800/256-7670
Mazomanie Chamber of Commerce: 608/795-2117
McFarland Chamber of Commerce: 608/838-4011
Medford Area Chamber of Commerce: 715/748-4729 or 888/682-9567
Mellen Area Chamber of Commerce: 715/274-2330
Menasha (Fox Cities Chamber of Commerce & Industry Inc.): 920/734-7101
Greater Menomonie Area Chamber of Commerce: 715/235-9087 or 800/283-1862
Menomonee Falls Chamber of Commerce: 262/251-2430 or 800/801-6565
Mequon-Thiensville Area Chamber of Commerce & Industry: 414/512-9358
Mercer Area Chamber of Commerce: 715/476-2389
Merrill Area Chamber of Commerce: 715/536-9474 or 877/907-2757
Merrillan Commercial Club: 715/332-2332
Middleton Chamber of Commerce: 608/827-5797
Millston Chamber of Commerce: (Mailing address, Millston, WI 54643)
Milltown Community Club: 715/825-2257
Milton Area Chamber of Commerce: 608/868-6222 or 866/645-8660
Metropolitan Milwaukee Association of Commerce: 414/287-4100
Milwaukee Minority Chamber of Commerce: 414/226-4105
South Milwaukee Association of Commerce: 414/762-2222
Greater Milwaukee Convention & Visitors Bureau: 414/273-3950
Mineral Point Chamber/Main Street: 608/987-3201 or 888/764-6794
Minocqua-Arbor Vitae-Woodruff Area Chamber of Commerce: 715/356-5266 or 800/446-6784
Mishicot Area Chamber of Commerce: 920/755-2525
Mondovi Business Association: 715/926-3866
Monona Chamber of Commerce: 608/222-8565
Monroe Chamber of Commerce: 608/325-7648
Montello Area Chamber of Commerce: 608/297-7420 or 800/684-7199
Monticello Community Club: (Mailing address, Monticello, WI 53570)
Mosinee Area Chamber of Commerce, Inc.: 715/693-4330
Mount Horeb Area Chamber of Commerce: 608/437-5914
Mukwonago Chamber of Commerce: 262/363-7758
Muscoda Chamber of Commerce: 608/739-9158
Muskego Chamber of Commerce: 414/679-2550

N
Nashotah Area Chamber of Commerce: 262/367-3374
Nebagamon Community Association: 715/374-2283
Neenah (Fox Cities Chamber of Commerce & Industry Inc.): 920/734-7101
Neillsville Area Chamber of Commerce: 715/743-6444
Nekoosa (Wisconsin Rapids Area Chamber of Commerce): 715/423-1830 or 800/554-4484
New Berlin Chamber of Commerce: 414/786-5280
New Glarus Chamber of Commerce: 608/527-2095 or 800/527-6838
New Holstein Area Chamber of Commerce: 920/894-3482
New Lisbon Area Chamber of Commerce: 608/562-3555
New London Area Chamber of Commerce: 920/982-5822
New Richmond Area Chamber of Commerce & Visitors Bureau: 715/246-2900 or 800/654-6380

O
Oconomowoc Area Chamber of Commerce: 262/567-2666
Oconomowoc Convention & Visitors Bureau: 262/569-2185 or 800/524-3744
Oconto Area Chamber of Commerce: 920/834-6254
Oconto Falls Area Chamber of Commerce: 920/846-8306
Omro: 920/685-6960
Oostburg Businessmen's Association: 920/564-2336
Oregon Area Chamber of Commerce: 608/835-3697
Orfordville/Footville Chamber of Commerce: (Mailing address, Orfordville, WI 53576)
Osceola Chamber of Commerce: 715/755-3300 or 800/947-0581
Oshkosh Chamber of Commerce: 920/303-2266

APPENDIX

Oshkosh Convention & Visitors Bureau: 920/303-9200 or 877/303-9200)

P
Palmyra Area Chamber of Commerce: 414/531-4357
Pardeeville Area Business Association: 608/429-3121
Park Falls Area Chamber of Commerce: 715/762-2703 or 800/762-2709
Pelican Lake Chamber of Commerce: 715/487-5222
Pepin Area Community Club: 715/442-3011
Peshtigo Chamber of Commerce: 715/582-0327
Pewaukee Chamber of Commerce: 262/691-8851
Phelps Chamber of Commerce: 715/545-3800 or 877/669-7077
Phillips Area Chamber of Commerce: 715/339-4100 or 888/408-4800
Pierce County Economic Development Corporation: 715/425-3881
Platteville Chamber of Commerce: 608/348-8888
Plover Area Business Association: 715/345-5258
Plymouth Chamber of Commerce: 920/893-0079 or 888/693-8263
Port Edwards: 715/423-1830 or 800/554-4484
Port Washington Chamber of Commerce: 414/284-0900 or 800/719-4881
Portage Area Chamber of Commerce: 608/742-6242 or 800/474-2525
Portage County Business Council: 715/344-1940
Potosi-Tennyson Area Chamber of Commerce: 608/763-2261
Pound (Coleman-Pound Area Chamber of Commerce): (Mailing address, Box 105, Coleman, WI 54112)
Poynette Chamber of Commerce: 608/635-2425
Prairie du Chien Area Chamber of Commerce: 608/326-8555 or 800/732-1673
Prairie du Sac (Sauk Prairie Area Chamber of Commerce): 608/643-4168
Prescott Area Chamber of Commerce: 715/262-3284
Presque Isle Chamber of Commerce: 715/686-2910 or 888/835-6508
Price County Tourism Department: 715/339-4505 or 800/269-4505
Greater Princeton Area Chamber of Commerce: 920/295-3877
Pulaski Area Chamber of Commerce, Inc.: 920/822-4400

R
Racine Area Manufacturers & Commerce: 262/634-1931
Racine County Convention & Visitors Bureau: 262/884-6400 or 800/272-2463
Randolph Chamber of Commerce: 920/326-4769
Reedsburg Area Chamber of Commerce: 608/524-2850 or 800/844-3507
Reeseville Area Chamber of Commerce: 920/927-5308
Rhinelander Area Chamber of Commerce: 715/365-7464 or 800/236-4386
Rib Lake Commercial & Civic Club: 715/427-5761
Rice Lake Area Chamber of Commerce: 715/234-2126 or 800/523-6318
Richland Area Chamber of Commerce/Main Street Partnership: 608/647-6205 or 800/422-1318
Rio Area Community Club: 920/992-3213
Ripon Area Chamber of Commerce: 920/748-6764
River Falls Area Chamber of Commerce: 715/425-2533
Rusk County Tourism: 715/532-2642 or 800/535-7875

S
St. Cloud Businessmen's Association: (Mailing address, St. Cloud, WI 53079)
St. Croix Falls Chamber of Commerce: 715/483-9737
St. Germain Chamber of Commerce: 715/477-2205 or 800/727-7203
Sauk City (Sauk Prairie Area Chamber of Commerce): 608/643-4168 or 800/68-EAGLE
Sauk Prairie Area Chamber of Commerce: 608/643-4168 or 800/68-EAGLE
Saukville Chamber of Commerce: 262/268-1970
Sayner-Star Lake Chamber of Commerce: 715/542-3789 or 888/722-3789
Scandinavia (Iola-Scandinavia Area Chamber of Commerce): (Mailing address, Box 167, Iola, WI 54945)
Seymour Chamber of Commerce: 920/833-6053
Sharon Chamber of Commerce: 262/736-6246
Shawano Area Chamber of Commerce: 715/524-2139 or 800/235-8528
Sheboygan Convention & Visitors Bureau: 920/457-9495 or 800/457-9497
Sheboygan County Chamber of Commerce: 920/457-9491
Sheboygan Falls Chamber-Main Street, Inc.: 920/467-6206
Shell Lake Chamber of Commerce: 715/468-2270
Sherwood (Heart of the Valley Chamber of Commerce): 920/766-1616
Shiocton Business League: (Mailing address, Box 44E, Shiocton, WI 54170)
Siren Area Chamber of Commerce: 715/349-5999
Sister Bay Advancement Association: 920/854-2812
Slinger Advancement Association: 414/644-5866
Soldiers Grove Community Development Corp.: 608/624-3264
Somerset Area Chamber of Commerce: 715/247-3366
South Milwaukee Association of Commerce: 414/762-2222
Sparta Area Chamber of Commerce: 608/269-4123 or 888/540-8434
Spencer Area Chamber of Commerce: 715/659-5423
Spooner Area Chamber of Commerce: 715/635-2168
Spring Green Area Chamber of Commerce: 608/588-2054 or 800/588-2402
Spring Valley Chamber of Commerce: 715/778-5015
Stanley Area Chamber of Commerce: 715/644-3333
Star Lake (Sayner-Star Lake Chamber of Commerce): 715/542-3789 or 888/722-3789
Stevens Point (Portage County Business Council): 715/344-1940

Stevens Point Area Convention & Visitors Bureau: 715/344-2556 or 800/236-4636
Stone Lake Area Chamber of Commerce: 715/865-2080
Stoughton Chamber of Commerce: 608/873-7912 or 888/873-7912
Stratford Area Chamber of Commerce: 715/687-4466
Strum Commercial Club: 715/695-3308
Sturgeon Bay (Door County Chamber of Commerce): 920/743-4456
Sturtevant Area Chamber of Commerce: 262/886-7200
Sun Prairie Chamber of Commerce: 608/837-4547 or 800/400-6162
Superior-Douglas County Chamber of Commerce: 715/394-7716 or 800/942-5313
Sussex-Lisbon Business & Professional Association: (Mailing address, PO Box 24, Sussex, WI 53089-0024)

T
Tennyson (Potosi-Tennyson Area Chamber of Commerce): 608/763-2121 or 608/763-2261
Theresa Chamber of Commerce: 920/488-3800
Thiensville (Mequon-Thiensville Area Chamber of Commerce & Industry): 414/241-8186
Thorp Business Association: 715/669-5707
Three Lakes Information Bureau: 715/546-3344 or 800/972-6103
Tigerton Advancement Association: 715/535-3300
Greater Tomah Area Chamber of Commerce: 608/372-2166 or 800/948-6624
Tomah Convention & Visitors Bureau: 608/372-2166 or 800/94-TOMAH
Tomahawk Regional Chamber of Commerce: 715/453-5334 or 800/569-2160
Turtle Flambeau Flowage Association: 715/769-3680
Twin Lakes Chamber & Business Association: 414/877-2220
Two Rivers (Manitowoc-Two Rivers Area Chamber of Commerce): 920/684-5575

U
Greater Union Grove Area Chamber of Commerce: 262/878-4606
Unity Commercial Club: 715/223-4537

V
Verona Area Chamber of Commerce: 608/845-5777
Vilas County Chamber of Commerce: 715/479-3649
Viroqua Chamber: 608/637-2575

W
Wabeno Area Chamber of Commerce: 715/473-2311
Washburn Area Chamber of Commerce: 715/373-5017 or 800/253-4495
Washington Island Chamber of Commerce: 920/847-2179
Waterford Area Chamber of Commerce: 262/534-5911
Waterloo Chamber of Commerce: 920/478-2500
Watertown Area Chamber of Commerce: 920/261-6320
Waukesha County Chamber of Commerce: 262/542-4249
Waukesha Area Convention & Visitors Bureau: 262/542-0330 or 800/366-8474
Waunakee/Westport Chamber of Commerce: 608/849-5977
Waupaca Area Chamber of Commerce: 715/258-7343 or 888/417-4040
Waupun Area Chamber of Commerce: 920/324-3491
Wausau Area/Marathon County Chamber of Commerce: 715/845-6231
Wausau/Central WI Convention & Visitors Bureau:715/355-8788 or 888/948-4748
Wausaukee Area Business Association: 715/856-5678
Waushara (Wautoma) Area Chamber of Commerce: 920/787-3488
Webster Area Chamber of Commerce: 715/349-7411
West Allis Chamber of Commerce: 414/302-9901
West Bend Area Chamber of Commerce: 262/338-2666 or 888/338-8666
West Suburban Chamber of Commerce: 414/453-2330
Westfield Chamber of Commerce: 608/296-4146
West Allis/West Milwaukee Chamber of Commerce: 414/321-2585
Weyauwega Area Chamber of Commerce: 920/867-2500
Weyerhaeuser Community Club: 715/353-2731
Whitehall Area Chamber of Commerce: 715/538-4353
Whitewater Area Chamber of Commerce: 414/473-4005 or 800/499-8687
Wind Lake Chamber of Commerce: 414/895-6367
Winneconne Area Chamber of Commerce: 920/582-4775
Winter Area Chamber of Commerce: 715/266-2204 or 800/762-7179
Wisconsin Dells Visitor & Convention Bureau: 608/254-8088 or 800/223-3557
Wisconsin Dells/Lake Delton Chamber of Commerce: 608/253-5503
Wisconsin Rapids Area Chamber of Commerce: 715/423-1830
Wisconsin Rapids Area Convention & Visitors Bureau: 715/422-4650 or 800/554-4484
Wittenberg Area Chamber of Commerce: 715/253-3525
Woodruff (Minocqua-Arbor Vitae-Woodruff Area Chamber of Commerce): 715/356-5266
Woodville Economic Development Committee: 715/698-4150
Wrightstown (Heart of the Valley Chamber of Commerce): 920/766-1616

Index by Institutional Type

The Historic Tank Cottage over 100 years old, Green Bay, Wis.

INDEX

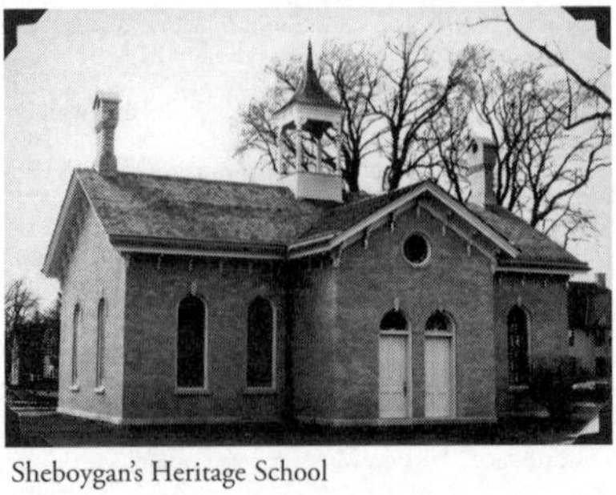

Sheboygan's Heritage School

Museums and Zoos That Have Closed

Layton Art Gallery, Milwaukee
The Layton Art Gallery was the first art museum in Wisconsin and sadly became the victim of urban renewal and expressway expansion in the late 1960s. Most of the art collection merged with the Milwaukee Art Museum, and the art school closed. The stately building was torn down.

Bathroom Tissue Museum, Madison
Dells Auto Museum, Wisconsin Dells
Doll Museum, La Crosse
Frank Palumbo Civil War Museum (will reopen in 2008 at Kenosha Public Museum)
Harmony Hall-Alford Mansion (again a private residence)
Hartland Depot, Hartland (might reopen)
Kaytee Avian Center, Chilton (They are open 2 days per year)
La Reau's Miniature Buildings, Pardeeville
Norman Rockwell Art Museum, Reedsburg
Point Beach Energy Center, Two Rivers (They just re-opened)
Sandstone Reptile Zoo, Wisconsin Dells
Ship's Wheel Gallery and Museum, Kewaunee
UFO Museum, Wisconsin Dells
Warbonnet Zoo, Hazelhurst
Wax World of Stars, Wisconsin Dells
Willie's Wildlife Zoo, Brandon
Winnebago Indian Museum, Wisconsin Dells
Wisconsin Folk Life Museum, Mount Horeb

Index by Institution

INDEX

Index by City

SCHRC

"Rajer's new book is a resource directory for museum professionals as well as the public."

Robert Teske
Milwaukee County Historical Museum director

"Wisconsin is well known as being a beautiful place. It deserves to be known for its man-made wonders too. Tony Rajer's new book will help in that journey of discovery for all visitors."

David Gordon
Director and CEO
Milwaukee Art Museum

"It's about time someone wrote a book to celebrate the cultural resources in Wisconsin. Bravo."

Robert Harker
Director
Sheboygan County Historical Society Museum

SCHRC

MANVILLE, 722 EIGHTH ST., Sheboygan, Wis.

"Finally - a comprehensive book on all the amazing museums, zoos and botanical gardens in Wisconsin. Enjoy your exploration of the known and little known!"

Mary Risseeuw
Genealogist

"A great guidebook to cultural, artistic, and historic Wisconsin Museums, Zoos and Botanical Gardens of Wisconsin by Tony Rajer."

University of Wisconsin Press
www.wisc.edu/wisconsinpress/books/2456.htm

Anton (Tony) Rajer is a native of Sheboygan, Wisconsin. He worked for many years at the Kohler Arts Center, Sheboygan and attended the University of Wisconsin-Milwaukee, where he majored in Art History. Later, he attended Harvard University for art conservation training as well as ICCROM in Rome, Italy. Additional studies took him to the University of Paris at the Sorbonne and the University of London. He is a specialist in heritage preservation and has been a Fulbright scholar for the US State Department in Brazil and Panama. For five years he was conservator at the Wisconsin State Capitol. He is the author of several books on art heritage preservation and teaches at the University of Wisconsin-Madison.